IT SEEMED LIKE NOTHING HAPPENED

ALSO BY PETER N. CARROLL

Puritanism and the Wilderness

The Other Samuel Johnson: A Psychohistory of Early New
    England

Religion and the Coming of the American Revolution (editor)

The Restless Centuries (with David W. Noble)

The Free and the Unfree: A New History of the United States
    (with David W. Noble)

The Twentieth Century Limited: A History of Recent America
    (with David W. Noble and David Horowitz)

IT SEEMED LIKE NOTHING HAPPENED

The Tragedy and Promise of America

in the 1970s

PETER N. CARROLL

A William Abrahams Book

HOLT, RINEHART AND WINSTON

NEW YORK

Published by Holt, Rinehart and Winston, 383 Madison Avenue, New York, New York 10017.

Published simultaneously in Canada by Holt, Rinehart and Winston of Canada, Limited.

Library of Congress Cataloging in Publication Data

Carroll, Peter N.
It seemed like nothing happened.
Includes bibliographical references.
1. United States—Civilization—1970—
I. Title.
E169.12.C29   973.92   82-1047
                          AACR2

ISBN: 0-03-058319-5

FIRST EDITION

Designer: Christine Aulicino

Printed in the United States of America
10 9 8 7 6 5 4 3 2 1

Lines from *Monster: Poems by Robin Morgan*, copyright © 1972 by Robin Morgan, reprinted by permission of Random House, Inc.

Lines from *Another Brick in the Wall* by Roger Waters. Copyright © 1979 by Pink Floyd Music Pub. Ltd., London. Published in the U.S.A. by Unichappell Music, Inc. All rights reserved. Used by permission.

Lines from "Words Unspoken" by Angela de Hoyos, from her unpublished book *Yo, Mujer*. Used by permission of the author.

ISBN 0-03-050319-5

For my children,

MATTHEW and NATASHA

born on the edges

of an era

· CONTENTS ·

· PREFACE ·

The seventies rest uneasily on the national conscience. "It was the worst of times, it was the worst of times," said *New West* magazine in 1979, urging that the decade be ended right then—"one year early and not a moment too soon." "Nobody," agreed *Time*, "is apt to look back on the 1970s as the good old days."

This sense of despair reflected the obvious disappointments of the era—the frustration of the apocalyptic dreams of the sixties, the failure of government and business to stabilize the economic order, the decline of American leadership in the world, the belief that major social problems remained forever insoluble. Few will wax poetic about the signs of chronic trouble—Vietnam, Cambodia, and OPEC; Watergate, Koreagate, and Billygate; inflation, unemployment, and Three Mile Island. By the late seventies, therefore, it was easy for the pundits to scorn the entire decade.

Beneath the dark headlines, however, beyond the snide journalism and the rhetoric of public figures, a quiet, almost subliminal revolution was altering the contours of the cultural landscape. As conventional answers failed to resolve the problems of the age, Americans looked increasingly toward alternative values and institutions to create a new sense of community. This search for alternatives and the pervasive crisis within traditional structures produced a complicated counterpoint that echoed through the politics and the culture of the seventies. It is this dialogue between established values and the emerging alternatives that forms the subject of this book.

PART ONE

THE LOSS OF CONNECTION

"THE ALLEGIANCE OF YOUTH"

Vietnam, Cambodia, Kent State

RHETORIC RAN FREELY IN 1970—
rhetoric about the war and about peace, rhetoric about social injustice and possibility. There was also considerable rhetoric about
rhetoric. It was a time when language itself became a subject for
political discourse, when the press corps interpreted presidential
rhetoric as "credibility gap," and when students shocked an older
generation with outspoken obscenities.

Richard Nixon understood better than most people the
power of the word. His campaign oratory of 1968 had promised to
bridge the great language barrier of the Johnson presidency, had
vowed to bring Americans back together again. "We are entering
an era of negotiation," he said in his inaugural address, and he
spoke effectively about the importance of softening language, of
controlling the word. The country "suffered from a fever of
words," he explained; "from inflated rhetoric. . . ; from angry rhetoric. . . ; from bombastic rhetoric." While antiwar protesters
staged a counterinauguration across the street from the White
House, the new President urged Americans to lower their voices,
to "speak quietly enough so that our words can be heard as well as
our voices." He promised, too, that "government will listen."

Nixon's sensitivity to rhetoric—more than a good politician's
ear—also reflected his skill at leaving so much unsaid. While Vietnam tore at the national conscience, undermining established loyalties and commitments, splitting families and friendships, Nixon

in his campaign had pledged simply that "the new leadership will end the war and win the peace in the Pacific." He presented, however, no specific plans. Disavowing any desire to weaken Johnson's chances of ending the war before election day, he had sworn to say "nothing during this campaign that might destroy that chance."

The candidate's vagueness offered a glimmer of hope to the war-weary electorate and, despite Johnson's last-minute bombing halt, enabled Nixon to obtain a solid majority. But the inaugural address added little light about the administration's policy. And when the new President finally did speak about Vietnam at a press conference five days later, the public heard the familiar language of demilitarized zones, mutual withdrawal, and an exchange of prisoners. "Where we go from here," said Nixon, "depends upon what the other side offers in turn." Hoping to maintain the honeymoon that traditionally accompanies a change of administrations, the White House pleaded for six months to effect the miracle that had eluded Johnson and Kennedy and Eisenhower. Later the administration asked for a six-month extension.

The war, meanwhile, continued. Determined to test the new President's mettle, the Hanoi government ordered new attacks on South Vietnamese cities, shellings which killed several hundred Americans. Nixon retaliated with new "pacification" drives, crop burnings, population removals, and bombing. Casualty figures continued to climb and in April 1969 the total number of American dead—33,641—surpassed the grisly toll of Korea. The next month, a battle at a place called Hamburger Hill symbolized the entire war effort. For nine days, American paratroopers made daily frontal assaults on the entrenched enemy, only to be repelled each time with high casualties. Frustrated by failure and overwhelmed by the sheer gore, American soldiers for the first time in significant numbers challenged military orders and threatened mutiny. On the tenth day, the Americans captured the hill. Then, since the position had no military value, the troops were withdrawn.

The continuation of the war assured the continuation of antiwar protest. Such dissent had swamped the Johnson presidency and Nixon strove to avoid the political errors of his predecessor. In his inaugural, he promised to "listen . . . to the voices of quiet anguish." But his foreign policy, like Johnson's, precluded serious attention to the words. "I understand that there has been and continues to be opposition to the war in Vietnam on the campuses, and also in the nation," the President told a press conference in September 1969. "We expect it. However, under no circumstances will I be affected whatever by it."

Despite Nixon's aloofness, the divisions caused by the war remained inescapable. "Old and young across the nation shout across a chasm of misunderstanding," he had admitted to a college audience in South Dakota in June 1969, "and the louder they shout the broader the chasm becomes." In identifying this generation gap, the President understood that political disagreement represented only the rippling surface of a culture in crisis. "Drugs, crime, campus revolts, racial discord, draft resistance"—the list seemed endless—"on every hand," said Nixon, "we find old standards violated, old values discarded, old principles ignored." The rise of a youthful counterculture, hostile to what the President considered "fundamental values," now threatened "the process by which a civilization maintains its continuity." For Nixon, the student shout seemed self-evident proof of the loss of reason.

To his horror, however, Nixon discovered that these voices of dissent had gained enormous support. In October 1969, the New Mobilization Committee to End the War in Vietnam organized a nationwide moratorium to protest the war—and drew gigantic crowds to the national capital and to peace ceremonies throughout the country. One public opinion poll revealed that 57 percent of the population supported the withdrawal of American troops by a specific date. "Sort of laughed at the Peace thing," wrote a frustrated sergeant from the combat zone. "I'm afraid they don't know Nixon. . . . Pressure will just freeze his stand on anything." More optimistic antiwar leaders announced a second moratorium for November 15.

Nixon bragged loudly about his indifference to Moratorium Day and spent the afternoon watching a televised football game. But his public posture belied a feverish attempt to undermine further dissent. Bypassing his speechwriters, the President drafted a rebuttal to the antiwar movement and asked for network airtime on November 3—midway between the two days of protest—to deliver it.

The speech illuminated Nixon's mastery of political oratory, his ability to use exalted rhetoric to muffle the voices of opposition. Making no concessions of policy, still insisting that he held a secret program to end the war and "win America's peace," Nixon denied the reality of mass protest. Acknowledging that "honest and patriotic Americans have reached different conclusions about how peace should be achieved," he nevertheless suggested that the hundreds of thousands who marched against the war, signed petitions, and balked at administration policy constituted only "a vocal minority." There was, he insisted, a larger group—"the great silent majority"—that supported the White House. "We've got those liberal bastards on the run now," Nixon exhorted his staff; "we've got them on the run and we're going to keep them on the run." Support from the "silent majority" poured into the White House—and to newspapers and television stations—which the President happily displayed to skeptical outsiders. Few realized then that many of these seemingly spontaneous messages had been manufactured by administration insiders to create the impression of massive support. In a war of words, a "silent majority," no matter how large, would appear ineffective.

To add decibel strength to the voice of the people, Nixon encouraged his Vice President, Spiro Agnew, to rally support. It was a role the President readily appreciated. As Eisenhower's second in command, the young Nixon had supplied the verbal ammunition for the anticommunist crusade and, in the process, developed a fondness for such alliterative verbiage as "Adlai the appeaser . . . who got a Ph.D. from Dean Acheson's College of Cowardly Communist Containment." Agnew, the tough-talking ex-governor of Maryland, welcomed the opportunity to find a niche in the American treasury of light verse.

The Vice President turned his guns on youthful antiwar demonstrators. "A spirit of national masochism prevails," Agnew remarked in a speech four days after the October Moratorium, "encouraged by an effete corps of impudent snobs who characterize themselves as intellectuals." Two weeks later, the Vice President returned to the stump to denounce "political hustlers" who led "shouting matches in the streets." Dropping any pretense of consensus, Agnew extolled the virtues of political warfare. "If, in challenging, we polarize the American people, I say it is time for a positive polarization," he announced. "It is time to rip away the rhetoric and to divide on authentic lines."

While Nixon attempted to rally support among the "silent majority," Agnew's barrages aimed at the institutions that seemed to stand between the people and their proper leaders. Ten days after Nixon's image-building speech, the Vice President attacked the television networks for undermining the President's message through "instant analysis and querulous criticism." In angry, barbed metaphors, Agnew suggested that "a tiny and closed fraternity of privileged men" controlled the national news media and imposed their parochial political views on the rest of the nation. Indignant protests from the press merely whetted the Vice President's invective. Refusing to circumscribe what he called "my rhetorical freedom," Agnew told the network commentators and the nation's major newspapers that the day of "diplomatic immunity from comment and criticism of what they said is over."

The great debate over the right to debate, the taut rhetoric about the uses of rhetoric, reflected a keen awareness of the potential power of language. Since World War II, American foreign policy had depended upon the willingness of the public to respond to certain charmed words and concepts—to such positive phrases as "the free world," "the democratic way," "responsible leadership"—as well as to recoil from such negative symbols as "communist menace," "totalitarianism," "enslaved peoples." The familiar litany enabled Presidents from Roosevelt to Kennedy and, for a time, Johnson, to carry American power to the corners of the earth. Vietnam, however, produced a fundamental change. Americans now disputed the borders of "the free world," questioned the distinctions between democracy and totalitarianism, and, most important, challenged the political leadership about its claim to resolve such ideological problems.

As the war grew increasingly unpopular, the invention of a "silent majority" enabled the administration to ignore unpleasant criticism. "Nothing would please me more than to see all voices lowered," claimed Vice President Agnew. But "a unilateral withdrawal" of rhetoric—like a unilateral withdrawal of American troops—would "abridge the confidence of the silent majority, the everyday law-abiding American who believes his country needs a strong voice." The people wanted "a cry of alarm," said Agnew, "to penetrate the cacophony of seditious drivel."

Despite the attempt to link dissent with treason, two counterforces—one pragmatic, the other psychological—prevented the suppression of the antiwar movement. First, as public opinion polls showed repeatedly, opposition to the war pervaded American society—by 1970 even reaching the higher echelons of government. Second, the myth of a "silent majority" provided a basis for permitting vocal dissent to flourish without altering the political structure or the government's decision-making process. "In this great free country of ours," Nixon explained in April 1970, "we debate—we disagree, sometimes violently, but the mistake the totalitarians make over and over again is to conclude that debate in a free country is proof of weakness." In domestic terms, Nixon's analysis meant that it was important to sustain a façade of debate—to maintain a semblance of participation—while preserving the undiminished power of the presidency. No one doubted that the United States government functioned on the principle of majority rule. By defining the antiwar movement as a minority position, the administration could justify its refusal to listen. Those who formed a mere minority and so had been defeated in political debate could be said to have lost fairly. Political rhetoric thus enabled the President to dismiss dissent even as it provoked it.

The Nixon leadership also appreciated the importance of language for maintaining appearances. One aspect of the attempt to control rhetoric emerged in the crusade against obscenity. Inside the White House, the President felt no need to silence, much less to criticize, such expressions as _____ [expletive deleted], or _____ [expletive deleted], or even _____ [expletive deleted]. But in his fiery speeches against antiwar protesters, Agnew commonly denounced the use of street language and "gutter obscenities."

This attack on dirty words served an important political purpose. Within the antiwar movement—and the burgeoning youth culture in general—the continuation of technological warfare in Vietnam itself appeared obscene, far more grievous than words like _____, _____, or _____. No less important for the nation's youth was the desire to use language to identify an alternative culture. "The new-style young people have adopted these ultimate words out of a sense of frustration," explained Robert Franklin, a chemistry instructor at Kent State University, "seeing our earlier vocabulary coopted by Madison Avenue." In a society which encouraged the rapid translation of street talk into advertising copy, suggested Franklin, "young people are devising a language which older people cannot steal from them."

Such statements seriously underestimated the possibilities for manipulation. Young people might refuse to clean up their language, but they remained susceptible to other types of appeals. "Sure I'm against pollution," said Jeffrey Miller, a freshman at Kent State in 1970, "but I don't like the way Nixon and the administration are giving so much publicity to the problem. I think they may be trying to co-opt the whole country, getting us so uptight about the environment that we forget about Vietnam." Less politicized youth could be distracted by more banal causes. Football, one of Nixon's favorite interests, appeared as a frequent diversion in presidential speeches. In a surprise predawn conversation with antiwar students, Nixon spoke amiably about the quality of the Syracuse University football team.

THE CONTROL OF CONVERSATION and language served not only to distort reality, but more fundamentally to conceal it. Believing that political success required utmost secrecy, the Nixon administration cultivated a protective rhetoric of deceit. "This war will be settled in private rather than in public," the President told the press in March 1969. Few doubted that the intricacies of diplomacy required some shelter from public scrutiny, a seclusion in which bold initiatives might be taken without risk of exposure or embarrassment. In this spirit, Nixon authorized his chief foreign policy adviser, Henry Kissinger, to commence secret negotiations with the North Vietnamese as early as 1969.

Nixon's insistence on secrecy, however, extended beyond the area of negotiation into the realm of policy. The celebrated plan to end the war in Vietnam, having no existence in reality, remained hidden beneath a morass of presidential verbiage and the casual announcement of a Nixon Doctrine in July 1969. Speaking to American journalists who were accompanying him on a trip around the world, the President remarked that Asia properly belonged to Asians, though the United States maintained vital interests in the Pacific. Forecasting a new American role in the area, he suggested that "we should assist, but we should not dictate" to our allies. Not until his postmoratorium speech of November 1969 did Nixon coin a word for his vision—"Vietnamization." In plain English, it meant that South Vietnamese troops would be trained to wage the ground war, enabling an "orderly" withdrawal of American forces. Such tactics offered the domestic advantage of reducing American casualties, perhaps weakening the antiwar movement. The President made no mention of long-term commitments, but American airpower and economic assistance constituted essential ingredients of future plans.

While Nixon spoke publicly about curtailing American involvement in southeast Asia, he simultaneously pursued a secret foreign policy that expanded the unpopular war. In one of his first presidential decisions, he authorized B-52 bombing raids against Cambodia, a neutral nation, in hopes of disrupting enemy supply bases and destroying a reported Viet Cong headquarters. The policy also served notice on Hanoi that the new President would not be intimidated by a "mini-Tet" offensive. In violating Cambodian neutrality, Nixon could cite precedents from the Johnson administration. But under Nixon, the Cambodian adventure had ominous repercussions.

Given the political climate in the United States, the illegal attacks on Cambodia required maximum secrecy. The military accordingly developed a secret system of false reporting that misinformed not only the general public but also such high government officials as the Secretary of the Air Force. Besides violating military laws, the deceptive practices demonstrated the seclusiveness of the policy-making elite within the administration. And despite the elaborate efforts at concealment, someone leaked information about the Cambodia bombings to *New York Times* reporter William Beecher, who promptly revealed the new policy. Most people ignored Beecher's story. But it did have an immediate impact on a presidential troupe basking in the sun at Key Biscayne, Florida. Furious at the breach of security, Nixon and Kissinger ordered FBI Director J. Edgar Hoover to initiate wiretaps on suspected informants. This domestic surveillance constituted the first major violation of domestic law by the Nixon administration.

The decision to expand the war reflected Nixon's unyielding belief that American military power could still prevail in Vietnam. Rejecting pessimistic assessments from the field, the President joined military leaders in affirming the efficacy of a bombing strategy. This misplaced confidence had serious political consequences, however, for the bombing of Cambodia swiftly undermined the precarious stability of that tiny republic. Under the benevolent despot, Prince Sihanouk, Cambodia had managed to walk a shaky tightrope between Vietnamese violations of its borders and United States pressure to interdict the Ho Chi Minh trail. But for all his past success as a neutral, Sihanouk no longer could preserve the balance of power in his country once American bombing pressured communist forces to move deeper into Cambodia. Dissatisfied by Sihanouk's ambiguity, anticommunists, led by Lon Nol, staged a coup d'etat in March 1970 and began a more aggressive war against the Vietnamese invaders. The Cambodian forces, however, were hopelessly outmatched. By April 1970, Nixon began to fear that a communist victory in Cambodia would destroy the possibility of reaching a satisfactory settlement throughout Southeast Asia.

While the Cambodian situation disintegrated, antiwar dissent had weakened. Nixon's announcement of Vietnamization, the steady withdrawal of American ground forces, and revisions of the draft laws undermined organized dissent. Lacking adequate funding, the Vietnam Moratorium Committee prepared to disband its Washington offices. But college campuses remained seedbeds of discontent. To deal with the continuing student protest, Vice President Agnew proposed drastic remedies: "Just imagine they are wearing brown shirts or white sheets," he advised, "and act accordingly."

As the White House studied the Cambodian crisis in secrecy, the President notified television viewers on April 20 that the success of Vietnamization justified the withdrawal of additional ground forces. "We are not a weak people," he declared. "We are a strong people. America has never been defeated in the proud one-hundred-ninety-year history of this country, and we shall not be defeated in Vietnam." The next day, Nixon turned his attention to the urgent question of reinforcing the Lon Nol regime in Cambodia. In evaluating the options, the President spoke with top policy advisers and personal friends, attended formal intelligence meetings, retreated to Camp David for contemplation, and, for spiritual comfort, he ordered several screenings of the movie *Patton,* a film which celebrated military toughness, high-risk attacks, and the disregard of formal channels. "Megalomania," remarked film historian Len Keyser of Nixon's cinematic choice, "is always its own best friend."

On April 30, 1970, the President announced a bold change of policy. In a remarkable television address, filled with rhetorical bombast, mild deceptions, and outright lies, Nixon endeavored to convince the public that an American invasion of Cambodia served the national interest. He began by distorting recent Vietnamese activities in Cambodia, claiming that long-existing troop movements constituted fresh aggression. "American policy," Nixon then lied, "has been to scrupulously respect the neutrality of the Cambodian people. . . . For the past five years, we have provided no military assistance whatever and no economic assistance to Cambodia." Pointing to a large wall map, the President presented a misleading description of communist strategy, confusing the withdrawal from the border bases with a two pronged attack on South Vietnam and Cambodia. To justify his momentous decision, Nixon maintained that Cambodia had issued "a call . . . for assistance." That statement, too, was dishonest, for Lon Nol had asked only for economic assistance and supplies—and was not even notified of the impending invasion until *after* Nixon's speech. The President then offered an Orwellian distinction: "This is not an invasion of Cambodia," he stated. The United States intended only a temporary "incursion" to capture and destroy Vietnamese military bases that made possible aggressive warfare in South Vietnam.

Nixon's manipulation of language was obviously self-serving. But in international relations, rhetoric also functioned as an adjunct of power. Subtle expressions—a nuance, a threat—constructed a context for policy, set boundaries and intentions around power relations. The speech of April 30 illuminated underlying themes that motivated presidential action. Criticizing Hanoi's "intransigence at the conference table," Nixon warned that American "credibility" was at stake. "We will not be humiliated," he insisted. "The world's most powerful nation" could not afford to act "like a pitiful, helpless giant."

The issue cut to the center of the national identity. "It is not our power but our will and character that is being tested tonight," said Nixon. "If we fail to meet this challenge, all other nations will be on notice that despite its overwhelming power the United States, when a real crisis comes, will be found wanting." The illusion of power, then, required a sturdy defense. By April 1970, American military efforts in Vietnam had stalled, the nation had lost its will to fight. Yet Vietnam had always symbolized American fortitude in the face of communist aggression; the little countries of Southeast Asia served as whipping boys in the real power struggle between American freedom and the red tide. Nixon's action, he believed, would stem the flow.

THE CAMBODIA INVASION, as predicted by Nixon insiders, unleashed storms of outrage in the nation. "This is madness," exclaimed Senator Edward Kennedy, expressing widespread congressional shock. A few weeks earlier, the Senate Foreign Relations Committee had warned the administration against sending assistance to Cambodia. "We recognize that if we escalate and we get involved in Cambodia with our ground troops," Secretary of State William Rogers had assured a House committee, "that our whole [Vietnamization] program is defeated." Senator Vance Hartke of Indiana called Nixon's decision "a declaration of war against the Senate," and Senator Stephen Young of Ohio introduced a resolution censuring the President for his "unconstitutional" action.

Newsweek magazine carried these statements in a cover story called " Nixon's Cambodian Gamble." It also printed a startling photograph of a National Guardsman jabbing a bayonet at the face of a protesting student at Ohio State University; the caption bore the ominous pun, famous from the days of Joseph McCarthy, "Point of order." The photograph captured the administration's attitude toward campus protest. During an informal tour of the Pentagon, Nixon characterized student dissenters as "bums," a provocative remark that soon returned to plague the American conscience.

On May 1, 1970, some three hundred students at an obscure midwestern campus staged a symbolic protest against the invasion of Cambodia. From the back pages of an American history textbook, they tore a copy of the United States Constitution and, with great solemnity, they buried it. "We do not harbor any malice towards this document," they asserted. "We only recognize the fact" that "President Nixon has murdered it." By invading a neutral country without congressional approval, the President had violated "our legal rights." "It is now our task," declared one speaker, "to see that it is resurrected in its original form . . . in its true meaning." The setting was Kent State University.

That evening, in a combination of antiwar zeal and old-fashioned spring fever, some students smashed windows in downtown

Kent, leading the town's mayor to declare a state of emergency. The next night, students attacked a dilapidated ROTC building, burning it to the ground. On Sunday, as weary National Guardsmen occupied the campus, Governor James Rhodes arrived on the scene and loudly castigated student radicals as "worse than the Brown Shirts and communist element and also the nightriders and the vigilantes. They're the worst type that we harbor in America." An emergency faculty meeting quickly condemned the governor's histrionics. The burning of ROTC was "no accident," they maintained. "It must be viewed in the larger context of the daily burning of buildings and people by our government in Vietnam, Laos, and now, Cambodia." They also reaffirmed the importance of defending constitutional rights "against any challenge, even from the Department of Justice itself."

On Monday, May 4, however, they could not prevent gross violations of constitutional rights. As students congregated for a noon rally to protest the presence of military force as well as the Cambodia invasion, the National Guard ordered them to disperse. There was no legal basis for that order, no right to claim martial law or to abridge the right of assembly. But General Robert Canterbury had his own ideas about constitutional rights. "These students are going to have to find out what law and order is all about," he remarked. Minutes later four students were shot dead, nine others seriously wounded.

The killing of four college students at Kent State—followed soon after by the murder of two black students at Jackson State in Mississippi—awakened profound anxieties in American society. A widely circulated photograph of a young woman kneeling above the inert bleeding body of Jeffrey Miller captured the stark impotence of death, a blood immersion that haunted this generation of Americans. Mass annihilation hovered almost as a cliché around American children born in the baby boom of World War II. "We may be the last generation in the experiment with living," Tom Hayden grimly remarked in the Port Huron Statement that announced the birth of the radical Students for a Democratic Society in 1962. Hollywood movies, doomsday novels, presidential addresses, reiterated that apocalyptic vision. Death imagery permeated the culture.

In the sixties, this sense of imminent extinction had exploded dramatically on November 22, 1963. The assassination of John F. Kennedy suddenly transformed the possibility of mass death to human proportions. Other public murders—Malcolm X, Martin Luther King, Robert F. Kennedy—reinforced those anxious feelings. After 1963, the dread of nuclear holocaust, too terrible to accept in its reality, turned into a fascination with the death of symbolic leaders. But while public attention focused on political assassinations and related questions of domestic violence, the ultimate issues of mass death quietly drifted across the Pacific Ocean into the jungles of Vietnam. There, a Strangelovian assortment of technological inventions devastated the countryside, while Pentagonese wrapped the atrocities in the neutral language of free fire zones, protective reactions, and body counts. Such destruction, thanks to American electronics, then recrossed the Pacific and slipped into the nation's living rooms where civilians also could experience a powerful death encounter in the form of self-immolating Buddhist monks and napalmed children, amid the crack of automatic fire and buzzing helicopters on the national news. Regardless of one's politics, the war inevitably pierced the self-protective armor that ordinarily separated the living from the dead.

The murders at Kent State accomplished what antiwar demonstrators had demanded—they brought the war back home. Sprawled on an Ohio campus were no oddly dressed Vietnamese or uniformed soldiers trained to kill. These were not symbolic leaders like Kennedy or King who lived exceptional lives and consequently assumed great risks. Nor were they anonymous numbers stacked like woodpiles in concentration camps or buried beneath the rubble of wartime cataclysm. Allison Krause, Sandy Scheuer, Bill Schroeder, and Jeffrey Miller symbolized the immediacy of all death and its arbitrary arrangement.

A sense of horror flashed through the student community. Hundreds of colleges suspended normal operations in the first national student strike in American history. Tens of thousands poured into Washington, D.C., to protest the war, leading the administration to prepare plans to station armed troops in the basement of the White House. But opposition reached even the highest levels of government. Robert Finch, a longtime Nixon ally and Secretary of Health, Education, and Welfare, condemned Agnew for "heating up the climate in which the Kent State students were killed," and Secretary of the Interior Walter Hickel argued that "youth in its protest must be heard." Never in the twentieth century had the nation been so divided.

Refusing to accept responsibility for the domestic crisis, the administration denounced the antiwar protest. "This should remind us all once again," said Nixon upon learning of the killings, "that when dissent turns to violence it invites tragedy." Agnew, speaking that evening to the American Retail Federation, called the shootings, "predictable and avoidable" and launched another tirade against "psychotic and criminal elements" which hid behind the Bill of Rights. The White House marked dissenters like Finch and Hickel for dismissal, once the national mood became calm.

Nationwide outrage nevertheless forced the administration to adopt more conciliatory language. On May 8, the President held a prime time news conference and suggested that he shared the goals of the antiwar protesters—peace. Nixon also ordered Agnew to "keep the rhetoric cool," and the Vice President dutifully edited from a speech sentences which criticized "a gloomy coalition of choleric young intellectuals and tired, embittered elders." Troubled beyond sleep, Nixon rambled through midnight telephone calls (fifty-one on the evening of May 8–9) before bolting off to the Lincoln Memorial at 5:00 A.M. to chat with antiwar demonstrators. "I know that probably most of you think I'm an SOB," he conceded, "but I want you to know I understand just how you feel." Ordering a federal investigation, Nixon created a special presidential commission, headed by former Pennsylvania Governor William Scranton, to gather evidence on the state of "campus unrest." The shootings at Kent State, the report concluded, "were unnecessary, unwarranted, and inexcusable," those at Jackson State constituted "an unreasonable, unjustified overreaction." To Vice President Agnew, the study merely offered "Pablum for the permissivists."

The Scranton report traced the origins of student alienation to an emerging counterculture that was dedicated to "humanity, equality, and the sacredness of life" and appalled by the country's loss of "human purpose." The killing of middle-class college students reaffirmed those feelings. But the "moral recoil" of the youth culture was hopelessly unprepared for armed soldiers firing live ammunition. "I saw the same disbelief on everyone else's face," recalled an eyewitness survivor. In July 1970, the bombing of a military research center at the University of Wisconsin killed a late-working graduate student, magnifying a shockwave of helplessness that spread around the nation's campuses. In psychological terms, the human slaughter had come too close for comfort. Amid this despair, Hollywood released three movies about other wars—*Tora! Tora! Tora!, Catch 22,* and *M*A*S*H*—but found audience reactions so unsettled that the movie industry silently imposed a moratorium on war films. The terrifying issue of violent death, nestled deep in the national psyche, receded from public discourse.

Such patterns also reflected the conservative counterforces operating in the larger society. A special *Newsweek* public opinion poll, taken days after the Kent State slayings, indicated that 58 percent of the respondents blamed the students for the shootings, only 11 percent felt the National Guard was at fault. Half the people polled supported the invasion of Cambodia and 46 percent approved Vice President Agnew's criticism of dissent, while disapproval of these positions amounted to only 39 percent and 30 percent respectively. By contrast, a simultaneous Harris poll of college student opinion showed that 76 percent believed that "basic changes in the system" were necessary to improve the quality of life in America and 44 percent believed that social progress required "radical pressure from outside the system."

The clash of values appeared dramatically in the pages of the Kent, Ohio, newspapers in the form of letters to the editor. "Authority, law and order are the backbone of our society," maintained a local "housewife." "The sooner the students of this country learn they are not running this country, that they are going to college to learn, *not teach*," wrote "concerned citizen," "the better." Even the "silent majority" joined the chorus of bitterness. "If the National Guard is forced to face these situations without loaded guns," warned one writer, "the silent majority has lost everything. The National Guard made only one mistake—they should have fired sooner and longer." "The score is four," ran a local jingle, "And next time more."

While heated citizens gloated about the show of force, the Nixon administration rushed nervously to control mass protest. Shortly after the Cambodia invasion, the White House ordered the installation of illegal wiretaps on newsmen and several government officials. In June 1970, the President endorsed an elaborate plan to intensify surveillance of dissident groups. Only the opposition of J. Edgar Hoover, who objected to surrendering FBI power, prevented its implementation. But Nixon continued to support the CIA's program of domestic spying and allowed administration officials to plan alternative enterprises. "Kent State," Nixon aide H. R. Haldeman later stated, "marked a turning point for Nixon, a beginning of his downhill slide toward Watergate."

The administration also remained steadfast against rising antiwar sentiment in Congress. In June 1970, the Senate repealed the Tonkin Gulf resolution of 1964, the only legislative sanction for American action in Vietnam. But the administration fought back, managing to defeat the McGovern-Hatfield "end the war" amendment which would have denied military expenditures in Vietnam after 1970. And when the Senate approved the Cooper-Church amendment to halt all American operations in Cambodia, the White House persuaded the House to squash it.

The failure of antiwar legislation enabled the administration to pursue its policy in Cambodia. Though Nixon claimed that the invasion represented a great American victory, the sixty-day operation hardly interrupted Vietnamese infiltration and completely failed against the communist offensive in Cambodia. Long after American troops departed that country, United States and South Vietnamese air forces treated Cambodia as a free fire zone, unleashing heavy bombardments that brought only negative political consequences. By the autumn of 1970, Lon Nol had become a puppet of American policy-makers and an enemy to many of his own people.

But as the military failure in Cambodia complicated the problems of achieving peace in Indochina, American policy compounded these difficulties by expanding the war in Laos. Still hoping to win a military victory, Nixon ordered a South Vietnamese invasion of Laos in February 1971. Establishing a "news embargo" to prevent premature protest, the President limited United States involvement to air strikes. But again Nixon underestimated enemy resources and exaggerated South Vietnamese prowess. Within a month, the invading forces reeled backwards in one of the worst military catastrophes of the war. Yet Vice President Agnew insisted that the rout was really "an orderly withdrawal," and the President maintained that the defeated troops emerged "with greater confidence and greater morale than before."

As the war continued in the spring of 1971, antiwar demonstrators became more desperate. Attempting to "shut down" the government, thousands of protesters arrived in the capital for May

Day demonstrations. The government responded by staging mass arrests, eventually detaining over ten thousand citizens, sometimes without charging them with crimes. The courts subsequently ruled the roundup a massive breach of constitutional rights. From his retreat in San Clemente, California, however, the President attacked the protesters, asserting that "the right to demonstrate for peace abroad does not carry with it the right to break the peace at home." In waging war against dissent, the administration showed as little regard for civil rights as for the limits of executive authority.

Frustrated by Nixon's imperviousness to legal dissent, enraged by the continuing war and the perpetuation of official lies, one government insider decided to speak the truth. On June 13, 1971, *The New York Times* printed the first installment of secret government documents supplied by a former intelligence adviser, Daniel Ellsberg. The *Pentagon Papers*, originally compiled for former defense secretary Robert McNamara to prove the continuity of American policy in Vietnam, revealed a long history of government lies—of lies spoken to foreign governments, lies transmitted to Congress, lies offered to the American people. The Vietnam "quagmire," it now became obvious, resulted not from accident or miscalculation. It constituted no aberration of American foreign policy. The war, in all its cruelty, represented a deliberate extension of national policy-making which repeatedly flew in the face of national opinion.

The appearance of the *Pentagon Papers* alarmed White House officials, who initially feared the revelation of other diplomatic secrets. But even after learning the limited nature of Ellsberg's documentation, the administration attempted to protect the principle of secrecy by suppressing further publication. When the federal courts refused to back the government's demand for censorship, the White House slid beyond the law. In July 1971, the administration ordered a special "Plumbers" group, responsible only to the White House, to stop further "leaks." Seeking to complete this illegal mission, the Plumbers brazenly burglarized the offices of Dr. Lewis Fielding, Ellsberg's psychiatrist.

"I call it a common, cheap fencing operation," said Spiro Agnew about the publication of the *Pentagon Papers*. Charging Ellsberg and his cohorts with common theft, the administration moved quickly to suppress further revelations. At issue was the entire system of documentary classification, the bureaucratic rules that enabled the government to control public access to information and so permitted the pursuit of policies that violated the law. "The Constitution is larger than the executive branch," Ellsberg told a reporter, and he determined to challenge the government's right to withhold information from the American people.

"IF WE DON'T BELIEVE IN OURSELVES," asked Agnew about the release of the *Pentagon Papers*, "who can believe us?" The Ellsberg case touched the root of the nation's trust. But in June 1971, most people sided with the government. A public opinion poll, quoted by a delighted Agnew, showed that three-quarters of the respondents opposed the publication of Ellsberg's documents. The administration, so far, had preserved its credibility.

The same survey, however, showed that 15 percent of the people polled—not an insubstantial number—desired to penetrate the veils of government secrecy. Agnew and Nixon might still bow to the "silent majority." But by then many Americans already had become disenchanted with their leaders. For them, the burned flesh of Vietnam, the rough treatment from public officials, had created raw, painful, unhealing wounds.

"I feel about as alienated from my Government as you can get," a Kent State student told *The New York Times*.

"I feel too much hatred and bitterness within me to let this occurrence fade away," said a shocked schoolmate.

"I realized that my sympathy lay with the students," remarked a third, "and would forever remain with them."

"I felt the futility of trying to stop the massive flow that is America going down the drain," asserted one of their teachers.

Such statements, taken together, revealed a gaping crack in the American identity. "A nation that has lost the allegiance of part of its youth," warned the President's Commission on Campus Unrest, "is a nation that has lost part of its future."

The dishonesty of the Vietnam War struck first at the hearts of the young people in the vanguard of the antiwar movement. Perhaps because this postwar generation had matured in an idealistic world of infinite possibility, perhaps because it possessed a special sensitivity to the terror of extinction, the antiwar youth experienced deep feelings of revulsion and disaffiliation from the policies of the national leadership. In subsequent years, other events traumatized different segments of American society, producing a similar sense of betrayal, disgust, and anger. "They feel they must remake America in its own image," the Scranton commission said of the nation's youth. During the seventies, millions of other Americans came to share that hopeful vision.

· 2 ·

"TO OPEN ONE'S EYES"

The Rise of Women's Liberation

She was inside a federal court-room in New York City pleading guilty to a bombing conspiracy indictment when a news bulletin announced the mass shooting at Kent State. An outspoken critic of the Vietnam War, twenty-three-year-old defendant Jane Alpert saw the Ohio slayings as another battle in the armed struggle between "serious militant leftists" and an entrenched, unyielding establishment. "The anger of youth and all oppressed people is mounting against [the] mockery of justice," she had written on the eve of the second moratorium protest of November 1969, the day she was arrested, along with her lover Samuel Melville and two accomplices, for bombing "military and war-related corporate buildings," including the Armed Forces Induction Center in Whitehall Street, in an attempt to disrupt the war-making process. Free on twenty thousand dollars bail, Alpert agreed, in the spirit of revolutionary camaraderie, to plea-bargain with the federal judiciary to mitigate Melville's sentence. In June, he received a thirteen-to-eighteen-year term and was sent to do his time in New York's maximum security prison at Attica.

By then, Alpert's life had veered in another direction. Facing a stiff prison sentence, which would sepatate her from Melville and from the movement they shared, she decided to thwart the legal machinery. On a warm evening in mid-May 1970, she dressed in good clothing, daubed her face with makeup, bleached her hair, and disappeared into the night. Expecting help from the radical Weather Underground, Alpert fantasized a dramatic jail raid to release Melville. But shortly after becoming a fugitive, Alpert lost contact with the radical left and decided, as she later explained, "to take off on my own." For a while, she drifted through the West, sometimes traveling alone, sometimes with small groups of hippies; later, she worked as a waitress in a ski lodge in New England and, after that, as a medical technician near San Diego. In sunny California, she joined a YWCA-sponsored women's "rap group" and met regularly with six women "brought together only by our common desire—or desperate need—to talk with other women about our lives." And these friends supported her, though they never knew her background, through the agony of Melville's death behind bars.

As a fugitive, Alpert became a classic underground person, stripped of identity, lacking connection to social class, geographic locale, or traditional family. In a sense, she personified the archetypal modern American—individualistic, mobile, self-consciously rootless. Yet, to her surprise, Alpert discovered one constant that pursued her everywhere, one personal certainty that clung to her skin like the pigment of race: "I was a woman." Everyone she met "related to me as Woman," she wrote, "all my other interests or characteristics being in their eyes mere modifications of that one essential. Whether I was desired, rejected, abused, admired, ignored, treated with kindness or hostility, it was basically because I was a female."

Startled by this perception, Alpert began to reexamine her political commitments, her relationship to radical politics and to the men who dominated it. Lacking a fixed persona, she simultaneously searched for self-definition. Yet, despite her unique situation, Alpert's quest for identity was a shared experience. "We had come to the group each in a private panic of no longer knowing who we were," she said of her San Diego friends, and "we discovered in each other . . . the pulse of a culture and a consciousness which was common to us as women."

OTHER WOMEN THROUGHOUT THE COUNTRY were making similar surprised discoveries. "We have suddenly and shockingly perceived the basic disorder," wrote journalist Jane O'Reilly, "in what has been believed to be the natural order of things." What she called "the housewife's moment of truth" became a puzzle-solving "click!" as pieces of social reality snapped into place, revealing generations of unspoken assumptions about the place of women in American society. "The initial feminist understanding," recalled *Village Voice* columnist Vivian Gornick, "came as a kind of explosion: shattering, scattering, everything tumbling about, the old world within splintering even as the new one was collecting." The recognition that sex—and often sex alone—determined one's identity came as a traumatic truth to American women—not only because the idea contradicted timeworn rhetoric about social equality, but also because it underscored the relative deprivation of most women's lives.

The unexpected discovery of the importance of women's sexual identity reflected basic changes in American attitudes toward the human body, including a new pattern of values associated with the sexual revolution. Though surveys of sexual behavior suggest that the loosening of Victorian morality began early in the twentieth century, the introduction of effective birth control pills in the early sixties eliminated a major deterrent to freer sexual relations. The possibilities offered by the Pill, moreover, were reinforced by the pioneering sexual research of Virginia Masters and William Johnson, published in 1966 under the title *Human Sexual Response*. According to these investigators, women possessed as much sexual energy as men, if not more, and could enjoy a variety of sexual responses, including multiple orgasms. Most significant, laboratory study overturned the traditional distinction between vaginal and clitoral orgasm and so undercut an established truism that heterosexual intercourse was "naturally" superior to self-stimulation or homosexuality.

These scientific discoveries, besides altering conventional wisdom about female sexuality, were themselves products of a changing sexual style that permitted candid discussion of what previously was considered private terrain. The popularity of quasi-sexual dances, the appearance of nudity in Hollywood films and of see-through fashions in New York, the acceptability of explicit sexual detail—all were signs of a new celebration of the body. As guilt about bodily activities diminished, women became more sexually active and imitated the more liberal sexual patterns that Dr. Alfred Kinsey had once described exclusively for men. Even in the conservative bastions of Catholicism, attitudes about sexuality

changed dramatically, as more couples admitted they approved
sexual intercourse "for pleasure alone," accepted intercourse for
engaged couples and remarriage after divorce, and opposed official
church teachings about birth control and abortion.

Liberated sex flourished especially among younger women.
Surveys of female college students, for example, showed a significant increase in premarital sexual relations after 1965, while regis-
tering a decline of disapproval of homosexuality, abortion, and
casual sex. The new sexual freedom inevitably aroused the jeal-
ousy and then the anger of an older and more sexually repressed
generation. "It's disgusting the way the girls sleep around,"
snorted a businessman of Kent, Ohio, in explaining the town's
hostility to the university community. Others complained that the
local movie theaters had been taken over by students who preferred sex-related subjects, leaving family-oriented audiences without a theater. And novelist James Michener, surveying the impact
of the Kent murders, found a remarkable antipathy to the liberal
clothing styles of college women. "If I've had to wear a bra all my
life," the women of Kent repeated, "why can't she?"

In rejecting the sexual values of their mothers, younger
women asserted their right to control their bodies. Yet ironically
the affirmation of sexual liberation often involved the substitution
of one type of sexual exploitation for another. "According to most
men," charged writer Anselma Dell'Olio, "a liberated woman was
one who put out sexually at the drop of a suggestive comment,
who didn't demand marriage, and who 'took care of herself' in
terms of contraceptives." Pressured by the new morality, women
experienced sex more frequently, but did not necessarily find sexual satisfaction. "The Achilles' heel of the Sexual Revolution,"
explained Dell'Olio, "is the persistent male ignorance of the female orgasm."

These problems were compounded by a liberated sex style
that was still defined and dominated by men. In treating genitals
as interchangeable parts, exponents of the sexual revolution justified open sexuality by denying the importance of emotional involvement. Yet most women regarded sex not as an isolated act,
but as an integral part of a loving relationship. The eagerness of
men to engage in detached sexuality thus created enormous pressure for liberated women either to conform to male sexual standards or to appear prudish and unsexual.

By the early seventies, feminists began to rebel against this unpleasant choice. "When women feel powerless and inferior in a relationship," explained the Boston Women's Health Collective in an immensely popular publication *Our Bodies, Ourselves,* "it is not surprising to feel humiliated and unsatisfied in bed." "Orgasms," they concluded, "are not that important in life." Seeing the sexual revolution as an extension of male supremacy, some women declared celibacy a better alternative. And even more significant numbers announced their conversion to lesbianism. Challenging the myth that homosexuality was a clinical perversion, gay feminists inverted the standard argument. "If hostility to men causes Lesbianism," reasoned Martha Shelly, "then it seems to me that in a male-dominated society, Lesbianism is a sign of mental health."

The defense of sexual autonomy also led feminists to demand ultimate control of the birth process. Sharing that common goal, women's opinion nevertheless varied considerably. "Pregnancy is barbaric," declared Shulamith Firestone in her polemic *The Dialectic of Sex,* and she urged women to seize the technology of reproduction, create artificial wombs, and so end female subordination to biology. The idea especially appealed to lesbians, who desired motherhood without the cost of heterosexual relationships. But other women, by contrast, insisted that childbirth was a natural experience, "a process of the female body," best liberated from the "physician-centered bureaucracy." Both positions, though polar opposites, assumed that the male-oriented medical professions had needlessly turned childbirth into "a terrifying and inhumane experience."

These pervasive antiprofessional feelings spilled into the political arena over the sensitive issue of abortion. Despite the increasing availability of birth control information, several states in 1970 still prohibited the sale of contraceptive devices to minors and high medical costs often made them unavailable to the poor. In addition, many prophylactics were ineffective. As a result, several hundred thousand women in America each year became pregnant against their will. Unhappily pregnant women took one of three paths. The majority resigned themselves to nature and either gave their babies up for adoption or integrated them into their lives. A second group, approximately 25 percent of the total, terminated their pregnancies through legal abortions, and of these women, ninety percent were white. The remainder, of unknown size, chose illegal abortion, endangering their lives in what otherwise was a simple medical procedure. Each year, feminist Robin Morgan pointed out, more women died of abortions than Americans were killed in Vietnam.

The demand for unlimited voluntary abortions, however, confronted powerful groups that viewed conception, pregnancy, and birth not only as moral issues, but also as the natural extension of female existence. In 1967, the only justification for abortion in any state of the union was the need to save the mother's life. But the abortion movement exerted strong counterforces of its own—attracting a large constituency that cut across sex, class, and race. It appealed, moreover, to a popular fascination with the possibility of manipulating the life process, of establishing scientific hegemony over nature. In 1970, after a bitter political debate, the New York legislature agreed to reform the state's century-old abortion law, permitting the termination of pregnancies resulting from rape or incest, as well as those threatening the physical or mental health of the mother. One year later, demographers noted a significant drop in the state's birthrate. By mid-1971, eleven other states had enacted similar abortion reforms. As feminist protest against existing laws continued to mount, federal judge Gerhard A. Gesell ruled that "a woman's liberty and right to privacy . . . may well include the right to remove an unwanted child." The question eventually moved to the Supreme Court—from which it would later emerge as the most controversial constitutional issue of the decade.

The feminist challenge to antiquated abortion laws, like the rejection of the sexual revolution, represented a deliberate departure from traditional expectations of female images and roles. In defying the status of "sex object," women also attacked pervasive corporate values that perpetuated sexual stereotypes in order to maximize economic profits. "Our legs, busts, eyes, mouths, fingers, hair, abdomens, and vaginas," protested the Boston Collective, "are used to sell stockings, bras, fashions, cosmetics, hair coloring, a multitude of birth-control products that men would not consider using in any form, powders, sprays, perfumes (again to make us smell 'nice' for men because our own smells are not good enough), and such obscene things as deodorants for our vaginas." Emphasis on such products established uniform standards of beauty by which all women were judged (and judged themselves).

By these arbitrary criteria, exceptional women might attain a modicum of social success, much as blacks had occasionally found opportunities through physical activity in sports or entertainment. For most women, however, beauty contests were competitive, divisive events.

The repudiation of traditional fashion soon became a visible assertion of women's liberation. At the 1968 Miss America pageant, radical feminists from a New York group called WITCH (Women's International Terrorist Conspiracy from Hell!) flaunted their discarded underwear as they disrupted the proceedings. Women pointed to the impracticality of most fashions and criticized the tendency to standardize the female form. Dresses, skirts, and stockings now went the way of the whalebone corset. And with legs no longer in sight, women felt more comfortable about letting their body hair grow, though, as one feminist observed, "even the most liberated women backslide when beach weather arrives." For conservatives, however, it was the departure of the brassiere that epitomized the recklessness of the feminist crusade, and the term "bra-burner" emerged as a nasty term of derision.

The confusion between sexuality and liberation seemed most perplexing in an issue that found radical feminists and archconservatives on the same side, in opposition to mainstream liberals—the question of pornography. Since the late fifties, the expansion of first-amendment rights served as an important stimulus to the sexual revolution, providing the legal basis for the liberalization of language and rules about public nudity. Conservatives saw this trend as bedrock evil. In May 1969, President Nixon called for "a citizen's crusade against the obscene," and Vice President Agnew attacked the "radical-liberals," who, he said, "wore themselves into a lather over an alleged shortage of nutriments in a child's box of Wheaties—but who cannot get exercised at all over that same child's exposure to a flood of hard-core pornography that could warp his moral outlook for a lifetime." But in 1970, the President's prestigious Commission on Obscenity and Pornography reported that there was "no evidence" linking pornography to delinquent behavior and recommended that the government avoid any legal restrictions on "explicit sexual materials." Nixon promptly denounced his committee's findings and, in a rare display of support, so did a vast majority of the Senate.

While the politicians fulminated about the morality of pornography, feminists introduced complex questions about the relationship of commercial sex to the subordination of women. Although the presidential commission denied that pornography altered popular attitudes toward women and insisted that females seemed as interested as men in sex-related products, it did admit that very little pornography was aimed at a female clientele. Moreover, in determining the nature of pornographic material, the commission excluded from its purview the contents of newspapers, radio, and television, thus deliberately overlooking the varieties of lascivious appeals used by business to sell nonsexual merchandise. These unexamined issues, feminists argued, obscured the omnipresence of pornography and its oppression of women.

As pornography penetrated polite circles, however, its exploitative nature became more apparent. Goaded by profits, the pornographic industry reduced participants and spectators alike into orgasm-seeking objects. Just as capitalistic enterprise depended upon efficiency and expertise to maximize profits, so pornography became increasingly slick and professional to maximize orgasmic expenditure. Popular exhibitionists such as Linda Lovelace, Marilyn Chambers, and Xaviera Hollander dropped their anonymous exteriors and, as porn "stars," took public credit for their sexual performances. The content of pornography nevertheless continued to depend upon the treatment—and often maltreatment—of women as objects of male pleasure. Lovelace's *Deep Throat*, for example, hinged on an improbable male fantasy that a woman's clitoris was lodged in her esophagus. Though conservatives continued to view fellatio as perversion, such pornography was tolerated—and became economically successful—precisely because it reinforced prevailing beliefs about social and sexual relations.

Mainstream media, unlike pornography, avoided gross sexual expression, but they endorsed the same conservative themes in more subtle ways. At a time when women were challenging a traditional dichotomy that divided females into angels (virgins, housewives) and whores (independent, economically self-sufficient), major Hollywood movies continued to define good women as appendages of men (*Straw Dogs, Carnal Knowledge*), sheltered from worldly affairs (*The Godfather*), while portraying working women as prostitutes (*Klute*). Television's "All in the Family" not only caricatured Edith Bunker as a willing victim of her husband's chauvinism, but in the early shows, cast their daughter, Gloria, as a sexy newlywed playing the stereotyped roles. Serious newspapers like *The New York Times* occasionally opened their editorial columns to feminist protest, but one beneficiary of this largesse, Robin Morgan, noted angrily that "The *Times* can congratulate itself on the liberalism of 'permitting' such dissent in its pages— and thus retain the ability to 'permit' what is a human right." In the regular news stories, women's status remained unchanged: they were described by marital status, physical appearance, and dress ("Miss Alpert, a petite brunette wearing a dark green sweater, black slacks and no makeup . . .").

Such editorial and programing content, however, revealed only the surface of the media message. More than half the space in *The New York Times* carried advertising, other national magazines strove for a similar percentage, and one-fifth of television airtime transmitted commercials. These marketing techniques had proven enormously effective not only in selling products, but also in altering opinion about public issues. Yet advertisers had little incentive to change old sexual stereotypes.

Depicting traditional images, advertisements of the early seventies accentuated female domesticity, characterizing women primarily as consumers—seldom as workers—whose main purpose in life was to please the opposite sex. American women in advertisements waged endless warfare against sinister subversion, usually portrayed as an invisible conspiracy of germs or dirt. Laundry detergent ads commonly placed women in competition over the whiteness of their clothes. But women's most effective weapon, a feminist analyst observed, was the aerosol spray can, used to fight body odor, keep hair under control, and halt the ravages of bacteria and bugs. (Coincidentally, the nation's largest manufacturer of aerosol sprays was Robert Abplanalp, President Nixon's closest confidant and financial backer, who ploughed his earnings from the Precision Valve Corporation into real estate in San Clemente, California, and Key Biscayne, Florida, and then kindly transferred some of the property to the chief executive and leased some to the secret service.)

In exaggerating the pleasures of domestic bliss, advertisers appealed to women who felt threatened by the feminist challenge to traditional roles. By placing females in ridiculous situations, such commercials made women into objects of derision. Antifeminist humor became a stalwart defense of the sexual status quo. "Let me make one thing perfectly clear," said President Nixon about the subject of women's liberation, "I wouldn't want to wake up next to a lady pipe-fitter."

NEITHER THE PRESIDENTIAL WIT nor the aerosol spray can, however, could protect American housewives from a contagious unhappiness that had spread like wildfire across the land. Though national media campaigns continued to assert that a female's proper place was in the home—a cook in the kitchen, a lady in the parlor, a whore in bed—women expressed great dissatisfaction about those conventional roles. "I want something more than my husband and my children and my home," dozens of women assured Betty Friedan as she documented the housewife's malaise in her pioneering book of 1963, *The Feminine Mystique*. By decade's end, these sentiments compelled a major reevaluation of the role of married women in American society.

The subject of housewife frustration emerged in the early seventies as a central theme in American fiction. Where traditional male literature placed the major crises of life in late adolescence, a time of career choice and marriage, a series of women's novels emphasized the deep frustrations of married heroines. Alice Adams's *Families and Survivors*, Paula Fox's *Desperate Characters*, Joan Didion's *Play It as It Lays*, Alix Kates Shulman's *Memoirs of an Ex-Prom Queen*, Marge Piercy's *Small Changes*—all focused on the collapse of female identity when conventional domestic relations became sour.

"Now I lie in the sun and play solitaire," lamented Didion's Maria Wyeth, who in the course of the brief novel is separated, impregnated, aborted, and divorced. "I mean maybe I was holding all the aces, but what was the game?"

Shulman's heroine moved with similar despondency from marriage to a psychiatrist's couch to extramarital affairs to divorce to pregnancy to abortion to remarriage and childbirth.

Psychiatrist Alexandra Symonds, observing a significant number of housewives "who seem to shrivel up after getting married, who seem to lose all interests and involvements, who constrict their inner life, and who become depressed, anxious, and excessively dependent," concluded that many women fled into marriage to avoid confronting difficult problems of emotional development. "They feared the consequences of taking life into their own hands."

But if some women retreated into passive marriages to avoid reality, others suffered what psychoanalyst Robert Seidenberg called "the trauma of eventlessness." Describing the case of a twenty-eight-year-old housewife who feared "losing her mind" and who experienced "apprehension in the street and in stores, and fear that she might harm her three-year-old daughter," Seidenberg suggested that neurosis was a form of rebellion, in this case a reaction to the woman's realization "that in her life 'nothing would happen'! " Living vicariously through their husbands, such women faced a future without serious challenge, without personal destiny, and developed paralyzing feelings of worthlessness.

The frustrations of American housewifery resulted in an epidemic of psychological symptoms associated with depression, self-deprecation, and suicidal impulses. In 1964, the number of women requiring psychiatric care began to increase significantly, and many of these patients embarked on a peculiar female "career" of recurring hospitalization. Sheltered from reality, these women could regress to total dependence, free from the burdens of adult relationships, including sexuality. Psychologist Phyllis Chesler found that many of these patients blamed their mothers for failing to provide protection from traditional submissiveness and viewed older women with distrust. Ironically, women in psychiatric institutions remained under the control of male-dominated professionals, and feminist researchers reported numerous cases of sexual manipulation delivered under the guise of therapy.

AS MORE WOMEN REALIZED that conventional marriage produced spiritual disaster, the nation experienced a dramatic increase in the number of independent households headed by females. A rising proportion of women, apparently fearful of duplicating their mothers' mistakes, decided to delay marriage (the 1970 census indicated a one-third increase of unmarried women under age twenty-four), adding to a burgeoning population of adult "singles." Meanwhile, unhappily married women increasingly opted for divorce. The national divorce rate, the highest in the world, had grown slowly but steadily since the beginning of the twentieth century; between the mid-fifties and 1970, it leaped by two-thirds for women under forty-five. The highest category of divorce was the age group twenty to twenty-four, an indication that early marriage no longer satisfied a woman's need for identity. More divorced women were now mothers and, unlike an earlier generation of divorced women with children, preferred to support their families rather than seek remarriage. Poor families, which often could not afford the high cost of divorce, simply separated, though frequently women were then left with inadequate means of support. Female-headed households remained among the poorest in the land.

Women's willingness to live without men reflected the growing opportunities within the work force. At all economic levels, the number of female workers increased tremendously in the years after World War II. In 1940, only 25 percent of women had jobs, but by 1970 that proportion had nearly doubled. At the same time, the percentage of married women who worked tripled and those with children increased at an even faster rate. Besides augmenting family income, the entry of women into the labor force provided important precedents for a younger generation, offering an attractive alternative to the ideology of female domesticity. For married women, work not only brought liberation from loneliness and the passivity associated with watching television, but also bridged the isolation that traditionally separated women from each other.

In acquiring jobs, however, women encountered serious obstacles to satisfactory careers. Believing that females were unreliable workers, employers were reluctant to hire women for responsible tasks. During the sixties, some women managed to breach sex barriers in skilled occupations, and the rate of female entry into the professions rose considerably. But women remained disproportionately employed in low-paying nonunionized jobs—as secretaries, domestics, waitresses, and salespeople—which held little possibility of advancement. To compound these problems, women traditionally received lower wages than men, even when their work skills required superior training. Reflecting these discriminatory patterns, women's income remained substantially lower than that of men, a ratio that actually *declined* from 63 percent of male income in 1945 to 57 percent in 1973. "I've suffered more discrimination," claimed Representative Shirley Chisholm, "as a woman than as a black."

Drawing on the experience of the black civil rights movement, women began to exert pressure on government to eliminate discrimination in public life. In 1966, author Betty Friedan led a group of women in forming the National Organization for Women (NOW), a body pledged "to confront with concrete action, the conditions which now prevent women from enjoying the equality of opportunity and freedom of choice which is their right as individual Americans, and as human beings." NOW's initial program emphasized the end of sexual discrimination in employment and the establishment of day-care centers to supervise the children of working mothers. But membership pressure soon led the group to endorse a broad range of issues, including liberalized abortion laws, specific programs to equalize education opportunities, revision of marriage, divorce, and rape laws, and adoption of an Equal Rights Amendment (ERA) to the Constitution. With one hundred chapters and over three thousand members by 1970, NOW liberals expected to win changes by influencing the established political structure.

While liberal women lobbied for legal reform, feminists with roots in the civil rights movement, Students for a Democratic Society (SDS), and antiwar groups began to protest against male domination and sexual discrimination within the radical movement. Declaring that "the personal is political," radical feminists formed "consciousness raising" groups that encouraged women to define a political identity as the first step for achieving social equality. Unlike liberal feminists, radical women sought not equal rights, but equal power, a much more grandiose objective that envisioned a fundamental revolution in American sexual relations.

Despite differences about tactics and goals, liberal and radical feminists recognized an essential unity of purpose in attacking the male establishment. On August 26, 1970, the fiftieth anniversary of the adoption of the Nineteenth Amendment that guaranteed women's suffrage, tens of thousands of women gathered in most major cities to demand abortion reform, child-care centers, and equality of opportunity in employment and education. REPENT, MALE CHAUVINISTS, read some typical placards, YOUR WORLD IS COMING TO AN END; DON'T COOK DINNER TONIGHT—STARVE A RAT TODAY; DON'T IRON WHILE THE STRIKE IS HOT. "This is not a bedroom war," Friedan reminded the crowd at New York's Bryant Park, "this is a political movement."

Responding to this pressure, legislators moved to remedy obvious political inequities. In 1971, Congress approved the Child Development Act, which authorized federal funding of child-care centers. The next year, federal legislation guaranteed rights of equal pay, prohibited sex discrimination in educational programs receiving federal monies, and extended the jurisdiction of the Equal Employment Opportunity Commission to prohibit job discrimination based on sex. And after five decades of inaction, Congress overwhelmingly approved the ERA, which asserted that "equality of rights shall not be denied or abridged . . . on account of sex." Hailing this legislative victory, Senator Birch Bayh predicted ratification by the states within two years.

The optimism was short-lived. In a ringing veto message, President Nixon rejected the Child Development Act, arguing that day-care centers would "commit the vast moral authority of the National Government to . . . communal approaches to child rearing" and undermine the nation's "family-centered" traditions. Public opinion widely supported the President's position, effectively killing child-care reforms. Similarly, despite a broad legislative mandate, the EEOC proved desultory in forcing compliance with the antisex discrimination provisions of the Equal Employment Act. And the ERA, after quick passage by thirty-three states, soon bogged down in a quagmire of local politics.

These political defeats testified to the strength of traditional values and persuaded feminists of the importance of attacking the underlying assumptions that defined social roles. In March 1970, New York feminists staged a day-long sit-in at the offices of the *Ladies' Home Journal* to protest the magazine's demeaning image of women. "It's not a matter of atoning for the past," wrote publisher John Mack Carter in agreeing to publish a special women's liberation supplement, "but [of] building for the future." The next year, a group of journalists led by Gloria Steinem launched *Ms.* magazine. "Eliminating the patriarchal and racist base of existing social systems requires a revolution—not a reform," they explained. "But it's not a revolution we die for—it's one we live and work for. Every day." As the title of the new publication suggested, feminists insisted on developing a nonsexist vocabulary to eradicate distinctions of gender, and to expand the horizons of a younger generation, the magazine offered innovative stories for "liberated children."

Attempts to alter popular consciousness through the mass

media, however, greatly underestimated the ability of the established order to absorb dissent while offering mere appearance of change. *Ms.* magazine might publish Alix Kates Shulman's marriage contract as a way of suggesting alternatives to female domesticity, but in listing the varieties of household chores, the same article handed critics an avalanche of trivia to bury serious attention to the issues. "Even the brightest movement women," Joan Didion observed, "found themselves engaged in sullen public colloquies about the inequities of dishwashing and the intolerable humiliations of being observed by construction workers on Sixth Avenue." In a similar way, *The New York Times* coverage of a feminist protest march highlighted Betty Friedan's rallying speech with a witty sidebar about her delay at the hairdresser. "The women's movement is going to be the biggest movement for social and political change in the nineteen-seventies," she told a cheering throng. But a casual reader more likely noticed Friedan's remarks about being "as pretty as we can. It's good for our self-image and it's good politics."

These diversionary tactics held the potential of undermining the women's movement from within. The women's liberation supplement to the *Ladies' Home Journal*, for example, appeared as part of a regular issue which featured the usual articles about beauty and marriage as well as full-page advertisements for feminine products that treated women as decorative objects. Similarly, the premier version of *Ms.*, packaged with the advertisements of *New York* magazine, contained considerable sexist material. *Ms.* editors might boast about their "editorial control," but the countersymbols of the ads communicated a different message. Concern about surface language—the invention of terms like "chairperson"—sometimes seemed more important than substantive changes.

The political consequences of misplaced trust appeared in the very first issue of *Ms.*, in an article that rated the 1972 presidential candidates. Of the major entries, *Ms.* gave highest scores to Senator George McGovern of South Dakota, calling him "the only candidate who consistently makes women's concerns a part of his campaign." As chairman of the Democratic Commission on Party Reform, McGovern had advocated changes of delegate selection procedures to increase female representation. He had, moreover, criticized Nixon for failing to name a woman to the

Supreme Court and had promised to appoint women to important offices. Given the choices, the South Dakotan seemed most likely to support women's causes. But in the coming campaign, women would discover that even the liberal McGovern viewed feminism as a risky—and disposable—commitment.

FOR WOMEN, THE CONNECTION between sexuality and politics remained inescapable. ". . . all of us are underground," wrote Robin Morgan, in a public prose poem to the fugitive Jane Alpert:

> . . . thousands of years in hiding, and only now
> beginning to surface. Ready.

Sharing this apocalyptic faith, the poet Adrienne Rich celebrated the feminist revival: "The sleepwalkers are coming awake," she announced, "and for the first time this awakening has a collective reality; it is no longer such a lonely thing to open one's eyes."

On her twenty-sixth birthday, Jane Alpert surfaced in an open letter which proclaimed her "conversion from the left to radical feminism." Traveling incognito through middle America, she had seen the futility of social revolution. Yet the wide acceptance of women's liberation seemed to presage a new era of social relations. "Because the Women's Movement gets lumped with the left in many people's minds," she observed, "it is mistakenly regarded as narrowly 'political.' Yet feminism concerns more than political power, essential as *that* is. It is closely tied," she remarked, "to theories of awakening consciousness, of creation and rebirth, and of the essential oneness of the universe." Alienated from the mainstream, feminists would follow a path taken by other oppressed groups, seek unity in opposition and build a culture of their own.

3

"THIS TERRIBLE DIVISION BETWEEN US"

The Politics of Race

THE NEWS FROM KENT STATE SENT shockwaves through the land, but some citizens had good reason to feel little involvement. "They're starting to treat their own children like they treat us," stated a dry-eyed black woman riding a bus in Harlem. In Buffalo, New York, a black student recalled the complaisant silence that had followed the shooting of several black students at Orangeburg, South Carolina, in 1968. "The contrast," he observed, "teaches us a lesson." A week after the killings at Jackson State, fifteen black college presidents journeyed to the White House to reiterate that lesson, telling the President of "the anger, outrage and frustration of the Black people of this nation." In Jackson, Mississippi. meanwhile, a white grand jury investigating the incident absolved the trigger-happy highway patrol and warned students to expect similar reactions to civil disobedience. The "depth of bitterness among black students," the Scranton commission reported, "surpassed anything found among white students."

This hostile atmosphere reflected a profound disillusionment at the failure to achieve racial justice after more than a decade of protest. Following the 1954 Supreme Court ruling in *Brown* v. *the Board of Education*, which established the principle that biracial facilities were "inherently unequal," blacks had optimistically anticipated a new era of race relations. Challenging legal obstacles to equality, the civil rights movement inspired mass protests—sit-ins,

38

freedom rides, marches to Birmingham, Washington, and Selma—
that eliminated obvious forms of racial discrimination as it won
support from sympathetic whites.

In the mid-sixties, however, blacks experienced a major revolution of consciousness that carried black protest beyond the limited demands of racial integration. Seizing power from the middle
class leadership of the civil rights movement, black radicals like
Stokely Carmichael and H. Rap Brown condemned the tokens of
racial "progress," proclaimed the importance of preserving a
unique black culture, and demanded recognition of black power.
Purging white liberals who advocated peaceful racial accommodation, a young generation of black leaders committed the movement to winning a mass base among blacks. Militant rhetoric, no
longer restrained by middle class proprieties, soon aroused a festering anger than had slept uneasily in the squalor of American cities.
Shouting "Burn, baby, burn," ghetto blacks ignited a series of
violent upheavals that spread from Harlem to Watts to Newark
and Detroit. Facing the collapse of public order, the Johnson administration responded by expanding liberal programs designed to
alleviate the misery of ghetto conditions. But such partial remedies failed to abate black rage. As a sign of the times, Brandeis
University established a Center for the Study of Violence in 1966;
it reported 167 cases of urban riots in 1967. The next year, the
assassination of Martin Luther King provoked riot conditions in
most major cities.

The increase of black violence intensified fears throughout
white society, producing a conservative backlash against black demands. "This country cannot temporize or equivocate in this
showdown with anarchy," wrote Richard Nixon in a *Reader's Digest* article. "Opinion-makers have gone too far in promoting the
doctrine that when a law is broken, society, not the criminal, is to
blame." The issue, explained Nixon, involved nothing less than
"the decline in respect for public authority and the rule of law."
Just as black militants rejected the limited advantages offered by
middle-class liberalism, now white conservatives criticized the failure of liberal gestures to satisfy black demands.

This erosion of liberalism from both the left and the right
provided the background for the Republican campaign strategy of
1968. Never sympathetic to a liberal race policy, Nixon decided to
ignore the black vote, most of which traditionally went Demo-

cratic anyway, and instead appealed to white conservatives. Though this tactic was called by the press a "southern strategy," the Republican candidate also sought to attract northern conservatives who feared black militance. When the President's National Advisory Commission on Civil Disorders, headed by Governor Otto Kerner, reported in March 1968 that the country was "moving toward two societies, one black, one white—separate and unequal," candidate Nixon scorned its refusal to condemn the "perpetrators" of urban riots. "Until we have order," he declared, "there can be no progress." Hoping to avoid needless offense to black voters, Nixon conceded that there was "a great deal of prejudice" in American society. But he criticized the frank language of the Kerner Report because it tended "to divide people." "What we need is more talk about reconciliation," he said, "more about how we're going to work together, rather than the fact that we have this terrible division between us." Proving remarkably effective at the polls, the Republican strategy enabled Nixon to carry several southern states (George Wallace, running as an independent, took the rest). But Republicans obtained only 13 percent of the black vote.

The election of 1968 consequently accentuated the alienation of black voters. Having been denied black support, however, the new President felt no obligation to reward a black constituency. He appointed no blacks to the cabinet, picking his campaign manager, John Mitchell, architect of the "southern strategy," to head the racially sensitive Department of Justice. "It is hard for the average white or black American," complained the NAACP's Roy Wilkins, "to see how a Wall Street lawyer can appreciate the police and courtroom hocus-pocus that snuffs out the liberties and lives of many helpless citizens each year." Columnist Tom Wicker, writing in *The New York Times*, pleaded with the President to reconsider the appointment, arguing that blacks and poor people deserved "a symbolic assurance" that the administration really cared about their problems.

Nixon responded with conciliatory promises "to do more for the underprivileged and more for the Negro" than any other President. In his inaugural address, he borrowed a phrase from the emotionally powerful civil rights song "We Shall Overcome," summoning "black and white together" to move forward toward an era of racial equality. And in an early press conference, he expressed hope of gaining "the respect and . . . eventually, the friendship of black citizens and other Americans." But the President had no intention of destroying his political base among conservatives. Blacks would receive little from this administration beyond words—and even these, as a secret document revealed, would come grudgingly.

"THE ISSUE OF RACE," read the memorandum to the President, "has been too much talked about . . . has been too much taken over by hysterics, paranoids, and boodlers on all sides. We may need a period in which Negro progress continues and racial rhetoric fades." The manipulation of language, the message implied, would diminish black expectations, allow the inertia of American institutions to absorb and soften the demands for change. It was time, said presidential adviser Daniel Moynihan, to adopt a policy of "benign neglect." This private statement, leaked to the press in February 1970, aroused storms of anger among liberals. In the Senate, Edward W. Brooke, the only black member of that body, castigated the administration for its "cold, calculated political decision" to reject the needs of black people in favor of a strategy of accommodating southern whites.

The most significant reaction to the Moynihan letter, however, was scarcely noted. As a historical symptom, silence is an elusive document, impossible to verify or quote. But while black leaders and liberals denounced the cynicism of administration attitudes, the mass of blacks hardly blinked at all. For them, presidential machinations simply reinforced a sense of separation, a feeling that government was a white man's game in which a handful of exceptional black leaders were permitted to participate, sometimes as equals. Few blacks, the silence indicated, were genuinely surprised by the unexpected glimpse behind the scenes.

But while most blacks remained outside the political dialogue, their fate provoked bitter debate among white politicians. Nixon's position on racial issues, initially designed to attract southern votes, held broad ramifications for the entire society. In seeking to overcome Dixiecrat prejudices against Republicans, Nixon denied the uniqueness of southern racial attitudes and instead emphasized the more complicated problems of racial justice throughout the country. This strategy thereby diverted public attention from what Nixon people called "regional" issues and undermined the national crusade for civil rights. To the frustration of liberals, Nixon took the racial question into the north, where it helped to fragment the shaky Democratic alliance.

The issue crystallized on that old symbol of American democracy—the public school. Despite the historic *Brown* decision, years of litigation, the use of federal troops, and a variety of other tactics, by the time Nixon entered the White House, 68 percent of the black children of the south still attended all-black schools. During the Johnson administration, the Department of Health, Education and Welfare (HEW) had made significant gains in integrating schools by threatening to deny funds to school districts that violated the desegregation provisions of the Civil Rights Act of 1964, and Nixon's Secretary of HEW, Robert Finch, announced his intention to continue that policy. In keeping with the administration's southern strategy, however, Finch introduced a novel idea when he said that school desegregation would be enforced "nationally, not just in the South. You've got *de facto* segregation in every part of this country," he explained, "and we're going to go after it."

While southern conservatives applauded this shift of operations, the administration abruptly backtracked on its support of desegregation. In the summer of 1969, on the eve of the new school year, the White House ordered a delay of desegregation in Mississippi, claiming there was insufficient time to produce alternative plans. But government lawyers already had developed an effective program and had introduced it earlier as legal evidence. The administration was lying. "It's almost enough to make you vomit," complained Roy Wilkins.

Such protests forced the President to elucidate his position on civil rights. Prudently, he made no mention of the political bargain he had recently struck with Mississippi Senator John Stennis—a tradeoff of school desegregation for support of the controversial ABM missile system. Instead, Nixon discussed civil rights as a matter of pragmatic politics. "There are those who want instant integration and those who want segregation forever," he told a press conference. "I believe that we need to have a middle course." The great moral force of school desegregation, however, could not so easily be undone. Two months later, a unanimous Supreme Court, defending the 1954 *Brown* decision, ordered the end to segregated schools "at once." The President promised to enforce the order. But at year's end, Secretary Finch returned to court to plead for additional delay. Again the High Court rebuffed the administration. But its ruling revealed the beginning of an important shift of opinion. For the first time since 1954, two justices, one of them Nixon's first appointee to the Court, dissented on a school desegregation case.

Southern school districts, lacking further legal recourse, now accepted desegregation with minimal upheaval. Though a white mob attacked a school bus carrying black students to a previously all-white high school in Lamar, South Carolina, this incident proved to be exceptional and government officials loudly condemned the violence. Many white students, in what became a pronounced trend in subsequent years, began to abandon public schools altogether, seeking white educations in suburban schools or in private academies. But by September 1970, only 14 percent of southern blacks attended all-black schools.

Nixon, meanwhile, having demonstrated his defense of southern principles, could safely endorse what he could no longer forestall. "The Constitutional mandate will be enforced," he announced in a statement released in March 1970. According to his "personal belief," Nixon agreed that racial segregation "by official action" was legally and morally wrong. But the President drew a hard line against ordering government action in cases of de facto (nonofficial) segregation. With an eye on northern conservatives, he pointed out that 78 percent of blacks in Los Angeles attended nearly all-black schools; in Chicago, the figure was 85 percent, the same as Mobile, Alabama; nationwide, 61 percent of blacks went to schools that were 95 percent or more black.

These statistics reflected the existence of urban ghettos throughout the north, patterns of residential segregation that once had been supported by official government policies. To overcome the impact of segregated housing on public schools, civil rights leaders advocated the busing of students. Nixon, however, in one of his most popular anti-civil-rights decisions, rejected that proposal. Transporting pupils "beyond normal geographic school zones for the purpose of achieving racial balance," he declared, "will not be required." The statement carried the civil rights struggle into the courts, where school busing became the central race issue of the decade.

In moving the burden of school desegregation to the judicial branch of government, Nixon not only avoided responsibility for unpopular decisions, but also placed the question of race within the most conservative of all federal institutions. Under Johnson, civil rights lawyers had discovered that government lawsuits proved less effective in enforcing desegregation orders than the termination of HEW funds to state and local school boards. The Nixon administration nevertheless decided to shift enforcement procedures back to the courthouse. More cynically, the President determined to fill crucial judicial posts with "strict construction-ist" judges, regardless of their position on civil rights.

These policies climaxed in bitter debates about two men nominated by Nixon to the Supreme Court—Clement Hayns-worth and G. Harrold Carswell. Believing that the political character of the Court promised a more durable impact than any legislation or executive action, Nixon determined to reverse the liberal trends which under Chief Justice Earl Warren had led not only to the reversal of segregation, but also to the reinterpretation of personal civil liberties. When Warren retired in 1969, Nixon chose the conservative Warren Burger, who was easily confirmed by the Senate. To fill a second vacancy, the President nominated Haynsworth. But in this case, Senate investigators discovered an antilabor, prosegregationist record as well as a conflict-of-interest ruling in which the judge presided in a case involving one of his holdings. When liberals challenged Haynsworth's qualifications, Nixon refused to retreat, instead charging the critics with "vicious character assassination." Despite the presidential lobby, the Senate, for the first time since the days of Herbert Hoover, rejected a Supreme Court nominee.

Furious at this rebuff, Nixon proposed Carswell, another southern judge with conservative credentials. But Senate investigation found Carswell even less qualified than Haynsworth. As an archsegregationist, Carswell had harassed civil rights lawyers from the bench, campaigned on a segregationist platform, and had participated in a shady business deal to prevent the integration of a municipal golf course and then lied about it to a Senate committee. As opinion turned against Carswell, Nixon attacked the Senate for infringing his right to select Supreme Court justices. But in April 1970, the Senate defended its own constitutional prerogatives of "advice and consent" and rejected the nomination. "I understand," retorted Nixon, "the bitter feelings of millions of Americans who live in the South about the act of regional discrimination that took place in the Senate yesterday."

The idea of "regional discrimination" involved more than rhetorical indignation. In seeking an alliance with southern conservatives, the administration recognized the importance of preserving the political status quo within the South, even though this objective threatened one of the most impressive gains of the civil rights movement: the expansion of black suffrage. The Voting Rights Act of 1965, which eliminated literacy tests and authorized federal supervision of voting procedures, had stimulated a huge leap in southern black voter registration, from 29 percent to 52 percent. If this trend continued, black voters might obtain sufficient power to topple the conservative regimes of the southern states, upon which Nixon's southern strategy depended. The liberal law, however, was scheduled to expire in 1970.

As Congress prepared to reenact its provisions, Attorney General Mitchell announced the administration's refusal to support "essentially regional legislation." He proposed instead a weakened voting rights measure that would apply to all fifty states. The NAACP promptly denounced the scheme as a "deadly way of thwarting the progress we have made." But the administration continued to lobby the revised bill through the House of Representatives. The Senate, however, again rejected the southern strategy and forced an extension of the original law. The measure assured increasing importance to black voters. "The time for racial discrimination is over," stated one beneficiary of the law, the newly elected governor of Georgia, Jimmy Carter, in 1971. But as blacks entered the Democratic fold in greater numbers, more southern whites departed the party.

In the northern states, Nixon's racial strategy produced a similar effect. Insisting that racism constituted a national phenomenon, the administration introduced the much publicized Philadelphia Plan, by which government contractors in the construction industry pledged to hire a specific number of minority workers. By attacking the interests of white construction workers, the program placed liberal labor leaders in the embarrassing position of opposing their own rank and file, and at the same time aggravated tensions between urban whites and blacks. Yet the Philadelphia Plan, which the administration extended to major cities throughout the country, did not lead to a consistent fair employment policy. Having made a token gesture, Nixon cynically allowed the antidiscrimination provisions to remain unenforced. Similarly, while cabinet member George Romney tried to persuade northern suburbs to accept subsidized low- and middle-income housing, the President announced his opposition to "forced integration" and promised "not . . . to impose economic integration on existing local jurisdictions." These vacillating pronouncements, by stirring passions in urban areas, created serious divisions within the liberal Democratic coalition.

The contradictions of Nixon's statements especially offended black leaders. To celebrate Independence Day 1970, fifty black clergymen bought a full page advertisement in *The New York Times* to announce a "Black Declaration of Independence" "from the injustice, exploitative control, institutional violence and racism of white America." Three weeks later, three members of the congressional black caucus, angered by the President's refusal to meet with them, issued a public letter warning that "the patience of many black Americans is exhausted." Still unsatisfied six months later, members of the black caucus boycotted Nixon's state of the union message, citing the President's failure "to give the moral leadership necessary to guide and unify this nation in time of crisis."

Such criticism underscored the absence of a coherent administration policy on civil rights. More concerned with creating appealing presidential images, the White House deliberately clouded its political intentions. Speaking to indignant civil rights workers in 1969, Attorney General Mitchell offered some paradoxical advice: "You will be better advised to watch what we do instead of what we say."

LISTENING TO THE WHITE HOUSE, however, distracted attention from what was obviously the President's primary concern—the achievement of a semblance of peace in the nation's ghettos. Urban violence threatened not only the authority of government, but also imperiled the corporate structure. "If the cities continue to deteriorate," remarked the president of the Western Electric Company, "our investments will inevitably deteriorate with them." The White House responded to such fears by offering a series of highly publicized programs to dampen black anger. In the event that these measures failed to work, however, the administration also prepared a racial strategy that was deliberately concealed from public view. It was an alternative that seriously jeopardized the rights—and the safety—of black citizens.

Nixon's public policy emphasized the importance of stabilizing the black community. "People who own their own homes," he stated, "don't burn their neighborhoods." By encouraging the emergence of a black middle class, the administration hoped to weaken the appeal of black militants. Such a policy would split the black population along class lines, offering some blacks the opportunity to enter middle-class positions. As symbols of success, upwardly mobile blacks, like an earlier generation of white immigrants, would demonstrate to their less favored brothers and sisters the advantages of working within the American system.

To achieve this ambitious goal, the administration reverted to conventional Republican wisdom, conservative to the core: the federal government, Nixon announced, would support black business. Shortly after taking office, the President created an Office of Minority Business Enterprise to coordinate government and private efforts to help black entrepreneurs. "We believe that every American should have the opportunity to share in the profits of our free enterprise system," declared Nixon. Using funds from the Small Business Administration, the federal government raised the number of its loans to minority businesses, tripling economic assistance in Nixon's first three years in office. The government also increased purchases from minority small businesses. And to attract support from private sources, the administration sponsored minority small-business investment corporations to protect private loans.

These efforts, presented as a generous departure of policy, nevertheless concealed a fundamental deceit—a false, anachronistic vision of the nation's economic system as well as a crude distortion of the nature of government aid. Despite Nixon's extravagant promises, the age of small business had long since vanished from the land and black enterprise, no matter how vigorous, had little chance of penetrating the corporate mainstream, much less of altering the pattern of economic relations dominated by huge conglomerates. To claim otherwise merely raised false hopes. Nixon's support of minority business, moreover, when measured against government assistance to other business interests, remained minuscule. Despite large increases in total funds made available to minorities, the rate of expansion remained slower than that of loans made to nonminority businesses. Nixon's policies scarcely affected the structure of business relationships, in which white companies not only controlled a disproportionate share, but under Nixon increased their relative holdings. A 1972 survey by *Black Enterprise* magazine found that only 26 black companies exceeded $5 million in annual sales and that the *combined* totals of the nation's top 100 black businesses would have ranked only 284 on the *Fortune* 500 list of leading corporations. "There's been lots of rhetoric in Government about helping blacks," concluded Philip Pruitt, who resigned as head of the minority entrepreneur program, "but no money has been forthcoming."

While creating an illusion of expanding black capitalism, the Nixon administration took more serious steps to defuse the sense of crisis among the more volatile ghetto population. In April 1969, with another long hot summer approaching, Nixon assigned $9 million of emergency funds to the Department of Housing and Urban Development (HUD) to rebuild riot-torn cities, and later approved other supplementary allocations. "There could be no more searing symbol of governmental inability to act," he remarked, "than those rubble-strewn lots and desolate, decaying buildings, once a vital part of the community's life and now left to rot." In subsequent years, Nixon approved large increases in HUD funding for low-income housing and for urban renewal. Federal allocations for housing subsidies leaped from under $1 million in 1969 to nearly $3 billion by fiscal 1973. The Model Cities Program, a much criticized legacy of Johnson's Great Society, also received substantial funding increases.

Through the Office of Economic Opportunity (OEO) and HEW, the federal government financed job programs to alleviate black unemployment, particularly among youth. With the black jobless rate running double that of whites and with black teenage unemployment over 30 percent, government jobs eased a major source of complaint. To deal with the inequities of welfare, the administration proposed an elaborate Family Assistance Program designed to provide minimum incomes for the working poor. But a combination of conservative opposition and liberal suspiciousness killed the measure in Congress. In signing an Emergency Employment Act in 1971, the President expressed hope that federally backed employment would have a "steadying" effect, leading blacks to permanent jobs. Such expectations proved illusory. But the administration's intentions may have been better expressed by presidential adviser Moynihan. More important than the economic impact of government programs, he suggested, was "the evidence of attention being paid, care being expressed"—the idea that the government had not ignored the plight of the ghetto.

For Nixon, outward appearances seemed more important than substantive racial policy. While offering token support to blacks, therefore, the administration concealed its policies lest conservatives take offense. In proposing a revision of welfare laws, for example, the President denied that the program represented a form of guaranteed income, even though its major author, Moynihan, insisted that it was precisely that. "Money for social programs was substantially increased," admitted one HUD official. "But this did not gain verbal support and acknowledgment of Administration leaders because the majority of white constituents did not perceive that as beneficial to them." In only one department did Nixonian rhetoric match action with word: "I think this is an institution for law enforcement," said John Mitchell upon taking over the reins of Justice, "not social improvement."

THE PRESIDENT MIGHT UTTER rhetorical platitudes, offer sums for urban renewal and unemployment, but in secret the administration operated on different assumptions: in planning racial policy, the White House assumed that the ultimate weapon for achieving racial peace was military force. Under Nixon, the Department of Justice prepared for armed war against blacks. With riot control its main objective, the Law Enforcement Assistance Administration, established by the Omnibus Crime Control and Safe Streets Act of 1968, saw its budget appropriations increase from $63 million in 1969 to $268 million in 1970 to almost $700 million by 1972. Most of this money went for police hardware—crowd control equipment, weapons, even an armored transport. Attorney General Mitchell also endorsed electronic surveillance of suspected dissidents and coordinated Justice Department operations with the illegal spying activities of the CIA and the military.

Mitchell's determination to crush black radicals culminated

in a systematic program to destroy the Black Panther Party. Founded in 1966 in Oakland, California, by Bobby Seale and Huey Newton, the Black Panthers embodied the new militance of black urban youth dedicated to protecting the black community from harassment by white police. The charismatic Panther leadership won wide support among poor blacks and, with a popular "Breakfast for Children" program, expanded the Panthers' base even among nonviolent, nonmilitant blacks. These successes alarmed FBI chief J. Edgar Hoover, who feared the formation of a national black coalition around some black "messiah." In 1967, Hoover unfolded an enlarged Counterintelligence Program (COINTELPRO) to "expose, disrupt, misdirect, discredit, or otherwise neutralize the activities of black nationalists."

Mitchell's Department of Justice enthusiastically endorsed these FBI activities against the Black Panthers. In one of his first official decisions, the attorney general authorized electronic surveillance of the Panther organization, and he included Bobby Seale in the indictment against the Chicago 8, charged with inciting riots at the Democratic National Convention of 1968. Hoover's claim that the Panthers represented "the greatest threat to the internal security of this country" aroused sympathy among Mitchell's top advisers. "The Black Panthers," said Jerris Leonard, head of the Civil Rights Division, "are nothing but hoodlums and we've got to get them."

Instigated by Hoover and sanctioned by Mitchell, the FBI joined local police departments in attacking Panther groups around the country—raiding thirty-one Panther headquarters in 1968–69, arresting hundreds of Panthers on spurious charges, demanding high bails, and disrupting party operations through secret "disinformation" programs. Panther protests simply raised the level of police violence which, in turn, raised the level of rhetoric. "Richard Nixon is an evil man. He is the man that unleashed counterinsurgent teams against the Black Panther Party," charged Panther chief of staff David Hilliard in a Moratorium Day speech in San Francisco. "We will kill Richard Nixon. We will kill any motherfuckers that stand in the way of our freedom." Hilliard soon found himself under arrest for threatening the life of the President.

Having immobilized Hilliard, the FBI moved against his likely successor, Fred Hampton of Chicago. In a surprise raid, federal authorities and Chicago police unleashed a terrible fusillade on a Panther apartment, killing Hampton while he lay in bed. Mark Clark, another Panther, died with him. Though substantial evidence indicated that the massacre was unprovoked, a grand jury excused the incident as justifiable homicide. In southern California, police attacked other Panther offices, leaving two more dead, wounding many others, and carting bystanders off to jail. In New York, twenty-one Black Panthers lingered in jail for two and a half years, unable to raise sufficient bail—and were subsequently acquitted of questionable crimes. In another celebrated trial in New Haven, Connecticut, Seale and Erica Huggins faced murder charges in the death of a Panther informant, but also won acquittal. Such accusations not only preoccupied the Panther leadership, but also drained the party treasury.

As the number of Panthers in prison approached one thousand, the focus of black militance shifted from ghetto streets to the maximum security lockups around the country. For many poor blacks, prison had become an extension of normal life. In 1970, nearly 2 percent of the total black male population—4 percent of those aged eighteen to thirty-four—lived behind bars, and nonwhites represented 40 percent of the total prison population. Prison conditions, like the ghetto slums that fed them, remained atrocious, and entrenched correctional officials blocked significant reforms. Penal reformers questioned the value of a system that caged human beings and still left society unprotected from a soaring crime rate. But the attorney general rejected the idea of a moratorium on prison construction, announcing instead new funding for additional facilities in 1971.

The arrival of black militants in prison served to politicize the inmate population, leading to new demands for prison reform. "They are fighting for human dignity," explained a black ex-convict, "for empowerment, for self-determination, for political rights—which many believe will lead to the eventual overthrow of the system that enslaves them." Blacks won recognition of black cultural and political groups, such as the Black Cultural Association at California's Vacaville prison, which offered "alternatives to the Black Offender in his apathy." Such groups attracted not only political radicals, but also ordinary criminals who sought comradeship and an end to racial oppression. Racial conditions inside prisons reflected the worst features of American society. At Soledad

Prison in California, for example, authorities maintained rigid separation of races. But on January 13, 1970, for reasons which remain unexplained, prison guards allowed blacks to mingle with whites in the yard. A fight erupted; three unarmed prisoners, all black, were shot dead. Black convicts later retaliated, killing a prison guard. Prison officials charged three convicts, known as the Soledad Brothers, with murder. One of them was the legendary George Jackson.

For prisoners of every background, Jackson served as a model of resistance. Serving a one-year-to-life sentence for armed robbery, he had endured a decade of harsh prison treatment, including beatings, solitary confinement, and arbitrary refusal of parole. In the process, Jackson had become an eloquent, impassioned revolutionary. His prison letters, published as *Soledad Brother*, won international acclaim for its exposure of racism and its demand for militant opposition. On August 7, 1970, while Jackson was standing trial for the Soledad case, his young brother Jonathan entered the courtroom, pulled a gun, and marched off with several court officials, hoping to exchange his hostages for George Jackson's freedom. In the ensuing shootout, Jonathan was killed, and police issued a warrant for the arrest of an alleged accomplice, a well-known black philosophy instructor and activist in the Soledad Defense Committee, Angela Davis. Still behind bars, George Jackson was promoted to field marshal of the Black Panthers, responsible for military planning.

Prisoners throughout the country closely watched Jackson's strange saga. In August 1971, however, San Quentin officials announced that he had attempted to escape, and while running toward the high prison wall, had been shot and killed. Few inmates believed the official account of Jackson's death. In distant Attica, New York, the state's maximum security facility, convicts staged a silent protest, wearing black items on their clothing and refusing to eat the midday meal. "No one can remember anything like it here before," reported Sam Melville, one of the few white inmates on good terms with blacks, who proudly signed a group condolence letter sent to Jackson's mother.

Like other prisons, Attica represented a microcosm of the larger society, pitting tough urban minorities against violent prison guards, most of them, as Tom Wicker observed, rural, white,and often racist. In the days after the silent protest, tension mounted inside the walls. "All the rules are now *strictly* enforced," Melville told his lawyers. "Attire, haircuts, lining up, not talking, no wearing hats—everything. . . . We are treated as dogs." One week later, Attica exploded, as convicts seized control of the institution. "WE are MEN!" they announced, demanding basic reforms ranging from religious freedom to a healthy diet. "We are not beasts," the inmates said; "we only want to live." Despite pleas from a delegation of neutral observers, however, New York Governor Nelson Rockefeller refused to negotiate with convicted criminals. "There was the whole rule of law to consider," Rockefeller later explained, "the whole fabric of our society, in fact." To the governor, the prisoners' demand for amnesty shook the foundations of justice.

Preoccupied with what one observer called the "Kent State psychology," prison guards itched to retake the facility. Ignoring Black Panther leaders who promised a peaceful solution, Rockefeller decided to act. At dawn of the fourth day, prison guards and state police charged over the wall, their guns blazing. It was "the swiftest and most skillful revolutionary offensive since the 1968 Tet attack in South Vietnam," boasted a state prison official. The result was shockingly bloody: forty-three dead, including ten hostages—all killed by police bullets. "I was amazed at Kent State," remarked a shaken observer, "shocked by Jackson State. But this . . . to see a decision being formulated that leads to so many deaths. . . . I don't believe I'll ever forget this." Here died Jane Alpert's lover, Sam Melville, whose resistance to "senseless authoritarianism" had led inexorably from the radical underground to the advocacy of prisoner rights.

The massacre at Attica epitomized official attitudes toward lower-class rebels, most of them black. Government might flirt with minority entrepreneurs, provide summer jobs for unemployed students, dole out welfare checks to "dependent children." But the yawning poverty of urban America remained untouched. "In prison," concluded an official investigation of the Attica rebellion, "inmates found the same deprivation that they found in the street. . . . Like the urban ghetto disturbances of the nineteen-sixties, the Attica uprising was the product of frustrated hopes and unfulfilled expectations."

In every major city, a large proportion of blacks—perhaps as much as 10 percent—no longer participated in the labor force or even collected unemployment insurance. These statistics suggested the existence in the seventies of a black "underclass" which lived outside the regular institutions of society and remained unassimilated to the larger culture. "We are a year closer to being two societies," declared the Urban Coalition on the first anniversary of the Kerner Report in 1969, "black and white increasingly separate and scarcely less unequal."

The Nixon administration nevertheless found satisfaction in the tangible results of its racial policy—the dramatic decline of urban riots. As blacks learned to expect less from government and as examples of police repression appeared more frequently, blacks retreated from the barricades of urban revolt. "Our cities and ghettos seem to be quieter today than they were a few years ago," observed Senator George McGovern. "But it is a stillness born more of resignation and despair than from any confidence in progress or the future."

In 1973, Brandeis University marked "the end of an era" when, for lack of business, it closed the Center for the Study of Violence. Few could be optimistic about its farewell statement. "There are still many events of severe conflict in neighborhoods, around schools, in prisons," it conceded. "But these phenomena remain localized and are much more susceptible to mediation and what we now call conflict-regulation." There was little chance, the group admitted, of attaining the more desirable goal of "conflict-resolution."

Faced with massive government suppression, the Black Panther Party also moderated its demands. "We've rejected the rhetoric of the gun," Huey Newton told an interviewer in 1972: "it got about 40 of us killed and sent hundreds of us to prison. Our goal now is to organize the black communities politically." In March 1972, black political leaders, most of them with roots in the lower class, organized a Black Political Convention in Gary, Indiana, in hopes of influencing the national elections, and Representative Shirley Chisholm of Brooklyn, New York, announced her candidacy for the presidency. For the first time in a decade, black dissent seemed institutionally safe. But the 1972 elections also produced strong, unyielding counterpressures to change, forces that were beyond the control of black leaders.

The situation for most blacks remained unchanged. The inadequacy of government programs, aggravated by a declining economy, increased black alienation from white America. Yet the transformation of consciousness created by black power established new values within the black community.

"The next generation may not be Black Panther in name," predicted an ex-Panther named Virtual Murrell. "But they will be Black Panther in mind." No longer would blacks burn their own homes or look to the federal government for help. Rather, they would nurture their own culture, seek a place in America on their own terms.

"Black men have no country," explained Joseph Langstaff, a retired carpenter and mason, "but they are a country in their hearts."

"I get tired of that one-nation-under-God boogie-joogie," protested a middle-aged black named John Oliver. "We are ourselves. We are our *own* nation or country or whatever you want to call it. We are not one-tenth of some white something! That man has got his country and we *are* our country."

4

"NOBODY CALLS IT THE WORKING CLASS"

Hard Hats, Blue Collars, and Ethnics

TALL, HANDSOME, BEAMING BEFORE the cameras, New York City Mayor John V. Lindsay embraced the microphones at the National Magazine Awards dinner of 1970. Yet he had little to beam about. Outside, his city seethed with anger. Two days after Kent State, student strikes were disrupting the city's campuses. At the evening rush hour, antiwar protesters occupied the major thoroughfares, bringing the heavy traffic to a halt. The municipal board of education, fearing outbursts of violence, announced the closing of public schools to honor the dead. On Wall Street, the stock market plunged to the lowest levels since the Kennedy assassination.

"The country is virtually on the edge of a spiritual—and per-haps physical—breakdown," the mayor warned. "For the first time in a century, we are not sure there is a future for America." Calling for "antiwar legions" to challenge administration policy, Lindsay pleaded that dissent be kept "peaceful, orderly, and reasonable." Friday, May 8, 1970, he proclaimed, would be set aside as a "day of reflection," a time "to reflect solemnly on the numbing events at Kent State University and their implications for the future and the fate of America."

Lindsay's appeal soon aggravated the very tensions he was attempting to abate. As antiwar demonstrators gathered at the federal Subtreasury building near Wall Street to protest Kent State and Cambodia, a shining wave of yellow and orange surged through the crowd. A contingent of two hundred construction workers, decked in bright plastic hard hats and armed with pliers, hammers, and other hand tools, pounced on the "longhairs." As police watched tamely, the peace protesters raced for safety inside Trinity Church. The workers banged on the heavy doors, found them immovable, then marched their anger down the street toward Lindsay's City Hall, where the American flag, in homage to the Kent Four, hung at half-mast. To the chant "Alla way with the U.S.A.," one worker returned the banner to full height.

Standing in front of City Hall, the workers admired their success. "We just wanted to show how we felt," one participant later explained, "that we support Mr. Nixon." But to the amazement of the workers, one of Lindsay's assistants climbed onto a ledge and relowered the flag. A new rage ignited the men, who now burst the police lines and stormed the building. Fearing further violence, the deputy mayor conceded the point, personally reraising the flag. Shouting approval, the workers moved away from City Hall. But as they passed Pace College, antiwar posters drew their attention. Smashing glass doors and windows, some of the men turned their fury on the students inside. Then, as the lunch-hour whistles blew retreat, the workers returned to nearby construction sites, leaving behind seventy victims, many of them hospitalized, and only six of their own under arrest. "They went through those demonstrators like Sherman went through Atlanta," gloated a correspondent in Kent, Ohio. "That's exactly what we need."

Mayor Lindsay fumed at the "wanton violence," and liberal journalists warned of a protofascist uprising. But the unrepentant construction workers, backed by their union leader Peter Brennan and encouraged by the building contractors who employed them, took to the streets daily to harass antiwar dissenters, to condemn "Mao Lindsay," and to show their support for President Nixon. On Wednesday, May 20, one hundred thousand building workers and longshoremen paraded for three hours, carrying patriotic placards, shouting pro-American doggerel, and slugging bystanders who wore long hair or peace buttons. The liberal mayor was burned in effigy. Six days later, Brennan journeyed to the White House to present the President with an honorary hard hat, a gift that Nixon described "as a symbol, along with our great flag, for freedom and patriotism to our beloved country."

Though Nixon and Brennan extolled this old-fashioned

Americanism, the revolt of the hard hats spoke less about patriotic duty than the burning indignation within the white working class against the beneficiaries of sixties liberalism. These feelings had surfaced the previous year during Lindsay's reelection campaign, a contest characterized by unusual rhetorical violence in which white ethnic voters scorned the mayor for his "softness" toward black militants and welfare cheats, while a coalition of streetwise blacks and well-heeled liberals attacked the workers' candidate, Mario Procaccino, as an ethnic bigot. With Lindsay's election, the white working class felt squeezed by the alliance of poor blacks and upper-middle-class whites. In an incisive article that attracted the attention of President Nixon, columnist Pete Hamill warned in 1969 that New York's white lower middle class ("nobody," he remarked, "calls it the working class any more") was "on the edge of open, sustained and possibly violent revolt." In the construction trades, the specific grievances involved racial integration (the celebrated Philadelphia Plan that Nixon held as a powerful political cudgel), unemployment (in 1970, 30 percent of the nation's construction workers were unemployed at one time or another, one-third of these for more than four months), and cutbacks in public works caused by inflation and budgetary shifts. More generally, white workers felt, in the words of a witness of the Wall Street riots, that "they are almost the only segment of the population government hasn't paid much attention to . . . , that they were in a kind of limbo."

Two issues symbolized this sense of powerlessness: the massive expansion of welfare rolls in the sixties and the prolongation of the war in Vietnam.

Welfare, by 1970, had become synonymous with black power. As urban blacks demanded basic improvements of ghetto living conditions, municipal, state, and eventually the federal government used welfare as a way of providing minimal assistance while avoiding major reforms that might have upset entrenched political interests. In the decade ending December 1970, therefore, nationwide welfare lists swelled by 225 percent, half of which occurred in the Nixon administration when the President's anti-inflation strategy produced higher unemployment. Welfare funds nevertheless remained grossly inadequate and blacks continued to protest against economic inequities. But these complaints seemed particularly outrageous to working-class whites, who themselves teetered on the brink of economic disaster.

"I'm working my ass off," said a blue-collar worker of south Boston, "and I'm supposed to bleed for a bunch of people on relief."

"I work my ass off," a New York ironworker told Hamill. "But I can't make it." People on welfare were demanding credit cards, he explained, when he, a hardworking man, was unable to get one, either. "You see that," he said somberly, "and you want to go out and strangle someone."

"There's a lot of people," said another ironworker, "who ain't gonna put up with it much longer."

The war in Vietnam produced similar expressions of frustration. Labor leaders like Brennan and AFL-CIO chief George Meany might rally unquestioningly to the flag, but public-opinion polls repeatedly indicated that rank-and-file workers were substantially less hawkish than college-educated, upper-middle-class respondents. "The whole goddamn country of South Vietnam is not worth the life of one American boy, no matter what the hell our politicians tell us," declared one construction worker. "I'm damn sick and tired of watching those funerals go by." Working-class youth, more vulnerable to the draft than the college crowd, remained suspicious of the military effort, caring less about the outcome of the war than their personal well-being. These "grunt" soldiers viewed mutiny as a satisfactory alternative to risky assignments and occasionally assassinated officers who insisted on executing all orders. Stateside, military bases became seedbeds of antiwar sentiment.

But precisely because a disproportionate number of working-class men were drafted and sent to Vietnam, blue-collar Americans bitterly resented the role of college students in leading antiwar protest. At issue was not a difference over foreign policy, but plain class antagonism. One worker whose son was serving in Vietnam lamented the inability of poorer boys to "get the same breaks as the college kids." "We can't understand," he added, "how all those rich kids—the kids with beads from the fancy suburbs—how they get off when my son has to go over there and maybe get his head shot off."

"If I had a chance to get an education," stated one envious factory worker in May 1970, "I wouldn't be wasting my time on the streets."

The antipathy to student protest stemmed less from a conflict of interests than from the simplified manner in which the mass media, especially television news coverage, dispensed information. "You can't turn on the television," said an exasperated factory worker, "without seeing them do something else." In presenting news as drama, television highlighted the exceptional story, transformed rhetoric into role playing, created images of unrelieved tension, and ultimately persuaded audiences to sit through commercials about headaches and banking to glimpse the next unresolved crisis. Screened in this form, the news came as segments and fragments, bits and pieces of scenes that, no matter how banal, received equal exposure and, most important, appeared separate from any cultural or social context. The black militant, posturing about burning the city, stood as the random demagogue—eccentric as any Dallas assassin, a "loner"—unconnected to social problems of unemployment, inflation, war, or racial discrimination. From this perspective, the white worker understandably opposed political dissent.

"Why the hell should I work with spades," one worker asked Hamill, "when they are threatening to burn down my house?"

In the White House, the President pondered these words. "What is our answer?" he asked.

The administration responded with campaign oratory, a concerted effort to capture the congressional elections of 1970. "This country is going so far right," predicted Attorney General Mitchell, "you are not going to recognize it." Sent to the hustings, Vice President Agnew launched the first blast. "The time has come for someone . . . to represent the workingmen of this country," he declared, the hardworking, family-oriented, churchgoing, tax-paying patriot, the average American, member of the "silent majority" who, he claimed, had become "the Forgotten Man of American politics."

Nixon also pleaded with the electorate to reject the antiwar caricatures that populated the evening news. "You hear them night after night on television," he insisted, "people shouting obscenities"—not blips!—"about America and what we stand for. You hear those who shout against the speakers and shout them down. And then you hear those who engage in violence. You hear those, and see them, who, without reason, kill policemen and injure them and the rest." These images, figments perhaps of the presidential imagination, could be exorcised, Nixon said, by initiating a powerful four-letter counterforce—the vote.

But in November, Nixon's Forgotten Man did not forget his own interests. With unemployment running high, the war unresolved, voters rejected the party in power. The Democrats obtained significant gains in the House and the state capitals and lost only two seats in the Senate. To the surprise of the administration, rhetoric alone could not rally the white working class. Yet even as the White House contemplated this discovery, a new symbol of blue-collar outrage prepared for his debut.

TWO MONTHS AFTER THE ELECTION, he entered public life, bearing a vision of America as "the land of the free where Lady Liberty holds her torch sayin' send me your poor, your deadbeats, your filthy . . . so they come from all over the world pourin' in like ants . . . all of them free to live together in peace and harmony in their little separate sections where they feel safe, and break your head if you go in there. That there is what makes America great!" He was ignorant, raw, and angry—dictatorial to his wife, Edith, gruff to his daughter, Gloria, contemptuous of his Polish son-in-law, Mike; he was Archetypically full of Bunk, inhabiting a besieged "bunker" mentality, hero of the most popular television series of the decade: "All in the Family"'s Archie Bunker.

"Why fight it?" Archie's liberal son-in-law asked in the series' first episode. "The world's changing."

But Archie preferred an older, simpler America, expressed in his theme song, "Those Were the Days," a nostalgic time when sex roles were clearly defined, when men worked hard, and music was no more complicated than the tunes of Glenn Miller. "If your Spics and Spades want their rightful share of the American dream," Archie replied to Mike, "let 'em go and hustle for it just like I done."

Caught in a world he had not made, Archie thrashed against the forces of change, revealing an undisguised hatred for imagined enemies—minority groups ("hebes," "spics," "spades," "dumb Polacks"), nonconformists ("pansies," "fags," "fruits"), especially liberals (the "pinkos" who spouted "Commie crapola"). Never before had such words passed the television censors. Norman Lear, creator of the program, also defied convention by transforming that citadel of American stability—the idealized American family, usually seen as a refuge from the real world—into a political battleground. If blue-collar Americans resented the intrusions of the liberal state, which forced them to support wars, racial integration, and welfare, Archie had his hands full fending off the liberal invasion of his live-in son-in-law, personification of the generation gap, pervasive reminder of Archie's entrapment. "I'm against all the right things," Archie yelled, listing an orthodox liberal litany— welfare, busing, women's lib, and sex education.

The brazenness of "All in the Family" unleashed a serious debate about the implications of unexpurgated bigotry. Whitney Young, in practically his last public statement before his sudden death in 1971, deplored "the creative liberals who find racism a fit subject for television comedy" and contrasted the evils of Archie's verbal abuse with "the decency and lack of racism" articulated by the recently inaugurated governor of Georgia, Jimmy Carter. On the other hand, John Leonard, writing in *Life*, suggested that Archie's uncensored language might well rob "the words of their subterranean powers to shock or destroy." Whether Archie was legitimizing racism or betraying its idiocy, however, became a moot issue because of the passive nature of the television audience. The content of the programing, researchers discovered, seldom altered spectator opinion. Rather, through a process called "selective perception," viewers found reinforcement for their personal preconceptions. With 40 million people watching the show each week, "All in the Family" apparently offered something for everyone.

Archie's appeal to middle-aged workers, however, illuminated basic strains within American society.

"I wish there were more Archie Bunkers," said a storekeeper in Oregon. "You just can't change their ways, that's all. Like me, they're asking me to go along with these new ways today, but I can't see it. Me and Archie—it's too late for us."

"What's great about that show," agreed a railroad switchman, "is that . . . it's just like you feel inside yourself. You think it, but ole Archie, he *says* it, by damn."

"Dad is like Archie," observed one college son, after hearing his father praise the Bunker patriarch.

Underlying such identifications lay an ironic, often neglected dimension of the relationship of television to the American consciousness. Carroll O'Connor, the actor who portrayed Archie, complained about being stopped in the street by friendly bigots who confused his own identity with that of Bunker. To working-class viewers, the personality of Archie seemed more "real" than the glamorous stars who usually beamed into their living rooms. "I think they [!] enjoy making Archie look a little bit foolish," said a worker in a lumber mill. "I don't think he *really* means what he says about people." "I think a couple more shows with *real* people is needed," offered another enthusiastic viewer. Unnoticed by these commentators was the obvious truth that Archie Bunker was not at all real.

These remarkable transformations demonstrated television's ability to absorb and deflect working-class frustration. For in idolizing a fictitious character, viewers inadvertently accentuated their passive relationship to the larger society. Endorsing Archie's harangues might release tension, focus anger, week after week create an illusion of power. But each week a flick of a switch effectively silenced "ole Archie" and O'Connor returned to his liberal convictions. Meanwhile, the television spectator, who really was left with nothing, clung to the false impression that there were famous people who supported his opinions, that someone, somewhere *really* cared about his malaise. The televised fantasy of discontent became an electronic substitute for real life. In this way, television appeased its loyal followers, while simultaneously accomplishing its commercial purpose.

AT THE APEX OF SUCCESS, "All in the Family" found its niche in the *Guinness Book of World Records*: as the most widely seen television program, it commanded the top advertising dollar in the industry—$128,000 for one minute. Although viewers remained wary of advertising promises, few realized the intimate relationship between the ideology of shows like "All in the Family" and the commercials themselves. While Archie Bunker's rages distracted attention from the authentic sources of working-class dissatisfaction—the structure of the economy—the advertising station breaks assured audiences that the consumption of products brought personal improvement. Television, the ubiquitous salesman's foot-in-the-door, served to perpetuate the conservative mythology that in America any moral and hardworking citizen could obtain, if not success, at least happiness through materialistic consumption.

Belief in the values of self-improvement permeated the culture. "Work," assured Vice President Agnew, "will always be re-warded." On Labor Day, 1971, the President presented a major address, praising "America's competitive spirit, the work ethic." In Nixon's eyes, success was equivalent to mobility, what he de-scribed as "the right and the ability of each person to decide for himself where and how he wants to live." On a popular level, mobility translated into a fascination with vehicles of escape. By 1970, mobile homes had become, in the words of journalist The-odore White, "a golden growth industry"; in the colder states, a new apparatus, the snowmobile, made its appearance; and auto-mobiles, despite lagging domestic sales, continued to dominate the consumer economy.

The idealized vision of a mobile society, however, conflicted with the realities of American life. Despite the President's rhetoric or the assertions of Madison Avenue, most people lived very close to the economic class they were born into and worked at occupa-tions similar to those of their parents. "The blue collar worker," a special task force reported to the Secretary of HEW, "sees his mobility and his children's mobility blocked." This sense of immo-bility pervaded the working-class consciousness. In response to in-terviews about job changes, workers invariably defined their lives in the passive voice—"I was just in the right place at the right time," "I was lucky," "they picked me." Such passivity, by separat-ing individuals from the causes of their fate, provided crucial psy-chological defenses against feelings of failure. But paradoxically most workers continued to blame themselves—their personal lim-itations—rather than the economic structure, for their failure to succeed.

This sense of passivity represented a basic ingredient of the most popular comic form of the seventies, the television situation comedy, of which "All in the Family" was the prototype. "He'll never be more than what he is now," Edith Bunker said of her husband, "even though he had dreams once, like you." Such pa-thos usually remained hidden beneath the comic exterior, indeed functioned as the essence of the comic device. In this format, characters established distinct, fixed personalities, and then re-acted to a variety of external situations that befell them. Laughter came as the audience tried to anticipate exactly how the stock character would respond. It was this very predictability that made "ole Archie" a "lovable bigot" and distinguished this stereotype from the more vicious portrait of the upwardly mobile Joe, hero of a 1970 Hollywood movie of the same name, who in his frustration committed violent murders.

The dark side of Archie's passivity, the lack of social opportunity, was obscured from viewers by the separation of the home life from his job. Archie was seldom seen at work. His fury thus appeared to be temperamental, part of his character, rather than the result of situational conflict. In real life, of course, the evasion was impossible. "The workplace," explained Irving Bluestone, vice-president of the United Auto Workers union, "is probably the most authoritarian environment in which the adult finds himself. Its rigidity and denial of freedom lead people to live a double life; at home they enjoy substantially the autonomy and self-fulfillment of free citizens; at work they are subject to constant regimentation, supervision and control by others." To maintain the myth of infinite mobility, however, the television hero was spared these psychological gymnastics.

Television's antiseptic view of industrial work prevented an understanding of the causes of worker discontent. In the most simple sense, work in America was dangerous. In 1970, for example, there were 10 to 20 million industrial accidents, 27,000 each day, producing fifty-five deaths a day, 14,200 for the year, a figure that paralleled and sometimes exceeded the casualty rates of Vietnam. Occupational risks included exposure to substances that caused chronic illness and, in 1970, about 100,000 deaths. Only after considerable lobbying did Congress pass a weak Occupational Safety and Health Act in 1970, but subsequent analyses revealed a poor record of enforcement. Even this minimal legislation provoked loud corporate complaints about the overregulation of business by government.

Besides its physical hazards, work for most people was plagued by a feeling of meaninglessness. Assembly-line tasks had changed little since the days of Henry Ford and Charlie Chaplin, except for speedups, forcing workers to struggle with unrelenting monotony. Even new middle-management jobs, part of the growth of service industries after World War II, required repetitive activity rather than personal endeavor. Trapped in unsatisfying jobs, workers remained vulnerable to even less favorable temptations. IF YOUR JOB PUTS YOU TO SLEEP, offered an army recruiting poster, TRY ONE OF OURS.

The frustrations of work were particularly acute because personal identity in America was traditionally linked to occupation. Despite the drudgery of most jobs, therefore, workers strove to develop a sense of uniqueness about their achievement. Interviews with workers showed that most sought pride even in the most menial activity and deeply resented the indifference of management to the quality of performance. Moreover, work for most people represented the only avenue toward the establishment of some sense of higher purpose, the feeling of having contributed to human life. "I can look back and say, 'I helped put out a fire. I helped save somebody,'" said a city fireman. "I did something on this earth."

Younger workers, by contrast, still hoping to build a meaningful future, resisted the demands of industrial life, sought more than bread and butter from their jobs. Raised in the relative affluence of postwar society, they scoffed at the compliant habits of their elders, including union leaders, and adopted numerous strategies of rebellion. Lateness, absenteeism, violation of company rules, and, ultimately, job turnover reached epidemic proportions by 1970. "They're different, all right, no damn question about it," said one union leader about the new breed. "They're better educated, make more demands, and generally raise hell when something is wrong."

This rebelliousness erupted dramatically at General Motors' Vega plant in Lordstown, Ohio, when assembly line workers, averaging only twenty-four years of age, went on strike in March 1972 not for wage benefits, but for better working conditions. The factory, billed as the fastest line in the world, reflected GM's attempt to increase production (and compete with foreign imports) by maximizing efficiency. But the rate of one hundred cars per hour overwhelmed the men. "I'm getting the shit kicked out of me," protested a twenty-year-old, "and I'm helpless to stop it." The president of the UAW local put the logic of the company's efficiency experts and their time-motion studies into perspective: "When you talk about that watch," he said, "you talk about it for a minute. We talk about a lifetime."

Although labor commentators saw Lordstown as a symbol of a new type of unionism, the strike soon exposed the classic divisions within the American labor movement. Factory men from industrial cities like Youngstown and Warren felt little affinity for their coworkers from Appalachia, considered them "hillbillies." Both these groups agreed, however, in disliking the "hippie" element that flaunted a counterculture life-style. And blacks and Puerto Ricans, constituting 15 percent of the Lordstown work force, distrusted the white union leadership. These divisions forced the union to settle for old-fashioned issues of security—the reemployment of discharged workers. In exchange, labor acquiesced to the breakneck pace of the work. The strike, which lasted three weeks, cost GM $150 million (the large number of recalls in subsequent months suggested an even higher price-tag). But once again in American labor history, differences of culture established preeminence over the interests of class. In the end, the Lordstown affair revealed less about the difficulty of humanizing the workplace than about the illusions of another historical myth—the idea that America was the great homogenizer of culture.

"THE MELTING POT of our nation works wonders," boasted the son of a Greek immigrant, who now held the second highest office in government. "It builds unity out of diversity; all we have to do is give it a chance." For Spiro Agnew (aka Anagnostopoulos), assimilation, like the work ethic, offered the high road to success. But just as economic mobility encountered the insurmountable obstacles of the corporate economy, so, too, did the tenacity of ethnic identity obstruct entry into the cultural mainstream. For ethnic Americans, the problems of class and culture were thoroughly intertwined. "The Ethnic American is forgotten and forlorn," asserted Baltimore councilwoman Barbara Mikulski, with typical blurriness; "The status of manual labor has been denigrated." Many blue collar employees, frustrated by the limits of the workplace, now turned for sustenance to their ethnic heritage.

The resurgence of ethnicity represented an alternative to competitive individualism. "Our children," explained a supporter of working-class interests, "stripped of a strong group self-identity, will become defenseless and will be unable to cope with the pressures which are a prominent part of our society today." This image of a hostile world, besides reflecting ethnic alienation from the WASP leadership, had important political ramifications, drawing inspiration, ironically, from the most vocal antagonists of white ethnics, the black militants. If Afro-Americans could cherish their heritage, wear dashikis, and let their hair grow "natural," ran the argument, why not also celebrate the traditions of Italians, Slavs, and Poles? In an era of confrontation politics, group solidarity offered obvious advantages.

The new ethnicity also repudiated basic tenets of the modern state. Melting-pot values had traditionally assumed that the erad- ication of European culture and the acquisition of "Americanism" symbolized a transition from "backwardness" to "progress." A sim- ilar logic supported the exportation of the American way overseas. As a superior people, Americans could uplift benighted cultures throughout the world. In the Vietnam war, for example, the removal of peasant populations into barricaded concentration camps called "strategic hamlets" could be defined by political leaders as accelerated urbanization. The destruction of tropical forests by toxic chemicals like Agent Orange constituted the first stage of urban renewal.

These rationalizations served as instruments of cultural impe- rialism. But as the war in Vietnam came under attack, revealed itself in its technological horror, the values of ethnocentrism also lost power. The assertion of ethnicity, after generations of as- similationist teachings, constituted a declaration of independence from WASP hegemony, an anticolonial rebellion. Rejecting WASP cultural leadership also involved a reexamination of such elitist values as efficiency, quantification, and objectivity. As Michael Novak argued in his influential book of 1973, *The Rise of the Unmeltable Ethnics*, the new ethnic consciousness articulated "disillusionment with the universalist, too thinly rational culture of professional elites." The ethnic legacy promised to restore a sense of soul.

For second- and third-generation descendants, however, eth- nicity required a self-conscious commitment. In 1971, the Ital- ian American Civil Rights League of New York City sponsored "Unity Day," attracting thousands of people, many wearing KISS ME, I'M ITALIAN buttons to celebrate cultural pride. The next year, Congress passed the Ethnic Heritage Studies Act "to legitimatize ethnicity and pluralism in America" and appropriated funds for groups "whose members define themselves as a people claiming historical peoplehood." On a more subliminal level, ethnicity ob- tained reinforcement from the proliferation of stereotyped jokes, a form of humor that disguised aggression while simultaneously lending sanction to ethnic differences. These contrivances of ethnicity belied an underlying conflict within the ethnic communities.

The concealed tensions between ethnicity and assimilation emerged as the major theme of the best-selling novel of the decade, Mario Puzo's *The Godfather*, a work that sold over 13 million copies by 1980 and also became a two-part Hollywood box-office success. In the opening scene, Amerigo Bonasera (goodnight America), a hard-working immigrant who prospered in pursuit of the American Dream, discovered that his faith in American legal institutions had been misplaced. In the second scene, a sexually liberated woman betrays the immigrant son, Johnny Fontane, calling him "a dumb romantic guinea." Both characters, victims of the false ideology of the melting pot, turned to the Italian patriarch "for justice." "You found America a paradise," the Godfather sneered. "You never armed yourself with true friends." Puzo proceeded to describe a culture that despises the individualistic ethic of WASP America and instead venerates Old World virtues of respect, friendship, and especially loyalty.

THE AWAKENING OF ETHNICITY, like the brooding anger that surfaced at Lordstown and in Wall Street, indicated deep fissures within the national identity. The old Democratic coalition, in which working-class ethnics, blacks, and liberals joined forces against rural conservatives and wealthy Republicans, could no longer embrace the varieties of interest. As the Democratic party slipped into the hands of a liberal leadership that was dedicated to ending the war in Vietnam and to eliminating racial and sexual discrimination, the white working class abruptly realized its inability to stop this reversal of policy, found itself powerless in a rapid transformation of values. "They learned the Puritan work ethic and the system of meritocracy," explained Father Paul Asciolla of Chicago, "and now they're caught in a game where the rules are changing. They were just about to cross the goal line with the football when they were tapped on the shoulder and told to give the ball to a black to carry over." Believing in traditional patriotic duties, the white working class was also shocked to see the futility of the Vietnam War.

These discoveries—indicative of the decline of American virtue, the loss of a sense of national greatness—undermined established commitments and left working people vulnerable to the blandishments of their traditional enemies. Peter Brennan, leader of the construction workers, acknowledged the confusion of priorities when he supported Nixon "not because he's for labor, because he isn't, but because he's our President." And Father Asciolla underscored the consequences of that confusion when he predicted the white ethnic vote in 1972: "They know God is a Democrat," he said, "but this year they're voting Republican."

5

"POLITICS IS EFFRONTERY"

The Election of 1972

By 1972, THE ONLY HOPEFUL VISION of the American future seemed to exist in the past. The breakup of the Beatles two years earlier had symbolized the end of an era, and the big hit of 1971, Don McLean's "American Pie," forecast the death of rock 'n' roll. As the music industry embraced the introspective songs of James Taylor, John Denver, and Carole King, a major public-opinion survey found that most Americans believed the country had declined in the past five years. Even President Nixon, after announcing in his state of the union address of 1972 that Americans were "now . . . recovering our confidence . . . now renewing our sense of common purpose," reluctantly admitted that "our recovery is not complete."

The sense of having lost touch with the true America, of having fallen away from history, nourished a new enthusiasm for the American past. Taking advantage of the wistfulness for better times, the popular culture industries launched "nostalgia" campaigns to merchandise new products. Fashion designers, attuned to the advantages of sartorial obsolescence, celebrated the twenties style ("The Gatsby Look") and introduced "midis" that evoked the thirties, before fixing on the images of the forties and fifties. Hollywood contributed the sepia tones of *Butch Cassidy and the Sundance Kid*, the black and white of *The Last Picture Show*, sentimental glimpses of the Great Depression, and dozens of other grade-B historical romances. In 1972, *Life* magazine, known for its photographic realism, went out of business, but an enterprising publisher reissued the defunct *Liberty* magazine, which reprinted stories that were over thirty years old.

It took a politician with a genuine passion for American history to challenge this escapist fare. He had earned a Ph.D. degree in American history from Northwestern University, written a book about the Colorado coal strike of 1914, and quoted freely from the nation's historical documents. "I shall seek to call America home to those principles that gave us birth," declared the senator from South Dakota, George McGovern. Believing that the country was "drifting so far from those ideals as to almost lose its way," he offered to help the American people "seek a way out of the wilderness." In January 1971, one year earlier than the customary time for tossing one's hat into the ring, McGovern announced his candidacy for the presidency.

The source of America's malaise seemed easy to identify. "Vietnam is the wound in American life that will not heal," stated *Time* magazine in reporting the conviction of Lieutenant William Calley for the massacre of civilians at My Lai. Vietnam, said McGovern, "is a moral and political disaster—a terrible cancer eating away the soul of the nation." Having served as a bomber pilot during World War II, McGovern knew intimately the devastation of airborne explosives. He had voted in 1964 with most of the Senate—Wayne Morse of Oregon and Ernest Gruening of Alaska were the only dissenters—in approving the Tonkin Gulf Resolution which gave President Johnson a blank check to wage war in Vietnam. Within months, McGovern regretted his vote and remonstrated with Johnson to shift course. "Don't give me another goddamn history lesson," answered the Commander in Chief. McGovern carried his case around the country, spoke against the war at college campuses, and, in the wake of the assassination of Robert Kennedy, launched a brief and futile candidacy against Hubert Humphrey.

After Nixon's election in 1968, McGovern continued the struggle in the Senate. One day before the invasion of Cambodia, he introduced an "End the War" measure to terminate American military activity in Southeast Asia by December 31, 1971. "Every senator in this Chamber is partly responsible for sending fifty thousand young Americans to an early grave," McGovern declared. "This Chamber reeks of blood. . . . And if we do not end this damnable war, those young men will someday curse us for our pitiful willingness to let the Executive carry the burden that the Constitution places on us." The bill drew thirty-nine votes in favor; fifty-five opposed. McGovern began to plan for 1972.

NIXON, TOO, WAS MAKING PLANS—most of them in secret. As early as August 1969, he had encouraged his foreign-policy adviser, Henry Kissinger, to undertake private discussions with representatives of Hanoi. While public attention fixed on the stalemated formal negotiations that had been held in Paris since 1968, Kissinger met secretly with Vietnamese officials, offering subtle and slight concessions to the public stand. But since the administration refused to consider a coalition government in South Vietnam, these conversations also deadlocked. When the United States continued to back South Vietnamese President Nguyen Van Thieu, despite his obvious violations of democratic principles during a fraudulent election campaign in 1971, the North Vietnamese decided to shift strategies, broke off the secret meetings, and began mounting plans for a major military offensive the following spring. Unaware of this reversal, Nixon nevertheless gained an important domestic advantage when, in a televised address in January 1972, he revealed the details of the secret diplomacy. Blaming Hanoi for the failure of negotiations, the White House undercut the criticism of Democratic politicians who, in this election year, accused the administration of prolonging the war.

The news about secret negotiations surprised the public, but even this revelation paled by comparison to a previous announcement. Six months earlier, the President had unexpectedly ordered a revolutionary change in American foreign policy: the decision to normalize relations with the People's Republic of China. The State Department earlier had hinted at a new policy by loosening restrictions on trade and travel to the Chinese mainland. But neither the press nor the public knew about Kissinger's secret diplomacy in Peking. Now Nixon, once the nation's most outspoken anticommunist, accepted an invitation to visit the country with which the United States had permitted no formal relations since the boycott began in 1949.

As Nixon and Kissinger embarked on a new China policy, the administration also initiated high-level discussions with the Soviet

Union about arms control. The Strategic Arms Limitation Talks (SALT) raised extremely complex questions about the relative values of various weapons and delivery systems and were further complicated by mutual suspicion and the secrecy of both governments. In early 1971, however, the two powers signed the Seabed Arms Control Treaty, which banned nuclear weapons from the ocean floor. Sensing a relaxation of the Soviet position, Nixon pressed Moscow to concentrate on limiting antiballistic missiles (ABMs) and persuaded the Soviets to make a simultaneous public announcement promising to break the stalemate. In September 1971, the Soviet Union joined the Western powers in signing a pact that stabilized the status of Berlin, long a thorn in Cold War diplomacy. By October, Nixon was prepared to announce an impending visit to Moscow in the spring of 1972, partly to ease Soviet fears about a Sino-American alliance, partly to accelerate the SALT negotiations.

These dramatic diplomatic shifts, heralded by the White House as the dawn of a new era of global peace, seemed to contradict the essential reason for waging war in Vietnam: the belief that communism was an absolute evil that had to be driven from the face of the earth. Yet in seeking détente with communist leaders in China and the Soviet Union, Nixon made crucial distinctions between the political status of big powers and the rest of the world. For one thing, both communist superpowers possessed immense military strength that could embroil the United States in global holocaust. Secondly, both countries held enormous economic power which had direct consequences for the health of the American economy. The national interest, Nixon understood, required a reassessment of the international settlement that had been established after World War II.

American foreign policy traditionally functioned on two contradictory principles—first, that all nations should have free access to the trade and resources of all other nations, a capitalistic doctrine known as the "Open Door" which envisioned American industry competing successfully with the less dynamic economies of other nations—and, second, that certain areas of the world, particularly Latin America, were a special sphere of American influence in which other countries must have only minor interest. It was the refusal of communist governments to permit capitalistic penetration through the open door that contributed to the cold war divisions between "free nations" and "enslaved peoples." But in freezing economic relations with communist countries like China, the United States had thwarted its own capitalistic goal of maximizing world trade to keep the domestic economy flowing freely. As a cold warrior, Nixon had loudly defended the policy of nonrecognition toward China. But 800 million potential customers, whatever their political ideology, could no longer be ignored. "What we have done is simply opened the door," Nixon explained, "—opened the door for travel, opened the door for trade."

While confirming American commitments to free trade, Nixon also endorsed the idea of big-power spheres of influence. "What we see as we look ahead five years, ten years, perhaps it is fifteen, but in any event, within our time," he remarked to a group of newspaper editors in 1971, "we see five great economic superpowers: the United States, Western Europe, the Soviet Union, mainland China, and, of course, Japan." The list, with the exception of Japan (ironically America's great economic rival of the seventies), was only slightly different from the "Four Policemen" that Franklin D. Roosevelt had attempted to institutionalize in the United Nations Security Council in 1945. Roosevelt's vision had been stymied by the postwar anticommunist crusade, which had attempted to "roll back" Soviet dominance in Eastern Europe, the communist victory in China, and the emergence of indigenous revolutionary movements in European colonies, such as Indochina. But the new Nixon, more flexible than Eisenhower's Vice President, could accept this imperfect world.

The United States under Nixon now supported the concept of spheres of influence. The Berlin treaty of 1971, for example, acknowledged Soviet hegemony in eastern Europe, and the formulation of a "two China" policy conceded communist control on the Asian mainland. The President also acted to preserve United States domination in Latin America. Though he boasted that "the hemisphere community is big enough, mature enough and tolerant enough to accept diversity of national approaches to human goals," Nixon maintained the boycott of Castro's Cuba and ordered clandestine CIA operations against the communist regime of Salvador Allende in Chile. In yet another area, Nixon promptly moved to fill the power vacuum caused by the withdrawal of British forces from the Persian Gulf in 1971, providing vast economic and military support for the anticommunist Shah of Iran.

Nixon refused, however, to apply such sphere-of-influence

reasoning to Southeast Asia. First, like the four Presidents before him, he had staked the nation's prestige on a defeat of Vietnamese communism. More subtly, he may have feared that Chinese or Soviet dominance in the area would imperil the ability of the United States and Japan to expand trade in Asia without challenging each other. In an ironic replay of the issues that had led to Japanese-American rivalry before World War II, the United States insisted on maintaining an open door of economic competition in Southeast and central Asia as a way of discouraging future conflict with its Pacific ally in a shrinking marketplace.

With this paradoxical philosophy in mind, Nixon journeyed to Peking in February 1972, arranging his arrival in the Chinese capital to coincide with prime-time television viewing in the United States. All parties well understood the historic nature of the visit. "What we say here will not be long remembered," said Nixon in a paraphrase of Lincoln's Gettysburg address. "What we can do here can change the world." Then, in a series of cautious negotiating sessions with China's top leaders, the President sought common ground for agreement. The ensuing joint communiqués, carefully edited to express differing national interests, revealed the lines of future accord. Both sides shared the principle of "self-determination" for the countries of Indochina, though the idea remained subject to different interpretations and ignored the issue of Vietnam. They also agreed to relax tensions in Korea and southern Asia. The United States reaffirmed its "close ties" with Japan, including an unspoken military commitment, while the Chinese expressed opposition to the "revival and outward expansion of Japanese militarism." Finally, Nixon conceded that Taiwan remained a part of China and promised a gradual withdrawal of American forces from the island "as the tension in the area diminishes." "We have been here a week," the President said in farewell. "This was the week that changed the world."

Returning triumphantly to Washington, Nixon basked in the image of a peacemaker, issued licenses for trade with China, and prepared for his visit to Moscow, where he hoped to sign a SALT agreement. But he soon discovered an unexpected deficiency of big-power diplomacy—the inability or unwillingness of strong nations to dictate absolutely to their weaker allies. Pursuing its own national interest, North Vietnam waited for spring to launch a major military offensive, caught the South Vietnamese armies—and American intelligence—by surprise, and quickly captured important areas previously believed to have been "pacified." The weakness of South Vietnam's defenses further demonstrated the futility of "Vietnamization" and threatened to undermine the American negotiating position.

Recognizing the gravity of the situation, Nixon moved to take decisive military action, even at the risk of the Moscow summit. For the first time since 1968, the White House ordered B-52 bombers into action against North Vietnam and extended the targets to include Hanoi and Haiphong. The damage of four Soviet merchant ships created a brief period of crisis. But the Soviet Union, also pursuing a policy of détente, issued only a cursory protest and indicated a willingness to continue negotiations. Kissinger flew to Moscow to arrange for Nixon's visit, while the President appeared on television to justify the military escalation. "If the United States betrays the millions of people who have relied on us in Vietnam," he said, "the President . . . will not deserve or receive the respect which is essential if the United States is to continue to play the great role we are destined to play of helping to build a new structure of peace in the world."

Unimpressed by Nixon's rhetoric, undaunted by B-52s, Hanoi rejected another cease-fire overture and continued the successful spring offensive. In early May, Nixon decided to raise the stakes. Ignoring strenuous congressional opposition, Nixon announced to a television audience that the United States would block foreign trade to North Vietnam by mining the harbor of Haiphong and by bombing rail lines that led to China. Though Kissinger had speculated that there was an even chance that Moscow might cancel the summit, Nixon appealed to the Kremlin not to "permit Hanoi's intransigence to blot out the prospects we together so patiently prepared." The administration waited nervously for a reply.

The domestic response came more quickly. "This new escalation is reckless, unnecessary, and unworkable," protested McGovern, "a flirtation with World War III." "I think it is folly," exclaimed Senator Edward Kennedy. The President risked "a major confrontation," warned Senator Edmund Muskie, "and is jeopardizing the major security interests of the United States." Other voices, not so eminent, disagreed. "We are headed for a major defeat in South Vietnam," admitted the conciliatory governor of Georgia, Jimmy Carter, but Americans, he insisted, should "give President Nixon our backing and support—whether or not we agree with specific decisions." To reinforce such sentiments, the White House produced twenty thousand telegrams praising the President's policy; later, the public learned that most of the correspondence had been sent by Nixon's own reelection committee.

Despite the hostile reaction of the American public, Soviet officials chose to continue negotiations and made no mention of the crisis. Nixon had apparently won the war of nerves. In mid-May, he departed for Moscow, expecting a prompt conclusion of the SALT talks. Though some preliminary agreements had been reached through lower level negotiations, numerous complicated issues remained unsettled. Yet in his desire to return with a treaty in hand, Nixon imposed a rigid timetable for resolving these delicate matters. For unknown reasons, moreover, the President decided not to bring his technical advisers to Moscow, leaving himself to negotiate in unfamiliar territory.

The resulting treaties appeared extremely ambiguous and possibly unenforceable. Although the two powers agreed to a moratorium on ABM defensive missiles, specific restrictions on offensive weapons proved difficult to establish. Nixon not only compromised American demands on the size of Soviet arsenals, but also offered "unilateral statements" that were not official parts of the treaty, in hopes of establishing qualitative limits. Even after the final signing of documents, both nuclear powers diverted public attention from the real meaning of SALT: rather than providing for military cutbacks, the treaty simply institutionalized the nuclear arms race.

The President nevertheless returned in triumph to Washington and immediately went to Capitol Hill to address a joint session of Congress. "Everywhere we went," he declared, "we could feel the quickening pace of change in old international relationships. . . . Everywhere new hopes are rising for a world no longer shadowed by fear and want and war." Savoring his success, Nixon urged Congress to build a lasting peace by ratifying the SALT agreements. Within weeks, however, the President revealed a paradoxical commitment to military expansion. "If we have a SALT agreement and then do not go forward with [new weapons] programs," such as the Trident submarine and the B-1 bomber, he told a press conference, "the Soviet Union will, within . . . a very limited time, be substantially ahead of the United States overall."

While Congress grappled with these contradictions, the administration announced a new dimension to détente, one that might well explain the Soviet reluctance to cancel the summit conference when Nixon blockaded North Vietnam: the Soviet Union, facing a serious grain shortage, would purchase the huge sum of 17 million tons of surplus wheat. Such a sale, by promising to boost United States exports, fit nicely with the doctrine of the open door. Managed by Secretary of Agriculture Earl Butz, however, the wheat deal proved less a boon to American farmers than a boondoggle for a few large grain-exporting companies which, with inside information, bought cheap and sold high, leaving American consumers to face grain shortages of their own along with substantial increases in domestic prices. Nor did this transaction lead to a general commercial agreement between the two powers. Opponents of détente, led by Senator Henry Jackson of Washington, demanded that any additional commercial arrangements depended on the lifting of Soviet restrictions on the emigration of Jews. At that point, economic détente reached another impasse.

WHILE CAPTURING INTERNATIONAL ATTENTION, the administration's elaborate diplomacy also furthered the political aspirations of the President. Recognizing the advantages of seeking reelection as an incumbent, Nixon cultivated an image as Chief Executive, too burdened by presidential decisions to launch a partisan campaign. The missions to China and to the Soviet Union served these political purposes, and the President remained ever conscious of the proximity of television cameras that beamed his performances back to his constituents. On the crucial journey to Peking, for example, Nixon found room on Air Force One for his wife's hairdresser and amused his Chinese hosts by appearing in public wearing television makeup. *Newsweek* magazine headlined the feverish SALT negotiations as "the Moscow primary."

Though the President appeared untainted by the mundane world of electoral politics, his White House staff controlled a secret program of campaign warfare designed to discredit the opposition party. It began first with a series of "dirty tricks"—forged letters that attributed insulting words to Democratic candidates, late-night telephone calls that accentuated racial and ethnic antagonism, phony campaign literature intended to divide Democrats irrevocably, and the use of political spies. One night, during the President's visit to Moscow, a White House team of burglars (the "Plumbers") entered the headquarters of the Democratic National Committee at the Watergate office building, copied documents, and planted a telephone wiretap. Two weeks later, they returned to repair a faulty connection. Clumsy in their movements, five burglars were captured by Washington police, who soon reported that one of the crooks, E. Howard Hunt, carried a notebook that suggested some connection to the White House.

The executive branch moved quickly, in the parlance of the day, to stonewall further revelations. "I'm not going to comment," said presidential press secretary Ron Ziegler, "on a third-rate burglary attempt." Meanwhile, presidential advisers John Ehrlichman, H. R. Haldeman, and John Dean began to conceal incriminating evidence. Campaign manager John Mitchell, once the top law enforcement officer in the government, denied any connection to the Watergate break-in and soon announced his resignation because of family pressures. When queried about the case, his successor, Clark MacGregor, unconnected to the illegal operation, could maintain a better façade of righteous indignation. These pious reactions, coming from the most prestigious government leaders, appeared irrefutable and most voters, according to a subsequent Gallup poll, considered the affair "just politics."

Seemingly impervious to the fiasco, the President supervised preparations for the Republican National Convention, which was scheduled in Miami Beach, Florida, in August. So thorough were these plans, so detailed and precise, that Republican delegates found they had nothing to do but follow a carefully orchestrated scenario and applaud on cue. A convention timetable paid rigid attention to the television audience, even scheduling specific times for "spontaneous" demonstrations. Covering the proceedings for *Life* magazine, Norman Mailer realized that "since there would be no possibility for anything unsettling to happen in the hall," the only purpose of the convention was to create the *image* of a convention—"the communication itself," he explained, "would be the convention."

The national party platform, written inside the White House and concealed from most delegates, relied heavily on amnesia to celebrate the Nixon administration. "The choice is between going forward from dramatic achievements to predictable new achievements, or turning back toward a nightmarish time," the Republicans averred. "It is so easy to forget how frightful it was. There was Vietnam—so bloody, so costly, so bitterly divisive. . . . At home our horrified people watched our cities burn, crime burgeon, campuses dissolve into chaos. . . . Working men and women found their living standards fixed or falling, the victim of inflation. To millions of Americans it seemed we had lost our way." Under Nixon, however, the problems had vanished; "a new leadership with new policies and new programs has restored reason and order and hope."

The nomination ceremony was equally contrived. Nelson Rockefeller, Nixon's rival in 1968, introduced the President's name and reiterated the amnesia theme. "Four years ago . . . America was in deep trouble," he stated, but Nixon's "skilled management and leadership" had reversed the tide. "We need this man." Former Secretary of the Interior Walter Hickel, forced from the administration for criticizing the Cambodia invasion, returned to second the nomination and was followed by a bevy of other speakers, each carefully selected from a specific constituent group. The foreordained balloting proceeded on schedule, and convention chairman Gerald Ford announced, amid prepackaged cheers, that President Nixon had indeed been renominated. Spiro Agnew, considered by many Republicans a liability to the ticket, was again chosen as running mate. "Agnew is a monster," confided a White House insider, "but he's Nixon's monster."

Still following the script, Nixon waited until the next evening to make the last acceptance speech of his career. "I shall not dwell on the record of our Administration, which has been praised, perhaps too generously, by others at this Convention," he declared modestly, but he did take credit for having changed America and the world. "Let us reject, therefore, the policies of those who whine and whimper about our frustrations and call on us to turn inward. Let us not turn away from greatness." Then in a repetition of the television speech he had broadcast to the Soviet people the previous May, he quoted from the diary of a Russian girl who, with her entire family, had been killed during World War II. Nixon summoned his American audience to "build a peace that our children and all the children of the world can enjoy for generations to come." At a time when the President was still ordering "protective-reaction air strikes" against Vietnam, Norman Mailer discovered a curious omission in Nixon's version of the poignant diary: "For the last five weeks," wrote the ill-fated Tanya, "the airplanes have been coming over." In Nixon's lexicon, concluded Mailer, "politics is effrontery."

Having effectively sidestepped the major predicament of his tenure in office—the continuing war, the failure of Vietnamization, the escalation of bombing—Nixon left the convention feeling no obligation to discuss these troublesome issues. Under the television industry's "fairness doctrine" every minute of Democratic coverage required equal time for the Republicans. Yet Nixon held only one press conference in the fall of 1972, instead relying on administration surrogates to speak on his behalf. This strategy of aloofness left the more open Democratic campaign the only target for serious editorial criticism. Nixon's absence also exempted him from having to confront the festering matter of Watergate. When McGovern told a group of UPI editors that the Nixon regime was "the most corrupt administration" in American history, the press dismissed the charge as electoral hyperbole. Of the more than eight hundred newspapers that expressed an opinion, Nixon obtained endorsement from 93 percent. "After all," commented one reporter, "most editors thought Nixon was going to win, so why go out of the way to alienate him."

NIXON'S MASTERY OF THE MEDIA became the unspoken but crucial theme of the 1972 elections. As President, he not only controlled airtime wherever he traveled, but also deliberately accentuated an image of statesmanship, against which no other politician could effectively compete. It was perhaps no coincidence that the President visited China, drawing national television attention as a respected international figure, on the very day that Senator Muskie, then the Democratic frontrunner, lost the respect of the national press corps—and with it his status as a winning candidate.

The circumstances, seemingly bizarre and ephemeral, nevertheless typified the entire campaign. On the eve of the New Hampshire primary, long considered an important bellwether of election success (it was here that Eugene McCarthy knocked President Johnson out of the 1968 race), a peculiar letter appeared in the controversial Manchester *Union Leader*, sent from a mysterious Paul Morrison of Deerfield Beach, Florida. Subsequent investigation failed to locate Morrison and he may well have been a figment of the Republican "dirty tricks" campaign. The impact of his letter, however, was quite real. For Morrison claimed that Muskie had referred to New Hampshire's large minority of French Canadians as "cannocks." The *Union Leader's* editor, William Loeb, had accepted the letter as truth and aimed an editorial blast at Muskie for his insensitivity, and he followed this comment with other attacks, including an unfavorable description of Muskie's wife. Responding to these charges, the senator from Maine denied the truth of Morrison's claim and proceeded to denounce Loeb for criticizing his wife. "A good woman . . ." he said, and then, overcome by emotion, he began to cry. Gaining control, Muskie started again, but could not contain his tears. "He's talking about my wife. . . ." He paused, and then continued this staggered speech for a moment until he recovered his composure.

Muskie's "breakdown," treated as normal frustration and anger, might have meant nothing. But political pundits quickly seized its subtle implications. The "trouble," explained David Broder of *The Washington Post*, was that Muskie had failed "to solve the problem of how a rational man should behave in an irrational situation." Once praised for his "reasonableness" and "calm good judgment," Muskie now appeared vulnerable under pressure. He later won the primary by a clear plurality (9 percent), but the press declared his margin too slim to be viewed a victory.

This emphasis on a politician's public self-control boomeranged tragically for the one candidate who had learned better than anyone else to control his political rage, who in recent years had discarded a rough public exterior for one of moderation and self-discipline: George Wallace. Once a symbol of white racism, the Alabama governor had run as an independent candidate in 1968, capturing nearly 14 percent of the poll and forty-five votes in the electoral college. Four years later, Wallace returned to the Democratic Party, offering a populist campaign on the theme Send Them a Message. "The American people are fed up with the interference of government," said Wallace. "They want to be left alone." Carrying his message into the Florida primary, where Wallace's opposition to school busing had special appeal, the Alabaman swamped all the other contestants, taking 42 percent of the vote. "The George Wallace victory . . . is a threat to the unity of this country," complained Muskie, who was beginning to imitate his vitriolic media image. But McGovern defined the Wallace vote differently, seeing it as "an angry cry from the guts of ordinary Americans against a system which doesn't give a damn about what's really bothering people in the country today." Moving to Wisconsin, a northern and presumably less friendly state, Wallace finished second. McGovern, who shared Wallace's attack on "the Establishment Center as an empty, decaying void," won by only 7 percent.

One Wallace observer was particularly disturbed by the Alabaman's success in the north. "I wish I could give it to the Nixonites who crossed over and made Wally-boy look strong," he wrote in his diary. From his native Milwaukee, this political dilettante followed the Wallace campaign closely, attended suburban rallies as far distant as Michigan and Maryland. Wearing red, white, and blue clothing, a big Wallace button pinned to his jacket, he would stand at the front of the crowds, cheer the governor's "send 'em a message" finale, and yell for a handshake. Once, when Wallace approached, twenty-one-year-old Arthur Bremer blasted five bullets into the candidate.

The shooting of George Wallace awakened familiar memories of similar political assassinations and led observers to draw parallel conclusions. Comparing Bremer to other assassins, Lee Harvey Oswald, James Earl Ray, and Sirhan Sirhan, psychiatrist David Abrahamsen maintained that American assassins were "mentally ill persons driven by twisted forces in their own mind." "He seems like a shallow, mixed-up man," an arresting officer described Bremer, "but not an ideologue." "He must have been pretty sick," offered the assassin's father. Bremer pleaded not guilty to state charges of attempted murder on grounds of insanity and heard his attorney describe him as schizophrenic, mentally ill from birth, "if not before." But three court appointed psychiatrists and the jury found Bremer "legally sane" and he received a fifty-three-year sentence. Federal charges were later dropped.

The insanity argument, as in other cases of political assassination, effectively prevented any analysis of the defendant's motives. Though the FBI discovered no accomplices, Wallace believed he had been the victim of conspiracy, partly because White House aide Charles Colson asked the Plumbers to search Bremer's apartment soon after the shooting. When investigators did uncover Bremer's diary, they learned that earlier he had attempted to shoot President Nixon and perhaps also had stalked candidates

Humphrey and McGovern. But no one seriously considered the assassin's political commentary as anything but symptoms of schizophrenia. When queried by a court reporter about his post-assassination behavior, Bremer retorted: "Nixon doesn't have to give press conferences; neither do I." There the matter rested. Ignoring the possibility that assassination might reflect the failure of the political system to absorb extreme passions, Americans instead assumed that violent political acts, by definition, were insane.

WITH WALLACE REMOVED from the race, the way for McGovern seemed clear. Having stumbled in New Hampshire and Florida, Muskie could never recover his old image of "calm good judgment." New York Mayor John Lindsay, a recent convert from Republicanism and the only big-city candidate in the contest, attempted to project his good looks and charismatic style into a television-based campaign, but instead left voters suspecting an absence of substance beneath the media camouflage. Hubert Humphrey, the standard bearer of 1968, tried to rejuvenate his old Democratic following, but for reasons of credibility, he, too, failed to persuade the voters. "It was the horror of his career," wrote Norman Mailer about Humphrey, "that as he came to the end of it, his constituency was real (if antipathetic to one another . . .) but he was not real, not nearly so real as the constituency, more like some shattered, glued, and jolly work of art."

McGovern's success in the primaries gave him control of the Democratic convention. But as the delegates gathered in Miami Beach, they, too, communicated an aura of unreality. Following the Democratic debacle of 1968, party leaders had issued a "mandate for reform" and established a commission, headed by McGovern, to build "an open party" by increasing representation for women, minorities, and youth. The 1972 convention reflected these fundamental changes. Four years earlier, 13 percent of the delegates had been women; now they totaled 38 percent; the number of black representatives tripled to 15 percent; and people under the age of thirty increased from 2.6 percent to 23 percent. Old-line Democrats, squeezed from the proceedings by new guidelines, scarcely recognized their party. They've "reformed us out of the Presidency, and now they're trying to reform us out of a party," complained Ohio Congressman Wayne Hays. "I don't think those people represent the mainstream of the party." Other statistics confirmed this impression: 39 percent held postgraduate degrees; 31 percent earned more than twenty-five thousand dollars a year; the black delegates were inordinately educated and rich.

Internal controversy exaggerated the importance of these demographic configurations. Ethnic voters, traditionally associated with the big city machines, bitterly resented their exclusion in Miami. "Anybody who would reform Chicago's Democratic Party by dropping the white ethnic," scoffed columnist Mike Royko, "would probably begin a diet by shooting himself in the stomach." Meanwhile, the women delegates, who hoped to attach a proabortion plank to the party platform, encountered stiff resistance from McGovern forces who feared alienating the political mainstream in the general election. After considerable backroom bickering, the proposal failed. Feminist politicos, enraged by what they considered a last-minute betrayal, loudly questioned the advantages of working within traditional political structures. Even the black caucus, considered sturdy McGovern supporters, turned at last to one of their own—Shirley Chisholm.

Surviving by the skin of his teeth, McGovern worked to rebuild party unity with the theme Come Home, America. "We will call America home to the ideals that nourished us in the beginning," he addressed the convention. "From secrecy, and deception in high places, come home, America. From a conflict in Indochina which maims our ideals as well as our soldiers, come home, America." From wasteful public spending, from tax privileges, from prejudice and discrimination, he summoned the nation to "seek a newer world," a "joyful . . . homecoming."

But before setting the course, the McGovern campaign foundered in a squall of contention. Harried by the convention procedures, the candidate had hastily chosen as his running mate the handsome and vigorous senator from Missouri, Thomas Eagleton. Reporters soon learned, however, that the vice-presidential nominee had a history of mental strain. Three times the young politician had been hospitalized for fatigue, twice undergoing electroshock therapy to overcome depression.

The idea of ghosts lurking skin deep terrified the political leadership. McGovern's campaign contributions dropped precipitously, and most of the major newspapers urged the candidate to scuttle his running mate. Hoping to avoid such drastic remedies,

McGovern offered Eagleton "1000 percent" endorsement. But as the pressure persisted, McGovern developed second thoughts and consulted Eagleton's physicians. Their prognosis, McGovern later confirmed, was hardly reassuring. Meanwhile, a public opinion poll published by *Newsweek* indicated that the continuation of the Eagleton candidacy might cost the Democrats as much as 17 percent of the vote. McGovern decided to ask for the resignation.

This public reversal ironically increased opposition to McGovern. Having forced the hapless Eagleton from the slate, public opinion now rallied to his defense. And McGovern, unable to divulge the private medical reports, could not refute Eagleton's claim to have fully recovered. Nor, Eagleton made clear, would he resign voluntarily if McGovern deemed him mentally unfit for high office. Instead the Democrats announced that Eagleton would be dropped not because of illness but because his continued candidacy weakened the entire ticket. In taking this tack, however, McGovern tarnished his image as a man of principle, revealed himself no less opportunistic than all other politicians who sought high electoral office.

Even without the Eagleton affair, McGovern would have had difficulty preserving the Democratic constituency. His strenuous antiwar position and his willingness to consider amnesty for draft resisters offended supporters of Kennedy and Johnson and Humphrey who thought the war effort vital to the national interest. Several southern governors, led by Jimmy Carter, declared McGovern's views "completely unacceptable to the majority of the voters" and refused to risk their own careers by endorsing the national ticket. Carter even declined to appear in public with McGovern's new running mate, a Kennedy brother-in-law, R. Sargent Shriver.

These divisions undermined McGovern's ability to challenge the administration's foreign policy. A Gallup poll in September revealed that 58 percent of Americans believed that Nixon could do a better job in ending the war than McGovern, while only 26 percent backed the senator. McGovern might condemn United States support "of dictators, dope-runners and gangsters in Saigon," but his pleas proved far less persuasive than a surprise press conference held by Kissinger in late October which announced that "peace is at hand." Though McGovern correctly denounced administration optimism as premature—President Thieu, in fact, refused to accept the pending offer—voters preferred to believe Nixon's assurances that "the President of the United States is not the number-one warmaker in the world."

McGovern's dovish foreign policy also weakened his grip on the Democrats' traditional labor constituency. "He's become an apologist for the Communist world," complained AFL-CIO president George Meany on Labor Day. "My goodness, doesn't this man know there are no countries in the world where people chose communism?" The crotchety union leader could not completely ignore labor's Democratic sympathy, but the nation's largest federation refused to endorse any candidate, for the first time in its history. Nixon, meanwhile, solicited the votes of other unions. Two days before Christmas 1971, he pardoned former Teamster president Jimmy Hoffa, and a few months later was repaid by a strong union endorsement. His support of Peter Brennan—leader of New York's hard hats—and his cancellation of the unpopular Philadelphia Plan further broadened the President's base among organized labor. But despite these defections, most unions maintained a formal allegiance to the Democratic party, and the rank and file split nearly evenly.

McGovern's inability to keep the support of labor was closely related to his alienation from ethnic voters. "I feel a little like Al Smith addressing the Baptist League of Eastern Texas," he quipped to a Catholic audience in Manhattan. While McGovern's refusal to endorse abortions infuriated his feminist supporters, his assertion that such matters were a point of personal conscience won few friends from the Catholic community. Nixon, by contrast, publicly supported the Catholic hierarchy's opposition to all abortion reform.

On school busing and welfare—two other emotionally charged issues—McGovern's stand diverged sharply from the sentiments of white ethnics. In January, a federal court in Richmond, Virginia, had ordered local school districts to bus students across political boundaries in order to compensate for patterns of racial segregation. The case had wide ramifications for northern states, where residential segregation created de facto racial imbalances in public schools. Many white ethnics, having struggled to get their children away from poor inner-city school systems, now faced the prospect that court ordered busing would reverse their meager gains. Nixon, with an eye on the ethnic vote, promptly denounced the court ruling and asked Congress to enact a "moratorium" on new busing programs. But McGovern rejected Nixon's stand, calling it "a sneak attack on the Constitution." Nixon also spoke directly to ethnic resentment when he condemned liberal welfare programs, while McGovern preferred to attack more subtle loopholes that benefited the rich.

THE DISAFFECTION OF TRADITIONAL DEMOCRATS emerged dramatically on election day when President Nixon accomplished the greatest landslide in American history. Winning 60.7 percent of the vote, the Republicans carried every electoral ballot with the exception of Massachusetts and the District of Columbia. Capturing the Wallace vote from the Democrats, Nixon swept the once solid South. He garnered a majority of the ethnic vote, the Catholic vote, the white-collar vote, even the union vote. Only the Spanish-speaking, Jews, and blacks opted for McGovern, though even these groups gave more votes to Nixon in 1972 than they had four years before. "This may be one of the greatest political victories of all time," boasted the President on election night. McGovern, with less to gloat about, found solace in the thought that his campaign may have "pushed the day of peace just one day closer."

While the President celebrated his overwhelming triumph, political observers noticed a striking contrast in the congressional vote. Though the Republicans gained twelve seats in the House of Representatives, they remained a distinct minority (192–243), and in the Senate the Democrats added two seats, increasing their control to 57–43. Such statistics demonstrated a new pattern of ticket splitting among American voters, a significant decline in party loyalty, and a growing emphasis on political *issues* rather than partisan identification. In other words, blue-collar Catholic ethnics might desert the national party on ideological grounds, but at the same time they remained sensitive to the positions of local candidates who more closely reflected their interests. "The blue collar worker," remarked Senator Fred Harris of Oklahoma, "will continue to be progressive so long as it is not progress for everyone but himself."

Besides the disintegration of party allegiance, the 1972 poll confirmed another significant trend in American voting behavior—the steady erosion of voter participation, the unwillingness of people to ballot for *any* candidate. In 1960, 63.8 percent of the eligible electorate went to the polls; in 1964, the figure slipped to 62.1 percent; four years later, to 61 percent; in 1972 participation fell to 55.7 percent. "The low voter turnout," warned Shirley Chisholm, "was a disturbing barometer of the air of apathy and resignation which permeates the nation's political atmosphere." Subsequent analysis of public opinion suggested that nonvoters were not indifferent to the election, but rather attempted to make an explicit political statement by withholding their franchise. Disenchantment with the political process—not apathy—increased among nonvoters from 18 percent in 1964, to 26 percent in 1968, to 42 percent in 1972. Besides those nonvoters, over one million Americans registered a protest against both major parties by supporting right-winger John Schmitz of the American Party. Such choices, combined with the rise of split tickets, revealed an underlying alienation among voters, a grass-roots repudiation of traditional politics that would spread in later elections.

LOOKING BACK AT THE CAMPAIGN, McGovern acknowledged that he had made some serious mistakes. But "the other side," he said, "made deliberate deceptions. There's a vast difference, which . . . the public did not comprehend." Misled by the media, "they equated mistakes of the heart as being serious—in fact, more serious—than massive crimes, like the bombing of innocent civilians in Indochina or sinister plots . . . carried out by the Committee for the Re-election of the President, or secret campaign funds. . . . Those," he said, "were not mistakes." It would take another twenty months, however, before most Americans would come to share McGovern's analysis.

By 1972, most citizens had become unwitting accomplices in a national policy they neither wanted nor chose. Yet precisely for that reason, they were unwilling to admit their mistake, seek other leadership. "Vietnam is the shared crime that has turned our country into . . . a pact of blood," wrote columnist Garry Wills one month after the election. "Now patriotism means the complicity of fellows in a crime . . . ; we excuse each other; we keep the secret." It was for this reason that American voters turned overwhelmingly back to Richard Nixon—"a war criminal," said Wills—and it was the same logic that led them to look with hatred and horror at the one politician who decried the national lie. "They resent him because he is free," wrote Wills. "His mouth is not gagged by the knowledge of his own guilt "

6

"THE WAR ISN'T OVER"

The Imperial President

WHEN THEY FOUND HIS BODY sprawled on the floor beside the bed, his skin already had turned blue. Within moments former President Lyndon Baines Johnson was pronounced dead of a heart attack at his Texas ranch. Thirteen hours later, on January 23, 1973, President Nixon announced that, after a dozen years of fighting, agreement had been reached on a settlement of the Vietnam war. "No man would have welcomed this peace more than he," said the President of his predecessor. Johnson, the accidental President, chief architect of the liberal Great Society, had allowed United States involvement in Southeast Asia to escalate into the longest war in American history, a conflagration that drained the nation's resources, destroyed Johnson's liberal consensus, and finally drove the Democratic leadership from the White House. "His tragedy—and ours," stated Senator Muskie, "was the war."

Johnson's death—like some primordial rite of sacrifice—seemed to corroborate the promise of Nixon's second inaugural address, presented just three days earlier, that "we stand on the threshold of a new era of peace." But instead of assuaging a decade's grief, Johnson's demise removed the most obvious scapegoat for the war and spread the burden of responsibility through American society. "We had to realize that it wasn't just him," said a member of Vietnam Veterans Against the War (VVAW). "It was the whole country—and then there was nowhere to place the rage." The Vietnam war—no aberration of history, no "mistake," no mere presidential perversity—was instead a logical outcome of deeply held values and assumptions about American destiny, and these values would continue to influence American society. The war had ended—but the culture that had made it remained firmly entrenched.

Nixon's proclamation of "peace with honor," therefore, evoked little jubilation.

"There was no dancing in the streets, no honking of horns, no champagne," reported *The New York Times* from Washington, D.C.

"I'm not going to get excited till they quit fighting," asserted an older woman from Beallsville, Ohio, a small town whose sons had suffered a disproportionate number of war casualties. "I welcome peace, but you can't trust politicians anymore."

"This is a false ending," protested a Vietnam veteran, angered at the country's refusal "to face what did go on there."

"All I know," said a man in a Harlem bar nodding toward the street, "is that the brothers are still out there fighting every day."

"You can tell that bastard," shouted a black veteran in Times Square, by way of confirmation, "the war isn't over."

HAVING WON AN OVERWHELMING electoral victory the previous November on assurances that peace was "at hand," Nixon had promptly squandered public support by inexplicably ordering a massive twelve-day terror bombing of North Vietnam during the Christmas season to force the enemy to capitulate at the treaty table. Angered by Nixon's repudiation of election promises and incensed by the refusal of the White House to offer explanations, several members of Congress boycotted the President's inauguration to participate in peace demonstrations at the National Cathedral. Speaking at Oxford University the next day, McGovern condemned Nixon's haughty silence and charged the President with "abusing executive privilege."

Despite the savage Christmas bombing of North Vietnam, which amounted to ten times the total explosives dropped between 1969 and 1971, and despite heavy losses of B-52s and American flight crews, Nixon presented a treaty that scarcely differed from the preliminary settlement reached the previous October. In exchange for American prisoners of war, the United States agreed to withdraw its remaining ground forces from Vietnam within sixty days, and the Vietnamese people were "guaranteed the right to determine their own futures, without outside interference." This political understanding permitted Thieu to remain in power in South Vietnam—but only for what Kissinger called "a decent interval," because agreement to the principle of a unified Vietnamese government promised to remove the artificial divisions which had split that country since the United States had refused to sign or support the Geneva Accords of 1954.

The uncertain political future of Vietnam assured the continuation of fighting. As early as October, Nixon had personally authorized Operations Enhance and Enhance Plus to maximize Thieu's military strength before a cease-fire prohibited additional deliveries. The Pentagon also developed elaborate plans to violate the peace treaty by redefining military advisers as civilian employees of the Defense Department and by establishing a military command inside the American embassy in Saigon. With such covers, the United States intended to continue covert operations against North Vietnam as well as intelligence gathering in Laos and Cambodia. In November 1972 and again in January, Nixon sent confidential letters to Thieu, offering further assurances of American military assistance if the enemy violated the peace. Meanwhile, in Vietnam, both sides seized as much territory as possible, seeking military and political leverage in preparation for the final denouement.

Unable to prevent violations of the cease-fire in Vietnam, the administration resolved to preserve American power elsewhere in Indochina. In negotiations with Hanoi, Kissinger persuaded the North Vietnamese to support a truce in Laos. But fighting in Cambodia between the communist Khmer Rouge and the pro-American Lon Nol regime continued to devastate the countryside. Fueled by American military activity after the "incursion" of 1970, intense rivalry among Cambodians blocked a negotiated settlement. After the signing of the Paris treaty, Nixon decided to bomb the Khmer Rouge into submission, partly as a warning to North Vietnam. In the spring of 1973, American air raids increased dramatically. These attacks further disrupted Cambodian society, driving millions of peasants into the capital city of Phnom Penh, where crowded refugee camps became utterly dependent on American supplies. Yet the bombing proved militarily ineffective, and when the last American troops departed from South Vietnam, the Cambodia bombing lost any military rationale. "The justification," stated Deputy Assistant Secretary of State William Sullivan as an explanation for the policy, "is the re-election of the President."

Such logic finally aroused the long dormant congressional opposition to the administration's foreign policy. In June 1973, Congress approved a measure that prohibited the allocation of funds for the bombing of Cambodia. But Nixon vetoed the bill, arguing that it imperiled a negotiated settlement, threatened the survival of Lon Nol, and consequently jeopardized American credibility. Congress lacked the votes to override the President, but Senate Majority Leader Mike Mansfield notified the White House that Democrats would block all legislation "until the will of the people prevails." Nixon countered by threatening to veto any bill that undermined his diplomatic hand. As the federal separation of power moved toward a constitutional stalemate, however, the two branches of government agreed to compromise: Congress consented to the bombing of Cambodia—but only until August 15, 1973, when all American military activity in Indochina would finally cease. "Congress cannot sanction an unconstitutional and illegal endeavor for 'just a little while,' " objected Senator Eagleton. But it did so anyway.

The prolonged debate about the limits of executive authority now impelled Congress to establish a clear definition of its constitutional power to declare war. Ever since President Harry Truman ordered a "police action" against North Korea in 1950, American Presidents had ignored the constitutional mandate that located war-making power in Congress. But in November 1973, both houses of Congress overrode a presidential veto and passed the War Powers Act. It required that the commitment of American troops overseas without formal congressional approval be limited to sixty days and that CIA activities be reported to Congress "in a timely fashion." Such limitations still permitted considerable executive autonomy. But they signified that Congress, for the first time since the end of World War II, had acted to regain its foreign-policy powers.

THE BELATED AWAKENING of congressional power reflected the traumatic impact of the Vietnam war on the American identity. In 1961, President Kennedy had offered to "pay any price, bear any burden, meet any hardship, support any friend, oppose any foe to assure the survival and the success of liberty." Twelve years later, the loss of over fifty-six thousand American lives, three hundred thousand American wounded, more than one million Vietnamese dead, and $140 billion in war costs no longer seemed an acceptable payment to preserve American hegemony in the world. "The time has passed," stated Nixon's second inaugural address, in a mirror image of Kennedy's rhetoric, "when America will make every other nation's conflict our own, or make every other nation's future our responsibility, or presume to tell the people of other nations how to manage their own affairs."

More than the loss of life and property, more than the erosion of American power, Vietnam symbolized a failure of national purpose, a weakening of the historic values that had welded American omnipotence with its assumption of cultural superiority. American industrial technology, believed to be the finest in the world, failed not only to defeat the armies of North Vietnam—a fantastic psychological shock in itself!—but also revealed the monstrous impersonality of a society capable of turning its magnificent creations against the very values that gave them birth. The American warrior ethic, carried to a logical extreme in Vietnam, had produced only pain and suffering, horrible violence and impotent defeat. "There was a time when the red, white and blue meant something to me and I loved this country," stated a Marine survivor of Khe Sanh, "but I can tell you now that a country that burns yellow babies and starves black babies is a blood-sucking whore whose death I hope to see."

"As far as I'm concerned, we lost," stated a veteran suffering from a festering wound in his hip. "If one guy got killed over there for no reason, we lost."

"We've lost more over there than we'll ever get back," commented a middle-aged Ohio resident on the day the treaty was announced, "but it seems like people are trying to forget about the war before it's even over."

"You're forgetting a lot of people [who] shouldn't be forgotten," warned the wounded vet. "You just put it out of your mind, and this bullshit is going to go on forever."

Rather than facing the complicated issues raised by the Vietnam debacle, however, the President merely reiterated the achievement of "peace with honor." "I know it gags some of you to write that phrase," he told the first press conference of his second term, "but it is true, and most Americans realize it is true."

"It isn't peace," fumed a frustrated veteran in New York. "And there's no honor."

Having asserted an American victory, the administration shifted public attention toward "Operation Homecoming," the return of 587 men held as prisoners of war in Vietnam. With the consent of Lady Bird Johnson, the former President's widow, Nixon ordered American flags restored to full staff on the day the first contingent of prisoners flew from Hanoi to Clark Air Force Base in the Philippines. The returning captives, many of them career officers, shared the President's view of the peace. "We are honored to have the opportunity to serve our country under difficult circumstances," stated Captain Jeremiah Denton, the senior officer on the first planeload of POWs. "We are profoundly grateful to our Commander in Chief and to our nation for this day. God bless America!" "It's almost too wonderful to express," agreed the ranking officer on the second flight. "I would like to thank our President and the American people for bringing us home to freedom again." "When anyone can say that after six and a half years in prison," gloated Nixon, "it has all been worthwhile."

Besides an undiminished patriotism, the returning prisoners brought terrible stories of confinement—physical deprivation, torture, and forced confessions—a litany of communist atrocities that helped to blunt public outrage at American criminality in Vietnam. "We are over-publicizing the war criminals who are coming home," protested antiwar activist Philip Berrigan. "But what else would you expect from the Government, but to destroy the true nature of the war?" The administration accepted the testimony of the POWs as a convenient reason to cancel promised economic assistance for the reconstruction of North Vietnam. Some POWs also levied charges against their comrades for collaborating with the enemy. But when two former POWs committed suicide, the Pentagon decided to bury the allegations.

The return of the POWs—a journey not only from bleak jungle prisons to antiseptic military hospitals, but also a leap across months, even years, of captivity—dramatized extensive changes in American society. Though the military provided the repatriated prisoners with glossaries and guidebooks, shielding them from unfriendly encounters with the public and the press, the returning prisoners glimpsed a world they hardly recognized. On the first flight from Hanoi, a surreptitious copy of *Playboy* magazine stunned the hardened veterans with its blatant nudity. "I find it a little disconcerting," confessed one captain, "to find women wearing pants and men wearing women's hair styles." Many POWs now faced a difficult adjustment to family life based on their wives' acceptance of women's liberation.

The joyous homecoming also obscured a transformation in the political climate of the nation. Obsessed with their personal sacrifices, the former POWs failed to question the administration's interpretation of the war, as expressed by a military attaché assigned to the prisoners: "the South did not lose and the North did not win." "We walked out of Hanoi as winners," insisted one repatriated soldier. "It's about time we started raising the flag," remarked a freed captain, "instead of burning it." Such statements—the rhetoric of victorious armies and heroes—denied the reality of military failure and defeat. "What's disturbing," warned psychiatrist Robert Jay Lifton, an authority on war prisoners, "is the image being created of simple, old-fashioned American military virtue, as though nothing happened in Vietnam, and as though the understandable emotion around these men can wipe away 10 years of an ugly, unjust war."

The celebration of the returning POWs contrasted starkly with public indifference to the ordinary veterans of the war. "How many veterans are there whose heads are screwed up?" asked Cora Weiss, head of the Committee of Liaison, an antiwar group concerned with the POWs. "How many guys are hooked on drugs and can't get help?" A 1971 Harris poll revealed that most Americans believed that soldiers who went to Vietnam were "suckers, having to risk their lives in the wrong war, in the wrong place, at the wrong time." Younger than the veterans of other American wars and often perplexed by the political and moral issues of the conflict, Vietnam veterans experienced great trauma upon returning home. Under the military system of service rotation, the veterans arrived not with their units, but as individuals, who then faced the formidable task of reentering an unsympathetic society. "Coming back to America is not a coming back at all, it is starting again," remarked one veteran. "I wasn't ready to start again, I had to get used to it. . . . I was pretty lost for a couple of months."

Statistics about Vietnam veterans attested to the difficulties of readjustment. Between 1968 and 1974, the unemployment rate among Vietnam veterans was 22 percent, for nonwhites 50 percent—far higher than national averages. Some of these economic problems reflected the widespread military practice of using "less than honorable discharges" to rid the service of unwanted personnel. "I was busted for having two joints and given a General Discharge after three years and nine months of my four-year enlistment," recalled one subject of military justice. "Adjusting back to society wasn't easy. I couldn't find a job because I had 'bad paper.' This caused financial problems for my family and later resulted in my getting divorced." The military issued more than five hundred thousand "bad" discharges to Vietnam-era soldiers. Yet an analysis of the military justice system by Ralph Nader's Center for the Study of Responsive Law found the military guilty of numerous substantive and procedural violations of servicemen's rights.

The failure to deal with the material problems of Vietnam veterans was compounded by a general insensitivity to the psychological costs of the war. One clue to the inner turmoil of American soldiers was a soaring divorce rate among married veterans, 38 percent of whom separated from their wives within six months of service. More ominous still was the high suicide rate, 24 percent higher than that of their age peers. Others quietly suffered a common malady that psychiatrists labeled "post-Vietnam syndrome," a haunting, nightmarish life of guilt, depression, anger, self-deprecation, and persistent distrust of authority. At the core of the syndrome lay a fear of feeling, a reluctance to confront the meaninglessness of the war. "One time [in] Vietnam," recalled a Marine veteran, "I came to realize that the people I was fighting were right, the Vietcong were right, the NVA [North Vietnamese Army] were right, and I was wrong. And when I realized that, then I hated myself for not stopping. I despised myself." Such treacherous feelings, too volatile, too confusing to be acknowledged openly, settled in the back corners of consciousness, where they set long-lasting ambushes of disaster against the defenseless veteran.

As the war in Vietnam dragged on, however, American veterans increasingly challenged the effort. Through organizations such as VVAW and The Winter Soldier, antiwar warriors attempted to purge their complicity by testifying against the military ethic. "The vets are the only people who really accept direct responsibility for the Vietnam war," explained Bob Hood, a founder of VVAW. "We have to because we were the tools in that war." In 1971, two thousand veterans staged a dramatic protest by throwing away their battle medals on the steps of the Capitol and pleaded with Congress to end the "mistake" in Vietnam. Their testimony revealed an impassioned need among Vietnam survivors to transform their personal guilt into life-giving activity.

At the war's end, antiwar groups called on the President to offer a generous program of amnesty for the thousands of conscientious objectors who had evaded the draft or deserted from military service. "Amnesty means forgiveness," Nixon replied at his first press conference after the peace. "We cannot provide forgiveness. . . . Those who served paid their price. Those who deserted must pay their price." To Vice President Agnew, deserters were no different from "malcontents, radicals, incendiaries, the civil and the uncivil disobedients among our youth, SDS, PLP, Weathermen I and Weathermen II, the revolutionary action movement, the Black United Front, Yippies, Hippies, Yahoos, Black Panthers, Lions and Tigers alike—I would swap the whole damn zoo for a single platoon of the kind of young Americans I saw in Vietnam."

War resisters ironically wanted no amnesty from the Nixon administration, believing that their moral position was beyond reproach and that they, rather than the government, were entitled to bestow forgiveness. Most opponents of the war, moreover, had managed to avoid any penalties for draft dodging or military infractions. The President's unwillingness to consider amnesty served only to intensify the wounds of war. By denying the validity of reconciliation—to forgive and to forget—the administration encouraged Americans only to forget. Instead of therapeutic amnesty, Nixon invited amnesia.

The refusal of amnesty not only silenced moral debate about Vietnam—an increasingly awkward subject for hawk and dove alike—but also shielded the public from its complicity in the unpopular war. A Harris poll taken in June 1972 reported that Americans opposed amnesty by a three-to-two ratio; in March 1973, the margin increased to three-to-one. "They did not hear what they did not want to hear," complained Daniel Ellsberg shortly after the publication of the *Pentagon Papers*. But as Ellsberg's long-delayed trial threatened to expose government manipulation of public information, revelations of illegal prosecution activity abruptly terminated the case in May 1973. "I would certainly prefer to have litigated [the case] to completion," acknowledged trial judge W. Matthew Byrne in closing the court, but "the conduct of the government . . . precludes the fair dispassionate resolution of these issues." To avoid a Supreme Court ruling in the case of a court-martialed conscientious objector, charged with refusing an order to bomb Cambodia—a case that hinged on the legality of those orders—the Nixon administration ordered the Pentagon to drop the court-martial proceedings and prevented further appeal, thus blocking judicial consideration of the bombing. These legal gymnastics speeded the psychological retreat from Vietnam.

The submersion of Vietnam as a public issue also ended debate about government accountability to the American people. For over a decade, the executive branch had engaged in deliberate deceit—falsifying official statements about the war, lying about government policy, distorting the nature of the peace negotiations. But the war had so drained the national spirit that most people yearned only to put the matter behind them. This willingness to overlook government betrayal of public confidence nevertheless depended on one basic assumption—one unspoken but unavoidable truism—that peace abroad would expedite the recovery of tranquillity at home. Domestic stability—the ease of middle-class Americans—remained the benchmark for judging the acceptability of Nixon's second term.

"WE HAVE LIVED TOO LONG with the consequences of attempting to gather all power in Washington," Nixon said in his second inaugural address. "Abroad and at home, the time has come to turn away from the condescending policies of paternalism." With the war over, Nixon wished to return to orthodox Republican ideas about limited government. "In trusting too much in government," he said, "we have asked more of it than it can deliver. This leads only to inflated expectations . . . , and to a disappointment and frustration that erodes confidence in what government can do and what people can do."

As an alternative to "paternalism," Nixon proposed what he called "a new feeling of self-discipline." His budget proposals for the new fiscal year demanded heavy cuts in social welfare spending—reductions of federal assistance for hospital construction, for urban renewal, for public housing, education, and scientific research. "The average American," Nixon explained to a reporter, "is just like the child in the family. You give him some responsibility and he is going to amount to something. . . . If, on the other hand, you make him completely dependent and pamper him and cater to him too much, you are going to make him soft, spoiled, and eventually a very weak individual."

Democrats in Congress promptly denounced Nixon's plan— "contemptuous of the real needs of the American people," objected Senator Harrison Williams of New Jersey—and warned that the battle of the budget would raise constitutional questions about which branch of government ultimately controlled public spending. Already the White House had challenged Congress by claiming the right to "impound"—and not disburse—authorized appropriations. Arguing that government spending accentuated inflation, the President also issued a series of legislative vetoes, which Congress failed to override. Nixon flaunted his power by appointing an acting director of the Office of Economic Opportunity (OEO) and ordered him to dismantle the program. A district court ruled, however, that the President's action was illegal. But Nixon made no budget requests for OEO in the next fiscal year and transferred its remaining programs to HEW.

The conflict between the President and Congress soon extended to broad constitutional issues that affected the political interests of many powerful groups. Treating the landslide of 1972 as an absolute mandate, Nixon attempted to centralize power in the White House and promulgated reorganization plans that eliminated internal dissent. With the right to veto and the dubious power of impoundment, he disregarded the voice of Congress, claiming that the legislative body did not represent the public interest. In February 1973, he announced a broad reinterpretation of the doctrine of executive privilege, forbidding his aides—and former aides—from presenting testimony to Congress. "The President's in the driver's seat," lamented Majority Leader Mansfield.

Concentration of power in the executive branch threatened the very structure of the federal government. "The authority of Congress has decayed till it is overripe and rotten," observed liberal columnist TRB in the *New Republic*. But the presidential assault on the balance of power also alarmed conservatives who feared the disruption of the republican form of government. Determined to dig to the root of the problem—the election that emboldened the President's claim of power—the Senate voted in February 1973 to create a Select Committee on Presidential Campaign Activities to examine alleged abuses of electoral laws. Its chairman was a conservative expert on constitutional law who called himself "a plain country lawyer," Sam Ervin of North Carolina.

7

"NOT AS STEPCHILDREN OR WARDS"

The Dilemma of Minority Cultures

WHILE THE POLITICAL LEADERSHIP attempted to resolve the constitutional impasse, Nixon's proclamation of a "new federalism" raised immediate problems of survival for impoverished people who depended upon government assistance. In 1973, minority groups—blacks, Mexican Americans, Puerto Ricans, and American Indians—comprised 15.4 percent of the population; according to the 1970 census, their mean per capita income was just 54 percent that of whites. Trapped by barriers of language and culture, these groups experienced disproportionate unemployment and suffered health and educational disadvantages associated with chronic poverty. Their relationship to the federal government, observed Chicano leader Reies Lopez Tijerina in 1972, "is like that of a foster child to a mother. Naturally, the deepest love and affection of the mother goes to her natural child. This means that the foster child goes unnoticed or unattended until its cries force the mother's attention." Two weeks after Nixon's rejection of "paternalism," the United States Commission on Civil Rights criticized the administration exactly on these grounds, asserting that "everyone must have the opportunity to share fully in the bounty of society—not as stepchildren or wards."

The administration's indifference to the problems of minority cultures not only intensified feelings of frustration, alienation, and anger, but also accentuated conflicts within minority groups. Despite the revitalization of ethnic culture in the seventies, equally strong voices advocated the rapid abandonment of minority values and urged full integration into the American mainstream. For minority peoples struggling for recognition and the redress of historical grievances, this tension between traditionalists and assimilationists constituted a central and unresolved dilemma.

AMERICAN INDIANS

The clash of culture among the poorest of all minority groups—American Indians—climaxed in armed warfare in February 1973. Angered by federal government policies that supported the rule of assimilationist tribal leaders, militant Indians seized the village of Wounded Knee on the Pine Ridge reservation in South Dakota. "We have bet with our lives," declared Russell Means, a leader of the American Indian Movement (AIM), "that we could change the course of . . . the history of Indian America." Exchanging gunfire with federal marshals and their Indian allies—regarded by the militants as "Uncle Tomahawks" or "apples" (red outside, white inside)—the radicals demanded a reconsideration of the treaty relationships that bound native Americans to the United States government.

The eruption of violence at Wounded Knee reflected not only political rivalries within the Indian community, but also the failure of the Nixon administration to implement promised reforms, a situation the President considered "inflated expectations." The administration initially seemed responsive to Indian demands. Despite Nixon's affirmation of "law and order," the White House had adopted a tolerant policy toward an Indian takeover of Alcatraz Island in 1969, allowing militants to occupy the site for eighteen months. In July 1970, moreover, Nixon rejected a policy of "forced termination," which had threatened the integrity of tribal life, and announced the return of forty-eight thousand acres of sacred land to the Taos Pueblo of New Mexico. Using OEO funds, the administration pumped federal money to urban Indian groups and asked Congress to increase appropriations through the Bureau of Indian Affairs (BIA).

The measures failed, however, to overcome bureaucratic and congressional opposition to American Indian claims. Native Amer-

icans responded with more militant tactics—seizing federal property and asserting traditional tribal rights—which, in turn,
provoked whites to retaliate with increased violence. Outraged by
the government's inability to stop these attacks, radical Indians
organized a cross-country protest march—the "Trail of Broken
Treaties"—to bring their complaints to Washington, D.C., on the
eve of the 1972 presidential election. But when the caravan arrived in the capital, the Interior Department offered inadequate
accommodations, and the Indians protested this reception by bar-
ricading themselves inside the offices of the BIA. After a week of
negotiations, the occupation ended peacefully when the White
House agreed to consider a proposal to alter the legal status of the
American Indian tribes. The discovery of extensive damage to the
BIA building and the theft of government documents, however,
quickly cooled the administration's interest in further negotiations. "To call for new treaties is to raise a false issue," the White
House announced in January 1973, "unconstitutional in concept,
misleading to Indian people and diversionary from the real problems." The Interior Department then authorized sixty-five thousand dollars in new funds to support police security on the Pine
Ridge reservation.

The government response inflamed a tense situation. In
South Dakota, the recent murder of an Oglala man had provoked
vigorous protest by AIM leaders against white law enforcement.
At the same time, tribal chairman Richard Wilson, an implacable
foe of Indian militants, banned AIM activities on the reservation
and even offered to lend tribal police to help white officials crush
the protest. Backed by the federal bureaucracy, Wilson strength-
ened his personal police force—by now known to residents as the
"goon squad"—and used his control of the tribal government to
defeat a movement for impeachment. "If we all die today," protested medicine man Pete Catches, "we'll all die as dogs because
we've let one man, Wilson, dictate to us." The dissidents, who
included many of the traditional chiefs, asked AIM for help.

The ensuing occupation of Wounded Knee, like the earlier
seizure of Attica, demonstrated the powerlessness of radical pro-
test. Though AIM won support from sympathetic public figures—
New York Times columnist Tom Wicker, the black caucus of the
House of Representatives, Angela Davis, and actor Marlon
Brando—and obtained valuable publicity which prevented precipi-

tous military intervention, the administration ended the siege peacefully after seventy-one days by agreeing to consult with traditional tribal leaders. After the meeting, the White House simply reaffirmed its unwillingness to reopen treaty negotiations—"another indication," protested AIM lawyer Ramon Roubideaux, "that the Government never really listens to us." The government indicted AIM leaders Means and Dennis Banks, but both won acquittal in 1974.

Fundamental to the Wounded Knee affair was the reassertion of American Indian autonomy. "We believe we are still a sovereign nation," maintained Frank Fool's Crow, "and the Government has no right to . . . tell us what we can and can't do in the way of governing ourselves." The argument had ramifications not only for American Indian political rights but also for the distribution of the vast mineral wealth on reservation lands. BIA officials customarily leased Indian holdings to white entrepreneurs at bargain prices, a policy that depleted reservation resources while leaving the population dependent on the federal government for 60 percent of its income. In the aftermath of Wounded Knee, native American leaders resolved to bring economic resources under the control of the tribes.

The success of red power nevertheless hinged on a resolution of the historical conflict between assimilation and the preservation of tribal ways. "Culture is fine," conceded Richard Wilson during the Wounded Knee crisis, "but it don't feed you." Such attitudes, supported by government policy, placed great pressure on American Indians to adopt white values. The Small Business Administration, for example, refused to support Navajo business unless it operated "within the competitive free enterprise system," an economic philosophy that contradicted essential Navajo ideals of cooperation and community.

Against such influence, the seizure of Wounded Knee represented a powerful counterforce. "The Indian was good until the white man, the liar, came," said Crow Dog with contempt. Many American Indians, having experienced the squalor and alienation of urban poverty, returned to Indian ways and the comforts of tribal community. "A member of the reservation . . . has something," explained a California Morongo. "He is not lost. He is not like people in an urban ghetto—where the only identity you have is your job."

MEXICAN AMERICANS

The rejuvenation of American Indian culture paralleled the awakening of another indigenous people, the 6.5 million Mexican Americans—or Chicanos—who concentrated in five southwestern states. Like the native tribes, Chicanos had been victimized by violations of American treaties, in their case, the Treaty of Guadalupe Hidalgo, by which the United States acquired California and most of the Southwest at the end of the Mexican War in 1848. Chicanos, too, had suffered from racial prejudice and Anglo pressure to reject their cultural roots. In 1973, the median income of Chicano families was 71 percent that of whites—though Mexican American families had more mouths to feed—and over a quarter of all Chicanos were classified as poor. "We . . . have made them strangers in their own land," acknowledged Senator Edward Kennedy.

During the sixties, however, Chicanos became increasingly militant in asserting their rights and in affirming their culture. "Attack until the [Anglo] invader gives us power to control our community," advised David Sanchez, founder of the Brown Berets, a self-defense group modeled on the Black Panthers. Angered by the disproportionate number of Chicano casualties in Vietnam, Mexican Americans supported antiwar demonstrations in Los Angeles in 1970 and 1971—though the Vietnam issue was quickly subsumed by a brutal police attack on the nonviolent protesters. "We are first in janitors, first in infantry units, last in equal opportunity," charged Senator Joseph Montoya of New Mexico.

"Tio Taco Is Dead," announced a popular wall slogan. Attacking racist stereotypes in the media, Chicanos succeeded in ending advertising campaigns for Arrid spray deodorant ("If it works for *him*, it will work for you") and "Frito Bandito" taco chips, which portrayed Mexican Americans as indolent, criminal, and filthy. Chicanos also supported the Bilingual Education Act of 1968, which curtailed the suppression of the Spanish language by Anglo educational institutions, and in 1970, the California Supreme Court declared literacy in Spanish sufficient to guarantee voting rights.

As Chicanos became politically self-conscious, they questioned their traditional allegiance to the Democratic party. To capitalize on this disaffection, Nixon appealed to Chicano voters by appointing Spanish-speaking Republicans to visible positions, and he supported federal funding for Chicano community projects. Such investments proved extremely profitable in the 1972 elections, for Nixon increased his Chicano base from 10 percent in 1968 to 36 percent. But the postelection decision to dismantle OEO rapidly undermined the President's support. Moreover, the administration opposed a lettuce boycott by Chicano farm-workers and encouraged the Pentagon to increase purchases of the proscribed food. "Spanish-speaking voters gave the President a vote of confidence," complained Tony Gallegos, chairman of the Chicano G.I. Forum, "and we've been left out in the cold."

Such betrayals reinforced Chicano interest in an alternative political movement. "The two-party system is one animal with two heads eating out of the same trough," declared Rodolfo "Corky" Gonzales, founder of Denver's Crusade for Justice. "There is no lesser of two evils." Beginning in Texas in 1969, Chicanos led by José Angel Gutierrez had formed La Raza Unida and had played a minor role in preventing the election of Republican senatorial candidate George Bush. Focusing on local elections in subsequent years La Raza Unida won several victories. In 1972, the party fielded candidates in five southwestern states and captured six percent of the gubernatorial ballot in Texas, enough to wield a crucial balance of power in that state. But the same election saw the fragmentation of the regional party as Gutierrez and Gonzales divided over strategy and Cesar Chavez, head of the United Farm Workers union, endorsed McGovern.

The splintering of Chicano politics reflected broader problems of cultural conflict: the clash between assimilation and ethnic integrity. "This country is based on the principle of private enterprise—competition in business," Henry Ramirez, a high-level Nixon appointee, reminded the Chicano community, "—and we will not be in the mainstream of American life until we, the Spanish-speaking, get into business on the same footing as everyone else." These aspirations led to the proliferation of private business organizations, such as the National Economic Development Association (NEDA), "to foster the free enterprise system among Spanish-speaking people." Through management assistance programs, loans, and legal advice, such operations encouraged the expansion of Chicano business, leading the chairman of La Raza Investment Corporation to proclaim the advancement of "the principle of self-determination from the stage of empty rhetoric to meaningful reality." Yet Chicano business remained small in scale and consequently more vulnerable to the vicissitudes of the economy. In the barrio, NEDA was frequently translated as "NADA"—nothing!

Recognizing upward social mobility as a threat to traditional values, many Chicanos reaffirmed their commitment to a noncompetitive society. "I hate the white ideal," exclaimed David Sanchez of the Brown Berets. "It's a disease leading to madness." Such opinion cherished the closeness of the unassimilated community. "The barrio is a refuge from the harshness and coldness of the Anglo world," wrote Robert Ramirez in 1972. "No, there is no frantic wish to flee. It would be absurd to leave the familiar and nervously step into the strange and cold Anglo community."

The commitment to community resources illuminated an obvious though seldom acknowledged reality: the sheer difficulty of leaving the barrio. One obstacle to Chicano mobility—the lowest educational achievement in the country—reflected what the United States Civil Rights Commission described as "a systematic failure of the educational process, which not only ignores the educational needs of Chicano students but also suppresses their culture and stifles their hopes and ambitions." Yet a Supreme Court ruling in March 1973 involving fifteen Mexican American families of San Antonio, Texas, protected the educational status quo. Indicating the growing influence of Nixon's conservative judicial appointments, the Court denied that state governments had an obligation to provide equal financing of public schools and upheld the use of property assessments as a basis for school taxes. Such procedures enabled wealthier areas to obtain greater educational resources than poorer neighborhoods. At a time when public opinion was turning against pupil busing, the Court refused to evaluate the quality of neighborhood schools. "The poor people have lost again," said defendant Demetrio Rodriguez.

BLACK AMERICANS

Though the Supreme Court spoke solely in economic terms, the decision had obvious consequences for the racial minorities that occupied the lowest strata of society. For black Americans, educational mobility had promised to overcome the historical disadvantages of racial discrimination. Earlier judicial decisions had eliminated educational barriers throughout the South. But in the northern and western states racial imbalances persisted, partly the result of deliberate municipal policy. Such discrimination violated the tenets of the *Brown* decision and in 1973, the Supreme Court ordered the end of school segregation in Denver, Colorado, the first nonsouthern city required to introduce a program of mandatory busing. But most northern school segregation reflected the patterns of residence that separated races. Residential segregation in the north often had resulted from past government policies that limited minority access to housing. But the Supreme Court refused to tackle the question of segregated housing as it related to education.

The concentration of blacks in urban centers and the flight of whites to the suburbs revealed a plain fact of American life that transcended class and region—the perpetuation of racial discord. "There may be a change in the atmosphere," admitted John Lewis, former head of the Student Nonviolent Coordinating Committee, in 1974, "but solid changes haven't occurred. . . . When it got to hard things, and when the problem started to touch the North, the whites turned around." Plans to introduce mixed public housing projects in middle-class neighborhoods, such as Forest Hills, New York, drew vicious community protest, and as part of his postelection budget cuts, Nixon ordered a moratorium on public housing construction. From Baltimore to Boston, Louisville to Detroit, public school boards prepared to fight desegregation in the courts. "Racism," remarked M. Carl Holman of the National Urban Coalition, "comes much more naturally, and to a much broader spectrum of whites, than we could have imagined."

Black economic gains, considered by many the acid test of racial advancement, often proved illusory. Despite improvement in education, affirmative action programs, and occupational mobility, the ratio of black family median income to that of whites *declined* from 61 percent in 1969 to 58 percent in 1973. Though black wages increased, white incomes grew at a faster rate, accentuating economic disparities.

The contrast in economic opportunity emerged clearly in unemployment statistics, which showed the black rate running twice as high as the white, regardless of fluctuations of the economy. In

1973, for example, black unemployment reached 8.9 percent, compared to 4.3 percent for whites. Between 1970 and 1974, unemployment among black teenagers averaged 32 percent. Such statistics, combined with the problems of job turnovers, discouraged black participation in the labor force, creating a class of nonemployed blacks who depended for income on public assistance, crime, or hustling. In 1972, 42 percent of all blacks were classified as poor or near-poor. "The real danger," warned black economist Robert S. Browne, "is that an enormous gap will develop between the blacks who have and those who don't. Then we're on our way to having a permanent black underclass."

The problem of economic inequality among blacks concealed a more subtle division within the black community. Between 1960 and 1972, real incomes of black men increased by 52 percent, while that of black women leaped by 112 percent. By 1972, black women earned about 96 percent as much as white women. But black female incomes remained substantially lower than male earnings of both races. The disadvantages of being black *and* female had grave social consequences. By 1972, one-third of all nonwhite families were headed by a woman—three times the proportion among white families and a noticeable increase from the 22 percent figure of 1960. The result was that two-thirds of all black families living in poverty were headed by women—victims not only of racial prejudice, but also of sexual discrimination.

The oppression of black women reflected the perpetuation of sexual stereotypes throughout society, including the black community. A series of highly successful Hollywood "blaxploitation" films—*Sweet Sweetback's Baadasssss Song, Shaft,* and *Superfly*—all of which were extremely popular among black audiences—celebrated the black pimp as a folk hero, outsmarting the white establishment, while portraying black women as whores. "I'm a success. I'm a winner," boasted black star Diana Ross in the film *Mahogany*. But in Hollywood style, she happily renounced her career to marry a black man who himself had traded sidewalk protest for party politics. Even in this conservative guise, black films failed to attract white audiences, and the genre quickly disappeared. During the 1972 presidential campaign, black television comedian Redd Foxx—whose role on "Sanford and Son" preserved the stereotyped image of the lazy black—provided an extraordinary moment of comic relief when he joked about his preference for

Raquel Welch over candidate Shirley Chisholm. To black feminists like Michele Wallace, the quip epitomized the enduring rift between black men and black women.

The problems facing the black community required common action to overcome the divisions of sex and class. "Black Americans have obviously been a more stubbornly unassimilable group than any of the others," explained Chisholm in her postelection book, *The Good Fight*. "But the point is that this is not a problem." Arguing that group identity was essential for economic and political success, she exhorted minorities to "be yourselves." But black culture remained too dependent on white power, white wealth, and white values to achieve the desired autonomy. "Just as men will be free when women are liberated," concluded Chisholm with an eye on some distant future, "blacks and whites will emerge as more vital and ennobled beings when they can meet . . . as men and women of equal worth and potential."

WOMEN'S CULTURE

The parallels between black liberation and the women's movement had more than metaphorical reality: both revealed the remarkable ability of traditional society to contain and disperse political dissent. Following congressional approval of the Equal Rights Amendment in 1972, women won several highly publicized decisions against sexual discrimination. In 1973, the Equal Employment Opportunity Commission forced the giant AT&T corporation to adopt a policy of affirmative action and to award back pay to women and minorities who had been penalized by the company's "discriminatory practices." Feminists saw the case as a powerful precedent and soon celebrated a series of other "firsts"—the first female director of physical education at Yale University, the first female vice-president of the American Physical Society, the first female professional boxing judge—all symbols of a new age.

Feminists also gained a major political victory in January 1973 when the Supreme Court ruled that unborn children had no standing under the Fourteenth Amendment and that abortions were legal. The surprise decision undercut a burgeoning "right to life" movement that was attempting to repeal liberal state laws. Public opinion, which before the ruling had generally opposed abortions, now shifted in its favor. And as legal abortions diminished the medical risks of the procedure, women more frequently chose this alternative. By 1974, the nation's total abortions numbered nearly one million annually.

The liberalization of birth control was closely related to the withering of traditional sexual standards. In New York City, two-thirds of the women undergoing abortion were unmarried and a majority were under the age of twenty-five. Such statistics reflected a growing acceptance of free sexual expression. In 1973, Erica Jong's celebration of female sexual fantasy, *Fear of Flying*, became a national best-seller, and the publishers of *Playboy* and *Penthouse* magazines prepared similar monthlies to appeal to the prurient interests of a female clientele. "Like blacks," announced Jong, "women will have to learn first to love their own bodies."

Assertions of female independence, however, aroused deep fears throughout society and stimulated a vocal backlash against women's liberation. "It's just unholy for middle-class Americans to equate themselves with blacks," protested antifeminist Midge Decter. Forming a "Total Woman" movement, Marabel Morgan extolled the bliss of female subordination. "A Total Woman caters to her man's special quirks," she advised such famous alumnae as Anita Bryant, "whether it be in salads, sex, or sports." The ERA, after quick passage in over thirty states, now stumbled into stiff conservative opposition. Women's economic advances also made little headway. In 1973, white women still earned only 56.3 percent of the income of white men. "We are triumphantly galloping toward tokenism," scoffed *Ms.* publisher Gloria Steinem. Even liberalized abortion laws encountered strong opposition from doctors and hospitals that refused to comply with the Supreme Court.

Resistance to women's liberation reflected the deep-seated anxieties caused by the challenge to traditional sexual roles. One measure of this discomfort was the popularity of sexual comedy, which enabled audiences to laugh at their fears while avoiding direct confrontation with the serious issues. Woody Allen's *Everything You Always Wanted to Know About Sex* poked fun at a popular concern about physical performance, while his *Play It Again, Sam* glorified the security of traditional roles. "Dames are simple," advised a reincarnated Humphrey Bogart. "I never met one who didn't understand a slap in the mouth or a slug from a forty-five."

Uncertainties about proper sexual behavior also fired more sinister emotions. A series of Hollywood movies—*Straw Dogs, Walking Tall, Death Wish*—depicted a latent violence among married men, driven to acts of homicidal rage by sexual attacks on their women. These images rested on a growing awareness of sexual violence throughout society. In 1973, the FBI reported fifty-one thousand cases of forcible rape—estimated to be one-fifth the real total—an increase of ten percent from the previous year and part of a 62 percent rise over five years. "The assumption is that men *are* rapists," protested Adrienne Rich, "that this is a simple fact of nature."

Feminists argued that rape was a political statement, an expression of male domination, a literal attempt to force women into submission. "Knowing our place is the message of rape," insisted Robin Morgan, "—as it was for blacks the message of lynchings . . . they are both acts of political terrorism." Emphasizing that rape required, in Rich's words, "the objectification of another's person, the domination of another's body," feminists criticized the proliferation of pornography as an ideological basis for sexual violence. "Pornography is the theory," said Morgan, "and rape the practice." Many women therefore welcomed a Supreme Court ruling of June 1973 that established a stricter definition of pornography and allowed the use of local, rather than national, standards in determining "offensive" material.

While numerous public opinion surveys documented the expansion of feminist consciousness, the strength of the opposition to women's liberation intensified frustration at the rigidity of established institutions. Some feminists sought relief by rejecting the male world. Throughout the country, women established alternative organizations—health centers, schools, publishing companies, bookstores, and recreational facilities—to minimize dependence on traditional society. "Until all women are lesbians," argued Jill Johnston in *Lesbian Nation*, "there will be no true political revolution." But most feminists, recognizing the impossibility of escaping all male relationships, advocated more reasonably the elimination of stereotyped roles.

The difficulty of building a feminist coalition reflected the fundamental divisions within American society. "The Women's Liberation Movement is basically a family quarrel between white women and white men," maintained Ida Lewis, editor of *Essence*, a black magazine. "And on general principles, it's not too good to get involved in family disputes." Black women resented feminist emphasis on what they considered trivial matters—the opening of male-only bars, the title "Ms."—rather than basic problems of survival. "I just wish white women would get . . . concerned about the health and well-being of the black babies who are born," one woman told Representative Chisholm. Mexican Americans shared this distrust. "Chicanas have no more faith in white women than in white men," stated a radical group in 1971. "In our struggle we identify our men, not white women, as our natural allies." Working-class women and older women also expressed greater doubt about the values of sisterhood.

THE SUSPICIOUSNESS OF MINORITY WOMEN toward the white leadership of women's liberation represented in microcosm the historical divisions that prevented minority groups from joining forces against the majority culture. Occasionally a broad symbolic issue like the Vietnam war or the occupation at Wounded Knee served to coalesce diverse social groups in opposition to government policy. But such alliances remained extremely fragile—not only because of mutual distrust but also because of internal disagreement within the separate movements. Red liberation, brown liberation, black liberation, and women's liberation—pockets of resistance to mainstream society—all shared a dynamic of conflict with assimilationists who paid homage to the superiority of white male culture. From these divisions came only the frustrations of defeat or unfulfilled fantasies of revenge.

8

"PINCH, SQUEEZE, CRUNCH, OR CRISIS"

Energy, Ecology, Economics

THE ALIENATION OF AMERICAN minorities—the frustrations that caused American Indians to have the highest suicide rate in the country, Chicanos to be the poorest educated, and blacks to crowd welfare rolls—the anger of feminists, Vietnam veterans, alumni of the antiwar movement—all could be thwarted by the majority culture as long as it closed ranks against the various dissidents. Nixon's electoral victory in 1972 had clearly demonstrated the political impotence of these outgroups. But the stability of the established order depended on its ability not only to silence critics, but also to preserve, if not expand, America's status as the wealthiest and most powerful country on the surface of the earth.

This historical position had been seriously damaged by the failure in Vietnam. Worse, as the Nixon administration struggled to minimize the consequences of military defeat, the United States confronted a series of new challenges that further eroded the preeminence of American wealth and power. But instead of facing the possibility of global weakness and seeking alternative values and symbols, Americans retreated to established ideals and old virtues—and they judged their leaders accordingly. By such traditional standards, Richard Nixon would lose, within twenty-one months, almost his entire constituency.

Nixon's political success hinged on his mastery of foreign policy. Henry Kissinger, Nixon's chief adviser on international affairs, may have dominated the news media—winning, along with North Vietnam's Le Duc Tho, the Nobel Prize for peace in 1973—but Nixon himself maintained close control over American diplomacy. Even his fiercest critics conceded that the President had formulated a skillful policy of détente by balancing the rivalry between China and the Soviet Union. But Nixon's interest in world affairs did not include the complex questions of international economics. In this area, he deferred to corporate advisers who too often confused the national interest with that of their multinational companies. Moreover, as the White House became increasingly preoccupied with domestic affairs in the President's second term, Nixon devoted less attention to international relations. When, within one year of his reelection, fresh problems of diplomacy arose, many dealing with global economics, he could no longer provide effective leadership. As his grasp of foreign relations faltered, so, too, did his hold on domestic power.

ADMINISTRATION FOREIGN POLICY suffered a stunning setback when, despite several early warnings, the White House was surprised by a full-scale Arab invasion of Israel on October 6, 1973, Yom Kippur on the Jewish calendar. The United States remained firmly pro-Israel, but Nixon and Kissinger decided to restrict the flow of military assistance to its ally, partly to avoid antagonizing the Arab oil-producing nations and partly to encourage the development of a military stalemate that might allow the White House to impose a durable settlement. The decision nearly strangled the Israeli effort. Only a complete reversal of policy—the massive airlift of war materiel—finally enabled the American ally to repel the Arab forces. This belated shift promptly eliminated the benefits of prior appeasement. The Arab-dominated Organization of Petroleum Exporting Countries (OPEC) now responded to American intervention by halting the flow of oil to the United States, Western Europe, and Japan.

The oil embargo, which lasted from October 16, 1973, to March 18, 1974, represented what may well be the most revolutionary shift of world power in the twentieth century; but its implications were initially misunderstood. Believing that Arab exporters needed American capital and technology more than the United States needed oil, public opinion assumed that the OPEC alliance would soon collapse. "The Arab cutback in output is expected to tighten an already tight American oil situation," commented *The New York Times* with guarded optimism, "but not to bring major rationing."

Such assurances greatly underestimated American dependence on Arab oil. Within weeks, the nation confronted what the President called "a very stark fact: We are heading toward the most acute shortage of energy since World War II." Nixon soon ordered a lowering of thermostats to sixty-eight degrees—his doctor, he claimed, assured him it was "really more healthy"—cut back air travel by 10 percent, called for the lowering of highway speed limits, requested a halt in the conversion of coal-to-oil consumption, and urged an acceleration in the licensing of nuclear power plants. In addition, the President asked for congressional approval of daylight saving time in winter, the relaxation of environmental regulations affecting energy consumption, additional funding for exploration, research, and development, and executive authority "to impose special energy conservation measures." THINGS WILL GET WORSE, warned a newspaper headline, BEFORE THEY GET WORSE. With bipartisan support, Congress endorsed much of the administration program. State governments promptly lowered highway speeds, dimmed nonessential lighting, and reduced hours of service. In Georgia, Governor Jimmy Carter announced limits on the use of state aircraft and ordered cuts in building temperatures to the recommended 68 degrees. By January, school children were leaving home in the dark (causing a rash of roadside traffic accidents), commuters relied more heavily on car pools and mass transit, colleges canceled midwinter sessions, and factories shortened the workday to conserve fuel.

The shortages persisted. Despite a doubling of gasoline prices, customers lined up for hours—New Jersey had lines as long as four miles—to acquire a few gallons of fuel. Frustrated at the pumps, motorists vented their anger on service station attendants and each other—fighting, stealing, even killing. To discourage needless driving, Nixon ordered the closing of gasoline stations on Sundays and several states introduced rationing programs. Many Americans viewed these measures as unnecessary, if not counterproductive, especially when the major oil companies posted fourth-quarter profits for 1973 that were 57 percent higher than the previous year. A Gallup poll revealed that instead of blaming OPEC, one-quarter of the sample placed responsibility for the shortages on the oil companies and another quarter condemned the President. "I think there was gas all along," the driver of a VW told *The New York Times* in a typical response.

Official explanations of the energy crisis pointed to the profligate public. "We are running out of energy today," Nixon told a television audience in November 1973, "because our economy has grown enormously and because in prosperity what were once considered luxuries are now considered necessities." With only 6 percent of the world's population, the United States annually consumed about 30 percent of the world's energy. In 1960, Americans used 9.7 million barrels of oil each day; ten years later, that figure reached 14.4 million barrels; and in 1974, it climbed to 16.2 million barrels. But domestic production of oil had peaked in 1970, forcing the United States to rely on an ever larger percentage of imported oil. In 1960, Americans imported 19 percent of their oil; ten years later, that figure reached 24 percent; and in 1974, it climbed to 38 percent. These statistics supported the President's message that "our growing demands have bumped up against the limits of available supply."

Underlying the decline of American oil production, however, was a long history of corporate decisions. As early as the 1950s, American oil companies voluntarily reduced oil exploration and development within the United States and invested in the Middle East in order to exploit the greater profitability of developing foreign oil. Only because American resources were more expensive to extract was the country "running out" of oil. Even during the Arab embargo, the oil companies continued to seek maximum profits by delaying shipments, raising prices through transfer payments to subsidiaries, and diverting oil to areas of highest profit. These motives emerged in a widespread advertising campaign launched by the oil industry in the spring of 1973, six months before the OPEC embargo. "A country that runs on oil," warned the American Petroleum Institute, "can't afford to run short." Arguing that producers needed incentives for capital investment, the industry advocated increases in utility rates, maintenance of oil depletion allowances, and other tax advantages. Though the public remained unpersuaded by such pleas, the rising cost of imported oil—which was itself a function of industry policy—accomplished the same effect, making domestic oil wells, once considered too costly to drill, economically competitive.

While the oil companies sought to maximize profits, the

Nixon administration pursued a policy of laissez faire. Shortly after taking office, the President appointed a cabinet task force to examine the nation's oil policy. After a year of study, the report criticized the existing import quota system, by which the oil companies controlled the size of the nation's oil supply to keep prices inflated, and recommended a flexible tariff policy. More attuned to the demands of the oil industry, however, Nixon rejected this advice and under the guise of "national security" preserved the quota system. The administration also waived antitrust regulations, enabling the oil industry to present a united front toward OPEC in negotiating world oil prices.

These decisions encouraged American dependence on imported oil, even after OPEC forced significant price increases in 1971. Besides its strategic importance, the cost of imported oil also affected the nation's balance of payments, leading one State Department official to recommend a national policy of oil conservation. But White House adviser John Ehrlichman dismissed the idea: "Conservation is not in the Republican ethic." The same spirit inspired Nixon's first message to Congress on energy policy in June 1971. Convinced that "the needs of a growing economy" would continue to stimulate the nation's demand for energy, the President focused exclusively on improving the technology of what he called "clean energy"—fast breeder reactors, sulfur oxide control, and coal gasification. He made no mention of OPEC and, except for Canada, said nothing about foreign oil.

The limitations of Nixon's energy proposals—and the unwillingness of Congress to act upon them—reflected a continuing optimism about the ability of American technology to solve the problems of an industrial society. In September 1971, three months after Nixon's speech, *Scientific American* devoted an entire issue to the question of "Energy and Power," warning that the United States faced critical shortages by the year 2000. But in casting the problem into the distant future, the study exaggerated the promise of nuclear power and minimized the issue of what were called "future wastes." A decade and a half after the licensing of the first atomic energy plant, the United States was getting only 1.4 percent of its energy from nuclear power. But scientists predicted a 25 percent capacity by 1980 and 50 percent by the end of the century. "If ever any energy source can be said to have arrived in the nick of time," concluded Claude M. Summers of

Rensselaer Polytechnic Institute, "it is nuclear energy."

Such scientific conclusions reinforced Nixon's confidence in American negotiating strength with the Arab oil producers. The annual foreign policy report, released in February 1972, omitted the entire question of OPEC and oil, and the issue of energy remained unexamined throughout the ensuing political campaign. "Energy won't get the public attention it deserves until people run out of it," predicted Nixon shortly after his reelection, "and then they'll blame the government." Yet the White House hesitated to arouse public opinion. "It is not the philosophy of this Administration to control demand by government fiat," stated a Nixon energy adviser in early 1973. "We are not going to ask everyone to heat their homes at 68 degrees."

The winter of 1972–73 presented the first evidence of serious energy problems. In Denver, Colorado, bitter cold forced the closing of public schools, and factories were shut in Alabama and Louisiana because of fuel shortages. "Popeye," exclaimed former Secretary of Commerce Peter Peterson, "is running out of cheap spinach." Continuing to oppose conservation, Nixon responded to the crisis by urging expansion of American domestic production. "We should not be misled into pessimistic predictions of an energy disaster," he advised. "But neither should we be lulled into a false sense of security." In a major energy address to Congress in April 1973, the President repealed the oil quota system, promised accelerated leasing of offshore oil wells, demanded approval of the controversial Alaska pipeline, additional funding for research and development, and a partial decontrol of natural gas prices to provide incentives for further exploration and production. Arguing that the energy crisis "can and should be averted," Nixon appealed for the rapid development of nuclear power as the nation's "major alternative to fossil fuel energy for the remainder of this century. . . . If our energy resources are properly developed," he concluded, "they can fill our energy requirements for centuries to come."

This tenacious confidence in American technology shaped the President's response to the Arab oil embargo of 1973. Evoking the memory of America's greatest engineering achievements—the Manhattan Project that built the atomic bomb during World War II and the Apollo Mission that placed Americans on the moon in 1969—Nixon proposed a national commitment to what he called "a major new endeavor"—to make the United States completely independent of foreign energy sources by 1980—"an endeavor," he said, "that in this Bicentennial Era we can appropriately call 'Project Independence.'" As the centerpiece of the President's plan were the rapid development of coal production and the proliferation of nuclear reactors.

Such a program disregarded substantial objections to intensive energy development. "He is really calling for massive stripmining for coal, massive destruction of the land and pollution of the land and water," protested Brock Evans of the conservationist Sierra Club. "He has too readily permitted a breach of environmental safeguards," warned Rod Cameron of the Environmental Defense Fund, "without sufficient emphasis on the conservation of energy." Besides criticizing the destruction of the countryside, opponents of coal consumption warned of the dangers of contaminating the air. A study by the National Academy of Sciences, published in 1972, suggested that air pollution probably explained the tendency of city dwellers to suffer twice the rural rate of cancer. Sulfur dioxide, the end product of coal-burning, "is an especially pernicious pollutant," advised ecologist Barry Commoner, "for it tends to interfere with the self-protective mechanisms in the lungs that help reduce the effects of dust and other pollutants."

Less problematic than the risks of burning coal were the hazards of exposure to radiation. Despite industry assurances about the safety of atomic energy, reactors remained extremely unreliable. In the nineteen months preceding the end of the OPEC embargo, for example, the Vermont Yankee nuclear plant had been shut down seventeen times. Moreover, when after a series of legal suits the Atomic Energy Commission in 1973 reluctantly filed environmental impact statements about the new breeder reactors, the obvious inadequacies led the Environmental Protection Agency to request postponement of the program. In his efforts to accelerate nuclear development, however, Nixon criticized elaborate safety procedures that created "unreasonable delays" and imposed "unnecessary costs." "I am not afraid," Nixon had remarked about the breeder reactors in 1971, "not because I know much about it, but because what I do know tells me that here we have a new source of energy . . . that is absolutely important to the future of the world."

Nixon's commitment to nuclear energy stimulated the industry's development. "Call it pinch, squeeze, crunch, or crisis," gloated the Atomic Industrial Forum, an industry organ, "the precarious state of our energy supply has suddenly stripped away many clichés of both boom and doom from nuclear-power generation." By January 1974, 42 plants were operable, 56 were under construction, 101 had been ordered, and 14 more were in the serious planning stage. Nuclear power, concluded energy expert Ralph E. Lapp, was "the only practicable energy source in sight adequate to sustain our way of life and to promote our economy."

Government scientists scoffed at suggestions of nuclear risk. "We can't live in a Garden of Eden," explained AEC head Dixie Lee Ray, "and still have a technological society." A fourteen-volume report, drafted for the AEC by Massachusetts Institute of Technology professor Norman C. Rasmussen, insisted that the chances of an atomic reactor accident were equivalent to the odds of a meteor crashing into a large metropolitan area—about once every million years. "The consequences of potential reactor accidents," assured the Rasmussen study, "are no larger and, in many cases, are much smaller than those of non-nuclear accidents." Within five years, however, the AEC's successor agency, the Nuclear Regulatory Commission, reappraised Rasmussen's statistical methodology—and repudiated its findings.

With the end of the Arab embargo in March 1974, however, the issue of energy receded from public view. In the wake of gigantic oil-company profits, Congress endeavored to cut back the price of domestic oil, but the President vetoed the bill, arguing that it reduced any incentive for the production of domestic resources. In subsequent years, much of the oil profits were ploughed into non-energy fields—Mobil Oil's acquisition of Montgomery Ward, for example—as the oil companies continued to pursue their economic goals. Such diversification removed investment funds from other energy sources. In the summer of 1974, two nuclear power plants—one in Massachusetts, the other in Michigan—were canceled because of the difficulty of raising sufficient capital. But despite such problems and despite higher energy prices, Americans quickly returned to their high-consumption habits—relighting outdoor signs, avoiding mass transit, and violating the fifty-five-mile-per-hour speed limits. "We don't worry about the President any more," stated a Brooklyn service station attendant.

THE EASE WITH WHICH AMERICANS dismissed the energy shortages contrasted with their response to another crisis of resources—the danger of environmental collapse. It was the supreme irony of American technology that at the moment of its greatest achievement—the pinpoint landing of astronauts on the moon—human beings glimpsed just how unique and how vulnerable was the condition of the planet earth. Seen against the dusty summits of the moon, the blue planet reaffirmed the limited horizons of the remainder of mankind trapped by inexorable, but ultimately friendly forces of gravitation. The word "ecology," derived from the Greek *oikos*, meaning "house," quickly entered the American vocabulary. The earth, the Apollo space program reported, was mankind's only home.

Concern for the human habitat also reflected a belated awakening to the ravages inflicted by industrial technology. Reliance upon fossil fuels not only depleted irreplaceable resources but also generated toxic residues that upset the life patterns of plants and animals. The widespread use of petrochemical fertilizers in American agriculture created vast nitrogenous wastes that drained into rivers and lakes, encouraging algae growth that absorbed precious oxygen; as a result, sometime in the sixties, Lake Erie "died." More obvious industrial pollutants contaminated other waterways, turning Cleveland's Cuyahoga river into a fire hazard. The popularity of artificial products—the use of plastics instead of metal and paper, for example, or detergents instead of soap—left enormous quantities of nonbiodegradable waste. "The present course of environmental degradation . . . is so serious," warned Barry Commoner in his widely read book *The Closing Circle*, "that, if continued, it will destroy the capability of the environment to support a reasonably civilized human society."

Such prognostications aroused popular enthusiasm for environmental protection. "There is a new kind of revolutionary movement under way in this country," declared Senator Henry Jackson. "This movement is concerned with the integrity of man's life support system—the human environment." In 1969, the Department of Agriculture prohibited the use of the pesticide DDT, one of the "miracle" chemicals of World War II, because it destroyed the ecological balance—weakening, for example, the shells of birds' eggs. Nixon, in what the *Scientific American* called "a spectacular gesture," unilaterally banned biological and chemical weapons from American arsenals (though exempting tear gas, napalm, and defoliants commonly used in Vietnam). Responding to public opinion, Congress enacted the National Environmental Policy Act of 1969, which required all government agencies to file environmental impact statements on virtually every public project and placed the burden of protecting the public interest on the government. Congress also passed the Endangered Species Act of 1969 which endeavored to protect animals that faced global extinction. "Ecology," remarked California Democrat Jesse Unruh, "has become the political substitute for the word 'mother.' "

In his first official act of the seventies, Nixon signed the environmental policy act into law. "It is now or never," he remarked. "America pays its debt to the past by reclaiming the purity of its air, its waters, and our living environment." In February 1970, Nixon presented a major program for environmental action, proposing legislation to "rescue . . . our natural habitat as a place both habitable and hospitable to man." Six months later, the newly created Council on Environmental Quality issued its first annual report, proposing legislative remedies and pleading for what Nixon called "environmental literacy." "In dealing with the environment," said the President, "we must learn not how to master nature but how to master ourselves, our institutions and our technology."

The acceptance of ecological responsibility, however, required a major transformation of cultural values, "a new social ethic," explained microbiologist René Dubos of Rockefeller University, a "religion . . . based on harmony with nature as well as man." An ecological perspective, unlike the Judeo-Christian tradition, denied that mankind reigned over nature, named God's creatures, or could stand as the measure of all things. Commenting on the attempt to sterilize America's returning astronauts, the biologist Lewis Thomas observed that any extraterrestrial life "would have a lonely time waiting for acceptance to membership here. We do not have solitary beings. Every creature is, in some sense, connected to and dependent on the rest." But like astronauts wobbling on the alien moon, Americans, in the words of Barry Commoner, "have broken out of the circle of life."

By raising what were fundamentally religious issues, the ecological movement attracted the support of young people, who were more attuned than an older generation to the new ethic of survival. Asserting their reverence for nature, college students rediscovered the words of the Oglala holy man Black Elk, who worshiped the unity of nature, and turned the teachings of the Yaqui Don Juan, translated by Carlos Castaneda, into cult books. On April 22, 1970, environmentalists sponsored "Earth Day," a national teach-in to publicize the problems of ecology, to demand environmental legislation, and to encourage youth to clean up the polluted landscape. "The Establishment sees this as a great big anti-litter campaign," advised California Representative George Brown. "Wait until they find out what it really means . . . to their life-style to clean up our earth."

The government's commitment to environmental quality quickly revealed its limits. On Earth Day, Secretary of the Interior Hickel commemorated the occasion by announcing approval of the eight-hundred-mile Alaska pipeline, considered by environmentalists a dangerous threat to the ecological balance. Similarly, in enforcing the ban on DDT, the administration allowed the export of the lethal chemical for use abroad, even though many contaminated foods entered the American diet as imported products and, of course, poisoned an environment that knew no national boundaries.

The most glaring example of Nixon's insensitivity to the ecological issue appeared in his vigorous endorsement of the supersonic transport (SST), despite evidence that the aircraft threatened to damage the ozone layer that protected the earth from excessive radiation. "The increase of skin cancer in man is probably one of the simpler and best known effects," warned Dr. Gio Gori in testimony before Congress. "Other momentous modifications of the environment may not turn out so tame." In a crucial test of political strength—a vote that one senator characterized as a choice between "the bird watchers" and "the hardhats" who might lose their jobs—Congress refused to support the new aircraft by a narrow margin in March 1971. "America must and will continue pushing outward the horizons of the unknown," protested the President as he continued to request funding for the plane. "We may have lost this one, but we're going to win the next one."

THE ADMINISTRATION'S EQUIVOCAL POSITION on environmental protection reflected the vulnerability of the American economy to major shifts in world trade. By supporting the SST, the Alaska pipeline, the export of pesticides, Nixon hoped to redress a severe deficit of the international balance of payments that had plagued the American economy since the late fifties. Much of this deficit was the result of overseas military activity, especially the costs of the Vietnam War. But the problems of government spending had been greatly compounded by increases of private corporate investment in foreign subsidiaries. To take advantage of cheap foreign labor and favorable tax incentives, United States-based multinational corporations developed innovative accounting techniques to evade restrictions on capital flow and built overseas manufacturing plants which "exported" products to American customers. This failure to reinvest capital in domestic plants made the American economy more susceptible to direct foreign competition. As a result, in 1971, for the first time since 1893 (the year historian Frederick Jackson Turner proclaimed the closing of the American frontier), the United States experienced a deficit of international trade.

Besides inheriting these long-term financial liabilities, the Nixon administration also took office at a time of substantial—6 percent—inflation. Persuaded that the rise of prices resulted from "the growth of total spending"—budgetary deficits caused by the Vietnam war and expensive social welfare programs—the President promised to "slow down" the economy by controlling fiscal and monetary policies. True to his Republican philosophy of laissez faire, Nixon rejected the idea of establishing price and wage guidelines. "The leaders of labor and the leaders of management," he told his first press conference, "have to be guided by the interest of the organization they represent."

The business community took the President at his word—and began to raise prices. But while Nixon's hands-off attitude encouraged continuing inflation, the severe contraction of the money market created what Nixon called "slowing pains"—the highest interest rates in one hundred years, a decline in the gross national product, plummeting stock market prices, and an unemployment rate of 6 percent. This unprecedented inflation *and* recession— "stagflation"—translated into "Nixonomics." As defined by Democratic Party leader Lawrence O'Brien, it meant "that all the things that should go up—the stock market, corporate profits, real spendable income, productivity—go down, and all the things that should go down—unemployment, prices, interest rates—go up." This anomalous situation seriously hurt Republican candidates in the 1970 elections, leading the President to make a remarkable turnabout. Accepting the importance of an unbalanced budget, Nixon told television's Howard K. Smith, "I am now a Keynesian in economics." It was, remarked Smith "a little like a Christian crusader saying 'All things considered, I think Mohammed was right.' "

The persistence of inflation—the result both of an 11 percent increase in the cost of fuel and "administrative" price hikes—impelled the President to take more drastic action. On August 15, 1971, Nixon announced a "New Economic Policy," ironically the very phrase that Comrade Lenin had used in temporarily embracing capitalistic remedies in 1921. Nixon, instead, moved toward the socialist idea of economic controls, ordering a ninety-day freeze on wages, prices, and profit margins. To bolster the nation's foreign trade, the President also took the dollar off the gold standard, allowing it to float in world money markets, ordered a 10 percent tariff surcharge, and lifted excise taxes to stimulate automobile sales. Overnight the stock market soared nearly thirty-three points. The reaction of labor, whose wage increases usually followed rising prices, was less favorable. "Robin Hood in reverse," protested George Meany, "because it robs from the poor and gives to the rich." "It's us they is always chokin'," grumbled a young Kentucky coal miner, "so that the rich folks can stay fat." But careful monitoring by government agencies reduced annual inflation under 3 percent, while cost-of-living wage increases allowed labor to keep pace.

As wage/price controls cooled the inflation, the administration worked to improve foreign trade. In December 1971, in what Nixon asserted was "the most significant monetary agreement in the history of the world," the United States accepted new international exchange rates that devalued the dollar by eleven percent. By lowering the cost of American goods, the adjustment proved especially beneficial in two areas of foreign sales: high-technology equipment, including multibillion-dollar arms shipments to oil-producing countries such as Saudi Arabia and Iran; and food, 75 percent of the 1972 wheat crop, 50 percent of soybeans, and 15 percent of feed grains. The China market, a mere $5 million in 1970, rose by 1973 to nearly one billion dollars in sales of cotton, wheat, and tobacco.

These exports stimulated a short-term boom, but they failed

to deal with basic structural problems. Stiff foreign competition and high tariff barriers abroad forced the administration to order a second devaluation of the dollar by 10 percent in February 1973. But such measures hardly influenced the policies of multinational corporations, which placed priority on profits. In the automobile industry, for example, rising imports of small foreign cars drastically reduced domestic sales, and in 1970 General Motors introduced a competitive car, the Vega, "to improve," as one Chevrolet executive explained, "this country's balance of payments." But despite serious production problems at the Vega plant in Lordstown, the major automakers continued to invest more capital in Taiwan, South Korea, and the Philippines in 1972 than in the small-car project. In 1973, American car sales dropped by eleven million; the next year, they slipped seven million more. The United States was becoming "a nation of hamburger stands," complained the AFL-CIO, "a country stripped of industrial capacity and meaningful work . . . a service economy . . . a nation of citizens busily buying and selling cheeseburgers and root beer floats."

The aerospace industry also faced serious shortages of capital. As bankers refused to back risky aircraft development, the Nixon administration sponsored special legislation to protect the Lockheed corporation from bankruptcy. "Too much was at stake to permit Lockheed to fail," a study of multinational policy suggested "—24,000 jobs, $2.5 billion in outstanding contracts, $240 million advanced by airlines." These interests explained administration advocacy of the SST, even after the legislative defeat.

In the euphoria of his reelection, Nixon predicted that 1973 and 1974 would "be the best years our economy has ever experienced." In January 1973, he abruptly ended mandatory wage/price controls and, in what was called "Phase III" of the economic "game plan," offered a series of voluntary guidelines to regulate the economy. "Holding the line on Federal spending," the President asserted, "will reduce the inflation rate further." Many economists disagreed. "The logic of the 1973 economic situation called for a continuation of price and wage controls," objected Paul Samuelson, "but I'm not sure logic applies to Nixonomics."

Inflation came sooner than expected, striking at the most basic aspect of American consumption—food. Nixon's appeal for voluntary restraint had ignored the devastating effects of his own agricultural policy. In seeking to boost American exports, the government not only had oversold the farm surplus, but to assure higher prices also had withdrawn from cultivation a huge amount of acreage—and even increased the size of nonproductive land by five million acres in September 1972, two months *after* the Soviet wheat sale. Bad weather conditions elsewhere in the world aggravated the shortages. By the winter of 1973, food costs began to climb quickly and consumer groups called for ceilings on the price of meat. Nixon, remembering his problems in the Office of Price Administration during World War II, refused to act, and Agricultural Secretary Earl Butz, chief administrator of the "Food Power" export program, dismissed proponents of price ceilings as "damn fools." But as prices continued to skyrocket, the President reluctantly ordered a freeze on meat prices.

He acted, once again, too late. By April 1973, angry consumers spontaneously declared a nationwide boycott of meat. Expressing anger at the President's inflated ceilings, shoppers formed groups like Operation Pocketbook, Fight Inflation Together, and Housewives Expect Lower Prices, set up picket lines (NUTS TO BUTZ—NIX-ON BEEF), and reduced meat purchases by as much as 80 percent. A subsequent Gallup poll found that 25 percent of all consumers—affecting perhaps fifty million people—participated in the protest.

The meat boycott was especially effective in middle-class neighborhoods, according to a *New York Times* survey. "Doing something about meat prices is true women's liberation," maintained a Brooklyn picketer. "The average housewife isn't getting a job as a bank executive—and she can't understand the life of someone like Gloria Steinem." For middle-class families, stated a Boston reporter, the boycott showed "an awareness that, for a whole new class of Americans like themselves, push has finally come to shove." In poorer neighborhoods, the protest made scant inroads. "How much can these people tighten their belts," asked a butcher in Harlem, "when they don't have too much under their belts in the first place?" A local resident responsible for feeding a family of twelve agreed: "Why, I've been boycotting since Phase I."

Nixon remained critical of the effort, serving beef at a White House dinner for South Vietnam President Thieu. "He's the Marie Antoinette of American politics," scoffed a Brooklyn shopper. But despite vows to continue the protest indefinitely, meat prices slackened only slightly and the boycott slowly lost its momentum. Nixon's opposition to consumerism nevertheless weakened his middle-class support. "It's going to be the housewives against Nixon," declared the leader of an Illinois group called Women War on Prices.

Food prices continued to climb precipitously, fueling an inflation rate of 9.2 percent during the first five months of 1973. "Everybody thinks that Phase III was a failure," admitted Treasury Secretary George P. Shultz. In another abrupt reversal of policy in June, Nixon imposed a sixty-day freeze on prices, while reiterating his opposition to economic controls. "We must put the American consumer first," he said. But in July, he conceded "there is no way with or without controls to prevent a substantial rise of food prices." Moreover, "the freeze," Nixon explained, "is holding down production and creating shortages." Phase IV, which became effective in August 1973, allowed a gradual loosening of controls on a complicated sector-by-sector basis. "We shall have to work our way out," the President said vaguely, "and feel our way out of controls." Inflation nevertheless persisted through 1973, reaching an annual average of 6.2 percent (14.5 percent in food).

WHILE CONSUMERS PROTESTED runaway food prices, they paid less attention to the slow but steady inflation in the price of fuel, which increased at an average annual rate of 3.7 percent between 1964 and 1973. The Arab oil embargo quickly awakened public concern. As the OPEC countries raised the cost of crude oil 300 percent between the fall of 1973 and January 1, 1974, American oil companies compounded the inflation by increasing their rate of profit from 11 percent in the years before 1972 to 19 percent in 1974. These economic shifts undermined the stabilizing effects of Nixon's Phase IV. "We have been caught with our parameters down," quipped economist Walter Heller in December 1973, "and we have to go back to the drawing boards."

The oil embargo intensified stress throughout the American economy. When Nixon's new Secretary of Labor Peter Brennan boasted that "1973 was a good year for working people," union leader Jerry Wurf asked ironically, "I wonder what Pete is smoking." A Gallup poll taken in December 1973 showed that 85 percent of the sample expected serious economic problems in 1974.

"There is going to be panic, hoarding and, in some cases, no cooperation," predicted a young Milwaukee housewife, "which will result in hard times for all." Unemployment rates, which ended 1973 at 4.9 percent, jumped to 5.2 percent in January and remained at that level through the winter.

"I'm helpless," complained a seventy-year-old traveling salesman. "I can't get gas to go on the road. Who knows what I'm going to do."

"A lot of people are saying that recalls will never come," stated a furloughed TWA pilot. "We've never had a crunch like this before."

"Things have got to get better," emphasized an idled automobile worker, one of about a hundred thousand laid off in the industry, "because they can't hardly get any worse."

While the energy shortage eliminated jobs, rising fuel costs aggravated inflation. Despite increased unemployment, a drop in real incomes, and a decline in manufacturing output, wholesale prices leaped 14 percent in the year ending June 1974. More than half this increase reflected the rising cost of energy; the remainder was the result of administrative price changes, especially in noncompetitive industries. A 1967 dollar in consumer prices was worth sixty-eight cents in 1974.

"I used to keep a budget," a San Francisco woman told a Newsweek interviewer. "But it got so discouraging, I gave it up. The whole economic picture scares me. It's so unreal."

"You always used to think in this country that there would be bad times followed by good times," added a Chicago housewife. "Now, maybe it's bad times followed by hard times followed by harder times."

"There's nothing left after the rent and food," explained a Boston mother on welfare. "Sometimes I feel like I just want to give up."

As the economy raced out of control, disillusionment spread through the country. Blue-collar workers, whose unemployment rates exceeded national averages, fumed at Nixon's economic policies. "The wheat deal with Russia really ticked me off," stated a California worker, "and since then I've lost faith in everything the government says." "We are in for a hell of a lot of trouble," predicted a labor leader. "We'll see riots in supermarkets, gasoline stations and other places."

The contraction of the economy affected workers in all income brackets, and disaffection, like joblessness, slowly worked its way up the social ladder. Unemployment among college graduates reached unprecedented levels, and the teaching professions entered an era of decline. Not only were there fewer jobs for teachers, but academic salaries also slipped 2.5 percent in real dollars between 1970 and 1973. "Teachers and social science majors can get loans," commented a banker about the doubling of defaults in the 1973–74 academic year, "but they can't get jobs." Such problems had an immediate impact on academic life, producing a drop in college enrollment, encouraging students to switch majors to marketable subjects such as business administration, and contributing to a political quiet on college campuses.

Unprepared for the downturn, middle-class workers expressed deep frustration at the economic predicament.

"I'm resentful, bitter, and bored about the wasted years in college," stated an unemployed teacher, one year after graduation.

"I have absolutely no prospects for a job," complained another college graduate.

The stress of economic deprivation produced a social phenomenon typically associated with depressions—an epidemic of ransom kidnapping. As in the Great Depression of the thirties, the targets of these crimes were usually connected to wealthy businesses or banks. The most famous victim of the seventies was Patricia Hearst, granddaughter of William Randolph Hearst, child of the publisher of the *San Francisco Examiner*. Taken by the "Symbionese Liberation Army" as a prisoner of war in February 1974, the nineteen-year-old heiress served first as a hostage to force her family to offer $2 million worth of food to "all people with welfare cards, Social Security pension cards, food stamps, disabled veteran cards, medical cards, parole or probation papers, and jail or bail release slips." "It's too bad," protested Governor Ronald Reagan, "we can't have an epidemic of botulism." This unorthodox redistribution of corporate wealth ended abruptly when the captive Hearst denounced the program—"it certainly didn't sound like the kind of food our family is used to eating," she complained on a tape recording to her parents—and joined the SLA to participate in another crime characteristic of hard times—bank robbery.

"The gravity of our current inflationary problem can hardly

be overestimated," declared Arthur F. Burns, head of the nation's banking system, in May 1974. "The future of our country is in jeopardy. . . . Inflation at anything like the present rate would threaten the very foundations of our society." Pointing to the overthrow of several governments in Europe, he emphasized that the economic malaise "contributed materially to distrust of government officials" and threatened "a significant decline of economic and political freedom for the American people." The unemployment rate, agreed Senator Edward Kennedy, was "clearly excessive" and "ominous."

Alarmed by such warnings and suspicious of administration remedies, members of the corporate elite moved independently to stabilize the economic order. Under the leadership of Chase Manhattan's David Rockefeller, the nation's most powerful business executives formed a multinational organization called the Trilateral Commission in 1973. Composed of businessmen, politicians, academics, and lawyers from the United States, Western Europe, and Japan, the consortium sought to facilitate international economic cooperation beyond government supervision, particularly in dealing with countries that produced raw materials, such as OPEC. Though the activities of the Trilateral Commission remained cloaked in secrecy, its emergence reflected a global orientation among business elites which were more concerned with the survival of multinational corporations than with separate national policies. Looking beyond the Nixon administration, the Trilateral leadership pursued fresh talent to direct favorable government policy. Among the charter members were a coterie of presidential hopefuls—Jimmy Carter, Walter Mondale, George Bush, and John Anderson—all prepared, if not eager, to fill the breach of power after Nixon's departure.

THE DEPTH OF THE ECONOMIC CRISIS overwhelmed public concern for the broader issues of environmentalism and ecology, the reconciliation of human society to nature. But rising unemployment and double-digit inflation contributed to a deepening pessimism about the American future. A series of book titles—Commoner's *Closing Circle*, the affluent Club of Rome's *Limits to Growth*, the Ehrlichs' *The End of Affluence*, even the counterculture's *The Last Whole Earth Catalogue*—underscored a sense of completion, the beginning of the end of an era. In a sober "inquiry into the human prospect," economist Robert Heilbroner described a "civilizational malaise"—"the pall that hangs over us"—caused by the failure of "material improvement . . . to satisfy the human spirit."

The "crises" of the early seventies—in energy, ecology, and economics—added up to a spiritual crisis of major proportions. "What is at stake," observed E. F. Schumacher in his widely read *Small Is Beautiful*, "is not economics but culture." While the future of the industrial economy appeared bleak—a shrinking pie divided among more people—a reorientation of industrial values offered a different type of prosperity. Arguing that food shortages resulted not from agricultural limits but from bad eating habits, Frances Lappe proposed a "diet for a small planet" based on vegetable protein. "Free people," agreed Ivan Illich in an essay entitled "Energy and Equity," "must travel the road to productive social relations at the speed of a bicycle."

Most Americans stuck to the freeways. Preoccupied with gasoline, jobs, and the price of food—worried about preserving their place in a depressed economy—they identified more easily with traditional symbols. The subject of Richard Bach's best-seller, *Jonathan Livingston Seagull*—a mutant bird with the speed and spirit of an SST—epitomized this refusal to confront the limits of individualism or the failure of the frontier ethic. "If you want to know how we got to Vietnam," wrote Philip Slater in his appropriately titled book *Earthwalk*, "read *Jonathan Livingston Seagull*." The undying belief that Americans could exercise hegemony over nature reached its ultimate absurdity in a popular fad of the era—the gift of a "pet rock"—an object so tangible yet so puny as to provide ironic proof of the impotence of human possessiveness.

These expressions of popular culture betrayed an underlying anxiety about the new world of ecological limits. Uncertainty about the future also produced a search for scapegoats. By failing to protect the nation from serious economic and social dislocation, the Nixon administration appeared as a likely target. In the aftermath of meat shortages and the oil embargo, middle-class Americans, like minority outgroups before them, expressed growing alienation from the political leadership. And as the Watergate investigations unearthed evidence of government corruption—of corporate bribes, tax swindling, and blatant conspiracy—public frustration turned to outrage. Without Nixon, Americans hoped, the old system might yet be saved.

PART TWO

THE CRISIS OF LEADERSHIP

· 9 ·

"ANIMALS CRASHING AROUND IN THE FOREST"

The Politics of Watergate

THE TRIAL BEGAN AS THE SYMBOL of one era and ended as the symbol of another. Presiding judge William Matthew Byrne, Jr., had launched his public career as executive director of the President's Commission on Campus Unrest and had supervised the research and writing of the Scranton report of 1970. Despite the commission's criticism of the President, Byrne obtained an appointment to the United States district court in southern California in 1971, three weeks before the publication of the *Pentagon Papers* added another politically sensitive case to the federal docket. As the Department of Justice brought Ellsberg into Byrne's court in the spring of 1973, the judge received another presidential call, inviting him to the western White House in San Clemente to discuss an even more prestigious appointment—the directorship of the FBI. Impressed by the offer, Byrne nevertheless hesitated to accept, wondering about the judicial ethics of considering an administration promotion while hearing the controversial trial. In two days, he arranged a second session with Nixon's top domestic adviser, John Ehrlichman, and reluctantly declined the job. Whatever his personal misgivings, Byrne told no one about the secret meetings.

The White House soon called again. As the Ellsberg trial headed toward the jury, a special message informed Byrne that the government had illegally burglarized the offices of Ellsberg's psychiatrist. "An inflated and erroneous conception of 'national security,' " editorialized *The New York Times*, "led to criminal behavior which has brought the office of the President into grave disrepute." Now Byrne's discussions with Ehrlichman assumed a more ominous meaning, raising questions about a White House attempt to obstruct justice by influencing the rulings of the trial judge. By May 11, 1973, when Byrne discharged the case, the trial had become ensnarled with another matter of political subversion—Watergate.

THE CAPTURE OF FIVE BURGLARS inside the Democratic National Committee headquarters at the Watergate complex in Washington, D.C., on June 17, 1972, had aroused widespread suspicion about White House involvement. Despite official denials, two investigative reporters of *The Washington Post*, Carl Bernstein and Bob Woodward, printed stories claiming that the burglars had obtained money from the Committee for the Re-election of the President (popularly known as CREEP) and that illegal campaign contributions had been "laundered" in Mexican banks. "What really hurts," replied President Nixon in a news conference on August 29, "is if you try to cover it up. . . . I can state categorically that no one in the White House staff, no one in this administration, presently employed, was involved in this very bizarre incident." Two weeks later, a federal grand jury indicted the five burglars as well as two former White House aides, Gordon Liddy and E. Howard Hunt, on charges of tapping telephones, electronic surveillance, and theft of documents. "We have absolutely no evidence to indicate that any others should be charged," announced a Justice Department official. Pleased with the result, the President personally congratulated his counsel, John Dean: "the way you've handled it, it seems to me, has been very skillful, because you—putting your fingers in the dike every time that leaks have sprung here and sprung there."

Few voters paid attention to what McGovern denounced as an administration "whitewash." "Watergate did not, demonstrably, change the minds of those who went to the polls and voted for Richard Nixon by 61 to 38 percent," concluded Theodore White in his quadrennial epic, *The Making of the President*. "For it would be no less than national tragedy if men came to regard the election of 1972 as fraud," he added; "or attempted to reverse the verdict of the people at the polls on the technicalities of a burglary, in a spasm of morality approaching the hysterical." An investigation by the Fair Campaign Practices Committee later condemned the existence of a "conscious conspiracy to violate laws, to manipulate voters and to make a mockery of the democratic system of self-government." But in the aftermath of the election, Democrats saw no practical alternative to the Nixon slogan, "Four More Years."

The trial of the Watergate burglars opened in January 1973 in the court of Judge John Sirica, known in the legal fraternity for his harsh sentences as "Maximum John." Four of the burglars, all connected to the anti-Castro Cuban community of Miami and believed to have participated in the CIA-backed Bay of Pigs fiasco, maintained silence by pleading guilty. Hunt, Liddy, and former CIA operative James McCord were also convicted. But unlike his codefendants, McCord held loyalty to an organization outside the White House—the CIA—and opposed the administration's attempt, as he put it, "to get political control over the CIA assessments and estimates, in order to make them conform to 'White House policy.'" Politicization of the intelligence community, McCord felt, "smacked of the situation which Hitler's intelligence chiefs found themselves in . . . which ultimately was one of the things which led to Nazi Germany's downfall." With such reasoning, McCord determined to protect the CIA—and in the process, save his own skin—by refusing to participate further in the Watergate cover-up. In a letter to Sirica in March 1973, McCord admitted that "political pressure" had led the defendants to plead guilty, that perjury had been committed, and that the web of complicity reached high into the administration. The disclosures threatened to swamp a White House "stonewall" that, Dean's fingers notwithstanding, hovered on the verge of disintegration.

In invading the Democratic party, the Watergate burglary challenged important interest groups that held a solid base of power in Congress. Persuaded that the Nixon White House would never adequately investigate itself and angered by presidential attacks on the prerogatives of the legislative branch, the Senate established the Ervin committee to probe possible violations of campaign law. Nixon, fearing exposure of the Watergate cover-up and confident in his ability to defy congressional power, promptly announced his refusal to cooperate with the Senate on the grounds of "executive privilege." "Under the doctrine of the separation of powers," asserted Nixon, "the manner in which the President personally exercises his assigned executive powers is not subject to questioning by another branch of government." Nor, added the President, could Congress question "members of his staff . . . , for their roles are in effect an extension of the Presidency." "Executive poppycock," retorted Ervin. White House personnel were not "nobility and royalty," he stated, and would face arrest if they refused to appear before a congressional committee.

While the Ervin panel prepared for public hearings, the Senate Judiciary Committee, another bastion of Democratic power, scrutinized Nixon's nomination of acting FBI director L. Patrick Gray as permanent successor to J. Edgar Hoover. In testimony to the committee, Gray acknowledged several contacts with John Dean about the Watergate investigation. But when the committee invited Dean to appear, Nixon's legal counselor declined, citing the doctrine of executive privilege. Leaving Gray, in Ehrlichman's words, to "twist slowly, slowly in the wind," the White House allowed the FBI chief to mislead the senatorial investigation until early April when, as pressure mounted, the President withdrew the nomination. (It was this vacancy that Ehrlichman discussed with Judge Byrne.) But Gray's attempt to avoid what he called a "mine field" of controversy exploded violently when Senator Lowell Weicker of the Ervin committee reported that the head of the FBI had destroyed evidence relating to the Watergate affair. In late April, Gray resigned from the FBI. "Right now," warned Senator Robert Dole of Kansas, "the credibility of the administration is zilch, zero."

The testimony of McCord, Dean's refusal to become an administration "scapegoat," and the imminent opening of the Ervin inquiry forced the President to act dramatically to avert further damaging confessions. On April 17, 1973, White House press secretary Ron Ziegler announced the discovery of new evidence that made all previous statements about Watergate "inoperative." Behind closed doors, Nixon rallied his cabinet. "We've had our Cambodias before," he exhorted. On the third anniversary of the ill-received "incursion," the President told a stunned television audience that four major advisers—H. R. Haldeman, John Ehrlichman, John Dean, and Attorney General Richard Kleindienst—had resigned because of the Watergate affair, but that Nixon alone, as chief executive, was responsible for what he termed "a series of illegal acts and bad judgments by a number of individuals." Claiming that "both of our great parties" had violated the law, Nixon pledged to bring "the guilty . . . to justice," and to see "that such abuses are purged from our political processes in the years to come, long after I have left this office." The President named as attorney general Elliot Richardson, "a man of incomparable integrity and rigorously high principle," and agreed to appoint an independent special prosecutor to deal with the Watergate case. In May, Richardson selected a Harvard-based Kennedy supporter named Archibald Cox. "I have the greatest confidence in the President," maintained House Minority Leader Gerald Ford, "and am absolutely positive he had nothing to do with this mess."

The Democratic leadership remained more skeptical. On May 17, 1973, Ervin convened what he considered "the most important investigation ever entrusted to the Congress." "The burglars who broke into the headquarters of the Democratic National Committee," he suggested in his opening remarks, "were in effect breaking into the home of every citizen of the United States. And if these allegations prove to be true, what they were seeking to steal was not the jewels, money or other property of American citizens, but something much more valuable—their most precious heritage, the right to vote in a free election." Though the administration attempted to minimize the significance of the hearings—a "beauty contest" with a "Perry Masonish impact," sneered Vice President Agnew—the proceedings provided a daytime television spectacle comparable to the Army-McCarthy hearings of 1954.

Television news lacked the investigatory capacity of the press. But in broadcasting plain two-dimensional symbols, the cameras crystallized a political style that communicated more information about the procedures and policies of government than all the arcane, devious vocabulary of the witnesses. John Dean, the boy-faced accomplice, turned state's evidence, projected adolescent sincerity, drawing on a remarkable memory for detail to support charges of White House complicity. Former Attorney General John Mitchell, confident and brusque, presented the sly bullishness of a masterful municipal bonds lawyer well-trained in saying absolutely only what was necessary to hasten his departure from the scene. Ehrlichman and Haldeman—"two of the finest public servants it has been my privilege to know," Nixon had described them on April 30—personified their reputation as "the German shepherds," "Fritz and Hans," "the Berlin Wall," crew-cut images of militaristic discipline and administrative efficiency. In all the hours of testimony, the multitude of events and names and transactions became hopelessly entangled in charges and counter-charges, admissions and denials. All these convulsions of government translated through television into a raucous carnival of political corruption.

Here the public learned about the existence of a White House "enemies list," designed to punish prominent opponents. Here they learned about the abuse of the Internal Revenue Service, nemesis of the middle class, to harass journalists and politicians, private businesses and public foundations. Here they learned about enormous campaign contributions from corporations and individuals, the creation of multimillion-dollar slush funds to finance political sabotage and to buy silence from convicted conspirators. Here they learned about dubious political decisions, the dismissal of antitrust proceedings against ITT, one of the world's largest multinational corporations, possibly in return for support of the Republican convention, and the inflation of price supports for the milk industry after illegal donations by milk producers to key politicians. Here, too, the public heard charges of political corruption raised against the very members of the Senate who were investigating White House corruption—Joseph Montoya conceding that signatures on his 1970 campaign funding reports were forgeries; Edward Gurney acknowledging receipt of campaign funds for 1974 from two of Nixon's closest cohorts, Murray Chotiner and Bebe Rebozo; Herman Talmadge accepting a paid vacation from a major government contractor; Lowell Weicker, in a heated argument with Ehrlichman about the legitimacy of spying on private lives, stating, "I'm no angel; I'm no angel."

These revelations emphasized the political dimensions of the Watergate affair. "You placed the expediency of the next election above your responsibilities . . . to advise the President of the peril that surrounded him?" asked Talmadge of Mitchell. "You have put it exactly correct," replied the former Attorney General. "In my mind, the reelection of Richard Nixon, compared with what was available on the other side, was so much more important." In this context, the Watergate investigation seriously eroded the President's political base. In February 1973, the month the POWs returned from Vietnam, Nixon held 68 percent approval as President; by July, his standing slipped to 40 percent. In August, a Harris poll showed that 55 percent of the sample believed that "President Nixon does not inspire confidence as a President should." Democrats found satisfaction in the President's distress. "Watergate has taken some of the self-righteousness away from the Republicans in Georgia," observed a smiling Governor Carter. "They've got a real problem now of how to stay away from Nixon without driving off the diehard Nixon supporters they depended on before."

While the politicians competed for the public limelight, lawyers for the Ervin committee interrogated witnesses in the basement of the Senate Office Building. On Friday, the thirteenth of July—a day of bad luck for the President—former White House appointments secretary Alexander Butterfield was describing the administration's office procedures when an investigator asked about the possibility of recording presidential conversations. "I was hoping you fellows wouldn't ask me about that," replied Butterfield. After the Cambodian invasion, he said, the President ordered the Secret Service to install voice-activated tape recorders in White House offices to preserve a historical record. Such tapes, besides holding new evidence, promised to resolve the conflicting testimony presented to the Ervin committee—would reveal at last who had told the truth and who had lied. "We were all struck by the enormity of the matter," recalled Don Sanders, one of the examiners.

The existence of a secret tape-recording system, triggered without the consent of even the powerful visitors to the President, stunned the Democratic leadership. "An outrage," remarked House Speaker Carl Albert about the violation of privacy, "almost beyond belief." "I wouldn't have minded," admitted Majority Leader Mansfield, "if they told me." But in preserving the spoken word, Nixon seemed more interested in obtaining control, not so much of politics, as of history. More than most Presidents, he was obsessed with demonstrating historical "firsts," with record-breaking statistics or mere assertions of presidential superlatives. To his cabinet officers, he gave special four-year calendars, each day marking the remaining days of his administration. "If we make the

most of the challenge and opportunity that these days offer us,"
he inscribed on the covers, "they can stand out as great days for
America, and great moments in the history of the world."

Beyond hyperbole, Nixon treated history as plastic—not the
cosmic infinite, but days and seasons subject to the human will. It
was the Nixon administration that rewrote the public calendar to
transform legal holidays (once, literally, "holy days") into three-
day weekends. On Independence Day 1971, the President announced a unilateral change of the dates of the nation's
Bicentennial celebration, so that the affair would culminate not
with the end of the Revolutionary War, but in 1976, the last year
of Nixon's second term. This secularized view of history explained
Nixon's fascination with documentation, whatever the legal implications. "White people like to have books for everything," observed Jackson Jordan, Jr., who, as the son of a former slave, had
been raised in an oral tradition. "Don't you find it amazing that
the Watergate people wrote down everything they did and even
went so far as to record their unlawfulness? . . . You couldn't pay
black criminals to do that."

The historical perspective, as Nixon shrewdly understood,
easily led into unfriendly terrain. "At this time in world history
when totalitarian government is in command of the two other
largest powers," wrote historian Barbara Tuchman in August 1973,
"it is imperative for the United States to preserve and restore to
original principles our constitutional structure." Citing the acrid
testimony presented before the Ervin committee, she urged the
nation "to grasp the nettle of impeachment if we must." In the
same week, Supreme Court Justice Harry Blackmun, a Nixon appointee of 1970, delivered a sermon to the American Bar Association that reflected the historical vision of the country's founders.
"One senses a laxness in public life," he preached in the style of a
Puritan jeremiad, "that in earlier years, if indulged in, could not
be politically surmounted. . . . The very glue of our governmental
structure seems about to become unstuck. . . . The Twentieth
Century, for which we had such high hopes, seems indeed a Twentieth Century Limited."

THIS HISTORICAL ANALYSIS underscored the broad implications of
the White House tapes, turning a political imbroglio between
professional politicians into a legal and constitutional epic about

the essence of the American republic, the accountability of government to the law. Having learned about the tapes, two separate investigations—one by the Ervin committee, the other by the special prosecutor—appealed to the President to surrender the surreptitiously recorded evidence. Invoking the doctrine of the separation of powers, Nixon rejected both requests. "Happily," answered Cox in announcing he would seek a formal subpoena, "ours is a system of government in which no man is above the law." "How did it happen that burglars were caught in the headquarters of the opposition party with the President's campaign funds in their pockets . . . ?" asked the bushy-browed Ervin. "I don't think the people of the United States are interested so much in abstruse arguments about the separation of powers or executive privileges as they are in finding the answer to that question."

The President's refusal to comply with the Cox-Ervin requests reflected not only the obvious problem of White House involvement in the obstruction of justice, but also a philosophical attitude about executive authority that Nixon shared with his most recent predecessors in the Oval Office. Since World War II, all American Presidents had justified violations of constitutional rights in the name of "national security." Coinciding with a general expansion of executive power, these illegal practices often served purely political purposes, such as the wiretapping of civil rights activists or the burglary of left-wing organizations. Under Nixon, the adoption of a secret foreign policy obscured the distinction between national security and partisan politics. Distrusting the existing intelligence bureaucracies, Nixon allowed the plumbers to blur the interests of the White House with those of the nation.

Nixon supporters took refuge in the doctrine of "higher law." "In the White House," testified Jeb Stuart Magruder, deputy director of the reelection committee (CREEP), "we saw continual violations of the law by antiwar, radical groups. There was a feeling of resentment and frustration in trying to deal with these matters on a legal basis." These events, added Ehrlichman, "included hundreds of bombings of buildings, a highly organized attempt to shut down the federal government, intensive harassment of political candidates and violent street demonstrations which endangered life and property." "The notion that the end justifies the means," stated Nixon in self-defense in August 1973, "proved contagious. Thus it is not surprising, even though it is deplorable, that some persons in 1972 adopted the morality that they themselves had rightly condemned [in others] and committed acts that have no place in our political system."

Such assertions, intended to end what Nixon described as a "backward-looking obsession with Watergate," failed to satisfy administration critics. On July 31, 1973, Representative Robert F. Drinan, a Catholic priest from Massachusetts, introduced a resolution listing four presidential actions—the bombing of Cambodia, the taping of conversations, the refusal to spend impounded funds, and the establishment of a "supersecret security force within the White House"—as grounds for impeachment. Public opinion polls found that large majorities doubted the President's honesty and most Americans believed he had an obligation to surrender the White House tapes. "If President Nixon defied a Supreme Court order to turn over the tapes," warned Senator Kennedy, "a responsible Congress would be left with no recourse but to exercise its power of impeachment. . . . The President has no argument from history for such defiance." "It may well be," wrote columnist William Raspberry in *The Washington Post*, "that the biggest threat to the presidency today is—the President."

As Nixon struggled to recapture public confidence, his administration received a severe blow from its sturdiest supporter—Vice President Agnew. On August 6, 1973, the Justice Department revealed that the second highest executive officer was under investigation for receiving bribes during his tenure as governor of Maryland. "I am innocent of any wrongdoing," asserted the Vice President in launching a rhetorical attack against his accusers— "masochistic persons looking for all that is wrong." But with the administration's credibility already suspect, Agnew could no longer rally public support. Moreover, with the President himself in a precarious legal position, Attorney General Richardson wished to expedite a settlement of the Agnew case, lest it complicate the presidential succession. Compounding the problem, Nixon opposed an impeachment proceeding, fearing it might set an unfortunate precedent for himself, and exerted pressure on the Vice President to resign. Facing incontrovertible evidence of bribery, even while serving in Washington, Agnew agreed at last to plea-bargain for a reduced sentence. On October 10, 1973, in exchange for his resignation, Agnew offered a "nolo contendere" plea—it was, interjected the trial judge, "the full equivalent to a

plea of guilty"—to a single count of income tax evasion, amounting to $13,551.47. In leaving government service, the former Vice
President received a three-year suspended sentence, a $10,000 fine,
and a letter from Richard Nixon ("Dear Ted") expressing "a great
sense of personal loss." After a televised farewell address that denied "scurrilous and inaccurate reports," Agnew slipped quickly
from the public scene.

Contrary to Nixon's hopes, however, Agnew's resignation intensified pressure against the White House. With the leading
apostle of "law and order" defrocked, the administration lost support from a conservative "silent majority" that had turned to the
Republicans of 1972 to preserve the traditional morality. The conviction of the Vice President for illegal financial activity also lent
credence to accusations that the President may have misused public funds to pursue what the October 1973 issue of *Fortune* magazine called "the monarchical life-style to which U.S. Presidents
have grown accustomed." The high cost of government-financed
improvements for the President's personal residences in California
and Florida—demanded, claimed Nixon, by the need for security—
contrasted with "the typical homeowner's need to economize."
Nixon's elaborate chronicle of real estate transactions with his
friends Rebozo and Robert Abplanalp, by which the President
had become a millionaire in office, further aroused public suspicion. "People have got to know whether or not their President is a
crook," asserted Nixon in a remarkable concession of his weakening stature. "Well, I'm not a crook."

The departure of Agnew also served the crucial symbolic role
of weakening public allegiance to the entire adminstration.
"We've demonstrated that we can replace a Vice President," remarked William Rusher, publisher of the conservative *National
Review,* "so I expect we could replace a President." After a decade
of assassination—the sudden loss of the two Kennedys, King,
George Wallace—the idea of finding substitute leadership no
longer seemed odd or implausible. "For nearly five years," wrote
Time magazine, "a man morally and intellectually unfit for national leadership has been just one life removed from the Oval
Office"; to which a correspondent from Stanford, California, responded: "Big Deal. For nearly five years a man morally and intellectually unfit for national leadership has been *in* the Oval
Office."

Two days after Agnew resigned, Nixon attempted "a new beginning" by nominating for Vice President the House Minority Leader Gerald Ford of Michigan, a choice that won genuine applause from the Democratic leadership of both houses of Congress. "Ford has the reputation of being a somewhat limited spear-carrier," observed columnist Elizabeth Drew. "There are no sharp edges on him—of brilliance or of meanness." Thinking ahead toward the presidential race of 1976, the Democrats wanted no incumbent who might pose a serious threat to their own candidate. "As emphatically and as strongly as I can," assured the nominee, "I have no intention of being a candidate for any office—President, Vice President or anything else—in 1976."

Nixon's attempt to consolidate congressional support came not a moment too soon. On the day he announced Ford's nomination, an appellate court denied the President's "incantation of the doctrine of separation of powers," rejected his claim "of special presidential immunities," and ordered him to produce the subpoenaed White House tapes for Judge Sirica. Nixon still had the right to appeal the ruling to the Supreme Court, but perhaps fearful of the outcome, he decided on a different strategy. Disregarding the court order, Nixon announced his intention to comply with the spirit of the ruling, while preserving his executive privileges, by providing written summaries of the tapes, which could then be verified in a private hearing by Senator John Stennis of Mississippi. The Ervin committee, which had been denied access to the tapes on jurisdictional grounds, consented to Nixon's compromise. But prosecutor Cox questioned the reliability of such secondhand evidence and rejected the proposal. "I think it is my duty as the special prosecutor," declared Cox in a televised news conference on Saturday, October 20, 1973, "to bring to the court's attention what seems to me to be noncompliance."

Enraged by his subordinate's audacity, Nixon immediately ordered Attorney General Richardson to fire Cox. But Richardson, having assumed office the previous April on assurances that the President would not interfere with the special prosecutor, refused the task and instead submitted his resignation. Nixon then ordered deputy Attorney General William Ruckelshaus to fire Cox. But he, too, refused and was promptly fired by the President. Solicitor General Robert Bork then assumed the attorney general's post and executed the order. "Whether we shall continue to be a government of laws and not of men," stated Cox on learning of his dismissal, "is now for Congress and ultimately the American people."

This Saturday Night Massacre, reported immediately by the television networks, provoked waves of protest that White House Chief of Staff Alexander Haig likened to "a fire storm." "The President has defied the courts, defied the Congress," warned Senator Robert Byrd. "This sounds like a Brown-shirt operation 30 years ago; these are Gestapo tactics." "The office of the President does not carry with it a license to destroy justice in America," objected Senator Robert Packwood. More than a quarter of a million telegrams denouncing the President's action poured into Washington, and on Sunday huge crowds surrounded the White House, urging passing motorists to "honk for impeachment." The next day, nine hundred delegates to the AFL-CIO convention in Florida adopted a resolution calling for Nixon's resignation or impeachment. "We believe the American people have had enough. More than enough," stated George Meany. In the House of Representatives, eighty-four congressmen sponsored twenty-two different bills calling for Nixon's impeachment, and the Democratic leadership instructed the judiciary committee, headed by Representative Peter Rodino of New Jersey, to begin an impeachment inquiry.

When Nixon's lawyer Charles Wright appeared before Judge Sirica on October 23, few expected his brief announcement. "This President does not defy the law," he told a hushed courtroom. Nixon had agreed to surrender the disputed tapes. The President also promised a public address to explain his shifting position, but a sudden crisis in the Middle East forced its postponement. This coincidental intrusion of foreign policy issues, not unprecedented in Nixon's efforts to distract attention from Watergate, created additional doubts, for the White House acknowledged that the President had placed all American military forces on "red alert," a halfway step toward the commitment of troops. Worried that the embattled President might take some drastic action to preserve his power, members of the business community quickly joined a rising chorus of alarm. Harried by such pressures, Kissinger pleaded for "a minimum of confidence that senior officials of the American government are not playing with the lives of the American people." But *Time* magazine headlined its story with a still unanswered question: WAS THE ALERT SCARE NECESSARY?

During a tart press conference on October 26, Nixon conceded the appointment of another special prosecutor, but anger and suspicion continued to spread through the country. Nixon's reversals, said George Meany, demonstrated his "dangerous emotional instability." "He must leave office for the common good," demanded Senator John Tunney. "The people do not believe him, and he has shamed them." The next day, Nixon's credibility slipped even more, when the White House announced that two of the nine subpoenaed tapes did not exist. "I have passed the point of reacting," snapped Speaker Albert. "Coincidence, coincidence, coincidence," said Representative John Moss. "It may be true, but it is regrettable that one even has to question a President's statement." "The public," warned Hubert Humphrey, "is fed up with this sort of business."

The erosion of congressional confidence in the White House mirrored the sentiments of influential constituents around the country. "Someone in the White House is guilty of either unbelievable stupidity or outright lies," editorialized *The Detroit News*, once a strong supporter of the President. "In either case, public confidence in this administration suffers the final shattering blow." *Time* magazine, in the first editorial of its fifty-year history, called for Nixon's resignation, emphasizing that the President had "irredeemably" lost the support of the nation. A Gallup poll, taken during the first week of November, found Nixon's popularity rate at an all-time low of 27 percent. These feelings soon acquired a momentum of their own, accelerating the withdrawal of confidence that, once taken away, could never be restored. Then, in mid-November, the public learned even more: crucial portions of the White House tapes contained mysterious gaps.

Recognizing the real possibility of Nixon's departure, Congress now moved quickly to assure an orderly succession by confirming the nomination of Gerald Ford. After perfunctory examinations of his finances, his political attitudes—"a virtually unbroken record of favoring big business during his 25 years in the House," remarked Senator Howard Cannon, "indicating an indifference to the needs of the disadvantaged"—and his mental health ("The truth is," said Ford, "I'm disgustingly sane."), both houses ratified the appointment on December 6. "In exactly eight weeks," the Vice President stated in a brief inaugural speech, "we have demonstrated to the world that our great republic stands solid, stands strong upon the bedrock of the Constitution." Ford personified that stability. "Integrity is the bottom line in the social contract," commented Eric Sevareid that evening, "not brilliance, eloquence or magnetism, and we've reached the bottom line."

"I'm a Ford," echoed the Vice President, "not a Lincoln."

With the vice-presidency secure, Nixon endeavored to prove his own integrity in a public relations campaign called "Operation Candor." On December 8, the President released a complex statement of his personal finances, including income tax returns for the presidential years, and agreed to abide by an IRS audit. Three days later, Senator Weicker told a news conference that Nixon's tax deductions of his vice-presidential papers were illegal. As the IRS reopened its examination of the President's tax reports, other aspects of the Watergate case—missing tapes, campaign financing, milk price supports, the ITT antitrust settlement, and illegal wiretapping—held public attention. "There are other things, animals crashing around in the forest," suggested Republican Senator Howard Baker at the end of 1973. "I can hear them, but I can't see them."

THE PRESIDENT'S HOPE to restore public confidence in the new year abruptly collapsed when a panel of expert technicians reported on January 15 that a particular eighteen-and-a-half minute gap in a conversation between Nixon and Haldeman had been deliberately erased. "This is the most serious single bit of evidence to date," declared Representative John B. Anderson, chairman of the House Republican Conference, "that there has been a conscious deliberate effort to obstruct justice." "We *know* that there is corruption in the precincts of the Oval Office," concluded political columnist George Will. Listing the names of all the White House aides who had left the administration because of Watergate—Haldeman, Ehrlichman, Colson, Dean, Strachan, Porter, Caulfield, Ulasewicz, Mitchell, Stans, Hunt, Mardian, Segretti, Liddy, Kalmbach, McCord, Chapin, Gray, and Magruder—a veritable scoreboard of conspiracy—Will asked, "Of all the significant men who were around the White House when the cover-up began, who are still there providing the continuity in this ongoing cover-up? One name," he said, "springs to mind."

The persistence of public disbelief in the President had consequences far beyond the political arena, threatening the stability of the nation's economic structure. At a time of inflation, high unemployment, and energy shortage, members of the corporate elite warned of the importance of preserving public confidence in government policy. "Uncertainties make business nervous," observed *New York Times* editor Clifton Daniel, after interviewing several corporate leaders. "They would be very happy if the President would resign," he quoted a banker. "That would remove one of the uncertainties in the political picture." Reports from Europe confirmed the belief that Nixon's departure would have "a very positive effect on the world's economy."

The fears of the nation's business elite paralleled the economic concerns of less affluent Americans. On New Year's Day, Representative Les Aspin declared that contributors to the President's reelection included officials and stockholders of 178 oil and gas companies as well as oil corporations that used international subsidiaries to conceal illegal donations. "President Nixon's hands are tied," stated Aspin, "preventing him from dealing effectively with the current energy crisis." In April, members of the construction workers union—the once loyal hard hats—cheered George Meany's assurances that "the American people have completely lost confidence" in the Republican leadership. And in that month of income tax reckoning, when millions of Americans struggled with government form 1040, the IRS reported that President Nixon owed nearly half a million dollars in back taxes for illegally changing the date of a gift of documents to the National Archives.

While moviegoers flocked to see the horror film *The Exorcist*—a saga of the violent purgation of foul-talking evil—the Republican party grappled with the similar dilemma of saving their cause from the taint of sin. In February, Ford's former congressional seat, long a bastion of Republicanism, fell into Democratic hands. "I want my party to succeed," responded Nixon to the political upset, "but more important, I want the Presidency to survive, and it is vitally important . . . that the Presidency . . . not be hostage to what happens to the popularity of a President at one time or another." Describing the atmosphere of the congressional cloakrooms, however, Representative Shirley Chisholm suggested that Republican leaders would force the President to leave office, "not because they feel deep in their hearts he should resign, but because many of them . . . are having trouble in their districts from their constituents." Republican Senator Jacob Javits, facing reelection himself, predicted his party was "doomed to disaster" in 1974.

The loss of political support leaped beyond public opinion polls or the aspirations of incumbent politicians, creating what conservative Senator James Buckley perceived in March 1974 as "a crisis of the regime." The idea, old as the republic, touched the central tenet of Jefferson's Declaration of Independence. In that document, the great Virginian had attacked a theory of government that assumed the king, as God's regent on earth, could do no wrong, and Jefferson had masterfully focused American protest directly at the "royal brute," reduced King George to human proportions, stripped away the sacred regalia that had mystified the body of the monarch. For the next two centuries, Americans shifted their loyalty to a different type of executive—the presidency—and through time and habit had allowed this office to acquire a quality of sacredness, almost of spirituality. Nixon, for nearly two years, found shelter behind these trappings, offering up other public servants, much as King George had sacrificed his ministers, to appease public indignation. But the crisis of Watergate, as Buckley explained, touched "every tissue of the nation, conspicuously including its moral and spiritual dimension."

In an audacious attempt to preserve his administration, Nixon commanded television airtime on April 29, 1974—"mounting his electronic throne," scoffed Representative James Mann—to offer dramatic evidence of his innocence. For five months, the House judiciary committee, investigating the impeachment of the President, had tried to obtain specific White House tapes. But Nixon had thwarted their efforts, insisting on "the necessity of protecting the confidentiality of presidential conversations." Facing a judicial subpoena, however, a violation of which might itself constitute an impeachable offense, Nixon decided to mask a strategic retreat by offering the public a dose of "brutal candor." Still maintaining that "the President has nothing to hide," Nixon released a 1,308-page edited transcription of the subpoenaed tapes, in place of the actual evidence.

The publication of the transcriptions revealed the most intimate details of White House conversations and stripped away the remaining shreds of presidential dignity. "We have seen the private man and we are appalled," commented the conservative *Chicago Tribune*. "He is humorless to the point of being inhumane. He is devious. He is vacillating. He is profane. He is willing to be led. He displays amazing gaps in his knowledge . . . his loyalty is minimal." "A shabby, disgusting, immoral performance," admitted Senate Minority Leader Hugh Scott. Finding their names in the presidential transcripts, leading politicians expressed baffled amusement that belied outraged feelings of betrayal and violation. "Nobody is a friend of ours. Let's face it," said Nixon on one of the tapes. Congressional leaders, embarrassed and angered by such disclosures, prepared to take him at his word.

Having staked—and lost—his political reputation on the release of the transcripts, Nixon possessed few resources to fend off the inexorable legal process. Informed by the House judiciary committee that he had "failed to comply" with the original subpoena, Nixon decided to block the flow of additional material. Vice President Ford, caught in a conflict of loyalties, objected to the President's "stonewall attitude," but continued to maintain that the "preponderance of evidence favors the President." Nixon also accepted support from Rabbi Baruch Korff, president of a National Citizens Committee for Fairness to the Presidency, which made the peculiar claim that Watergate was "the broadest but the thinnest scandal in American history." Unimpressed by such logic, the Judiciary Committee commenced formal impeachment hearings on May 9 and special Watergate prosecutor Leon Jaworski, who had succeeded Cox, appealed to the Supreme Court to resolve the constitutionality of the President's position.

Feeling surrounded by the crawling legal machinery, Nixon turned to foreign affairs to bolster his sagging image. Though suffering from a serious case of phlebitis that threatened him with sudden death, the President journeyed to the Middle East in mid-June, finding satisfaction in the huge crowds that greeted him, and reciprocating by offering Egypt and Israel nuclear reactors for peaceful energy. Six days after his return to Washington, he departed again for a summit conference with Soviet leader Leonid Brezhnev. But because Nixon lacked a firm base of power at home, negotiations about SALT reached no agreement. The President returned to American shores to find his political troubles mounting to another climax.

The Supreme Court that convened on July 24, 1974, to rule

on the case *United States* v. *Richard Nixon* reflected the conservative principles for which the President had appointed four of its members. The issue involved a conflict between the President's claim to executive privilege and the obligation to provide evidence necessary for the due process of law. The Court took a decidedly conservative stand on the matter. "Neither the doctrine of the separation of powers, nor the need for confidentiality of high-level communications," declared Chief Justice Warren Burger, "can sustain an absolute, unqualified, presidential privilege of immunity from judicial process." In this highest court of appeals, the President had lost his case—and with it, his cause. Through his attorney, James St. Clair, Nixon announced his willingness to comply with the ruling.

That evening, without waiting for the final transmission of documents, Representative Rodino gaveled the Judiciary Committee to order. "Make no mistake about it," he said solemnly. "This is a turning point, whatever we decide." Stirred by the gravity of the occasion, stimulated, too, by the presence of television cameras, the thirty-eight committee members attained an extraordinary level of political eloquence in debating the articles of impeachment. "I am not going to sit here," declared Representative Barbara Jordan in a riveting speech, "and be an idle spectator to the diminution, the subversion, the destruction of the Constitution." "You have left no stain upon your effort," concluded Rodino. "I am proud to be part of you, to be among you, to be of you."

Two days later, on July 27, the committee voted 27-11 to adopt the first article of impeachment, charging the President with obstruction of justice for blocking a full investigation of the Watergate affair. On July 29, the committee recommended 28-10 the second article of impeachment, accusing Nixon of abusing his powers of office to violate constitutional rights. On July 30, the committee approved 21-17 the third article of impeachment, citing the chief executive's violations of congressional subpoenas. Two other proposed articles, accusing the President of concealing the bombing of Cambodia and of filing fraudulent income tax reports—charges that tainted other powerful politicians, including Vice President Ford—failed to carry by votes of 12-26. "Richard Nixon did many things illegal and immoral," observed Garry Wills, "—the secret bombing of Cambodia, the violation of Geneva rules on weaponry, the intervention in the Calley and Manson trials, the mass arrests of May Day. But none of these things could be made to matter when the House drew up its impeachment counts."

The committee vote had crippled the President. Certain that the full House would ratify the recommendations, Nixon prepared to carry his fight to the Senate. He failed, even then, to recognize the full implications of his deeds. On August 5, in an act of apparent political suicide, the President released additional transcriptions of conversations which showed unmistakably that on June 23, 1972, six days after the Watergate burglary, Nixon personally ordered a halt to a full investigation of the crime. Shocked by this disclosure, Republican loyalists quickly withdrew their remaining support. The ten dissenting members of the Judiciary Committee publicly rescinded their vote, and on August 7, three of the most powerful Republicans on Capitol Hill—Senate Minority Leader Scott, House Minority Leader John Rhodes, and Senator Barry Goldwater—journeyed to the White House to confirm estimates of minimal support.

Facing certain conviction, the thirty-seventh President of the United States addressed the American people for the thirty-seventh time on August 8, 1974. "I have never been a quitter," he admitted. "To leave office before my term is completed is opposed to every instinct in my body." He spoke wistfully about the spirit of Theodore Roosevelt, one of his heroes, "about the man in the arena whose face is marred by dust and sweat and blood, who strives valiantly, who errs and comes short again and again because there is no effort without error and shortcoming." His struggle, he announced, would end the next day at noon. For the first time, an American president had resigned.

In a somber White House, Nixon bade farewell to the members of his administration on the morning of August 9. He quoted again from Theodore Roosevelt, the young man's shock at the death of his wife, and his subsequent triumph over personal pain. "Always give your best," advised the outgoing President. "Never get discouraged. Never be petty. Always remember: others may hate you. Those who hate you don't win unless you hate them. And then you destroy yourself." Driven from office by his own vindictiveness, the ruthless, often petty pursuit of enemies real and imagined, Nixon knew well about the power of those he had turned against himself, and the self-destructive risks of what he considered "the rugged life" of politics.

Flying over the Midwest on his way to San Clemente, Nixon had no interest in hearing the conciliatory address of his successor. "Our Constitution works," affirmed President Ford. "Our great Republic is a government of laws and not of men. Here," stated the country's first unelected national officer with no trace of irony, "the people rule." In Albany, New York, another Republican leader drew similar conclusions. "Out of the traumatic experiences of these past two years," exclaimed ex-Governor Nelson Rockefeller, "has emerged an awareness of the extraordinary strength and stability of the American people." Asked about his future plans, the man who had spent more private funds than any other politician seeking public office smiled: "This is Jerry Ford's show."

As the new President pleaded to "bind up the internal wounds of Watergate," the curtain slowly settled across a strange theater of politics. John Mitchell, testifying about political sabotage, described "White House horrors," and Ford, seeking to build a new consensus, hailed the end of "our long national nightmare." Like the world of dreams, Watergate easily evoked archetypal symbols of Good and Evil, an authentic morality play, what Ford in his inaugural speech characterized simply as "the Golden Rule." The rise and fall of Richard Nixon—from the largest majority in American history to the abyss of political disgrace—illuminated a classic tale of virtue rewarded, vice punished.

During the prolonged controversy, however, Americans for the first time pierced the veil of secrecy that surrounded the normal exercise of power in their country. In the complexity of names and dates, it was impossible to keep track of the lines that drew politicians to corporate interests, that knit campaign contributors to executive orders and congressional votes. "You don't get to the top in politics without doing a lot of crooked stuff," was the lesson drawn by a seventy-three-year-old cab driver in Washington, D.C., on the day of Nixon's resignation. Watergate confirmed that truism and, if anything, threatened to reveal too much about the inner workings of American politics. Nixon's machinations, the contorted evidence suggested, were not unusual; they aimed, rather, too darkly, too viciously, at other powerful interests. "In terms of morality," one senator told an interviewer, "we in politics have a double standard. We have high social motives but we are content to play the game." "We assume that politicians are without honor," agreed Adrienne Rich. "We read their statements trying to crack the code. The scandals of their politics: not that men in high places lie, only that they do so with such indifference, so endlessly, still expecting to be believed."

10

"MODEL T IN THE WHITE HOUSE"

Frustrations Under Ford

THE PRESIDENT MADE THE STATE-
ment about Representative John B. Anderson, but it really told
much more about himself. "He's the smartest guy in Congress,"
remarked Gerald Ford about his colleague from Illinois, "but he
insists on voting his conscience instead of his party." A product of
the congressional cloakrooms—for a quarter of a century the representative of Michigan's fifth district—Ford defined the world by
his own limitations. About this President, observed *New York
Times* reporter Israel Shenker, "there is no whiff of charisma."
After the flamboyance of Johnson and Nixon, the debacles of
Vietnam and Watergate, Ford offered trustful homilies of calm.
"I do not want a honeymoon," he told a joint session of Congress
three days after taking office. "I want a good marriage."

To stabilize his shaky foundations, Ford turned to the Old
Guard leadership for advice about the first order of business, the
choice of a Vice President. A secret poll of Republican governors
and congressmen, partisan politicians and cabinet staff produced
two unsurprising names, both tightly knit to the traditional networks of power and wealth: the chairman of the National Committee, George Bush, and perhaps the wealthiest man in the
country, Nelson Rockefeller. Looking toward 1976, Ford nominated the more famous scion of Standard Oil.

Rockefeller's vast personal wealth troubled the Watergate-
bruised nation. Testimony before congressional investigating com-

mittees revealed that the millionaire governor had habitually bestowed large sums of money on subordinates ($50,000 to Kissinger in 1969, for example), had underpaid his federal income taxes by 21 percent or nearly $1 million, had used his personal fortune to finance a scurrilous biography of political opponent Arthur Goldberg, and had concealed his complicity during the early stages of a Senate inquiry—"a throwback to what we have had over the past two years," protested Senator Robert Byrd. Perhaps these diverse activities explained Rockefeller's sympathy for departed President Nixon. "He's been hung," said Rockefeller; he need not also "be drawn and quartered." But Rockefeller's support of a pardon for Nixon, Angela Davis told a Senate committee, was "profoundly hypocritical" because the former governor's refusal to consider amnesty at Attica prison had provoked "one of the most wanton massacres in the history of the United States." Responding to such charges, Rockefeller conceded that at Attica he had made a "serious mistake"—by not acting more quickly!—and maintained that his presence would not have achieved any miracles. "I'm no messiah," snapped Rockefeller. Such admissions finally appeased the congressional opposition. In December 1974, Ford's vice-presidential choice took the oath of office.

Rockefeller's long ordeal before Congress reflected a deepening disillusionment about the integrity of the Ford administration. Despite initial praise for his honesty and candor, the President had spoiled his public image by abruptly terminating the investigation of his predecessor's criminality. On September 8, 1974, he granted Nixon "a full, free, and absolute pardon . . . for all offenses against the United States." In a formal acceptance statement the former President regretted his "mistakes over Watergate." But he made no confessions of guilt and so provided no catharsis for the anger and sense of betrayal that had ravaged the country. For his complicity in this failure, Ford's popularity rating collapsed overnight from 72 to 49 percent. The *Chicago Tribune* reported "a sour smell" in the White House, and presidential press secretary Jerry ter Horst resigned in protest. When the White House hinted that other Watergate defendants might also receive pardons, the Senate hastily passed a resolution urging the President to desist—at least until the judicial process had been exhausted. As criticism persisted, Ford decided to take another unprecedented step by testifying personally on October 17 before a House subcommittee about the reasons for the pardon. Emphasizing his priority on "healing . . . the wounds of the past," Ford denied any secret arrangements with the former President. "There was no deal, period," Ford exclaimed, "under no circumstances."

Ford's generosity to Nixon contrasted with his treatment of another class of unpopular criminals, the young men who had challenged the Vietam war by violating draft laws and by deserting military service. Ten days after his inauguration, the President shocked a convention of the Veterans of Foreign Wars by offering a program of conditional amnesty—"earned reentry," he emphasized, *"earned* reentry"—for those war casualties "still absent without leave from the real America." But where amnesty implied pardon, Ford stressed "clemency" and "mercy," and established a presidential panel to review particular cases and propose alternative service. Of some 350,000 eligible persons, 6 percent applied for the program; the rest failed to do so, partly out of ignorance and partly from disdain. One draft resister explained: "They want me to shuffle and scrape and mumble, 'I'm sorry folks, I shouldn't of done it—please forgive me,' all so Ford can feel good about letting Nixon off the hook. They can cram it." As in other aspects of draft law and military justice, the clemency program was enforced haphazardly, perpetuating old inequities and institutionalizing new ones. More concerned with the political benefits of the program—the appearance of rapprochement—Ford rejected his panel's plea to revise the rules. "I think we gave them a good opportunity," he maintained. "I don't think we should go any further."

FORD'S ATTEMPT TO PUT Vietnam and Watergate behind him underestimated the extent of public bitterness. Though the President campaigned strenuously for Republican candidates in the 1974 elections, Democrats gained 49 seats in the House of Representatives, five in the Senate, and four governorships. To bolster his sagging image, Ford released a three-page report on the achievement of his first hundred days in office, a paltry list of public appearances and vague programs. "Gerald Ford is an awfully nice man," concluded John Osborne in *The New Republic*, "who isn't up to the presidency."

Despite his domestic problems, Ford worked to preserve

Nixon's foreign policy, relying on Henry Kissinger to merge the doctrine of détente with the open door. After the November elections, the President journeyed to Japan and South Korea to cement the Pacific alliance, before meeting with Soviet leader Brezhnev in the Siberian port city of Vladivostok to discuss the second round of the SALT treaties. Seeking additional trade with the United States, the Soviets proved eager to reach agreement based on an equivalence of nuclear strength. To satisfy United States demands, the Soviets discounted American weapons in Western Europe and accepted, for the time being, American superiority of multiwarhead missiles (MIRVs). But Ford refused to cancel the B1 bomber or to count air-launched cruise missiles within the accepted limits, while insisting that the Soviets include the subsonic Backfire bomber. Such complicated details, the stuff of endless negotiations, obscured the obvious fact that weapon limitations already far exceeded the amount of firepower necessary to incinerate either enemy many times over. But the unsettled issues prevented a final treaty, despite Kissinger's assertion that agreement of principles represented an important "breakthrough."

Administration optimism soon collided with entrenched interests in the Pentagon and the Senate. As in previous nuclear agreements, the military establishment refused to concede American superiority, even in principle, and lobbied against the proposed limitations. Senator Henry Jackson, long an opponent of détente, took the opportunity to link Soviet opposition to Israel in the Yom Kippur war with the persecution of Jews within the Soviet Union and managed to amend the foreign trade bill to deny benefits to the Soviet Union without concessions on Jewish emigration policy. Besides indicating a resurgence of congressional power in foreign affairs, the measure undermined Kissinger's diplomatic leverage and removed a major reason for Soviet accommodation.

Jackson's position nevertheless won strong support from administration conservatives such as Defense Secretary James Schlesinger. In 1974, Schlesinger had introduced a strategic refinement to the existing Mutual Assured Destruction (MAD) nuclear policy that was called "counterforce." Instead of targeting American missiles at Soviet industrial centers—an attack on which inevitably would lead to total war—the United States, he suggested, might arm for a limited nuclear war by aiming at Soviet missile sites. Though scientists denied the possibility of limiting nuclear war—indeed suggested that the very idea made nuclear war more plausible—Schlesinger announced in July 1975 that the Pentagon viewed counterforce as compatible with a first-use strategy, implying that the United States was prepared to launch a nuclear war for limited ends. Schlesinger's comments coincided with a rise of anti-Soviet opinion. That month, *Reader's Digest* published the advice of former Defense Secretary Melvin Laird: "Don't try to reach agreements with the Russians because you can't trust them." On June 30, exiled Soviet author Alexander Solzhenitsyn had used his first public forum in the United States to denounce détente and "to call upon America to be more careful with its trust." Goaded by conservative Republicans to embrace Solzhenitsyn, Ford resisted a reversal of policy, demonstrating a stubbornness that offended Old Guard stalwarts.

Despite conservative objections, Ford attended a summit conference of European leaders in Helsinki, Finland, in August 1975, which formally ratified the national boundary settlements of World War II. The agreement acknowledged Soviet hegemony in Eastern Europe but, at the same time, it denied legitimacy to external interference in domestic affairs and affirmed the principles of human rights. "Peace is not a piece of paper," the American President declared. "History will judge this conference not by what we say here today but by what we do tomorrow—not by the promises we make but by the promises we keep." For Ford, the judgment came sooner than expected. Americans of Eastern European ancestry joined a loud chorus of cold warriors in rejecting the Helsinki accords. "I am against it," said former California governor Reagan, "and I think all Americans should be against it." Ford's participation, agreed Senator Jackson, took us "backward, not forward, in the search for a genuine peace." Aware of his eroding support at home, Ford lacked the flexibility at Helsinki to compromise differences with Brezhnev about SALT. During the next year, the two powers agreed to limit the size of underground nuclear explosions—at a higher seismological level than scientifically necessary—but an unfinished arms-limitation treaty remained Ford's legacy for the next administration.

The repudiation of détente, considered just a few years earlier a major achievement of the Nixon presidency, reflected an enormous upheaval in the nature of American foreign relations following the signing of the Paris treaty of 1973. Nixon's assertions of "peace with honor" had provided a rhetorical buffer against the realities of military defeat. But by the spring of 1975, the regimes of South Vietnam and Cambodia, stripped by Congress of American military assistance, could no longer withstand the armies of North Vietnam and the Khmer Rouge. In the waning days of the war, Ford pleaded with Congress to extend emergency aid, "put an end to self-inflicted wounds," and reassert "our strength, our authority, and our leadership." But the war had created chasms of disbelief, a bitter numbness, unshakable even by Operation Baby-lift, the evacuation of Vietnamese infants spirited from their homeland to American shores. "So at last it has come to this," wrote columnist Herb Caen. "The Sentimental American . . . is fondling babies, washing diapers and guilt, and still, with indifferent arrogance, making the same mistake all over again: trying to tell other people how to live and die, fighting to the last Vietnamese."

The collapse of South Vietnam, televised in America as a slugfest among survivors trying to catch the last helicopter to safety, reopened questions about the future of American military power and its international responsibilities. But the administration moved quickly to stifle these unsettling issues, calling on the public to end "recriminations," "to close ranks." "What we need now in this country, for some weeks at least, and hopefully for some months," Kissinger told a press conference, "is to . . . put Vietnam behind us and to concentrate on problems of the future." In its moment of bitter vindication, the antiwar movement looked awkwardly for new commitments, an activist in Boston urging a crowd to "carry the nostalgia we all feel for the war that brought us together further into other organizing opportunities." The focus of a decade's energy suddenly vanished in silence. "We have been piously commanded to avoid recriminations," wrote a Vietnam veteran against the war in November. "The dead are not only buried but they never existed, there was never a war."

The momentum of amnesia, useful as a domestic nostrum, threatened to destroy the international balance of power, and the administration strove to reaffirm America's commitments to its allies. "Let no potential adversary believe that our difficulties or our debates mean a slackening of our national will," Ford stated to Congress. "In an era of turbulence, uncertainty, and conflict," proclaimed Kissinger, "the world still looks to us for a protecting hand, a mediating influence, a path to follow." But the nations of the world now lacked confidence in an American response. "Although South Vietnam is far removed," warned South Korean president Park (who in seven years had committed three hundred thousand troops to support the United States in Indochina), "we cannot regard the situation there as a fire across the river." In the European capitals, headlines emblazoned the American defeat and predicted a decline of United States influence.

"At some point," Kissinger told an emergency session of the National Security Council, "the United States must draw the line." Two weeks after the Vietnam withdrawal, the situation was hardly ideal. "But," said Kissinger, "we must act upon it now, and act firmly." Sailing between Saigon and Thailand, an American container ship, S.S. *Mayaguez*, had been intercepted by Cambodian patrol boats and escorted into port. Fearing that a repetition of the *Pueblo* incident of 1968—in which North Korea held an American crew captive for more than a year—would further weaken the nation's global posture, the administration decided to minimize the subtleties of diplomacy and strike a decisive blow. Ordering warplanes to strafe suspected vessels immediately, the Pentagon authorized an elaborate attack plan to seize the *Mayaguez*, rescue the crew, and, in violation of the 1973 ban, to bomb Cambodia. Under the provisions of the War Powers Act, Ford was obliged to consult with members of Congress and he dutifully summoned legislative leaders to the White House. "I was not consulted," Majority Leader Mansfield later explained. "I was notified after the fact about what the administration had already decided to do." Despite Ford's determination, the response took more than a day to develop. By the time American forces moved into action, the Cambodian regime had already released the captured crew unharmed, except for minor wounds caused by American strafing. Unaware of this decision, the attack proceeded, causing major bombing destruction to the Cambodian port and embroiling United States Marines in a vicious crossfire that damaged several helicopters and produced high casualties.

The *Mayaguez* operation cost forty-one lives and forty-nine wounded to "recover" forty sailors. "We never anticipated it," concluded Ford. "Having it happen so quickly and so successfully." "It was wonderful," said an exulting Barry Goldwater. "It shows we've still got balls in this country." After weeks of despairing news from Southeast Asia, the press seized the occasion to extol American courage and resolution—"a daring show of nerve and steel," gloated *Newsweek*, "—and it worked." "It did not only ignite confidence in the White House," the President later boasted, "it had an electrifying reaction as far as the American people were concerned." Meeting the next morning with the Shah of Iran, Ford could overlook the failure of the helicopter assault and assure the Persian ally of "close cooperation . . . continued and intensified." And in Cambodia, the Khmer Rouge had yet another argument for ordering the evacuation of its cities.

Support for the *Mayaguez* action, however, failed to blunt growing congressional criticism of the administration's supervision of the American intelligence establishment. Soon after taking office, Ford had naively acknowledged the role of the CIA in toppling the Allende regime in Chile in 1973. In the aftermath of Watergate, the revelation provoked a storm of protest against what Senator Kennedy called "not only a flagrant violation of our alleged policy of non-intervention in Chilean affairs, but also an appalling lack of forthrightness with the Congress." Two months later, *New York Times* reporter Seymour Hersh, author of the My Lai exposé of 1968, aroused further indignation by revealing an elaborate pattern of domestic espionage by the CIA that included wiretapping, burglary, surveillance, and mail intercepts—all violations of the agency's statutory authority as well as of the constitutional rights of the American people. Having glimpsed the CIA's "family jewels"—secret incriminating evidence—Ford endeavored to control any investigation of the intelligence network by appointing a conservative presidential commission headed by Vice President Rockefeller. Fearing another administration cover-up, both houses of Congress authorized investigations of their own, chaired respectively by Senator Frank Church and Representative Otis Pike, and broadened the mandate to include the secret activities of the FBI. Inherent in all three investigations was the problem of balancing the obligations of national security against the preservation of constitutionally protected civil liberties.

"In the CIA," explained former agent Philip Agee, in an angry exposé published in 1975, *Inside the Company*, "we justified our penetration, disruption and sabotage . . . because we felt morality changed on crossing national frontiers." The report of the Rockefeller commission, released in June 1975, revealed a similar abrogation of morality—and the law—on the home front. Domestic surveillance, illegal experiments with drugs such as LSD, the subversion of dissident groups in the late sixties and early seventies (known as Operation CHAOS), and a willing submission to the "personal political ends" of the White House—all involved serious violations of constitutional rights that led the commission to recommend greater control over CIA activities. The Senate committee report, issued over vigorous presidential objections, provided even more startling documentation of other intelligence abuses—CIA involvement in assassination attempts against foreign leaders—Fidel Castro, Patrice Lumumba, Rafael Trujillo, and Ngo Dinh Diem; interception of private correspondence (including a letter from Senator Church to his mother-in-law!); an FBI counterintelligence program designed to discredit and disrupt political dissent, including attacks on the Black Panthers; the creation of half a million domestic intelligence files, burglaries against the Socialist Workers Party, and the wiretapping and bugging of Martin Luther King.

These revelations reiterated the lessons of Watergate. "I think a President ought to be accountable," Ford remarked in announcing a major reorganization of the intelligence apparatus in 1976. Establishing explicit lines of responsibility, the executive order proscribed domestic intelligence by the CIA and created an Intelligence Oversight Board to monitor compliance. The Senate, still unwilling to relinquish responsibility to the White House, also created a permanent watchdog committee. At the same time, FBI Director Clarence Kelley conceded that his agency had committed "wrongful uses of power," and in the summer of 1976 announced an internal reorganization plan to prevent further abuses.

The exposure of illegal CIA activities had immediate repercussions for administration foreign policy. In December 1975, the White House appealed to Congress to underwrite covert CIA operations against a pro-Soviet faction engaged in civil war in Angola. Fearing entrapment in another Vietnam and especially distrustful of CIA involvement, Congress bluntly rejected the request. "A great nation cannot escape its responsibilities," protested Ford. "Responsibilities abandoned today will return as more acute crises tomorrow." But Congress remained adamant and a frustrated administration reluctantly complied with this unusual expression of legislative control over foreign affairs. Instead of committing military advisers and weapons, Ford sent the secretary of state on a goodwill tour, where Kissinger affirmed American support of "self-determination, majority rule, equal rights, and human dignity for all the peoples of southern Africa."

FORD's CONFLICTS WITH CONGRESS exacerbated tensions within the White House and threatened the President's control over the Republican party. Unwilling to desert Kissinger's foreign policy, but equally opposed to domestic liberalism, Ford moved to strengthen his political base by reorganizing the executive branch in a conservative direction. In a series of bold presidential orders in November 1975—dubbed by the press as the Halloween massacre—Ford fired Schlesinger and replaced him with a loyal conservative, Donald Rumsfeld; summoned ambassador Bush from Peking to replace William Colby as head of the CIA; removed Secretary Kissinger from his dual position as National Security Adviser; and prevailed upon Rockefeller to renounce interest in a vice-presidential candidacy in 1976. Yet the overhaul weakened Ford's position more. "I'm certainly not appeased," scoffed candidate Reagan, while liberal columnist Joseph Kraft suggested that the personnel changes "stimulated new doubts as to whether [Ford] has the brains to be President." A series of unfortunate accidents—tripping on an airport runway in Germany, falling on a Colorado ski slope, bumping his head on the presidential limousine, and an automobile collision in Hartford—added to a presidential stereotype of bumbling incompetence.

The Democratic party, though remarkably successful in the 1974 elections, also suffered from internal divisions left over from 1972. Most pressing was the problem of determining minority and female representation at the national nominating convention, a reform measure that had alienated the traditional Democratic constituency in the previous campaign. In an unprecedented off-year national convention held in Kansas City in December 1974, the Democratic leadership managed to skirt this dilemma by simultaneously endorsing "affirmative action" while rejecting the quantitative principle of "mandatory quotas." Chicago Mayor Richard Daley, exiled from the scene in 1972, now told black leader Jesse Jackson, "I recognize when power moves." Eager to preserve a united front, delegates paid little heed to the creator of the party reforms, George McGovern, who urged that Democrats not "be bland . . . and blind to the evils before us." With Watergate a fresh memory, party leaders looked confidently to a spate of winning candidates—Henry Jackson, Hubert Humphrey, Morris Udall, and Jimmy Carter.

But the stench of scandal, easily detected in the clean post-Watergate atmosphere, soon clouded the Democratic prospect. For nearly two decades, Arkansas Representative Wilbur Mills, chairman of the Ways and Means Committee, had protected entrenched Democrats from unpleasant votes on questions of taxation by carefully packaging legislation behind the scenes. In exchange, he had been rewarded with considerable power, enough to encourage a brief foray into the presidential contest of 1972. Along with his power, Mills developed a fondness for the bottle. One night, Park Service policemen found the ruffled congressman visibly intoxicated in the company of a woman named Anabella Batistella, aka stripper Fanne Foxe, "The Argentina Firecracker." "My little Argentine hillbilly," Mills called her. When Foxe parlayed her newfound fame into a lucrative nightclub appearance, an inebriated Mills joined her on the stage. But the pressure of public notoriety proved incompatible with political responsibility, and the harried congressman sought refuge in a hospital to obtain treatment for alcoholism. By the time he returned to the floors of Congress, his political career had been wrecked.

Mills's unseemly departure may well have spared him the pain of political defeat. A sizable number of liberal Democrats, elected for the first time in 1974, held no allegiance to the traditional seniority system and had no need for Mills's protection from unpopular votes. In January 1975, three other entrenched chairmen lost their posts, and the chairman of the Administration committee, Wayne Hays, won reelection by a thread. But his victory was short-lived. In May 1976, one of Hays's secretaries reported she had been paid a congressional staff salary solely for sexual services. "I can't type, I can't file, I can't even answer the phone," declared Elizabeth Ray. Hays retaliated by charging Ray with "emotional and psychological problems," and to forestall a full investigation, the Ohio congressman sought relief in a bottle of sleeping pills. Like Mills, he survived hospitalization, only to find his power gone, and within weeks he had left the House. Less influential than Mills and Hays, Representative Allan Howe was arrested in a red light district of Salt Lake City for soliciting an undercover officer for immoral purposes. Claiming entrapment, the congressman nevertheless lost a bid for reelection in 1976.

THE LIMITATIONS OF THE POLITICAL leadership in Washington, D.C., precluded a concerted effort to resolve the nation's economic problems. In August 1974, Ford had inherited, according to *The New York Times*, "the worst inflation in the country's peacetime history, the highest interest rates in a century, the consequent severe slump in housing, sinking and utterly demoralized securities markets, a stagnant economy with large-scale unemployment in prospect and a worsening international trade and payments position." In his first press conference, the President asserted an orthodox Republican philosophy—"wage and price controls are out, period"—and placed priority on eradicating what he called "public enemy number one": inflation. At an economic summit conference in September 1974, Ford pleaded for voluntary restraint, urging each person to "make a list of some ten ways you can save energy and you can fight inflation."

The Democratic leadership quickly established clear lines of disagreement. "We have not one but two public enemies," insisted Senator Humphrey, "—inflation and recession"; and he advised the administration that "any policy that brings higher unemployment and lower real incomes . . . in the name of controlling inflation, is simply unacceptable." Objecting to Ford's proposed fiscal retreat, Speaker Carl Albert called for the creation of a hundred thousand public service jobs and a prohibition of administrative price increases in monopolistic industries. The economy, argued Senator Mansfield, could not remedy itself. "Inflation is social dynamite," he warned. "Recession is social dynamite. . . . They will not wait for the 'self-adjusting mechanisms' of the economy to self-adjust."

Disregarding these charges, Ford asked Congress to enact a 5 percent surtax to limit inflation and recommended investment tax credits and enlarged unemployment benefits. Committed to voluntarism, the President wore a lapel button with the motto WIN, explaining that it signified a new civilian crusade, "Whip Inflation

Now." In a speech before the Future Farmers of America, Ford offered personal vignettes from his mailbag about how Americans might scrimp and save in the war against rising prices. "Clean up your plate before you leave the table," the chief executive exhorted the nation. "Guard your health."

Such admonitions failed to reckon with the health of the economy. As inflation persisted, cutting into real incomes, consumption began to slacken, resulting in high overstocks of manufactured goods which, in turn, produced cutbacks in production and rising unemployment. In November, the administration conceded, "We are moving into a recession." But the President continued to insist, "Our country is not in an economic crisis" and stubbornly rejected "a 180 degree turn from inflation fighting to recessionary pump priming." December statistics revealed that the GNP had declined 9.1 percent in the last quarter of 1974, inflation soared at a rate of 13.7 percent, and unemployment reached 7.1 percent. "The state of the union," admitted Ford in his first annual address, "is not good."

As the nation entered the worst economic downturn since the Great Depression, the President argued with Congress about proper remedies. In a skirmish symbolic of their differences, Congress trounced the President's plan to raise the cost of food stamps. But despite large majorities in both houses, the Democrats lacked sufficient cohesion to sustain an alternative economic program. Congress managed to restore some of Ford's proposed tax cut and also included provisions to eliminate corporate tax loopholes and long-standing oil and gas depletion allowances. But attempts to pass a liberal jobs bill and provide generous support to home buyers faced a presidential veto, forcing Democrats to compromise. By the late spring of 1975, administration parsimony had helped cut inflation in half, but unemployment hovered around 9 percent and the economy remained sluggish.

Underlying the economic crisis was a steady rise in the cost of energy. "Americans are no longer in full control of their own national destiny," the President told a television audience, "when that destiny depends on uncertain foreign fuel." In endorsing Nixon's Project Independence, Ford vetoed limitations on coal mining and advocated support of synthetic fuels and nuclear energy. Both alternatives, however, required heavy capital investment, a scarce resource in time of recession. A nuclear power industry report described 1975 as a year of "consolidation," indicating a decline of new construction, and in June 1975, the much vaunted breeder reactor was relegated to research status.

The cornerstone of Ford's energy program remained Middle Eastern oil. To reduce consumption and encourage conservation, the President proposed increasing the import fee for crude oil, allowing rising prices to stimulate voluntary cutbacks. Convinced that "voluntary restrictions simply have not worked," Democrats countered with an elaborate program of increased gasoline taxes, mandatory allocations and rationing, and tax incentives against energy waste. But the Democrats recoiled from implementing their austere proposals, fearing that the public would not easily accept the full burden of the energy shortage. In the Middle East, Secretary Kissinger launched a dramatic round of "shuttle diplomacy," hoping that an Arab-Israeli settlement might restore a modicum of certainty to the energy future. But in June 1975, Ford concluded, "We are worse off today than we were in January."

Recognizing that the world no longer conformed to American standards, business leaders tried to force the United States to accommodate the changing demands of the global marketplace. In a gesture that symbolized the loss of economic hegemony, the administration approved in December 1975 the Metric Conversion Act—described by a Commerce Department study as "a decision whose time has come"—to encourage American exporters to mesh their productive gears with the nuts and bolts of foreign competition. To compensate for the deficiencies of American capital formation, multinational corporations such as General Electric and Westinghouse worked with the Energy Research and Development Administration (ERDA), formed in 1975 as successor to the AEC, to stimulate the sale of nuclear reactors overseas. "The worldwide nuclear industry is estimated to be on the scale of about one hundred billion dollars," explained columnist Elizabeth Drew, "—and the grim reality is that no one knows how to call the whole thing off."

The enhancement of foreign trade, however, offered few short-term advantages. "People are disturbed by the failure of the economy to pick up," remarked AFL-CIO economist Nat Goldfinger in the fall of 1975. "They hear optimistic talk from the White House that the recession is over and they see it's not true for them." Arthur Burns, speaking at the University of Georgia, noted some "ominous signs" on the economic horizon and warned they might "before long bring on another recession." "For several years America has been approaching a crossroads in our history," Ford told a television audience in October. "Today we are here." Calling for major cuts in both spending and taxation, the President urged Congress to "take a new direction" and bring "to a halt the momentous growth of government."

The choice became stark reality that month when the city of New York announced that it was teetering on the edge of bankruptcy. Swollen municipal budgets—the combined result of higher welfare expenses and the wage gains of public service unions—and a shrinking tax base caused by the flight of business and residences to suburbia had carried deficit spending to its logical conclusion. Unable to sell new bonds, the nation's largest city appealed to the federal government for financial assistance. But the President refused to help—FORD TO CITY: DROP DEAD, headlined the New York *Daily News*—arguing that the city required a major financial overhaul. Saved at the last moment by a loan from the city's teachers union, the municipal government proceeded to make budgetary concessions, overcoming the President's objections. "As we count our Thanksgiving blessings," said Ford, in announcing short-term loans in November, "we recall that Americans have always believed in helping those who help themselves."

The plight of New York City illuminated not only the perils of recession, but also the larger issues of the liberal state. "We thought we could transform the country through massive national programs," Ford argued in his state of the union speech of 1976, "but often the programs did not work. Too often they only made things worse." It was time, he said, "for a fundamentally different approach—for a new realism" about the efficacy of government spending. The speech dropped a gauntlet before liberal Democrats, drew hard the battle lines of 1976. "We must reject those of timid vision who counsel us to go back," Senator Muskie rebutted the President. "We cannot go back. We cannot give up. And we will not."

THE ADMINISTRATION'S INSENSITIVITY to the troubles of New York City underscored fundamental social changes in urban America. "As the cities of the Northeast have become more and more the preserves of blacks and Latinos," explained M. Carl Holman of the Urban Coalition, "they have come to be seen as expendable."

Although black unemployment remained twice the national average, the mass media preferred to glorify the emergence of a black middle class. Typical of this emphasis was the appearance of television's George Jefferson, erstwhile black neighbor of Archie Bunker, who moved into new affluent surroundings in a program of his own. "It's the American dream come true," boasted Jefferson. "Ten years ago I was this little guy with one store. And now look at me. . . ." "Now," interjected his wife, "you're the little guy with seven stores." During 1974, black business receipts did gain a full percent over the previous year, but at the same time the nation's largest corporations reported increases of 25 percent.

In recession conditions, the likelihood of minority social mobility diminished sharply, aggravating racial conflict among the poorer classes that competed in the shrinking marketplace. As upwardly mobile whites departed the inner cities for the suburbs, the racial composition of urban schools became increasingly black; in Detroit, for example, the black population in the public schools edged from 64.9 percent in 1971 to 69.8 percent in 1973. To redress the racial balance, a federal court demanded a merger of urban and suburban school districts around Detroit and ordered mandatory pupil busing to restore a racial mix. But in 1974, the Supreme Court overturned the ruling, arguing, in the words of Chief Justice Burger, that "no single tradition in public education is more deeply rooted than local control over the operation of schools." Suburban public schools, the Court implied, could remain white.

The rejection of metropolitan integration returned the burden of racial accommodation to the urban centers, where white and black residents remained substantially poorer than suburbanites. In the white ethnic neighborhoods of Boston, unemployment approached 15 percent, nearly as high as that of blacks, and average annual incomes remained low. Into these traditionally Irish Catholic districts rolled the first court-ordered school buses in September 1974. Furious at this invasion of ethnic turf, whites led by City Council representative Louise Day Hicks organized a group called Restore Our Alienated Rights (ROAR) to halt integration. In scenes reminiscent of Little Rock in 1957, angry mobs attacked school buses, beat black students, and instituted a reign of terror against the city's black population. Asked his opinion of the disturbances, President Ford fanned the fires of discontent: "I have consistently opposed forced busing to achieve racial balance as a solution to quality education," he told a press conference, "and, therefore, I respectfully disagree with the judge's order." To rousing cheers in Boston, a speaker of the Ku Klux Klan recast the President's euphemisms. "The real issue isn't education," admitted a visiting grand dragon. "The real issue isn't a school here or a school there . . . the real issue is *nigger!*" In the middle of the school year, the Supreme Court further reduced the power of white school administrators to use unequal punishments to eliminate black students. "Young people," declared Justice Byron White, "do not 'shed their constitutional rights' at the schoolhouse door."

The 1975 school year opened with a resurgence of violence. In Louisville, Kentucky, the only major metropolitan area required to bus between city and suburb, antibusing mobs erupted in mass rioting and vandalism, but prompt summoning of the National Guard, together with the city's traditional moderation, eased the tension. But the Boston crisis persisted, forcing the appearance of federal marshals, specially trained in riot control during the occupation of Wounded Knee, to supervise the Boston police. In protest, arsonists set fire to the birthplace of John F. Kennedy. But the presence of armed guards at the schools reduced further violence, and whites chose a less dangerous tactic of nonattendance and legal appeal. In June 1976, however, the Supreme Court refused to reopen the case. "There is no longer justice for the white people of this country," complained antibusing leader James Kelley.

Opposition to school busing won unexpected support in 1975 from University of Chicago sociologist James Coleman, an early supporter of racial integration, whose follow-up study blamed mandatory busing for encouraging white flight to the suburbs and so aggravating the very problems it attempted to relieve. In 1976, the Supreme Court issued two additional rulings that encouraged racial integration without busing—in one case, denying racial discrimination in private schools; in another, declaring public housing projects in the suburbs a legitimate alternative to residential segregation in the cities. Then, in a major reversal of priorities involving the public schools of Pasadena, California, the Court denied the obligations of school districts to maintain racial balance "in perpetuity," even if "random" population movements reinstituted patterns of racial segregation. In the same year, in a decision that would have powerful ramifications throughout higher education, the Court permitted whites to bring suit under the Civil Rights Act of 1964, paving the way for a series of hearings on "reverse discrimination."

The changing tenor of the Supreme Court mirrored the diminishing political power of the black community. "There is a gut feeling of being out of it," Holman remarked, "—outsiders in your own country—which was a feeling [blacks] began to lose in the sixties. And it's come back double-barrelled now." Attempts to form an independent black political party, begun at the Gary convention of 1972, failed to attract black leaders to a second meeting in Little Rock in 1974. "If our leaders abandon us," warned Mayor Richard Hatcher, "we are lost." But even the rump leadership divided over political strategies, and a follow-up meeting in Cincinnati in 1976 left the coalition in shambles. "For us," stated a delegate after California congressman Ron Dellums declined to head a new Independent Freedom Party, "it's back to Square One."

The backlash against black power foreshadowed a major confrontation between conservatives and feminists over the issues of women's liberation. The ERA continued to encounter insuperable obstacles in the state legislatures, but in a series of sex discrimination cases, the Supreme Court upheld the equality of women before the law. At a time when over 54 percent of the female population worked outside the home, the Court denied that "the woman's role" prevented full participation on juries. The judiciary also invalidated social security regulations denying equal rights to women's beneficiaries and overturned a Utah law establishing different ages of majority for men and women. "No longer is the female destined solely for the home and the rearing of the family," the Court ruled, "and only the male for the marketplace in the world of ideas." Carrying its logic further, the Supreme Court denied that state law could give husbands "a veto power" over the right of women to have abortions. Such decrees represented fundamental victories for the women's movement. But in 1976, the Department of Labor reported that the disparity between male and female incomes had increased since the sixties.

The failure of women's economic improvement reflected a stiffening resistance to feminist ideals throughout the country. In

Boston, a "right to life" movement charged a black physician who had performed a legal abortion with murder; "that nigger is as guilty as sin," remarked a member of the all-white jury that found him guilty. (The judgment was later reversed.) In southern California, the Roman Catholic hierarchy attempted to exert pressure against the women's movement by denying the eucharist to female parishioners who refused to disavow the proabortion plank of the National Organization for Women. And efforts to pass statewide ERAs in New York and New Jersey suffered smashing defeats in 1975. "People were fed up by all that radical nonsense," attested Annette Stern, leader of the anti-ERA "Operation Wakeup." "They have repudiated this fraudulent proposal prompted by a little bunch of military radicals," agreed antifeminist Phyllis Schlafly.

SENSING THE CHANGING MOOD, radical dissenters, once fired by dreams of social revolution, now abandoned their militance and turned reluctantly to established legal institutions to seek justice. "My goal is to stop living the life I have been living," declared the young woman ("wearing," according to *The New York Times*, "a two-piece yellow suit dress") upon surrendering to the court. After four and a half years underground, Jane Alpert acknowledged the futility of revolution. "Melville was dead," she said, "and so was the movement." Accusing her of "the Watergate mentality" in which "the ends justify the means," the prosecutor rejected her plea for compassion and in January 1975, Alpert ("wearing a tailored maroon jacket with gold buttons over a matching skirt and white blouse") received a twenty-seven-month sentence. Later, for refusing to inform on another fugitive, she received an additional four-month term, despite an emotional disavowal of her "radical-left" past.

Another quest for justice had carried the plaintiffs through the entire judicial system before the Supreme Court ruled in 1974 that the survivors of the shootings at Kent State University had the right to bring suit against the governor of Ohio and the National Guard for violating constitutional rights of free speech and assembly. The court opened in Cleveland in May 1975, amid doubts about the possibility of obtaining a fair hearing. "Any jury we get," maintained one of the survivors, "is going to think of themselves as protecting Ohio against a bunch of Communist hippies." Aided by a series of controversial rulings from the bench—later the basis of a successful appeal—the jury did just that, acquitting the guardsmen of all charges. "We don't blame you," a former student yelled to the jury. "We blame this rotten system."

Getting away with murder became official policy in the state of New York, according to government attorney Malcolm Bell. "There is a double standard of justice," he charged, in protesting attempts by a special prosecutor to suppress indictments against law enforcement officers in cases growing out of the Attica rebellion of 1971. After nearly four years of desultory investigation, the state had returned indictments against sixty-two inmates but, despite overwhelming evidence, had refused to prosecute any of the police or prison guards responsible for the shooting and beating of prisoners. Embarrassed by Bell's disclosures, Rockefeller's successor, Governor Hugh Carey, ordered a new investigation, which led finally to the indictment of a single state trooper for reckless shooting. But the trials of the inmates continued through 1975, resulting in a series of acquittals and dismissals. "The time has come," pleaded Tom Wicker, "to drop the weak prosecution." At the end of 1976, Carey at last decided to act. "Attica lurks as a dark shadow over our system of justice," he admitted. "The time has come to firmly and finally close the book." He then pardoned all the remaining defendants, including the only policeman in the case ever charged with a crime.

"The integrity of Government officials," declared the final report of the Watergate special prosecutor in October 1975, "depends . . . on the credibility of criminal statutes as a deterrent to misconduct." But partly because of Ford's pardon, the investigation of criminality in the Nixon administration had been abruptly short-circuited, leaving unanswered—perhaps forever—compelling legal questions involving the antitrust settlement with ITT; cash donations from Howard Hughes to Bebe Rebozo; wiretaps against government officials and journalists; and responsibility for the notorious eighteen-and-a-half-minute gap. A survey of business leaders involved in the Watergate scandals, conducted by *New York Times* reporter Michael Jensen, illuminated the ambiguous denouement. "Most are still ensconced in their paneled corporate offices," he found. "Few of the executives seem contrite. . . . For most . . . a lifetime of accumulating wealth and power was scarcely upset by the Watergate events."

WATERGATE, ATTICA, KENT STATE, the return of political fugitives—all symbols of legal excess—epitomized by mid-decade the resilience of the American system. "One must believe," concluded the Watergate report, "that unresponsive power can never overcome [the people's] will." The Attica pardon, assured Governor Carey, "will foster respect for our system of law." "You have to enforce the will of the people," stated an acquitted Ohio Guardsman. "The people of the state have been fantastic." "I'm not that person anymore," said Jane Alpert, recanting "the craziness that came over me."

Beneath this façade of institutional stability, however, breathed a cauldron of anger and frustration. "The war continues, Nixon's pardoned, Model T is in the White House," lamented a Kent State University professor in 1975. "*What* changes? What good did it all do?" No channels vented this passion. No politics consumed this rage. It could erupt only outside the formal structures of society, in the interstices of power, in the open air, like a fist arching through a crowd.

"I saw a hand coming up behind several others in the front row," recalled the President, "and obviously there was a gun in that hand." Lynette "Squeaky" Fromme, twenty-six-year-old member of the Manson family, responsible for a spree of bloody murders, had carried her mad rage to the brink of assassination. "This country is a mess," she yelled. "This man is not your President."

"He is not a public servant."

"The President sanctioned building 145 or more nuclear power plants," she told a reporter. "Nuclear power is dangerous. Nuclear power kills."

"Clean up the earth," she screamed to her judge.

"Cutting down redwood trees is like cutting down your arms and legs."

"When people around you treat you like a child and pay no attention to the things you say," she remarked to a jailer, "you have to do something." In the court of Judge Thomas MacBride there was no room for what he called "political statements, or any statements on ecology—how bad things are because trees, air, water or land are concerned [sic]." Found by a psychiatrist to be "mentally competent," stripped of her defense, Fromme's conviction was inevitable. "You have only ten years of air and water," she pleaded as Judge MacBride denounced "the false and distorted belief that only terror and violence can save our environment and natural resources." He gave her a life sentence.

Two weeks after the assassination attempt, the most famous fugitive in the country was captured in San Francisco, after 591 days in the underground. "Urban guerrilla," she described her occupation, "radical feminism," her ideology. For fifteen months, Patricia Hearst had traveled in a world of revolutionary secrecy, participated in a reborn SLA that claimed credit for bombings and bank robberies, and boasted a feminist identity that placed her in the vanguard of "the coming revolutionary struggle." Authorities swiftly ordered psychiatric tests and, after receiving "a psychiatric profile of what is clearly a troubled young woman," ruled her competent to stand trial for bank robbery. In a remarkable alchemy of justice, the kidnaped heiress had become the stepchild of revolution. Basing her defense on the dubious grounds of "brainwashing," Hearst failed to persuade a jury of her innocence. Her ordeal ended only when a presidential pardon interrupted her prison sentence in 1978.

During Hearst's long absence, a middle-aged housewife had become obsessed with the fugitive. "For months," recalled Hearst's fiancé, Steven Weed, Sara Jane Moore "would call me up at odd hours, often in the middle of the night, to talk about Patty, the SLA." She had worked as a volunteer for the food giveaway demanded as ransom by the SLA and had remained on the Hearst staff as a bookkeeper to clear up the confused accounts. She claimed to have connections with the political underground, but she also served as an informant for the FBI. She told reporters she had been converted by the radicals she had once despised. In these contradictory roles, Moore's politics became confused. Suspect on the left, hostile to the establishment, she craved some clear affirmation of political identity.

"It was a kind of ultimate protest against the system," said Moore of her attempt to shoot President Ford in San Francisco, two weeks after Fromme had failed. "I am not a berserk woman." "In every case of violent political protest," she told interviewer Andrew Hill, "there is a serious attempt to put it down as a kook's act and as quickly and quietly as possible sweep it under the rug, where we try to hide the growing discontent of the people of this country." Calling Ford "a nebbish," Moore claimed that the succession of Nelson Rockefeller would have revealed "the actual leaders of the country" and "just might have triggered the kind of chaos that could have started the upheaval of change."

Having passed her psychiatric examinations, Moore pleaded guilty in an effort to publicize her politics. "No one has been charged with . . . the assassination plots against Castro, Allende, Lumumba or other foreign leaders, nor for the actual assassinations in this country of Fred Hampton, George Jackson and the Attica inmates, to name only a few of the comrades deliberately murdered by the police," she told the court. "When any government uses assassination . . . to put down dissidents . . . , it must expect that tool to be turned back against itself." Criticizing these violent impulses, the judge asked, "Whatever happened to 'The pen is mightier than the sword'?" To which Moore replied, "Why don't you ask the people in Washington the same thing?" She, too, received a life sentence.

THE WAVE OF ASSASSINATIONS touched a raw nerve in the culture, arousing haunting visions of catastrophe. Beyond the usual psychiatric interpretations—the mad cravings of lonely people for fame and power—there were no satisfactory explanations for the eruption of political violence. Comedy, more than lunacy, furnished insight. "I cannot vouch for what ensued as it is possible it was all a result of my brainwashing," offered Woody Allen in a piece called "The Nefarious Times We Live In," "but I was then brought into a room where President Gerald Ford shook my hand and asked me if I would follow him around the country and take a shot at him now and then, being careful to miss. He said it would give him a chance to act bravely and could serve as a distraction from genuine issues, which he felt unequipped to deal with." Though hardly deliberate, Ford's vulnerability did win public sympathy, which helped to blunt criticism of his political failings.

More subliminally, Americans became preoccupied with scenes of disaster. In an imaginary community named Amity on the eve of the July Fourth weekend, the invasion of nameless calamity served as a perfect metaphor for America under Ford. "The town is dying," wrote Peter Benchley in *Jaws*. "People are out of work. Stores that were going to open aren't. People aren't renting houses, let alone buying them. And every day we keep the beaches closed, we drive another nail into our coffin." For the nation's birthday, the town leaders decide to open the beaches. There is joy in the air—until the killer shark returns. Released as a film in 1975, *Jaws* brought the disaster genre to an unprecedented level of popularity. "Such movies," observed novelist Gore Vidal, "distract people from the thoughts of robbery and deceit to which they are subjected daily by oil companies, politicians, and banks."

Americans approached the nation's two hundredth birthday with the ambivalence of tourists dipping their toes into shark-infested waters. Under Nixon, an American Revolution Bicentennial Commission had attempted to turn the festivities into a partisan event, forcing Congress to legislate an alternative organization to supervise the activities. But the spirit of Watergate undermined efforts to sponsor a national celebration. "The common wisdom of the day pictures Americans as a people sunk in malaise—the legacy of Vietnam and Watergate, inflation and recession, the decline of civility at home and authority in the world," reported *Newsweek*. "And yet their ethos somehow endures." "The country is old, old, old," agreed Gloria Steinem. "But estrangement itself is a sign of life. Perhaps it is a nationwide growing-pain, a warning that the majority of Americans have progressed beyond their leaders."

On July 4, 1976, President Ford presented a series of patriotic speeches. "Liberty is a living flame to be fed, not dead ashes to be revered," he remarked at Independence Hall, "even in a Bicentennial Year." But most people paid more attention to a dramatic flotilla of sailing vessels in New York harbor, watched gigantic fireworks displays, heard the jazzy arrangements of Arthur Fiedler and the Boston Pops. "The feeling of the day sort of crept up on many of us, took us by surprise," noticed Elizabeth Drew. "For those of us who had been in despair about this Bicentennial . . . , who feared the worst, the surprise was a very pleasant one. But," she emphasized, "it was a people's day. . . . No doubt the good feeling one observed today, even the patriotic feeling, comes out of confidence in our country, as distinguished from confidence in our government."

11

"CALCULATED APPEALS AND EMPTY PROMISES"

The Election of 1976

PUBLIC DISTRUST OF THE POLITICAL leadership emerged in 1976 as the central theme of the presidential election. Watergate hung like a shroud around the body politic, symbol of the collapse of moral authority in government. The loss of global hegemony—the fall of South Vietnam, the exposure of the CIA, impotence in Angola—further testified to the failure of traditional policy. In the 1974 congressional elections, voter participation had dropped to 38 percent, the lowest since World War II, and public opinion surveys predicted a more grievous decline. "DON'T VOTE," urged one bumper sticker, "IT ONLY ENCOURAGES THEM." "THE LESSER OF TWO EVILS," declared another, "IS STILL EVIL."

Haunting the campaign was the ghost of Richard Nixon, still the main catalyst of political behavior. The fallen President represented the negative identity of the culture, all those traits the country seemed to affirm but hesitated to implement in their extremes—individualism carried to the point of personal aggrandizement; rootlessness to the verge of frenetic mobility; moral righteousness for the purpose of deceit; and a yearning for power that justified total sacrifice and total war. No politician after Nixon could afford such blatant displays. "Basically I found that I did not have the overwhelming desire to be President which is essential for the kind of campaign that is required," announced Minnesota Senator Walter Mondale in withdrawing from the contest in November 1974. "I don't think anyone should be President who is not willing to go through fire."

While conceding the corruption of power by past politicians, political leaders insisted that the structure of politics remained sound: the purge of Richard Nixon, went the refrain, proved that the American system endured. To avoid further abuses of power, Congress enacted the Fair Campaign Practices Act of 1974, which established limits on campaign contributions and required strict accounting of the disbursement of funds. By encouraging a multitude of contributors, however, the law not only equalized the economic strength of the two major parties (eliminating a traditional financial edge for the Republicans), but also discouraged the emergence of third-party contenders who could expect only a small base of support. Running as an independent candidate in 1976, former senator Eugene McCarthy tried unsuccessfully to overturn the restrictions on "fat cat" contributors, which doomed minority parties to economic shortage. Nor could McCarthy overcome the "fairness" doctrine of the communications industry, which promised equal time for political candidates while effectively limiting the beneficiaries to the established parties. In its formal terms, the election of 1976 indeed verified the survival of the old political system.

The rejuvenation of two-party politics mirrored the conservative mood of the electorate. "Great dreams still live within the collective heart of this nation," declared Governor Jimmy Carter in December 1974, one month before the expiration of his single term in office. "Our political leaders have simply underestimated the innate quality of our people." It was time, he announced, "to reaffirm and to strengthen our ethical and spiritual and political beliefs." It was time "for this chasm between people and government to be bridged, . . . time for new leadership and new ideas to make a reality of these dreams, still held by our people." Announcing his presidential candidacy, Carter promised "to restore in our country what has been lost."

Inside the White House, President Gerald Ford also grappled with the problem of public confidence. He, too, found inspiration in an earlier age of simpler values, a time of limited government. "The people are about as fed up with the petty tyranny of the faceless federal bureaucrats today," he declared in the spirit of the Bicentennial, "as they were with their faraway rulers in London in 1776." In his first bid for the presidential election, Ford offered to lead "the party of change." But he was no more forward looking than Carter. "We have turned our back on those old ways," he told a Republican Leadership Conference in January 1976. "We have turned away from the discredited idea that the federal government can solve every problem by spending more of your tax money on it. Yes," he explained, "we know that a government big enough to give us everything we want is a government big enough to take from us everything we have."

THIS YEARNING FOR A SIMPLER STYLE of politics provided the framework for the Democratic challenge to Republican leadership, and none benefited more from this climate than the former governor of Georgia. He was an underdog named "Jimmy Who?" in a year when voters felt contempt for incumbents. He was an outsider at a time when Washington politics were inherently suspect. He spoke the language of old-fashioned virtue, promising—in the words of George Washington's cherry-tree fable—"I would not tell a lie," and he offered an idiom and cadence sufficiently unfamiliar outside the South to appear both exotic and self-evident, refreshing to the ear and old as the hills.

In this era of spiritual malaise, Carter represented the politics of morality. "There is no need for lying," he declared in his campaign autobiography, *Why Not the Best?* "Our best national defense is the truth." He quoted frequently from the neo-Calvinist theologian Reinhold Niebuhr that "the sad duty of politics is to establish justice in a sinful world," and he seemed to personify that philosophy nearly every weekend when he interrupted an arduous campaign to return to his home in Plains, Georgia, to take his turn teaching the Bible class in Sunday school. "We might have the most incredible intellects in the world, we might study under the greatest philosopher or theologian, we might have a Ph.D. or understanding of the interrelation between people, but without a solid base under our lives," he explained, "all of this learning is superficial, and there's no foundation for a meaningful existence." Asked to sum up his campaign in one word, Carter replied, "That word would be faith."

Carter's candor about religion, hardly the standard fare of American politics, established a public image of a man of assurance and tranquillity. "The bickering, squabbling, hatred, and animosities, and blame handed back and forth in our great nation's capital in Washington," he chided a people grown weary of political chicanery, "is not good for our country." Carter provided instead a vision of cohesion and nurturance. NOTHING WRONG WITH AMERICA, read one of his earlier advertisements, THAT SOME STRONG COMPASSIONATE LEADERSHIP CAN'T FIX. His frothy smile seemed part grimace, part bite—a cartoonish attribute that Carter shared with the most popular pinup of the year, television's buxom Farah Fawcett-Majors—suggesting an ambivalent blend of kindness and aggression, a sensual warmth edged with scolding wrath, the ability to be both human and tough, a latter-day Theodore Roosevelt. With deep roots in his native town, Carter symbolized the stability of a vanished America, a common man from a common town, comfortable within its narrow borders and yet eager to carry the missionary's message to the ends of the earth.

These provincial leanings gave Carter a limited constituency, but the candidate transformed this apparent handicap into a major asset. Lacking an established base of power, he adopted a campaign strategy to attract a diverse electorate. The decision of the Democratic party to embrace "affirmative action" had encouraged the proliferation of primary elections, by 1976 numbering thirty states and the District of Columbia, largely because open balloting eliminated the problems of apportionment by race and sex. The Democrats also disallowed "winner take all" primaries, providing instead for proportional representation. These revisions meant that nearly three-quarters of the delegates to the Democratic nominating convention would be chosen by popular vote. Yet the proportion of voters who participated in primary elections remained quite small, only one-sixth of the eligible electorate. As a relatively unknown politician, Carter would benefit even by modest success, and he determined to enter every delegate contest. With his departure from the Georgia statehouse in January 1975, Carter also obtained a considerable advantage over contenders with other time-consuming responsibilities. He possessed, finally, an extraordinary personal stamina that sustained the campaign at its most obscure beginnings.

Carter's lack of notoriety gave him unique political advantages. Though he promised "not [to] avoid a stand on a controversial issue," voters held few prior assumptions about the upstart politician, enabling Carter to flourish, in the words of one journalist, as "the Lon Chaney of 1976, the man of a thousand faces." A survey by CBS and *The New York Times* found that liberal voters believed Carter was a liberal, conservative voters viewed him as a conservative, and moderates thought he was a moderate. To which Carter replied on a "Face the Nation" broadcast, "it indicates . . . that people don't like to be put in boxes." More concerned with his image as a candidate the people could trust, Carter adroitly evaded delicate subjects that might produce unfavorable reactions. "He has more positions," snapped one critic, "than the *Kama Sutra.*"

By expressing razor-fine distinctions, Carter managed to straddle the most controversial issues of the campaign—abortion, busing, and amnesty. "I am personally opposed to abortion," he assured leaders of the right-to-life movement. "I am personally opposed to government spending for abortion services." But he also opposed a constitutional amendment to alter the Supreme Court ruling of 1973 and he dodged related questions about the use of Medicaid funds to pay for abortion services. "I'm not in favor of mandatory busing," he told a television audience. "Also, I do not favor a constitutional amendment to prohibit busing, [because] I think it would be a very divisive thing." When Senator Henry Jackson ran an advertisement in *The Boston Globe* proclaiming I AM AGAINST BUSING, Carter reproved his opponent for raising "an emotional issue . . . that has racial or racist overtones." On the treatment of Vietnam war resistance, the candidate split hairs about the difference between "amnesty" and "pardon," fully renouncing the former term while embracing the latter. In exasperation, his liberal rival Morris Udall asked, "Who is Jimmy Carter?"

Carter's avoidance of controversy illuminated his respect for the power of the media. Though the candidate took considerable pride in his "close, personal, intimate relationship" with the electorate, effectively imitating McGovern's grass-roots campaign of 1972, he seldom took his eye off the red lights above the cameras. By running in all the primaries, Carter preempted media attention from his rivals and used one electoral episode to promote the next. Even before the New Hampshire primary, traditionally the first serious voter contest, Carter supporters packed a Democratic dinner in Ames, Iowa, and easily won the straw poll. "We knew the thing was going to be covered," said Carter's local organizer. "Politics is theater. We planned for that." In January, Carter captured

27.1 percent of the Democratic vote in the Iowa caucuses, substantially less than a slate of uncommitted delegates, in an election in which only 11 percent of the state's Democrats voted. But far from the final counting, Carter shrewdly spent the night in New York City, preparing for the next morning's news interviews. Having topped the other candidates, he appeared victoriously on NBC's "Today" show, CBS's "Morning News," and ABC's "Good Morning America."

The vigorous pursuit of media attention paralleled a less discussed but equally vital component of the Carter campaign—the winning of corporate support. Carter's early political career had benefited from the generosity of the Atlanta business establishment. "We have our own built-in State Department in the Coca-Cola Company," boasted the governor in 1974. Besides making timely financial donations to the nascent campaign, the state's largest corporation provided free transportation in company aircraft and contributed an international escort service of employees who gladly introduced Carter to various foreign leaders. The National Bank of Georgia, run by Carter supporter Bert Lance, made several generous and often unbacked loans to the Carter group. These southern business interests also brought the governor into contact with the nation's most powerful corporate elite, paving the way for Carter's membership on the Trilateral Commission. Participation in this Rockefeller-funded organization broadened Carter's international credentials—"a splendid learning opportunity," claimed the candidate—and established his credibility with other wealthy contributors. Though Carter portrayed himself as a simple peanut farmer, his campaign war chest in 1974 and 1975, years when the politician was still unknown, came largely from Atlanta business leaders and from industrial "fat cats" who tapped personal friends for contributions.

Carter's popularity with business leaders, in turn, facilitated his access to the media. "Stories in the *New York Times* and the *Washington Post* do not just happen," wrote Carter intimate Hamilton Jordan in a strategy synopsis in 1972, "but have to be carefully planned and planted." On the Trilateral Commission, Carter rubbed shoulders with such communications executives as the editor in chief of *Time* magazine, who proved sympathetic to his candidacy. Not only did that publication devote considerable favorable attention to the Carter organization—while castigating or ignoring his rivals—but even used a half-page picture of Carter (captioned: "His basic strategy consists of handshaking and street-cornering his way into familiarity") in advertising in other magazines the quality of *Time's* political coverage. Carter's image, said *Time* in 1975, was "elusive enough to qualify as that 'new face' many voters seem to be seeking." Such media support enabled Carter to survive several political setbacks—a poor showing in the Massachusetts primary, outrageous public statements about race, and his chronic vagueness on issues. "I would not be where I am now," conceded Carter on the eve of the nominating convention, "had the press not accommodated some of my errors."

CARTER'S APPEAL TO the established media and corporate leadership reflected not only the Georgian's essential conservatism, but more subtly and more importantly his promise to eliminate, once and for all, the most potentially dangerous threat to the relationship between big business and big government: the candidacy of George Wallace. In November 1975, almost a full year after Carter, the former Alabama governor launched another run for the White House under the slogan Trust the People. "The hierarchy of the Democratic party and the culture merchants who look down their nose at you and me—they're not supporting me," Wallace assured a campaign rally in Massachusetts. "But if you go out and vote we can s'prise 'em 'cause there are more of us than there are of them." Since the near-fatal shooting in 1972, Wallace had struggled heroically to rebuild his health and, with it, his stature as a national leader. Despite a self-congratulatory provincialism, he had journeyed briefly to Europe in 1975—his first trip abroad—not so much to claim, as Carter did, some international experience as to demonstrate his physical recovery.

The new Wallace candidacy endeavored to follow the successful blueprint of 1972—solid victories in southern primaries combined with daring forays into the north to harness the white backlash. In February 1976, Wallace parlayed his well-known opposition to busing into victory in Boston, while finishing third in the Massachusetts primary behind Jackson and Udall but ahead of Carter. The next week, the two southerners met again on their own turf in Florida, the scene of Wallace's dramatic upset four years earlier. But now Carter preempted the call to southern pride. Invoking Wallace's 1972 slogan, Send Them a Message, Carter pleaded, "Send them a President." Backed by a solid organization, including large volunteer contingents from neighboring Georgia, Carter won a narrow victory. The next week, he swamped Wallace in Illinois. Then, in a decisive triumph in North Carolina, Carter laid the Wallace threat to rest.

The defeat of George Wallace illuminated the crumbling of ideology within the Democratic party. "Everybody is now saying what I started out saying back in 1964," observed the losing candidate. "There are no longer any real regional differences." Wallace's attack on "pointy-headed" bureaucrats had been refined and supplanted by Carter into a proposal called "zero-based budgeting," an annual accounting procedure that "peeled the veil of secrecy from around bureaucracy by opening up for inspection and scrutiny the activities of every single [government] employee." Wallace's objections to court-ordered busing had been matched by Carter's emphasis on voluntary desegregation, the so-called Atlanta Compromise by which Georgia blacks dropped the busing issue for a greater voice in public school decisions. "Wallace and Carter," noted Elizabeth Drew: "the one dark, ugly, country, a fomenter; the other bland, well turned out, modern, cool." "Look out for phonies," Wallace had warned her.

Carter's quest for Wallace voters threatened his support at the opposite end of the political spectrum, especially among blacks who not only feared Wallace's popularity, but also his rightward drag on the Democratic party. Established black politicians remained skeptical of the southern politician whom Shirley Chisholm derisively called "blue-eyed Jimmy." "None of us are really emotionally involved in our candidates," conceded New York Representative Charles Rangel. "He'll be like most other white politicians," scoffed California's Willie Brown, "use the black vote and not pay off in the end." Pointing to low black turnouts in the primaries, John Lewis, head of the Atlanta-based Voter Education Project, lamented the "apathy and cynicism in our communities."

Offsetting the distrust of black politicians, however, was Carter's firm support in the black churches. "Blacks have always known that our best allies are those Southern whites who have dared to live by their religious principles," wrote Representative Andrew Young, once an associate of Martin Luther King, the first black representative from Georgia since Reconstruction, and an early Carter enthusiast. With endorsements from King's Baptist father, Martin Luther "Daddy" King, Sr., and his widow Coretta, Carter sidestepped the political leadership to develop grass-roots support within the black community. "This is a Christian when we need Christians in key positions," declared a black preacher in Chicago. "Why every Negro I ever met's goin' for Jimmy Carter," said an elderly black activist in Mississippi. "We just think he's the man. One reason, he seems to be a Christian man and then on top of that he's a Democrat. . . . He gonna get all the black votes." Such logic undermined the power of traditional liberals. "He caught a lot of black politicians sleeping in the black community," explained Chisholm.

The support of black spiritual leaders also enabled Carter to escape from the most grievous blunder of his campaign. On April 2, 1976, a day on which white ethnics in Milwaukee criticized President Ford for ignoring their demands for minority recognition, Carter ignited a storm of protest over the issue of ethnicity. In an interview with the New York *Daily News*, the Democratic front-runner used a peculiar choice of words to explain his opposition to low-income housing in the suburbs. "I see nothing wrong with ethnic purity being maintained," he said. "I would not force racial integration of a neighborhood by government action." Challenged by reporters, the candidate reiterated his antipathy to "the intrusion of alien groups" that compromised the "integrity" of neighborhoods. Seemingly impervious to the emotional impact of his vocabulary, Carter disavowed any racist intention. But his critics leaped for the jugular.

"Is there no white politician I can trust?" cried Atlanta's black mayor Maynard Jackson.

"We've created a Frankenstein monster with a Southern drawl," protested Gary's Richard Hatcher with a glance toward Wallace, "a more cultured version of the old Confederate at the schoolhouse door."

"A disaster," exclaimed Andrew Young, who promptly joined sixteen other black representatives to protest Carter's "Hitlerian connotations."

Though Carter soon apologized for his rhetorical lapse, suspicion about his motives lingered. "For a man who chooses every word with such precision, is such a master of language," remarked *New York Times* reporter Christopher Lydon, "I cannot believe he chose such a racist vocabulary [accidentally]. He wanted ethnic purity known." On the eve of primaries in Pennsylvania, Indiana, and Michigan, states with sizable ethnic populations, Carter's message certainly had no deleterious effects. "The burden is on Jimmy Carter," declared Tom Wicker, himself a native southerner with deep commitments to civil rights, "—not just to 'apologize,' not just to retreat, but to make clear where he really stands, what he really believes."

Carter responded with a dramatic display of black support. At a large noon rally in Atlanta, Daddy King, a stentorian brooding preacher of hellfire and brimstone, thrilled a vociferous black crowd by pleading for forgiveness. "I've always been able to let my religion and politics work together," he asserted. "And I always fitted in somewhere a statement for this man who I love and believe in. . . . I have a forgiving heart. So," he concluded, "Governor, I'm with you all the way." Armed with such endorsements, Carter easily mollified his liberal critics. "It would be ironic," soothed James Reston in *The New York Times*, "if 'purity' were turned into a dirty word."

The furor over Carter's language emphasized the impotence of the liberal wing of the Democratic party. By April, poor organization, insufficient funds, unfortunate timing—in general, bad politics—had stalled the campaigns of Indiana Senator Birch Bayh, Kennedy in-law Sargent Shriver, Morris Udall, and a handful of lesser lights. But the traditional New Deal coalition—labor, liberals, and northern blacks—still hesitated to join the Carter bandwagon, even when he belatedly embraced the most tangible symbol of Democratic liberalism, the Humphrey-Hawkins jobs bill, which promised to reduce unemployment to three percent through massive government spending. Udall remained an active candidate, but the professionals doubted his chances. Looking for an orthodox winner, liberals turned once more to the Happy Warrior from Minnesota, Hubert Humphrey. The temptation proved almost irresistible.

"Candidates who make an attack on Washington," Humphrey told the press, "are making an attack on government programs, on blacks, on minorities, on the cities. It's a disguised new form of racism, a disguised new form of conservatism." Recognizing Carter's challenge to a lifetime's commitment, the Minnesota senator inched his hat toward the ring. As organization Democrats urged his entry into the primaries, the former Vice President agonized for days, finally calling a special news conference in the historic Senate Caucus Room, scene of earlier campaign beginnings. Amid mounting tension, Humphrey described his political options. "One thing I don't need at this stage of my life," he said, "is to be ridiculous." Still, he hesitated. "I shall not seek it. I shall not search for it. I shall not scramble for it." He shrugged. "But I'm around."

Humphrey's ambiguous withdrawal left the liberal vacuum unfilled. But not for long. Two western Democrats waited in the wings to challenge Carter's lead—Frank Church of Idaho, who had delayed his candidacy while his Senate subcommittee completed investigation of the CIA, and Edmund M. "Jerry" Brown, youthful governor of the nation's most populous state. Both became active candidates in May, trying to divide the remaining primaries to confront Carter in strength. The Church campaign, lately organized and funded, nevertheless managed to topple Carter in Nebraska and proceeded to win minor victories on the senator's home ground, Idaho and Montana. But in Oregon, Church grappled not only against Carter but also a tough write-in campaign for Brown. "One of them has been campaigning in generalities to avoid the issues," he charged. "The other asks very good questions but has no answers." Together, Church and Brown smashed Carter in Oregon. But separately the Idahoan's victory appeared less than dramatic, less noteworthy than Brown's third-place 23 percent, all on write-ins, and Carter still accumulated his proportion of delegates. Even when he lost, Carter was winning. The Church campaign finally foundered after the senator fell ill and had to interrupt politics to return to Idaho when the huge Teton Dam burst.

The efforts of Jerry Brown, by contrast, offered genuine magic. A former Jesuit seminarian, frequenter of San Francisco's Zen Center, the California governor presented a style of spiritual politics that effectively challenged Carter on his own terms. "A lot of conventional thinking appears to say that everything is secular," Brown told an interviewer. "That's never [been] an interpretation that most humans in history have held and not one that most Americans hold today." Where Carter's born-again Christianity emphasized the importance of individual salvation through personal connection with God, Brown held a Catholic's respect for social organicism. As governor, he proposed equal wage increases for all state employees, regardless of salary base. "Whether you are a Governor or chopping wood or tending the fire," he explained, "any role is equal to any other role." Influenced by an ecological consciousness, Brown preached a politics of limits, questioning the ability of the liberal state to resolve social problems. He opposed busing, for example: the vehicle itself symbolized an artificial means of social integration. Besides a sophisticated politics, Brown projected charm, an off-beat charisma that drew voters. Moving into the campaign maelstrom, he tackled Carter in Maryland and won decisively. The next week, he carried Nevada, staged the powerful write-in show in Oregon, and nipped Carter in Rhode Island. He took his home state easily and scored a stunning victory in New Jersey. Against Carter, Brown never lost. But by mid-June, he had run out of primaries. With last-minute endorsements from Wallace and Mayor Daley, Carter had nibbled his way over the top.

The Democratic convention, held in New York City in July, exuded a spirit of unity. McGovern, who throughout the campaign had tried to represent the party's liberal conscience, squashed an "anybody but Carter" movement, reminding zealous aides that in 1972 similar efforts, sponsored by Carter, had "set the stage for the overwhelming Democratic defeat." The party platform, drafted in an atmosphere of compromise, reflected traditional Democratic concerns, endorsing more jobs, national health insurance, and the ERA, opposing a constitutional amendment against abortion, and describing school busing as "a judicial tool of last resort." Feminist leaders, such as Bella Abzug and Betty Friedan, endorsed the Carter candidacy; Mayor Daley, unseated in 1972, returned to center stage; George Wallace, whose perennial threats of an independent candidacy sent shivers down the Democratic spine, bade farewell to politics, casting a parting shot at "the monster bureaucracy . . . driving people in this country nuts." And an ever-optimistic Humphrey summoned the party forward. "There are new tories abroad in the land," he warned. "They appeal to cynicism. They cater to the people's mistrust of their own institutions." Rejecting their pessimism, the Democratic war-horse insisted "that our greatness is in the future. America's best days—America's great days—have only just begun."

The most impassioned issues of the decade—Vietnam and Watergate—scarcely made an appearance. During the primary campaign, Udall had attempted to expose Carter's hawkishness on Vietnam through television commercials, but the tactic backfired. "There's no sense in rehashing the past like that," protested one Ohio voter. "The present is too damn important." Hoping to overcome such deliberate amnesia, paralyzed war veteran Ron Kovic, author of a poignant autobiography about Vietnam service, *Born on the Fourth of July*, nominated another war resister, Fritz Efaw, for Vice President. But the symbolic protest had scant effect on the convention proceedings, and Efaw soon surrendered to Oklahoma authorities to face charges of draft evasion. Never again was Vietnam seriously considered in the campaign. The Democrats also remained remarkably mute about Watergate, allowing quiet symbols to convey the message. In her keynote speech, Representative Barbara Jordan's plea for "a national community" evoked memories of her brilliant speech before the House Judiciary Committee urging the impeachment of Richard Nixon. "Millions of Americans are disillusioned with government, disappointed with their political leaders, and disgusted with politics and politicians in general," observed another hero of Watergate, Peter Rodino. "They have a right to be. But the difficulty lies . . . not with our system of government . . . but with leadership, or lack of it." Carter's choice for Vice President, Walter Mondale, broke the strange silence, drawing loud cheers for his attack on Watergate and the "President who pardoned the person who did it."

Carter spoke more softly. "My name is Jimmy Carter," he began, "and I'm running for President." Admitting that "moral decay has weakened our country," Carter denied "that our best years are behind us." "It's now a time for healing," he said. "I see America on the move again." As party regulars surrounded the nominee, Daddy King pulled the convention back to its solemn task. "Surely the Lord sent Jimmy Carter to come on out and bring America back where she belongs," he preached. "We must close ranks now. . . . It's time for prayer." And the throng of Democratic delegates, caught in euphoria, clasped hands to sing "We Shall Overcome."

THE VULNERABILITY OF the incumbent President emboldened not only the disciples of King and Carter, but also powerful segments within the Republican party. "Our nation's capital," charged one GOP leader, "has become the seat of a buddy system that functions for its own benefit—increasingly insensitive to the needs of the American worker who supports it with his taxes. Today it is difficult to find leaders who are independent of the forces that have brought us our problems—the Congress, the bureaucracy, the lobbyists, big business and big labor." With these words, Ronald Reagan (sounding much like the other ex-governor seeking the White House), announced his candidacy in November 1975. That very day, he attained a dubious presidential distinction when a twenty-year-old college dropout named Michael Lance Carvin approached him with a plastic gun. "It doesn't change my view of campaigning," Reagan assured his entourage. (Like all the other potential assassins, Carvin was sent for psychiatric tests and found competent to stand trial. But even the judge recognized the youth had "problems." Sentenced first to psychiatric care, then to an indeterminate term, Carvin later tried to commit suicide.)

The Reagan candidacy crystallized an abiding dissatisfaction among conservatives with policies initiated by Nixon and prolonged under Ford. Criticizing détente, Reagan scoffed at "a foreign policy whose principal accomplishment seems to be our acquisition of the right to sell Pepsi-Cola in Siberia." "Americans," he told a Conservative Political Action Conference in Washington, "are hungry to feel once again a sense of mission and greatness." Conservatives also condemned deficit spending as needlessly inflationary. "Balancing the budget," Reagan liked to tell after-dinner audiences, "is like protecting your virtue—you have to learn to say 'no.'" And virtue itself became a sensitive subject when the President's wife, Betty Ford, told CBS reporter Morley Safer that she wouldn't be surprised if her daughter Susan had an affair, thought premarital sex might reduce the divorce rate, and considered the Supreme Court ruling on abortion "the best thing in the world, a great, great decision." A DISGRACE TO THE WHITE HOUSE, headlined William Loeb in the Manchester Union-Leader. "President Ford showed his own lack of guts. . . . As President of the United States, he should be the moral leader of the nation. . . . He should repudiate what Mrs. Ford said."

On the eve of the New Hampshire primary, Reagan's challenge to the President received an unexpected boost from the Republican pariah. Just as President Nixon's visit to China in 1972 had stolen the thunder from the Democratic race, four years later the exiled leader again grabbed the headlines by returning to Peking as a private citizen. "Gerald Ford's problem," remarked columnist Mary McGrory, "is that some members of his party who like him very much are not sure that he could run a two-car funeral. Richard Nixon's return to Peking has reinforced that sinking feeling. The memory of the pardon is like the smell of escaping gas over this first effort." Besides Nixon, the President had problems of his own. So weak was Ford's public presence that pollsters discovered a loss of support wherever he campaigned. But while Reagan enjoyed the star status of a Hollywood actor, his proficiency at making extravagant proposals—the investment of social security funds in the stock market, for example—raised doubts about his competence. In this trade-off of deficiencies, Ford won New Hampshire by a mere thirteen hundred votes. "When you lose such a close race," Reagan said in self-consolation, "it just means that it was a moral victory instead of a victory."

In their next contest, the Florida primary, Reagan focused attention on the inadequacy of Ford's foreign policy. Under Nixon, the doctrine of détente had not been incompatible with American omnipotence. The idea of spheres of influence had preserved United States domination in certain areas of the world—Latin America, the Middle East, the Persian Gulf—and Nixon's willingness to exert full American power, as in the toppling of the Allende regime in Chile or the Christmas bombing of Vietnam, assured that détente would not be translated into military weakness. But public reaction to Vietnam and Watergate placed heavy constraints on Nixon's successor. Détente with the Soviet Union and China easily blurred with the American retreat in Asia, Africa, and Latin America. "Under Messrs. Kissinger and Ford," Reagan told a cheering audience, "this nation has become Number Two in military power in a world where it is dangerous—if not fatal—to be second best."

Though Ford had made few concessions to the Soviet position on SALT, the administration had opened negotiations with the Torrijos regime of Panama about reducing American control of the Canal. Calling this diplomacy a capitulation to "blackmail," Reagan chastised the President's "mouselike silence." "When it comes to the canal," he declared, "we built it, we paid for it, it's ours, and we should tell Torrijos and company that we are going to keep it!" Forced to respond, Ford asserted "that the United States will never give up its defense right to the Panama Canal and will never give up its operational rights as far as Panama is concerned." But he conceded that treaty negotiations might well alter the status of the Canal in the future. Such disclosure lent credence to Reagan's claims, and the status of the Panama Canal came to symbolize the country's dubious determination to maintain world leadership.

Reagan's popularity and Ford's incumbency turned the Republican race into a dead heat. As delegates headed toward the national convention in Kansas City, each candidate worked to swing the small handful of votes that promised the nomination. In an effort to broaden his appeal, Reagan decided to risk an unprecedented act: he would reverse tradition, choose a vice-presidential running mate prior to his own nomination, and his choice would come from the party's liberal wing—Senator Richard Schweiker of Pennsylvania. But instead of attracting a flock of Republican moderates, the decision blurred the distinction between Reagan and Ford. The conservative wing, considered bedrock loyal to Reagan, now began to waver. Before conceding the President's victory, Reagan supporters managed to win adoption of a conservative party platform that criticized Ford's foreign policy—détente, Helsinki, the snubbing of Solzhenitsyn, and, in a thinly-veiled reference to Panama, "secret agreements."

Thirsty for victory, Ford swallowed his pride. On domestic issues, he shared the party's conservatism—opposition to "forced busing" and "compulsory national health insurance," support for constitutional amendments permitting prayers in the public schools and prohibiting abortions (while endorsing the ERA), and a general weakening of federal power ("less government, less spending, less inflation"). To unify the convention, Ford chose as his running mate a conservative midwesterner, Senator Robert Dole of Kansas, who had earned a reputation for vicious invective and absolute loyalty to American farmers. But as Vice President Rockefeller spoke on his successor's behalf, the Reagan faction took one last revenge on their liberal nemesis: they silenced his microphone. "We want Reagan!" they chanted. "This was no long, loud cheer for Ronald Reagan," observed one Ford supporter. "This was a long, loud scream of dismay over the defeat of the conservative movement for at least another four years."

Reagan's unification address—praising the party platform, overlooking the nominee—expressed that sentiment. "There is no substitute for victory," he concluded, quoting the conservative hero, General Douglas MacArthur. Recognizing his limited support in Kansas City, Ford aimed his acceptance speech at the television audience: "You are the people who pay the taxes and obey the laws. You are the people who make our system work," he stated. "It will take the voices and votes of many more Americans, who are not Republican, to make . . . my mission possible." But the President was optimistic. "This year," he said, "the issues are all on our side."

"IN 1976," NOTED JOURNALIST Kandy Stroud, "issues were no more important than the price of hoopskirts." A conservative Democrat running against a moderate Republican produced few areas of disagreement, especially in foreign policy. Though Carter criticized the administration for neglecting traditional allies in Western Europe and Japan, nations represented in the Trilateral Commission, and challenged the principle of secret diplomacy, the Democrats quickly closed ranks during the only international crisis of the campaign. In August 1976, two American soldiers stationed in Korea were brutally killed in the demilitarized zone for trying to cut down a tree blocking their view of the north. Calling the attack a "vicious and unprovoked murder," Ford ordered a dramatic display of military force, including B-52s from Guam, fighter bombers, helicopter gunships, and armed troops, to guarantee American access to the disputed zone. In campaign appearances, Carter endorsed this enormous show of strength, even hinting that the President's response might have been insufficient. An earlier Carter proposal, recommending the withdrawal of American forces from Korea, was quietly shelved. For an alternative position, Americans had to turn to a former candidate, McGovern, who denounced United States support of South Korea President Park Chung Hee, a "disreputable tyrant," and warned that "the forces . . . sent to Korea a generation ago as a trip wire could trip this generation into another wrong war in another wrong place at another wrong time."

Disagreements between the candidates on domestic subjects focused on the economy and closely followed traditional party lines. Carter attacked the President for tolerating high unemployment (averaging over 7 percent), while Ford predicted that Democratic spending remedies would aggravate inflation and bring higher taxes. Carter also criticized the administration for encouraging the sale of nuclear power plants abroad, but on the eve of the election Ford undercut the issue by ordering a moratorium on the transfer of reprocessing plants. Carter's caution about the domestic use of nuclear power nevertheless contrasted with the President's enthusiasm for a $100 billion nuclear program. On the most sensitive issues, however, on busing, abortions, the ERA, topics that swayed whole constituencies, the candidates remained safely within the conservative consensus described by public opinion polls.

The candidates' monumental fear of arousing the electorate produced a bland campaign. An early Carter attack against what he called the "Nixon-Ford administration" drew such negative reactions that the Democrat dropped the divisive reference, refusing even to comment on Ford's pardon of his predecessor. Another attempt to clarify his disapproval of the President's clemency program also failed. "I do not favor a blanket amnesty, but for those who violated Selective Service laws, I intend to grant a blanket pardon," he told a booing convention of the American Legion. "Amnesty means that what you did is right. Pardon means that what you did—right or wrong—is forgiven." For three minutes, the hall thundered, "No! no! no!" Senator Dole, following Carter to the podium, reaffirmed the administration's position. "No blanket pardon, no blanket amnesty, no blanket clemency," he assured the cheering veterans. But with a weak clemency program of his own, the President had no intention of dwelling on the touchy issue.

Ford's major concern, rather than Carter's, was his poor public image. "One of the incumbent's problems has always been to 'appear presidential,' " wrote Richard Reeves in *New York* magazine, "which, in his case, has come down to first proving he is not a dummy, that he can read and write." Recognizing this predicament, Ford advisers tore a page out of Nixon's campaign book and adopted a "Rose Garden" strategy, in which the President used formal White House occasions to make public statements. After a rousing campaign opener at the University of Michigan, in which Ford introduced the theme of public trust—"Trust must be earned," he declared; "trust is not being all things to all people but being the same thing to all people"—the Republican candidate stayed close to home. "Like a moderately dull marriage," concluded Norman Mailer, "Ford was endlessly endurable—one could even get fond of him in a sour way."

With few issues dividing the candidates, public attention focused on the effluvia of politics. Carter's suggestion that FBI Director Clarence Kelley be fired for using agency funds to remodel his home gushed into maudlin sympathy for the recent death of Kelley's wife. Nelson Rockefeller, attempting to help Ford among liberals, earned front-page photographic attention for jabbing his middle finger at hecklers. "It was done in the best schoolyard style," said a Ford communications adviser. "It looked like something he had wanted to do all his life." Ford's secretary of agriculture, Earl Butz, embarrassed the President by making a racist quip ("I'll tell you what the coloreds want. It's three things: first, a tight pussy; second, loose shoes; and third, a warm place to shit. That's all!"), which was promptly reported by John Dean, now a writer for *Rolling Stone*. Ford's hesitancy to fire Butz aggravated the controversy. "He had no interest in the matter," protested black columnist William Raspberry, "beyond its effect on his election campaign." Dole, in a public debate with Mondale, described the major wars of the twentieth century as "Democratic wars," earning the *Chicago Tribune*'s sobriquet, "street fighter of the year."

Amid such tawdry theater, both candidates welcomed the opportunity to appear "presidential" by participating in a series of televised debates sponsored by the League of Women Voters. The broadcasts promised to clarify the differences between the candidates, but as in the rest of the media-oriented campaign, matters of style and presence prevailed. As Carter began his final speech, a technical breakdown interrupted transmission for nearly half an hour. "Some people considered that silent stretch the intellectual high point of the campaign," remarked columnist George Will, "—for 27 minutes, neither man was misleading the nation."

The second debate, held two weeks later, saw a more confident Carter adopt the battle cry of Ronald Reagan to denounce the President's foreign policy. "Our country's not strong anymore," he charged. "We're not respected anymore." Criticizing "secret Lone Ranger-type diplomatic efforts," Carter condemned the huge weapons sales to Arab nations and Iran that had turned the United States into "the arms merchant of the world." Forced to the defensive, the President stressed the benefits of détente, including the Helsinki accord: "There is no Soviet domination of Eastern Europe," he stated, "and there never will be under a Ford administration." The remark rang in his ears. "I would like to see Mr. Ford convince the Polish-Americans and the Czech-Americans and the Hungarian-Americans in this country," objected Carter. THE BLOOPER HEARD ROUND THE WORLD, headlined *Time* magazine. "Ford's grasp of foreign policy and even his mere competence were called into question." For several days, the President stumbled through a series of clarifications, before finally admitting his mistake. But the damage was done. "It's something out of *Alice in Wonderland*," shrugged Wisconsin state representative Joseph Czerwinski. "Voters are going to question why the fellow sitting in the Oval Office has such an unclear picture of what's going on in Eastern Europe."

In the third debate, it was Carter's turn to address a major campaign blunder, one that his advisers likened to "the Eagleton thing." It involved Carter's relations with the media. "The traveling press have zero interest in any issue unless it's a matter of making a mistake," Carter had told a journalist. In the same interview, Carter fulfilled his prophecy. Explaining the dangers of religious pride, the usually careful candidate conceded he had "looked on a lot of women with lust . . . committed adultery in my heart many times." Assuring the reporter that "God forgives me for it," Carter proceeded to impugn the memory of Lyndon Johnson, comparing him to Nixon—"lying, cheating, distorting the truth." Even worse, the piece appeared in a magazine that few politicians admitted they read: *Playboy*.

Released amid great fanfare by the magazine's publishers, the article drew quick protest. New York sophisticates laughed at Carter's naiveté, wondering, "How can you put confidence in a man who's been faithful to the same woman for 30 years?" But conservatives were appalled for simpler reasons. "*Playboy* is known for its gutter approach to life, and its whole philosophy comes right from the barnyard," charged a leading pastor of the Southern Baptist Convention. "A lot of us are not convinced that Mr. Carter is truly in the evangelical camp." Such sentiments, according to Carter's pollsters, had great impact among women voters. In his final meeting with Ford, therefore, Carter apologized for his remarks and carefully crafted a polite image to win respect from the female audience. (Late in the campaign, the *Playboy* scandal was partially offset by revelation that a Ford photographer had filmed pornography. But the public never learned that Carter had once inadvertently filmed a television ad in a pornography studio.)

"In what is widely conceded to be the most trivial and vituperative campaign in history," concluded Tom Wicker, "the televised debates afforded the two candidates opportunity to make more misrepresentations, false claims, calculated appeals and empty promises than probably were ever offered so directly to a long-suffering electorate." These inadequacies, shared by both candidates, had a remarkable equalizing effect. At the start of the fall campaign, Carter held a commanding lead in public opinion polls, 50 percent to Ford's 37 percent. But the gap had steadily narrowed until by election eve, the major polls called it a "virtual tie." Louis Harris put Carter ahead by a single point; George Gallup saw the same margin, but picked Ford.

THE BALLOTING REMAINED extremely close, the final results unclear until a long night of counting and waiting. With a mere two percent margin in the popular vote, Carter won a thin electoral victory, 297–241. Ford carried twenty-seven states, Carter only twenty-three and the District of Columbia. In twenty-three states, including eight of the ten largest, the winner earned less than 52 percent of the poll. Ford received a majority of the white vote, carried virtually the entire West (benefiting in Oregon by the McCarthy draw on Democrats), and did better than Nixon in 1972 in attracting Jews and Catholics, who harbored suspicions about Carter's evangelical Protestantism.

Carter's great success was on native grounds. In carrying the southern states (except Virginia), the Democrat destroyed Nixon's southern strategy. Besides holding the white vote, particularly in low-income rural areas, Carter demonstrated extraordinary appeal among blacks. Nationwide, he took ninety percent of the black vote, which provided the margin of victory in numerous states; in Texas, the combined black and Chicano vote formed the winning difference. "I wish—Lord, how I wish—Martin were alive today," exulted black activist John Lewis. "Through it all, the lunch counter sit-ins, the bus strike, the marches and everything, the bottom line was voting." Yet black voter participation in the South declined from 1972.

The absence of specific campaign issues increased the importance of party affiliation. A *New York Times*/CBS poll found that 80 percent of Democrats voted for Carter; 90 percent of Republicans for Ford. Democrats, with a higher proportion of registered supporters, also benefited as the party out of power at a time of economic trouble. In the national elections, the amount of ticket splitting declined, and voters sustained the huge Democratic majorities brought into office in 1974. With a Senate margin of 62–38 and a House lead of 291–142, the Democratic President expected few legislative obstacles to his administration. But statistics also showed that three-quarters of the Democratic winners in Congress ran ahead of Carter in the polls, felt few obligations of gratitude for the Georgian's coattails, and recognized the importance of preserving an independent good standing back home.

The unimportance of political issues in the presidential contest also perpetuated the steady decline of voter participation. From 55.7 percent in 1972, the figure slipped still more to 54.4 percent. Carter, in effect, had the support of only one-quarter of the adult population. A survey conducted by *The New York Times* and CBS News found that nonvoters were younger, poorer, and less educated than those who went to the polls. But even active citizens voiced strong disillusionment with the political system, arguing that public officials cared little about ordinary citizens. Nonvoters expressed a deeper rage, feelings of separation from the political structure, a fundamental sense of powerlessness. "I consider it my duty as a good citizen not to vote," explained a Manhattan advertising employee. "If sixty percent of the country did not vote, it might shake up the political process." A Nebraska politician recommended a slate called "None of the above," urging repeated balloting until satisfactory candidates emerged. "I don't vote," explained a California resident, "because I don't want to force a second-class decision on my neighbors."

Some nonvoters held more specific motives. "I'm not apathetic about nonvoting," maintained a supporter of Reagan. "I'm emphatic about it." On the morning after the election, Reagan promised to launch a new campaign: "to use the Republican platform to reach a new majority . . . for the G.O.P."

For Carter and for Ford, however, the running was over. "I think the sun's rising on a beautiful new day," rejoiced the victor, "a beautiful new spirit in this country, a beautiful new commitment to the future." Defining his election as a "broad-based" mandate, Carter envisioned no problems in grasping the reins of office. "The State of the Union is good," assured President Ford in a farewell to the nation. "Today we have a more perfect union than when my stewardship began." Eight days later, President Carter paused at the outset of his inauguration. "For myself and our nation," he said, "I want to thank my predecessor for all he has done to heal our land." With metaphoric finality, Carter hoped to put a decade of division to rest.

12

"A CRISIS OF CONFIDENCE"

The Politics of Jimmy Carter

"OUR PEOPLE WERE SICK AT heart," said Jimmy Carter, explaining his election victory, "and wanted new leadership that could heal us, and give us once again a government of which we could feel proud." Carter's inauguration symbolized this affirmation of traditional values. Instead of formal attire, the two chief executives, Carter and Ford, wore ordinary business suits, and the new President took the oath of office with the nickname "Jimmy." Then, he stirred the Washington crowds by leading the parade from Capitol Hill to the White House on foot. ("He's walking!" people shrieked. "He's walking!") "I have no new dream to set forth today," he admitted, "but rather urge a fresh faith in the old dream. . . . We must once again have full faith in our country—and in one another." Evoking "a new spirit"—the phrase appeared five times in his inaugural speech—Carter called for the restoration of political morality, a government "at the same time . . . competent and compassionate."

Carter's appeal for moral leadership, effective as campaign oratory, raised new problems once the mantle of authority passed to his own shoulders. "This is not the time to tax Mr. Carter again for his fuzziness on the issues," acknowledged *The New York Times* on his first day in office. "But he should recognize that he lacks the eloquence to hide it." With a paper-thin electoral victory and a rising proportion of citizens who refused to vote, the new administration took power in an atmosphere of persistent distrust. "One result was certain," observed veteran reporter Haynes Johnson. "The [new] president would be watched more critically than ever before."

Recognizing these suspicions, Carter attempted to demystify the operations of government and create an impression of rule by ordinary people. He reduced the size of the White House staff by one-third, ordered cabinet officers to drive their own cars, and required that government regulations be written "in plain English for a change." His administration instituted new ethical guidelines for executive employees, mandating public disclosure of financial holdings, divestiture of potential conflicts of interest, and closing what Carter called "the revolving door" between government service and corporate appointment. "Government officials can't be sensitive to your problems," the President remarked in a televised "fireside chat" two weeks after taking office, "if we are living like royalty here in Washington."

Carter's disavowal of professional politicians, partly a function of his own inexperience, partly the result of a self-conscious style, determined the structure of power within the White House. As his closest advisers, he retained the people who had shaped his campaign strategy—all Washington outsiders from Georgia: Hamilton Jordan, Jody Powell, and Charles Kirbo. More problematic was his nomination to head the Office of Management and Budget, Georgia banker Bert Lance, state highway commissioner under Carter and an early, generous contributor to the presidential campaign. "What has been Mr. Lance's experience in the federal government?" asked Senator William Proxmire scornfully. "He has none—zero, zip, zilch, not one year, not one week, not one day." Even more controversial was the choice for attorney general, former federal judge Griffin Bell, also from Georgia. Bell's political views—membership in clubs that excluded Jews and blacks, enthusiastic support for Nixon's nomination of Judge Carswell, and a legal ruling that upheld the removal from office of Georgia legislator Julian Bond for opposing the Vietnam war—aroused liberal suspicions about the administration's political sympathies. But despite unexpected angry rhetoric, the Democratic Senate indulged the President's preferences.

While public attention focused on questions of inexperience and cronyism, however, the bulk of Carter's high-level nominations revealed the administration's close ties to another, even more powerful interlocking establishment, the corporate elite that supported the Trilateral Commission. "If after the inauguration you find a Cy Vance as secretary of state and Zbigniew Brzezinski as head of national security," Hamilton Jordan told an interviewer during the recent campaign, "then I would say we failed." Yet Carter appointed Vance and Brzezinski to those very posts! And besides these two administrators and Vice President Mondale, Carter also turned to the Trilateral Commission for Secretary of the Treasury W. Michael Blumenthal, Secretary of Defense Harold Brown, United Nations ambassador Andrew Young, and a dozen other slightly lower appointees. "Conservatives with high integrity," consumer advocate Ralph Nader described them, who would "follow the wrong policies straight instead of crooked."

It was perhaps no coincidence, then, that the only Carter selection rejected by the Senate was an apparent insider who inadvertently had become associated with genuine outsiders, Theodore Sorensen, a former Kennedy adviser, nominated by Carter to head the CIA. Six years earlier, Sorensen had filed an affidavit in the *Pentagon Papers* case, in which he acknowledged leaving government service in 1964 with sixty-seven boxes of documents, including papers marked "classified." Such confessions confirmed Senate fears about Sorensen's antipathy to extralegal activities by the intelligence organization. "It is now clear," maintained Sorensen in withdrawing his name, "that a substantial portion of the United States Senate and the intelligence community is not yet ready to accept . . . an outsider who believes as I believe."

The orthodoxy of Carter's appointments, however, could not compensate for their lack of political experience. Within one month of the inauguration, the administration needlessly aroused the fury of the Democratic leadership of Congress, surely its most valuable political ally, by announcing the cancellation of nineteen water projects in the interests of fiscal austerity. Challenged by this attack on traditional "pork-barrel" legislation—the division of public spoils among the politicians in power—congressional leaders roared defiance, threatened to crush the remainder of the President's programs, and authorized the disputed appropriations anyway. In the face of such opposition, Carter prudently retreated, neither vetoing nor even denouncing the unwanted measure. He had lost not only the immediate issue, but considerable goodwill on Capitol Hill as well. Yet after one hundred days in office, Carter enjoyed rising popularity, garnering a 75 percent approval rating in the Harris poll. There was, observed the venerable presidential adviser Clark Clifford, "a return of the confidence of the people in our government."

Carter's ability to revitalize the public spirit nevertheless depended on the cooperation of Congress. Since the fall of Richard Nixon, congressional leaders had become especially jealous of legislative power, reluctant to compromise with any administration and, often, even with each other. Moreover, the elections of 1974, 1976, and 1978 brought to office a spate of new politicians—half the House Democrats had not served under Nixon—who remained uncommitted to the traditional committee system and hostile to the control of party leaders. A survey conducted at the University of Pittsburgh showed party loyalty and party voting within Congress at the lowest level in thirty-six years. "If this were France," grieved Speaker Thomas "Tip" O'Neill, "the Democratic Party would be five parties."

The administration's attempt to restore public confidence in the federal government also collided with a more sinister dimension of congressional independence: the penchant of numerous representatives for graft. On the eve of Carter's election, *The Washington Post*, chief sleuth in the Watergate scandals, accused over one hundred congressmen of taking bribes from South Korea lobbyist Tongsun Park in exchange for enacting favorable legislation. The resulting "Koreagate" investigation, headed by former Watergate prosecutor Leon Jaworski, found "substantial" support for the charges. But because of intelligence restraints on the evidence, only three sitting congressmen were reprimanded for their conduct, and one former representative, Richard Hanna of California, went to prison. In a separate case, thirteen-term Michigan Democrat Charles Diggs was convicted of taking illegal kickbacks from staff employees, but managed to win reelection in 1978. The next year, he became the first congressman since 1921 to be censured by the House of Representatives for padding his payroll and taking public funds for personal use.

The discovery of widespread congressional corruption also smeared the White House. When United States attorney David Marston, a former aide of Republican Senator Schweiker, probed too closely into a kickback scheme involving two Pennsylvania Democrats, one of the suspects, Representative Joshua Eilberg, telephoned the President to recommend cashiering Marston, a proposal Carter endorsed. "This was a routine matter for me," said the President in self-defense, "and I did not consider my taking the telephone call . . . nor relaying his request to the attorney general to be ill advised at all." But the Marston affair evoked memories of Watergate and kept the case alive. Indicted on conflict-of-interest charges and defeated at the polls, Eilberg pleaded guilty in 1979. Representative Daniel Flood, charged with similar violations, won a mistrial, then pleaded ill-health to avoid a retrial; he retired in 1980. Meanwhile, FBI investigators were gathering some remarkable evidence, including videotaped motion pictures of congressmen taking bribes from mysterious Arab millionaires. The cases, coded Abscam, broke the headlines in 1980.

For two prestigious senators—liberal Republican Edward Brooke of Massachusetts, the only black in the upper house, and Herman Talmadge, scion of southern conservatism—messy divorce trials led to revelations of the illegal accumulation of funds. The charges contributed to Brooke's electoral defeat in 1978. Talmadge, having recovered from alcoholism, staged a strong personal defense. But in 1979, the Senate denounced his "reprehensible" conduct for bringing "dishonor and disrepute" on that body, and he lost a bid for reelection in 1980.

The reluctance of Congress to discipline its members intensified public distrust of the political process. "For some citizens," warned Carter in his first state of the union message, "the government has almost become like a foreign country." Responding to the decline of voter participation, the President proposed a liberalization of voter registration, urging the removal of "antiquated and unnecessary obstacles." But a Congress content with its own rule felt no need for reform. In the 1978 elections, voter participation dropped under 38 percent, the lowest turnout since 1942. Though most congressional incumbents won reelection, party loyalty virtually disappeared. In the state elections, voters readily split tickets in response to single issues and candidate personality, and while Republicans made only modest gains in Congress, they captured 298 new seats in the state legislatures. "This is the most profound change for us," said a gloating Republican National Chairman Bill Brock. The mood of the citizenry emerged clearly in the low television ratings obtained by election-night news shows, which in New York City ran third behind a rerun of Peter Sellers's *The Pink Panther*. It was no surprise, then, that by the summer of 1979, a Gallup poll found public approval of Congress at an abysmal 19 percent.

The intractability of Congress severely diminished the political power of Jimmy Carter, leaving the nominal head of the Democratic party with a shrinking constituency in the country which, in turn, further weakened his influence on Capitol Hill. "Nixon had his enemies list," quipped Senator James Abourezk. "Carter has his friends list." As White House proposals vanished in Congress, the President's popularity steadily declined, raising what *Newsweek* magazine called "the Eptitude Question—the suspicion abroad in Washington's power factories that Carter and his Georgia irregulars have not yet fully mastered their jobs." After one year in office, Carter's approval rating slid below 50 percent. "He is a soothing flatterer and a sensible president," noted *The New York Times*, "but not yet a leader, or teacher, even for a quiet time." This disenchantment fed upon itself, the erosion of support causing presidential failure, which eroded still more support until the ominous summer weekend in 1979 when Carter's popularity statistics dropped even below those of Richard Nixon on the eve of resignation.

CARTER'S DECLINING FORTUNES surely reflected his political incompetence. But he suffered as much for his personal style as he did for the policies he pursued. The very traits that had made the Georgian such an attractive candidate in 1976—images of compassion, homeyness, innocence—contradicted popular expectations of presidential authority, the decisive manipulation of power. Where Nixon personified a callous imperiousness and Ford simple bumbling, Carter, by contrast, epitomized neither boldness nor dullness, instead communicated images of hesitancy, obfuscation, ultimately of impotence. Carter's attempt to exercise compassionate power, almost by definition, could satisfy no one.

The difficulty of balancing moral justice with raw power emerged during Carter's first full day in office when, to fulfill one of his most controversial campaign pledges, the President offered "full, complete, and unconditional pardon" to the draft resisters of the Vietnam war, provided only that they had not engaged in violent crimes. (With considerably less fanfare, Carter later commuted the prison sentence of the unrepentant Watergate burglar G. Gordon Liddy.) Such gestures attempted to separate the administration from the troubles of the past. But Carter underestimated the force of memory. "It's the saddest day in American history," complained the director of the Veterans of Foreign Wars upon learning of the presidential pardon, "sadder than Watergate and Vietnam itself." "The most disgraceful thing a President has ever done," protested Barry Goldwater. "If I had known this would happen," snapped one bitter veteran, "I would have gone to Canada, too, and hung out." A Harris survey found that public opinion opposed the reprieve, and the Senate nearly passed a resolution criticizing the President's action. "I don't intend to pardon any more people from the Vietnam era," Carter soon assured a radio audience.

Nor did the Vietnam pardon win the gratitude of the peace movement. By excluding military offenders—deserters and veterans with less-than-honorable discharges—the President ignored a far larger group of war resisters which was also, according to the American Civil Liberties Union, "more likely to be poor, from minority groups and less educated." Though Carter instructed the Defense Department to reexamine the status of antiwar veterans, the Pentagon established strict criteria for upgrading discharges, and Congress specifically prohibited the expenditure of funds to advertise the project. When the program terminated in October 1977, only 9 percent of the eligible veterans had applied for review. By then, the President had also signed the Cranston-Thurmond bill which denied veterans' benefits to participants in the upgrading program. Carter's much publicized moralism, in perpetuating the distinction between civilian and military opposition to the Vietnam war, thus surrendered to political expediency.

The President demonstrated considerably greater compassion for intimate associates accused of crimes—but also bore unfortunate consequences for this loyalty. In 1977, budget director Lance drew congressional criticism for his loose financial practices—taking large personal overdrafts from his bank—prior to assuming federal office. Carter remained staunchly supportive of his friend, dodging reporters' questions and denying any improprieties. But public pressure forced Lance's resignation anyway and the President suffered for his unswerving faith. Lance did not win acquittal until 1980. The President showed similar tolerance for the harmful commentary of his brother, Billy, who insulted Jews and blacks with impunity. But Billy Carter's financial transactions as a lobbyist for Libya smacked of corruption and the "Billygate" scandal tarnished the administration. Carter also defended his close adviser, Hamilton Jordan, against charges of personal misconduct, snorting cocaine at New York's Club 54. Such allegations called into question the President's own standards.

The blurring of morality and power politics also affected Carter's foreign policy—and returned to plague the administration when it encountered moral values different from its own. "Our commitment to human rights must be absolute," said Carter in his inaugural speech, "but let no one confuse our idealism with weakness." While pursuing détente with the Soviet Union and negotiating SALT II, the President determined to promote "human rights" within Soviet borders. Such a program contradicted the assumptions of recent diplomacy, the acceptance of big-power spheres of influence in which other powers exerted no leverage. "We must replace balance-of-power politics with world order politics," the Trilateralist had suggested in the recent campaign. Soon after taking office, Carter personally wrote to Soviet dissident Andrei Sakharov, assuring that "the American people . . . will continue our firm commitment to promote respect for human rights not only in our country but also abroad." By unexpectedly altering American policy, the administration challenged the Soviet leadership, which responded by hardening its position on SALT. "Washington's claims to teach others how to live cannot be accepted by any sovereign state," retorted President Brezhnev.

Besides delaying SALT, the human rights issue exposed obvious contradictions in United States policy. The State Department used Carter's stand to justify the cessation of military aid to repressive regimes such as Argentina and Uruguay, but for reasons of national security rationalized continuing aid to South Korea. Even worse, administration policy raised an ugly specter of revenge. Challenged by Carter's attack, the Soviet Union could not afford to retreat from its traditional suppression of dissent. "Carter painted himself into a corner," observed Harvard's Adam Ulam. Nor would the White House halt SALT negotiations in protest. "It's not worth going into another cold war," explained a Carter aide. To protest Soviet domestic conduct, the President ordered minor retaliations—the cancellation of a computer sale to Tass for use at the 1980 Olympics, the delay of a shipment of drill bits—and allowed such symbols to serve as a substitute for policy. Utterly ineffective in influencing the Soviet leadership, Carter's denunciations also made the idea of rapprochement unpalatable to the American public.

The defense of human rights soon embroiled the United States in a new type of diplomacy, the manipulation of individual lives as a way of rendering impotent the most powerful government on earth. Seeking to demonstrate his consistency of policy, Carter referred in his second press conference to atrocities committed by Uganda's Idi Amin which, said the President, "disgusted the entire civilized world." The African dictator promptly clamped travel restrictions on the two hundred Americans living in Uganda and ordered them to attend a personal meeting. Fearing reprisals, the White House briefly considered landing troops to defend American citizens. But the futility of such action persuaded the President to settle for a protest letter that denounced the taking of hostages. Scorning American hypocrisy, Amin kept the world in suspense over a long weekend, before conceding he had no evil intent.

Two weeks later, the seizure of hostages came closer to home when a small group of Hanafi Muslims occupied three buildings in Washington, D.C., holding 134 people at gunpoint to protest their persecution by Black Muslims. Sensitive to what *Newsweek* magazine called "the ghosts of Attica," the administration ordered negotiations with the invaders, finally ending the siege peacefully after three days. The result, said the President, "was a vivid proof that a slow and careful approach was the effective way."

Such takeovers, spawned in terrorist politics, reached epidemic proportions in the late seventies. In New York, an American Nazi held an entire factory at bay; in Indianapolis, an angry debtor wired a shotgun to the head of his mortgage holder for sixty-two hours. One gunman in Cleveland refused to surrender until he had talked to President Carter. "Taking hostages is a very creative act," explained an experienced police psychiatrist. "It gives you real power." In such situations, federal authorities recommended continued negotiations. "Society should aim to outwit the terrorist," advised a government manual, "rather than to outfight him." But indulging terrorism lent credibility to the tactic. Commenting on Carter's "dealing *viva voce* with hostage-holders," the recently paroled Watergate conspirator E. Howard Hunt expressed an ominous thought: "I'll bet he hasn't answered the telephone for the last time."

CARTER'S CONFIDENCE in the power of moral persuasion miscalculated the strength of entrenched interests to resist presidential appeals, an error that soon devastated the administration's attempt to settle what it considered the most pressing domestic issue of the age: the energy crisis. The terrible winter of 1977 underscored the problem. As record snowfalls and subzero temperatures forced the closing of schools and factories, causing layoffs for an estimated 1.6 million workers, a grim President told the nation to "face the fact that the energy shortage is permanent." "Live thriftily," he advised, "and remember the importance of helping our neighbors."

These moral homilies served as the centerpiece of the President's much-awaited energy program, unveiled in a series of televised speeches in April 1977. Comparing the crisis to moral warfare, Carter reiterated the importance of old-fashioned frugality: energy conservation. "It is the cheapest, most practical way to meet our energy needs," he told a joint session of Congress, "and to reduce our dependence on foreign oil." To stimulate conservation, the President proposed a tax package to penalize energy waste and to encourage greater efficiency. The program offered few alternatives to the continued reliance on imported oil (which by 1977 amounted to half the nation's energy supply), suggesting small tax credits for the installation of solar devices and describing nuclear power "as a last resort." Opposing the development of breeder reactors, Carter insisted that "effective conservation efforts can minimize the shift toward nuclear power."

The President's emphasis on reduced energy consumption immediately challenged entrenched corporate interests. "This country did not conserve its way to greatness," protested a defender of the Texas gas industry. "It produced itself to greatness." Carter's plan to raise consumer prices through taxation rather than deregulation threatened corporate profits; "a windfall loss," complained an economist at Standard Oil. "Our problem isn't a shortage of oil," stated Ronald Reagan, "it's a surplus of government." The wrath of the business community descended quickly on Congress, which rallied to protect its diverse constituents. "It's like it was the day after Pearl Harbor," suggested Representative Morris Udall, "and you interviewed the Congressman from Detroit and he said, 'The Japanese attack was outrageous, but before we rush into war, let's see how it would affect the [auto] industry,' and then somebody else said, 'It was dastardly, but consider the effect on oil,' and another Congressman said, 'War could be very serious for recreation and tourism.'" Such pressures rapidly transformed Carter's clarion call for the "moral equivalent of war" into its acronym, MEOW, a pussycat proposal that could not slide through the legislature.

Though the President obtained approval for a Department of Energy to coordinate government policy, the remainder of his program collapsed in shambles. Unable to rally public opinion ("I don't feel much like talking about energy and foreign policy," an unemployed steelworker told him at an "Energy Round Table." "I am concerned about how I am going to live."), the President watched helplessly while the Senate dismantled the energy tax program and even overcame a two-week filibuster to endorse the deregulation of natural gas. "The moral equivalent of the Vietnam war," exclaimed a White House aide. When the President took his crusade for conservation to yet another television audience, *The Boston Globe* extended that metaphor further, calling the speech "the moral equivalent of Sominex."

Having failed in 1977, the President renewed his battle for an energy program the next year. "Further delay will only lead to more harsh and painful solutions," he warned. But the absence of fuel shortages—indeed, the existence of surpluses on the West Coast—encouraged consumers to burn ever larger quantities of imported oil. "I don't see the inevitability of a crunch," assured a petroleum industry spokesman. "The possibility is there but it's not a crisis." On the anniversary of his first energy speech, Carter conceded the importance of stimulating new oil production and recommended the decontrol of prices paired with a windfall profits tax to allow rebates for the poor. But Congress rebuffed the proposal. Nor did alternative technologies attract political support. "To think of alternative energy sources," observed economist Lester Thurow, "is to think of vigorous well-organized opponents." On May 3, 1978, advocates of solar power sponsored a Sun Day, reminiscent of the environmentalists' Earth Day of 1970, but won no inroads in government policy. Nuclear power remained economically suspect. "It's time for it to compete," said a Carter official in rejecting additional government subsidies. "It's been too much a pampered child of the federal government."

The National Energy Act, finally passed in November 1978,

bore scant resemblance to Carter's initial program, leaving the nation ill-prepared for an impending crisis of resources. "I have not given up on my original proposal that there should be some constraint on consumption," said Carter in signing the bill, "and thus on oil imports." Within two months, news from the Middle East reinforced that advice. The eruption of civil war in Iran against the rule of the Shah sharply curtailed world oil production, and the OPEC nations took the opportunity to announce a 14.5 percent increase in oil prices. "Market conditions do not warrant a price increase of this magnitude," protested the White House. But the administration did little more than plead for reconsideration. To the American people, the President urged that they "honor the 55-m.p.h. speed limit, set thermostats no higher than 65 degrees and limit discretionary driving."

While the public calmly accommodated these inconveniences, the problem of energy resources suddenly escalated beyond the bounds of ordinary imagination. "The world has never known a day quite like today," announced Walter Cronkite on March 30, 1979. "It faced the considerable uncertainties and dangers of the worst nuclear power plant accident of the atomic age. And the horror tonight is that it could get much worse." Two days earlier, a stuck valve at the nuclear power facility at Three Mile Island, Pennsylvania, had overheated the reactor core, threatening to wash the countryside in a shower of deadly radiation. While technicians worked feverishly to avert a cataclysmic meltdown, one hundred thousand civilians fled their homes for safety. It took nearly two weeks to bring the errant reactor under control. "We were damn lucky," admitted a member of a special presidential commission established to investigate the calamity. "No one understood what was going on at the time, and it scares the hell out of me." The then popular film, *China Syndrome*, the story of a similar reactor failure, dramatized a growing public suspicion about nuclear power—an anxiety not just about the dangers of radioactivity, but about the failure of the industry and the regulatory agencies to tell the truth about the omnipresent risk.

Such fears sent a chill through the troubled industry. Even before the Three Mile Island calamity, the rising cost of nuclear reactors had caused cancellation of twenty planned projects. Soon afterward, eleven more were dropped and no new orders were made in 1979. The seventy-one plants remaining in operation provided about 11 percent of the nation's electrical energy, far below

earlier estimates. But despite sharp criticism of the nuclear industry as well as condemnation of the safety procedures established
by the Nuclear Regulatory Commission, the President's advisers
recommended the continuation of nuclear power. "We cannot
simply shut down our nuclear power plants," insisted Carter; they
"must play an important role in our energy future."

The near disaster at Three Mile Island, by exposing the limitations of technological performance, shocked the nation into a
reconsideration of the energy crisis. Taking advantage of the unsettled mood, Carter again appealed for support of his energy program. "The fundamental cause of our nation's energy crisis," he
told a prime-time television audience in April 1979, "is petroleum," and he warned about overdependence on "a thin line of oil
tankers stretching halfway around the earth . . . [to] one of the
most unstable regions in the world." To encourage domestic production, Carter announced the gradual decontrol of oil prices beginning immediately and pleaded with Congress for a windfall
profits tax to equalize the sacrifice. He also requested "standby
authority" to impose a national rationing plan. At a time when
gasoline cost seventy cents a gallon, pessimistic observers predicted that the President's scheme would produce an increase of
twenty cents per gallon.

Despite the recent peril, however, Congress remained unimpressed. While praising the decontrol decision, most congressional
leaders criticized the tax proposal. In May, the legislature handed
the President a major defeat by rejecting the plan for standby
rationing. "The members don't pay any attention to him," said
Speaker O'Neill. "They put their heads in the sand," Carter complained. "The average motorist is going to be faced with more
shortages of gasoline in the future. We ought to be ready for it,
and we're not."

The crisis came sooner than expected. By May, gasoline lines
in California ran as long as five hundred cars, and prices at the
pump already touched one dollar per gallon. "It's sort of like sex,"
assured an official of Gulf Oil. "Everybody's going to get all the
gasoline they need, but they're damn sure not going to get all they
want." Then, in June, OPEC announced a gigantic 50 percent
hike in oil prices. The news created panic conditions. Despite odd-
even rationing schemes, tempers steamed easily, causing fistfights,
stabbings, and shootings, and in Levittown, Pennsylvania, the cra-
dle of suburbia, gasoline shortages provoked a full-scale riot. To

make matters worse, the nation's independent truckers staged a wildcat strike to protest rising diesel costs, idling 60 percent of the long-haul interstate traffic. "When the President and all them senators can't get no steak," said a striker, "then they'll do something."

"The future of the Democratic Party is tied to energy," Carter had recently advised congressional leaders. "It could cost us control of the Senate and White House. It could be the issue that puts the Democrats out of power for a very long time." Cutting short a vacation, the President retreated to his Camp David hideaway to prepare another address on the energy crisis. But the speech never came. As his popularity ratings cascaded to all-time lows, Carter recognized the futility of moral appeal. "If I give this speech," he told an aide, "they'll kill me." Canceling the broadcast, the President summoned teams of consultants to Camp David to discuss the sorry state of the nation. Mayors, governors, congressmen, academics, and private citizens—135 in all—spoke candidly, while the President and his wife Rosalynn took notes. After a week of suspense, Carter returned from the mountain.

"All the legislation in the world can't fix what's wrong with America," a solemn President addressed the nation. "It is a crisis of confidence. It is a crisis that strikes at the very heart and soul and spirit of our nation . . . [and it] is threatening to destroy the social and political fabric of America." Stressing the decline of traditional values—"hard work, strong families, close-knit communities and our faith in God"—Carter lamented the growing loss of assurance about the American future. "Looking for a way out of this crisis, our people have turned to the federal government and found it isolated from the mainstream of our nation's life; Washington, D.C., has become an island. . . . This is not a message of happiness or reassurance," he concluded. "But it is the truth. And it is a warning."

The struggle for renewal, Carter suggested, should begin "on the battlefield of energy." For the third time in his administration, the President revealed a major energy package, promising to "win for our nation a new confidence—and . . . seize control of our common destiny." First, he ordered a freeze on the amount of oil imported from abroad and recommended additional cutbacks during the next decade. Second, he proposed the formation of an $88 billion government-funded corporation to produce synthetic fuel from coal and shale. Third, he suggested the creation of an "energy mobilization" committee to cut through bureaucratic red tape. "We will protect our environment," he pledged. "But when this nation critically needs a refinery or pipeline, we will build it."

Carter's dramatic appeal struck close to the national conscience, rapidly improving his political prospects. But just as quickly, the President destroyed his advantage. Two days after promising to restore a sense of national unity, the White House announced that the entire cabinet had offered to resign and that Carter had accepted the departure of five top administrators, producing a major reorganization of the executive branch. The upheaval shocked public opinion and renewed fears that the government had drifted out of control. By the end of July, surveys showed Carter's approval ratings at a dismal 25 percent—exactly the nadir on the eve of the Camp David meetings.

Emboldened by the administration's self-defeating maneuvers, Congress delayed enactment of the President's plan, carefully cultivating exemptions to the windfall profits tax. Not until the spring of 1980, after nearly a year of oil decontrol, did the legislature approve a modified profits tax, which brought substantially lower funds for the government. Congress also authorized stricter safety rules for nuclear power, ordering reactors kept away from population centers and establishing stringent penalties for violations. To encourage production, Congress established the U.S. Synthetic Fuels Corporation, provided a solar-energy bank, and authorized funding for an alcohol fuel program and for a Strategic Petroleum Reserve. "If OPEC tries to blackmail us," explained Majority Leader Wright, "we'll have a spare tire."

BY THE TIME CONGRESS ENACTED an energy program, however, the issue of resources had been subsumed by its larger consequences— an economy on the brink of collapse. The deterioration of the American economy under Carter reflected as much the failures of presidential policy as it did persistent and fundamental structural problems that no administration could meet. Basic to these difficulties was the question of faith—the impact of future expectations as a driving force for inflation and as a drag on corporate investment. Having inherited an inflation rate below 5 percent, Carter saw the figure increase to 6 percent in 1977, 9 percent in

1978, and 13.3 percent in 1979, while official unemployment statistics fell slightly from 7.4 percent to about 6 percent. Worse, the rate of productivity of United States business steadily declined, running at −.9 percent in 1979.

Upon taking office, Carter expected to speed recovery from the recession of 1974–75 by cutting taxes and increasing government spending. But his refusal to fund public works projects antagonized organized labor, and conservatives criticized the growing deficit. "The increase in the federal budget is stirring up new fears," warned Arthur Burns, "new expectations of inflation that to some degree may be a self-fulfilling prophecy." As unemployment continued to drop, however, and the severe cold boosted prices, the administration decided to scrap a promised tax rebate. Opting for fiscal restraint, Lance predicted "no new programs if we are going to . . . get a balanced budget by 1981." Retorted Senator Hubert Humphrey, "There is *no* way to balance the budget by 1981."

Even if Carter had managed, as he promised in April 1977, "to discipline the growth of government spending," the rate of inflation would have continued to increase. Cost-of-living escalators, built into labor and business contracts as a hedge against inflation, had developed a self-generating momentum, one increase automatically stimulating the next. A lag of investment in the modernization of facilities—partly because of preferred opportunities abroad and partly because of fear of inflation—contributed to a decline of productivity. "We already have so much capacity," explained Stanford economist Ezra Solomon, "it's much easier to buy a company ready-made than to add capacity." Such trends weakened American competition with foreign manufacturers, causing a decline of such basic industries as steel and automobiles. These losses, combined with a growing reliance on imported oil, produced unprecedented deficits in the balance of trade, reaching $28 billion in 1979. The result was a rapid depreciation of the dollar overseas, which returned in the form of further inflated prices for imported goods such as OPEC oil. Finally, the rising cost of energy added across-the-board increases throughout the economy.

By the late seventies, these economic trends were threatening the survival of the nation's tenth largest business, the Chrysler Corporation. After losing $205 million in 1978 and over $700 million in the first three quarters of 1979, the third largest automobile manufacturer appealed to the federal government for a billion-dollar tax credit to remain solvent. The misfortunes of Chrysler closely mirrored the general predicament of American capitalism. Slow to convert to small-car manufacturing, Chrysler chose not to build its own factory and instead contracted with Volkswagen to import four-cylinder engines. These arrangements severely limited Chrysler's productivity, especially when the small-car Dodge Omni and Plymouth Horizon became the corporation's best-sellers. Yet even these vehicles suffered from basic deficiencies—the only American cars ever rated "Not Acceptable" by Consumers Union. With a shrinking share of the automobile market, Chrysler sold its European holdings to foreign manufacturers and reduced its facilities at home.

Chrysler's appeal for public assistance ignited an angry debate about the limits of government responsibility for the economy. "You just can't have a free-enterprise system without failures," asserted Senator Proxmire. "Are we going to guarantee businessmen against their own incompetence by eliminating any incentive for avoiding the specter of bankruptcy?" But the collapse of Chrysler, warned its president Lee Iacocca, "would have a falling-dominoes effect" in the economy. "The people who made the bad decisions at Chrysler are no longer there," argued Michigan Representative James Blanchard. "No one should hold half a million workers responsible for the decisions of a few officials long since gone." After forcing Chrysler to make significant economic concessions, including renegotiation of its contract with the United Auto Workers, Congress finally approved a $1.5 billion loan guarantee in 1979.

The structural problems of the American economy were intensified by new government legislation—agricultural price supports, increases in the minimum wages, benefits for the steel industry, and higher social security payroll taxes. Together with rising food and fuel costs and a depreciated dollar, such expenditures sparked a new inflationary spiral in 1978. "You can't figure your real return, so you postpone investments," Treasury Secretary Blumenthal explained. "Your costs rise, your real profits shrink, your stock values go down; it costs more to borrow. It goes on and on." A May 1978 Gallup poll showed that a majority of Americans saw inflation as the nation's most serious problem. Yet the administration hesitated to act, pleading simply for voluntary restraint.

The relentless inflation, however, together with the trade deficit, imperiled the stability of the dollar in international markets, moving the economy closer to a crisis situation. At an economic summit conference in Bonn and in a subsequent meeting of the World Bank in Washington, the President pledged "my own word of honor" to fight inflation. "I do not have all the answers," Carter told a television audience in October. "Nobody does." But he proposed a program of voluntary guidelines, calling for 7 percent limits on wage gains and 6.5 percent rises in prices. "We must face a time of national austerity," he urged. "Hard choices are necessary if we want to avoid consequences that are even worse." But, commented *The Wall Street Journal*, "few believed that the Carter plan would win the battle."

The lack of confidence in the Carter remedy precipitated another run on the dollar, further toppling its value. To halt this erosion, the administration intervened boldly, raising the discount rate a full percentage point, tightening credit, purchasing dollars abroad, and accelerating the sale of gold. But the policy aroused new fears of a recession. "Using high interest rates to psychologically support the dollar and try to fight inflation is part of the old-time conservative religion," protested consumer advocate Roger Hickey. "Millions of Americans will be sacrificial lambs in the anti-inflation war."

The sudden announcement of a major boost in OPEC prices—they would soar sixty percent in 1979—quickly undermined the credibility of Carter's economic program. "Sometimes a party must sail against the wind," declared Senator Kennedy in protesting the administration's commitment to balance the budget. "The party that tore itself apart over Vietnam in the 1960s cannot afford to tear itself apart today over budget cuts in basic social programs." As the inflation rate soared to 13 percent in January 1979, labor leader George Meany called for "equality of sacrifice, not the sacrifice of equality." Ignoring the President's plea for wage restraints, the Teamsters and United Airlines workers went on strike while an AFL-CIO local in Washington won a lawsuit that denied the legality of the administration's voluntary guidelines. Lacking effective controls, the White House encouraged the Federal Reserve system to raise interest rates to a record-breaking 15 percent in 1979, virtually assuring a recession in the coming election year. "There are no economic miracles waiting to be performed," conceded Carter in his 1980 economic report to Congress.

THE WEAKNESSES OF the American economy and mounting concern about the nation's energy resources provided the framework for the implementation of a foreign policy. Like his Republican predecessors, Trilateralist Carter placed preeminence on stabilizing American trade with other nations, particularly the "lesser developed countries" that constituted the third world. After the failure in Vietnam, however, the traditional commitment to the Open Door was now tempered by a recognition, if not a fear, of the limits of American power. Not only had the United States suffered ignominious military defeat in trying to enforce a capitalist regime in a small country, but the rejuvenated economies of Western Europe and Japan also competed more aggressively for American markets and sources of raw materials.

By the time Carter took office, the United States could no longer expect easy accommodation even in its own backyard, Latin America. Recognizing the changes in international power, the nations in this traditional American sphere of influence had charted a more independent course by seeking trade with other economic blocs, including the Soviet Union. One obstacle to better relations in the Western Hemisphere was Latin American opposition to United States interventionism. To eliminate the most obvious symbol of American aggression—United States control of the Panama Canal—Presidents Nixon and Ford had discussed a new treaty relationship with the Torrijos regime of Panama.

Carter resolved to complete these unfinished negotiations. By the summer of 1977, he announced the signing of two related treaties which provided for the gradual transfer of the canal to Panama by the year 2000. "Fairness, not force," said the President, "should lie at the heart of our dealings with the nations of the world." Yet the administration carefully protected the right of the United States to intervene to preserve the neutrality of the canal beyond 2000 and retained certain privileges in times of emergency. To avoid misunderstandings, the two nations also signed a subsequent statement distinguishing between acceptable intervention in the name of neutrality and unwanted interference "in the internal affairs of Panama."

Revelation of the treaties provoked angry debate around the nation, which showed that public opinion generally disapproved the arrangements. "The fatal flaw," warned Ronald Reagan, "is the risk they contain for our national security and for hemisphere defense. We're turning one of the world's most important waterways over to a country no one can believe." Antitreaty groups promptly launched a massive advertising campaign to block ratification. "There is *no* Panama Canal," asserted the American Conservative Union. "There is an *American* Canal in Panama. Don't let President Carter give it away." To overcome this opposition, the administration developed an elaborate public relations strategy, flooding the nation with prominent supporters, including Kissinger and Ford. "If the treaties are rejected," lobbied Carter, "Communist radicals from Cuba and other places would have rich hunting ground in Panama." Such pressure slowly shifted the balance of public opinion. "After receiving thousands of letters opposing the treaties, we were so happy to receive protreaty letters," quipped one senator, "that we framed both of them." But by the spring of 1978, the administration had persuaded the requisite two-thirds of the Senate to approve the pacts.

The ratification of the Panama treaties represented a fundamental shift in American power, heralding what Carter called "a new era" in relations with small countries. "The Panama Canal," remarked a United States diplomat, "was to our Latin policy what Vietnam was to our global policy—blood poisoning. Now that's over." When Sandinista guerrillas attacked Nicaragua dictator Anastasio Somoza in 1979, the Carter administration refused to support the doomed regime beyond offering the fallen president exile in Miami. "We're trying to carve out a moderate solution in Nicaragua," explained one government official, "that would inspire moderate opposition in El Salvador." The age of Big Stick diplomacy seemed at an end. TODAY THE PANAMA CANAL, warned a picket at Capitol Hill, TOMORROW TAIWAN.

The prophecy came sooner than expected. In a major departure from past foreign policy, Carter told a surprised nation that effective January 1, 1979, the United States extended formal diplomatic recognition to the People's Republic of China and terminated its mutual defense treaty with the regime on Taiwan. "Normalization," explained the President, "—and the expanded commercial and cultural relations that it will bring—will contribute to the well-being of our own Nation . . . , and it will also enhance the stability of Asia." Though the President promised the temporary preservation of the Taiwan government, conservatives deplored what former ambassador to Peking George Bush called "a major blow to our already declining credibility." Reagan immediately cabled regrets to Taiwan's president, while Goldwater filed suit to block "an outright abuse of presidential power." Carter could find solace, however, not only in the courts, which upheld his decision, but also in the quadrupling of American exports to China in 1978.

The importance of advancing American trade also shaped the administration's policy toward the nations of Africa. In 1978, Carter became the first President to visit black Africa, making assurances to Nigeria, the second largest supplier of crude oil to the United States, of a "departure from past aloofness." Fearful of offending this crucial ally, the White House rebuffed congressional pressure to lift economic sanctions imposed against Rhodesia for its policies of white supremacy. Carter also placed priority on economic interests by joining France and Belgium in ousting Zairian rebels from the mineral-rich province of Shaba in 1978. But the administration carefully limited United States involvement to air transportation and criticism of alleged "external intervention."

Underlying these alterations of American foreign policy, one basic assumption remained unchanged: the Soviet Union constituted a menace to world peace. Like Nixon and Ford, Carter had no illusions about the possibility of ending Soviet-American rivalry. But he did hope to stabilize the arms race and reduce the likelihood of nuclear war. As the administration reopened SALT talks in 1977, therefore, Carter made several significant gestures of good faith. To the dismay of traditional cold warriors, he canceled production of the B-1 bomber, withheld approval of the deadly neutron radiation bomb, and announced opposition to the reinstitution of the draft. (Unknown to the public and to the Soviets, Carter did approve the "Stealth" bomber as an alternative to the B-1.) "Peace will not be assured," he told the United Nations General Assembly, "until the weapons of war are finally put away."

These conciliatory postures, however, brought few Soviet concessions. Evidence of Soviet intervention in Ethiopia and Zaire infuriated the President. In a series of public addresses in the spring of 1978, Carter rekindled the cold war. "We, like our forebears," he declared in a Kennedy-like call to arms, "live in a time when those who would destroy liberty are restrained less by their respect for freedom itself than by the knowledge that those of us who cherish freedom are strong." But despite this rhetorical militance, Carter opposed suspension of SALT negotiations. "If we spend all our time jawboning against the Soviet Union," observed a White House aide, "we're going to have a real problem convincing the American people that the Russians can be trusted."

The new SALT treaty, signed by Carter in Vienna in June 1979, satisfied neither dove nor hawk. The agreement established ceilings on strategic weapons, limited qualitative improvements, and assured a basic parity of numbers between the two powers, while permitting a doubling of the number of nuclear warheads. "SALT II will not end the arms competition," the President admitted to Congress, "but it does make that competition safer and more predictable, with clear rules and verifiable limits." Protesting the continuation of the arms race, liberal senators led by McGovern vowed to vote against the treaty. But the loudest objections came from conservative quarters. "The danger is real," advised Senator Jackson, "that seven years of détente are becoming a decade of appeasement."

The domestic attack on SALT produced a remarkable change in administration policy. With the likelihood of expanded trade in China, the United States no longer needed economic détente with the Soviet Union. Carter could afford more easily to clash with the Soviets. To silence his domestic critics, therefore, and at the same time demonstrate United States resolve to its allies, the President adopted the contradictory goals of arms limitations and greater military expenditures. He endorsed construction of advanced Trident submarines, pleaded for the mobile MX missile system, and supported the return of compulsory "national service" for men and women. The administration also resurrected the dormant Civil Defense system, calling for doubled appropriations to facilitate the evacuation of major cities. But even these proposals failed to persuade opponents of SALT. Seeking a reevaluation of "deterrence"—the idea that fear of retribution would prevent either power from launching a first attack—conservatives urged the implementation of a strategy capable of destroying Soviet missiles. Paired with a civil defense program that could protect American citizens from counterattack, such a scheme challenged the very essence of SALT, threatened to restore only a balance of terror.

The taut era before détente, symbolized by the Cuban Missile Crisis of 1962, assumed special relevance in 1979 when, in a curious replay of events seventeen years earlier, American intelligence reported the presence of a Soviet combat brigade in Cuba.

Carter quickly called the situation "unacceptable" and pleaded with the Soviet Union to make some token retreat. But when the Soviets refused, the President merely assured a television audience "that the brigade issue is certainly no reason for a return to the cold war." For conservatives, the President's willingness to tolerate the presence of Soviet forces in the Western Hemisphere dramatized the decline of United States world leadership. "We stood toe-to-toe with the Soviet Union," objected Senate Minority Leader Howard Baker, "and, unlike 1962, we blinked instead of the Russians."

CARTER'S DETERMINATION to assert American hegemony by peaceful means produced the most extraordinary diplomatic triumph of his administration—a peace treaty ending thirty years of warfare between Egypt and Israel. Taking advantage of Egyptian leader Anwar Sadat's willingness to confer directly with Israeli Prime Minister Menachem Begin, Carter invited the two leaders to a summit conference in September 1978 at Camp David. After thirteen days of intensive conversations, the three heads of state presented the world with "A Framework for Peace," heralded as the first step toward stabilizing power in the Middle East. Overnight Carter's rating in public opinion polls soared, the only significant interruption in what otherwise appeared as an endless decline.

Despite great fanfare, however, the arrangements left considerable unfinished business, not the least of which concerned the status of the Palestinian refugees and the legitimacy of the Palestine Liberation Organization. Even the staunch American ally, Saudi Arabia, the main supplier of oil to the United States, was outraged by the exclusion of Palestinian negotiators. To mollify the Saudis, Carter sent substantial military aid to North Yemen, a buffer state between Soviet-supported South Yemen and the Saudi border. Sensitive to the power of the pro-Israel lobby, however, the President refused to press for Israel's withdrawal from occupied territory. In an embarrassing showdown in the United Nations Security Council, the United States voted to condemn Israel, but the next day apologized for the "error" and reversed its stand. Supporters of both sides were indignant.

"We have no illusions," said Carter after signing a second accord with Sadat and Begin in March 1979, "—we have hopes, dreams, prayers, yes—but no illusions." In an attempt to bridge the stalemate, UN Ambassador Young initiated secret talks with a PLO representative. But revelation of the meeting, followed by Young's disingenuous denial, raised a storm of protest, which forced the ambassador to resign; "a scapegoat for the entire muddled mess in the Middle East," protested Shirley Chisholm. Though Carter had managed to forge a solid alliance with Egypt and Israel, obtaining added leverage in that tempestuous part of the world, a general peace eluded his grasp. Having failed by mid-1979 to persuade either Egypt or Israel to meet with the PLO, a government official admitted that "the credibility of the United States is eroding."

The frustrations of American policy in the Middle East reflected an inability to understand, much less encourage, the forces of revolutionary nationalism outside the context of the cold war, a myopia that soon undermined United States interests in the Persian Gulf. Despite the rhetoric of human rights, the Carter administration preferred to overlook State Department reports of violations committed by the government of the Shah against so-called "terrorists." "Because of the great leadership of the Shah," the President toasted his ally on New Year's Eve 1977, Iran was "an island of stability in one of the more troubled areas of the world." Following the policies of Nixon and Ford, Carter allowed Iran to receive the largest quantities of American arms with sales amounting to $15 billion between 1974 and 1978. So supportive was Carter of the Shah that the administration forbade American intelligence agents to establish contact with Iranian dissidents, lest their presence imply a weakening of the regime.

The eruption of revolutionary violence in Iran in 1978 caused no shift in Carter's policies. In public statements, he reiterated support for the Shah and authorized the continuation of the sale of arms and crowd-control equipment. As a show of strength, the President ordered a task force to sail in the Persian Gulf. But three days later, he countermanded the order. "We've learned our lessons the hard way," he said, "in Vietnam." Meanwhile, the State Department tried to instigate a military coup to ensure emergence of a friendly regime, but seriously underestimated the strength of the revolution. Nor could the United States protect American citizens from the harassment of crowds. Bell Helicopter employees in Teheran began wearing T-shirts emblazoned with bullet holes; KEEP A LOW PROFILE, they read. Not until January 1979 did the administration accept the inevitability of change, persuading the Shah to surrender his peacock throne.

Carter's prolonged support of the Shah undermined the possibility of accommodation with the new regime. Quickly the United States lost access to Iranian oil and saw the cancellation of $7 billion of uncompleted arms contracts, a serious blow to the balance of payments. The United States also surrendered sensitive listening posts used to monitor Soviet missiles, raising questions about the ability to verify the new SALT treaty. Within Iran, anti-American tempers continued to erupt. On Valentine's Day 1979, revolutionary forces in Teheran overran the United States embassy, seizing seventy employees. But other soldiers, loyal to the Ayatollah Khomeini, ended the siege after two hours. "There is no way we could get those people out by using force," admitted a White House official. "We just have to wheedle them out the best we can." Unable to protect American lives, the State Department prepared to evacuate the seven thousand Americans remaining in Iran. "This is a volatile world," concluded Senator Church, chairman of the Foreign Relations Committee. "The thing we must learn is that the U.S. can live with a great deal of change and upheaval. But the one thing we can't do is stabilize it. There's no way to put a lid on it."

While relations between the United States and Iran deteriorated, the Shah basked in exile in the Bahamas, visited frequently by associates of David Rockefeller and Henry Kissinger, who urged the administration to give the former ally refuge. "The 10,000 Iranian students in the U.S. make this a rather less safe place than other countries," explained one government official. "How would you like it," replied another in May 1979, "if the U.S. mission in Teheran were taken hostage and held in return for the Shah? It might make good copy, but it would also make for a hell of a tough decision."

Five months later, the fantasy turned to nightmare. When the President, responding to Rockefeller pressure, finally agreed to allow the Shah to enter the United States for a gall bladder operation, militants in Iran seized the American embassy, captured sixty hostages, and demanded the repatriation of the Shah and his fortune. Showing contempt for international laws that had protected diplomats even in major conflagrations, the militants threatened their captives with death, paraded them blindfolded in scenes that would reappear on American television screens for a year. "Death to Carter," chanted the angry crowds.

"My initial reaction," said Carter, "is to do something." But "none of us would want to do anything that would worsen the danger in which our fellow Americans have been placed." Frustrated by the impotence of government, citizens vented their rage by attacking Iranian students, burning Iranian flags, and boycotting Iranian products. NO MORE IRANIAN STUDENTS WILL BE PERMITTED ON THESE PREMISES, read a sign posted on the Mustang Ranch, a bordello near Reno, UNTIL THE HOSTAGES ARE RELEASED. The crisis instilled a new sense of patriotism as Americans closed ranks behind the President. According to a Gallup poll, Carter's approval ratings jumped from 30 percent to 61 percent in the four weeks after the capture of the embassy.

While the nation poised for action, the administration worked to soothe public passion. "It is a time not for rhetoric," advised Secretary Vance, "but for quiet, careful and firm diplomacy." But appeals to the United Nations, to the World Court, to American allies throughout the world, brought no relief. To eliminate economic pressure, the administration clamped an embargo on imported Iranian oil and to prevent the removal of Iranian assets from Rockefeller's Chase Manhattan Bank, it froze Iranian deposits. There the matter rested. "It would not be possible, or even advisable," Carter told a press conference one week before he announced his candidacy for reelection, "for me to set a deadline about when, or if, I would take certain action in the future."

Carter's credibility now hinged on the patience of the American people, their willingness to accept the limits of American power. "If one works for years at becoming a pitiful, helpless giant," observed former Energy Secretary James Schlesinger in a paraphrase of Nixon's plea on the eve of the Cambodia invasion, "one might just succeed. It all goes back to the retreat and rout of American foreign policy in recent years. Wild as he is, the Ayatollah Khomeini would not have touched the Soviet Embassy." Harkening to Carter's cold war metaphors, Americans recoiled from this vision of global impotence—and wondered, too, how it all had happened.

PART THREE

THE SEARCH FOR COMMUNITY

13

"TO HEAL THE FRAGMENTATIONS"

Redefining Authority at Mid-Decade

Public distrust of the political leadership represented only the tip of a massive iceberg of discontent. A national opinion survey of 1975 showed that 69 percent of the respondents felt that "over the last ten years, this country's leaders have consistently lied to the people." These suspicions implicated all the major institutions of American society. A Harris poll revealed that between 1966 and 1976, public confidence in the medical establishment dropped from 73 to 42 percent; for major companies from 55 percent to 16 percent (advertising agencies fell to 7 percent); the credibility of lawyers slid to 12 percent. "The social incentives to deceit are at present very powerful," concluded Sissela Bok in her seminal book, *Lying*. "Many individuals feel caught up in practices they cannot change."

The problems of confidence and credibility extended far beyond questions of willful dishonesty, touched the most basic foundations of American culture. The loss of faith in doctors and lawyers, the skepticism about corporate leaders, the omnipresent distrust of politicians—all produced a spreading disillusionment about the competence of the dominant institutions of society. More seriously—and more ominously—these doubts also nurtured a belief that powerful and entrenched groups, in order to perpetuate their positions and values, offered only the most limited visions of the shape and stuff of human existence, of the nature and meaning of ultimate reality. By the mid-seventies, this crisis of confidence leaped quickly from the projections of speculative science to the bastions of education to the definition of life itself.

IN SUBURBAN BOSTON an amateur astronomer, aroused from his house by the predictions of the professionals, peered through a telescope at one of the marvels of the winter sky. "Watergate, then the energy crisis," he moaned, "and now the comet." Heralded as one of the most spectacular events of the century, the comet Kohoutek had fizzled and dimmed. "The Cosmic Flopperoo," hooted Russell Baker in The New York Times, "the Edsel of the firmament." The celestial fiasco presented dramatic proof of the limits of scientific predictability and reinforced what Time magazine called a "deepening disillusionment" with the scientific community. "Too often, as we know from experience," Baker had written earlier, "a new scientific or technological advance means only that it will become easier to exploit, manipulate or exterminate us."

Popular distrust of science, a marked contrast to public optimism of the sixties, supported major cutbacks of government spending for scientific research. As part of the budget pruning of Nixon's second term, the administration slashed appropriations for basic research and development, reserving the bulk of scientific funding for short-term projects such as the cure of cancer and nuclear energy. Nixon also abolished the President's Science Advisory Committee and moved the Office of Science and Technology from the White House to the National Science Foundation. These decisions reflected a simmering conflict between the President and the scientific community over ABMs and SSTs. But Nixon's position, according to several public opinion polls, obtained widespread approval, especially among poorer and less educated segments of the population, groups "most often excluded from the mainstreams of society."

Threatened by budgetary reductions, scientific leaders protested the implications of what Harvard's George Kistiakowsky called "using up our intellectual capital." The prestigious academic journal Daedalus devoted an entire issue to the perilous state of American science, in which Edward Shils suggested "the possibility of a decline of science as a continuously expanding body of knowledge." Such arguments often belied a narrow defense of professionalism. Complaining about a "further decline in the role of scientists in government," the Federation of American Scientists pleaded for a reconsideration of "disinterested expertise." "The general public is not well enough informed about science and technology and their role in our society," explained physicist Hans Bethe, in a polemical defense of nuclear energy. "This allows any number of nuts to dispense misinformation couched in noble rhetoric."

The attack on the scientific establishment involved more than budgetary politics, reached to the core of the scientific method. "There is an essential element in science," conceded physicist Steven Weinberg, "that is cold, objective, and nonhuman." Those values had provided the stuff of popular nightmares for centuries—images of madmen from Doctors Faustus and Frankenstein to Jekyll, Caligari, and Strangelove—practitioners of scientific objectivity who strove to conquer the secrets of the natural world. But the triumph of reason, as it was defined by the scientific professions, provided no explanations of nonrational phenomena—such things as telepathy, extrasensory perception, biofeedback, the occult. "I think present-day reason is an analogue of the flat earth of the medieval period," observed Robert Pirsig in his popular tract, *Zen and the Art of Motorcycle Maintenance.* Conceded MIT physicist Henry Morrison, "Rationality has to include, so to speak, the irrational."

The apotheosis of reason not only allowed vast areas of rationality to remain terra incognita—the belated discovery of Chinese acupuncture, thanks to an emergency appendectomy on *New York Times* writer Harrison Salisbury, on the eve of détente dramatized this deficiency—but also stripped the natural world of ultimate meaning, transformed the mysteries of the universe into detached objects of perception that could be clocked and measured and learned. "He had built empires of scientific capability to manipulate the phenomena of nature into enormous manifestations of his own dreams of power and wealth," wrote Pirsig of the prototypical western man, "—but for this he had exchanged an empire of understanding of equal magnitude: an understanding of what it is to be part of the world, and not an enemy of it."

This assault on the values of the scientific method—reason, detachment, objectivity—raised profound questions about the nature of knowledge and learning, challenged the meaning of education and the professionals who controlled its institutions of distribution. "What we have mistakenly come to think of as 'bodies of knowledge' or 'fields of learning' or 'academic disciplines' or 'school subjects,' " argued educational reformer John Holt, "are not nouns, but *verbs*." Education, in other words, was a process of learning. But professional educators had usurped that function, becoming, in effect, legal monopolies that perpetuated what Ivan Illich called "the hidden curriculum." Through a system of self-certification, he explained, "educators . . . now tell society what must be learned and write off what has been learned outside school." Such controls, he charged, contradicted the goals of a free society. "Next to the right to life itself," wrote Holt, "the most fundamental of all human rights is the right to control our own minds and thoughts. . . . Whoever takes that right away from us, as educators do, attacks the very center of our being."

Lacking such articulate defenses, students relied upon more anarchistic devices to sabotage the educational establishment. According to a Senate report released in April 1975, American youth had precipitated an extraordinary surge of violence and vandalism in the nation's public schools. Between 1970 and 1973, homicides increased 18.5 percent, rapes 40.1 percent, and robberies 36.7 percent. In the previous ten years, crimes against students had escalated 3,000 percent, while attacks on teachers had jumped 7,000 percent. The amount of money spent to repair vandalized school property in 1972 equaled the total annual cost of schoolbooks. "The most serious aspect of vandalism," concluded the Senate investigation of juvenile delinquency, "is the set of messages it conveys: that students look upon the school as alien territory." "It's just that we're not interested in what our folks were interested in," explained a sophomore at a crime-riddled high school in rural Missouri. "Things have changed." "The kids are just fed up," reasoned a junior. "When people get bored, there's trouble."

The crimes of public education, however, also included the obvious failings of the nation's schools. In October 1975, the Office of Education published a four-year study of adult learning abilities which revealed that one-fifth of the adult population—23 million people—lacked sufficient educational competence to function successfully in contemporary society and that an additional one-third—some 40 million people—suffered serious deficiencies in basic skills. For the twelfth consecutive year, the College Entrance

Examination Board reported a decrease in verbal and mathematical aptitude scores, and a national study of writing skills demonstrated further decline. These findings reinforced a landmark decision of the Supreme Court in a civil rights case of 1971, *Griggs v. Duke Power Company*, which held that employers could not establish educational qualifications without proving that such requirements served as a "reasonable measure of job performance." "Diplomas and tests are useful servants," said Chief Justice Burger, "but . . . they are not to become masters of reality." "The embarrassing thing about the Griggs decision," admitted a personnel specialist at the University of Minnesota, "is that we simply do not know how to predict competence in any job really worth having."

The limitations of American secondary education inevitably affected attitudes toward institutions of higher learning. In a nationwide survey of college campuses, Caroline Bird discovered a "prevailing sadness" among students, a malaise she ascribed "to the limited role society has assigned to them." Living in isolation from what they considered "the real world," college students reacted apathetically to a liberal arts tradition that could provide no certainty of career success. In 1974, private colleges reported a significant decrease in applications for admission and even for financial assistance. This decline in college enrollment had immediate consequences for postgraduate education. In 1975, for example, six hundred new Ph.D.'s in American history competed for exactly thirty full-time jobs.

The rise of unemployed college teachers contributed to a major reevaluation of the academic professions and the traditional disciplines they taught. "History is in crisis," announced the executive secretary of the Organization of American Historians in September 1975. After investigating the state of history teaching in the nation's schools, the OAH report concluded that "confidence and interest in history are not nearly as widespread among students, educational administrators and politicians as they were only a few years ago." This trend reflected popular disillusionment with the content of traditional historical study, particularly the reluctance of academics to explore contemporary social issues. "The 'lessons' taught by the American past," lamented historian David Donald, "are today not merely irrelevant but dangerous." In the midst of endemic stagflation, similar problems plagued the field of economics. "Conventional thinking about stabilization policies is inadequate and out of date," Arthur Burns told a university audience. "We must at least be willing to reopen our economic minds."

The loss of confidence in the established professions provoked a major dispute about the quality of the nation's medical care. Frustrated by rising medical costs (10.8 percent in 1974) and unsatisfactory treatment, patients more frequently accused their physicians of malpractice. In one widely publicized case, twenty-two-year-old Gail Kalmowitz received $165,000 for damage to her vision caused by what was considered standard medical procedure when she had been a premature infant. "The cause of the medical malpractice crisis," claimed a leader of the trial lawyers' association, "is malpractice on the part of doctors." Responding to the generosity of juries, the major malpractice insurance companies announced in 1975 a tripling of doctors' premiums and a general cancellation of malpractice policies on July 1.

The medical profession responded by blaming lawyers for instigating needless suits and lobbied the state legislatures for immunity from civil claims. Throughout the country, doctors threatened to discontinue practice. TO MY PATIENTS, read a typical waiting-room sign. I MAY HAVE TO DISCONTINUE PRACTICE ON JULY 1 THIS YEAR. In May 1975, California doctors organized a month-long strike to protest rising insurance costs and slowdowns in health care spread to New York, Texas, and Pennsylvania. As public pressure mounted, however, the nation's largest states proposed the creation of statewide underwriting associations to reduce insurance rates, providing a compromise that the medical profession reluctantly accepted. But, observed New York legislator Abraham Bernstein, "you're doing nothing to curtail malpractice." Malcolm Todd, president of the American Medical Association, agreed that "malpractice is the number one problem that faces the American medical profession." Surveys by the nation's leading medical schools found that 3 to 5 percent of American doctors—some sixteen thousand physicians—were "incompetent." Each year, according to a Cornell University study, patients underwent 2 to 4 million needless operations, which caused some twelve thousand deaths; one-third of all hysterectomies and tonsilectomies probably were unnecessary; one-third of American hospitals lacked adequate facilities for patient safety; and thirty thousand people died each year from faulty prescriptions. According to a Gallup poll, 85 percent of the public desired a rigorous housecleaning within the medical profession. "The time has come," declared Eli Bernzweig, former director of the Federal Commission on Medical Malpractice, in 1976, "to recognize that the root cause of the current malpractice problem is the substantial number of injuries and other adverse results sustained by patients during the course of hospital and medical treatment."

Disillusionment with the medical profession also reflected an expanding sophistication about the complexity of controlling and treating disease. In 1971, an exuberant Congress had passed the National Cancer Act in expectation of a prompt, effective cure. But in the next five years, not only had scientific research failed to produce a miracle treatment, but the incidence of cancer, for both men and women, blacks and whites, had increased annually. Though the American Cancer Society, subsidized by federal funds, continued to search for viral carcinogens, statistical studies suggested that the epidemic of cancer in the United States resulted from environmental changes, specifically the proliferation of industrial pollutants in air, water, and food.

The search for environmental carcinogens implicated powerful segments of the business community, which traditionally pursued profits over safety. In 1974, for example, the Manufacturing Chemists Association belatedly released evidence that showed vinyl chloride, a plastic used in bottling, was linked to human cancer. "Because of the suppression of these data," charged the American Association for the Advancement of Science, "tens of thousands of workers were exposed without warning, for perhaps some two years, to toxic concentrations of vinyl chloride." Similarly, for over forty years the asbestos industry had publicly denied the hazards of exposure to asbestos, despite contrary evidence contained in what journalists dubbed the "Asbestos Pentagon Papers"; yet asbestos caused approximately fifty thousand deaths each year. In February 1974, the contamination of chicken feed by the pesticides aldrin and dieldrin forced the killing of thousands of chickens in Mississippi, but the manufacturer of the toxic chemical, Shell Chemical Company, delayed suspending production until it lost a prolonged court struggle. Such corporate politics, admitted Bendix president W. Michael Blumenthal, prior to his appointment to Carter's cabinet, raised "extremely grave questions about the moral standards or ethical behavior of the business world today."

Growing awareness of the most deadly industrial byproduct, atomic radiation, triggered increased opposition to the proliferation of nuclear reactors. In February 1976, three top-level engineers in the reactor division of General Electric resigned their positions to protest the hazards of nuclear energy. "There is no way you can continue to build plants and operate them without having an accident," declared Richard Hubbard. "The magnitude of the risks," added Dale Bridenbaugh, "have led me to believe there should be no nuclear power." Echoing these sentiments, a top safety officer at a New York nuclear power station publicly denounced existing procedures and resigned in protest. The Nuclear Regulatory Commission emphasized, however, that the charges related to "generic problems that were well known and were matters of public record." But after a vitriolic campaign, California voters overwhelmingly rejected a ballot initiative in June 1976 that would have blocked the development of nuclear power in that state, and a series of similar laws also failed in several other states in the fall elections.

Objections to nuclear development, dormant since the megaton rumblings of the early sixties, reflected an abiding dread of mass annihilation. "Neither the nuclear bomb nor the nuclear reactor," observed Barry Commoner, "can be excused by postulating the acceptability of the other." The fear of imminent holocaust swam in the undercurrents of the culture, surfacing unexpectedly in disaster movies or in ghastly wit. "Still obsessed by thoughts of death," wrote Woody Allen, "I brood constantly. I keep wondering if there is an afterlife and if there is will they be able to break a twenty?" Such anxieties expressed a pervasive sense of alienation from the life process. "Life does end," remarked journalist Gail Sheehy. "Each of us travels alone. No one else can always keep us safe."

The fear of death, long repressed in American culture, emerged in the seventies as a topic of popular discussion. In her widely read book, *On Death and Dying*, Elisabeth Kübler-Ross described specific stages of awareness—from denial and anger to ultimate acceptance—by which terminally ill patients confronted the inevitability of death. "A patient reaches a point when death comes as a great relief," she explained. "Patients die easier if they are allowed and helped to detach themselves slowly from all the meaningful relationships in their [lives]." This image of death as "a natural process" mirrored a rising sensitivity to the ecology of the human body, viewing it more as an interrelated organism than as a machine that abruptly broke down. "Death is not a sudden-all-at-once affair," suggested biologist Lewis Thomas. "Cells go down in sequence, one by one. . . . It takes hours, even days, before the irreversible word finally gets around to all the provinces."

These philosophical considerations influenced a fundamental reassessment of the meaning of life and death in American society. In 1975, the Roman Catholic parents of a twenty-two-year-old comatose patient named Karen Ann Quinlan sued her physician to disconnect an artificial respirator to allow their daughter to die "with grace and dignity." "The time had come," stated the patient's father, "to face the fact that death is part of life, it's going to happen to all of us, and there's no sense in hiding it under the rug anymore." But the trial judge insisted that the young woman was still alive. "The hope of recovery is remote," he admitted, "but no doctor talks in the absolute." In an age of organ transplants and technological innovation, the medical profession could no longer determine the time, or even the nature, of human death. By 1978, however, eighteen states had enacted legislation that proclaimed "brain death"—the cessation of meaningful brain waves—rather than stoppage of heartbeat or breathing as a legal definition of the end of life. Responding to these changes, an appeals court reversed the Quinlan decision, authorizing physicians to disconnect the artificial respirator. Karen Ann Quinlan then commenced to breathe spontaneously. But she lived in what was called a "persistent vegetative state" (a condition which has persisted to the present, 1981). "She's been returned to nature," explained the family priest. "So if she dies of . . . some infection, it's really nature unfolding."

THE LEGAL, MEDICAL, AND PHILOSOPHICAL uncertainty about so elemental a phenomenon as death illuminated a remarkable uneasiness about the basic traditions of Western civilization. Loss of confidence in professional elites and entrenched institutions—doubts about medicine, academia, science, and metaphysics—all left an enormous vacuum of values at the center of American culture.

Even the traditional paragons of American virtue—the heroes

of sport—rebuffed established stereotypes and values. During the sixties, football coach Vince Lombardi had developed a cult of competitive discipline—his motto, Winning Isn't Everything; It Is the Only Thing, hung proudly in Republican party headquarters during the Watergate-tinged campaign of 1972—but by the seventies a new breed of athlete emerged to glorify more relaxed values. As entertainment celebrities, stars such as quarterback Joe Namath exceeded their professional salaries by endorsing cosmetics and accessories and could afford to ignore traditional restraints. Headliners like baseball's Billy Martin and Reggie Jackson clashed openly with management, and sports announcer Howard Cosell rose in the ratings through irreverent commentary. In 1974, Henry Aaron surpassed Babe Ruth's all-time home-run record, but found himself embroiled in a nasty dispute with the commissioner of baseball over his right to choose when to play. "I should've been given the privilege of deciding for myself," maintained the usually phlegmatic slugger. Challenging management's control of player trades, major league baseball players successfully boycotted spring training in 1976 until they gained revisions of the standard contract.

The style of the new professionals was epitomized by world heavyweight boxing champion Muhammad Ali. Flamboyant, outspoken, a critic of the establishment, the Vietnam war, even Christianity, which he rejected for the Moslem religion, Ali jeered, "I am the greatest." But in March 1975, an eighth-ranked palooka named Chuck Wepner, aka "the Bayonne Bleeder," scored a surprising knockdown and almost went the distance against the champion. Inspired by the near upset, filmwriter Sylvester Stallone transformed a streetwise ethnic named Rocky Balboa ("the Italian Stallion") into a contender against Ali look-alike Apollo Creed, in the 1976 Academy Award–winning film *Rocky*. As the white ethnic underdog staggered through fifteen rounds of punishment, movie audiences erupted in frenzied cheers for what critic Andrew Sarris called "the most romanticized Great White Hope in screen history." "When they're cheering for Rocky," said Stallone, "they're cheering for themselves." The winner of the fight, nevertheless, was Apollo Creed!

The frustration of fantasy stimulated a desperate quest for connection that seemed equally futile. In the film *Nashville*, a work director Robert Altman called "my metaphor for America," twenty-four peripatetic characters search vainly for human contact. "What this country needs," intones a fictional third-party candidate modeled on George Wallace, "is some monosyllable answers." But when a peculiar young man shoots the star singer, a huge country-and-western audience finds solace in endless refrains of "It Don't Worry Me." Off the screen, the same search for companionship promoted a boom in citizens' band (CB) radio broadcasting. Between 1974 and 1977, CB sales approached 25 million sets as anonymous callers developed a new language based on locating friendly communicants and identifying potentially hostile authorities—the police, known as "smokies." "The voices are nasal and tinny," observed fiction writer John Sayles, "broken by squawks, something human squeezed through wire."

"The whole world is just becoming like a bad connection," said the most depressed and most popular television character of the 1976 season, Norman Lear's Mary Hartman. In a funky parody of the hopelessness of daytime soap operas, "Mary Hartman, Mary Hartman" brushed against a counterfeit world that all too realistically captured the tone of America at mid-decade. Frustrated by a collapse of moral authority—by a minister who cheats on his wife and carries a bottle of booze in a hollowed Bible; a doctor who confuses a pregnancy test; a shyster lawyer falsifying a malpractice suit; a psychologist without a morsel of compassion—the Hartman family circle experienced the absurdities of a world without meaning. "The hardest decision I have to make each day," admitted Grandpa Larkin, a geriatric exhibitionist, "is whether to play checkers in the park or go down to the Safeway and watch them unload melons."

Broadcast on nonnetwork television stations, "Mary Hartman" competed successfully with the late-night news shows. "You can always find something on the evening news to take your mind off life," explained Mary's slightly dazed mother. Viewers readily confused the characters with real personalities ("You must have planted a microphone under my kitchen table," wrote one fan) and sent letters of advice to the actors, a blurring of roles that reached bizarre proportions when the star of the series, actress Louise Lasser, defended herself against charges of cocaine possession by claiming that the strain of performance had produced confusion between Hartman's character and her own! Observed the television critic of the *Boston Herald American*, "there is something sick, sick and twisted, twisted about 'Mary Hartman, Mary Hartman.' "

The predicaments described by the pseudosituation comedy mirrored the plight of millions of other Americans trapped in what came to be known as the "midlife crisis." "The constant revision of moral standards and social rules," explained popular anthropologists Nena and George O'Neill, "has left some . . . people with a sense of paralysis." Traditional psychology, based on nineteenth-century assumptions about human nature and society, presumed the stability of adult identity and could offer little guidance for mature conflicts. Therapists turned increasingly to the work of C. G. Jung, whose theories of adult psychology stressed the dilemmas of maturity. Seeking more contemporary sources, Yale University's David Levinson launched an intensive investigation of the development of adult males. "The life structure evolves through a relatively orderly sequence during the adult years," he concluded, a regular oscillation between stable periods and times of major upheaval. Popularized by Gail Sheehy's best-selling book *Passages,* the very predictability of adult transitions offered a modicum of stability. "Times of crises . . . are not only predictable," she averred, "but desirable. They mean growth."

The commonness of psychological stress explained a surge of interest among Americans in a veritable alphabet soup of therapeutic movements and growth programs—including aikido, Arica, bioenergetics, Erhard Seminar Training (est), Feldenkreis exercises, Gestalt, humanistic psychology, primal scream, Silva mind control, transcendental meditation (TM), yoga, and Zen—a vast array of choices that together formed the "human potential movement." A Gallup survey of 1976 found that approximately nineteen million Americans participated in TM, yoga, charismatic religion, mysticism, and Asian religions. (Mary Hartman's group was called STET, an acronym for Survival Training and Existence Therapy, but also the printer's term for leaving things as they are.) These diverse, often overlapping activities shared a commitment to individual transcendence—the liberation of the self from ego conflicts and institutional restraint as a way of attaining expanded consciousness. Self-knowledge, they suggested, established the basis for a new cosmic awareness.

The extraordinary popularity of the new psychotherapies represented only the secularized dimension of a nationwide spiritual outpouring, equivalent to a major religious revival. After nearly two decades of steady decline, weekly church attendance of adults in the United States increased in 1976 from 40 percent to 42 percent and remained at 41 percent in subsequent years. A series of Gallup polls also found that the proportion of people believing that religion was becoming more influential in American society increased from 14 percent in 1970 to 44 percent in 1976. Sixty-five percent of the population expressed confidence in organized religion, higher than any other institution of American society. It was "a time of religious awakening," proclaimed historian Theodore Roszak. "From all sides," agreed religion scholar Walter Capps, "there is a prospect that something has been born among us that is genuinely new."

The rising enthusiasm for religion ironically coincided with—indeed, may well have been caused by—major desertions from the established denominations. A survey of religious opinion in the San Francisco area in 1973, for example, revealed that one quarter of the respondents chose no religious identity in preference to the affiliations of their parents. The established Protestant churches that were closely linked to other entrenched institutions—Episcopalians, Congregationalists, Methodists, and Presbyterians—suffered significant losses of membership, particularly on college campuses. The defection rate among Roman Catholics reached epidemic proportions, following the liberalization of the liturgy in the sixties along with refusal to alter traditional teachings on birth control. "The Catholic church finally decided to recognize the values of the modern world," noted University of California sociologist Robert Bellah, "just when American young people were beginning to find it valueless." With the introduction of fashionable ceremonies—"Hootenanny masses," lay communions, and altar girls—participation in the mass and baptism declined, while the number of apostasies among priests and nuns soared into the thousands. In 1973, only 27 percent of Catholics felt "very sure" while speaking to their children about religious beliefs.

Frustrated by the failure of orthodox religions, Americans pursued alternative spiritualities, in Roszak's words, "to awaken the God who sleeps at the root of our being." Within Christianity, the rise of pentecostal and charismatic movements underscored a growing thirst for religious renewal. Seeking salvation beyond Christian denominationalism, the spiritual quest focused on the ancient traditions of Asia—I Ching, Hare Krishna, yoga, Zen, and Tibetan Buddhism—which denied the validity of the rational intellect and instead stressed the importance of spiritual enlightenment and respect for a sacred presence that permeated the world. "Do you know," taught the youthful guru Maharaj Ji, whose Divine Light Mission attracted twenty thousand devotees to the Houston Astrodome in November 1973, "the devil is the son of man that comes to mind, through mind, from mind."

The distrust of the power of human reason encouraged experiments with a variety of mystical and occult traditions that included astrology, satanism, and witchcraft. Uri Geller, an Israeli psychic, enjoyed wide popularity during a 1975 tour of the United States, in which he mesmerized audiences by stopping watches and bending spoons through alleged telepathic powers. Academic scholars resurrected the occult literature of Rudolf Steiner, George Gurdjieff, and Madame Blavatsky—an esoteric tradition which, with tarot, alchemy, and astrology, claimed to preserve the hidden truths of antiquity. "Nobody who ever talked with a witch or walked with a zombie goes without an attentive audience these days," remarked Roszak with cautious wonder; "the market for supernatural amazements is inexhaustible and infinitely indulgent."

The search for spiritual alternatives provided a large following for numerous charismatic leaders, who seemed to combine religious vision with traditional social values. The Healthy-Happy-Holy Organization (3HO), under the leadership of Yogi Bhajan, proudly flew the American flag in tandem with the banner of Aquarius, promising to restore "a nation whose trust is in God." "Here," stated the holy prophet, "we want to build a nation which we have lost."

"America," echoed the Korean missionary Sun Myung Moon, founder of the Unification Church, "is destined to serve as the Messiah's landing site for the 20th century." Offering a "new future of Christianity," Reverend Moon drew twenty thousand spectators to New York's Madison Square Garden in September 1974 to hear the message "Heaven is quite near."

"I feel changed," exclaimed one of his youthful converts. "I have much more of an inner peace."

Tired of the hypocrisy of established religions, one midwestern preacher led an entire congregation to California to implement the social gospel. Calling themselves the Peoples Temple, parishioners in San Francisco established free meal service for the poor, a medical clinic, a drug rehabilitation program, and child care centers, while actively engaging in local politics for social betterment. Church coffers provided bail money for AIM leader Dennis Banks, donated funds for the families of slain policemen, and contributed to the Hearst ransom fund. "It was radical Christianity," exclaimed one journalist. Asked to describe "the number one problem with the American people today," the minister quickly replied: "Apathy." "Everyone is worried about their own narcissistic problems." Feeling threatened by outside critics, the group followed their prophet to a new Israel in South America, building a community in the Guyana jungle named Jonestown after their leader Jim Jones. But when American officials continued to investigate charges that members were being held against their will, Jones led virtually the entire community, some 916 members, in an apocalyptic ceremony of self-inflicted death. "We committed an act of revolutionary suicide," Jones's voice echoed in a tape-recorded speech, "protesting against the conditions of an inhumane world." In this way, explained psychiatrist Robert Jay Lifton, "the cult would, once and for all, defeat and transcend the evil of the outside world."

THE PROLIFERATION OF religious and secular sects that required as a condition of membership some voluntary surrender of individual free will aroused the fear and antipathy of people accustomed to more conventional expressions of faith. A 1977 Gallup survey found that the Reverend Moon "elicited one of the most overwhelmingly negative responses ever reported by a major national poll." The families of some converts to the Unification Church and Krishna Consciousness even resorted to kidnapping their kin to facilitate "deprogramming." Criticizing "the New Narcissism," journalist Peter Marin attacked the human potential movement as "a retreat from the worlds of morality and history, an unembarrassed denial of human reciprocity and community." Though refusing to attend Werner Erhard's program ("because I have never been able to subject myself to the kind of treatment *est* visits upon its participants, or to listen to the kind of nonsense it offers them"), Marin denounced "a kind of soft fascism: the denial, in the name of higher truth, of the claims of others upon the self."

"It's the Me-Decade," announced Tom Wolfe in *New York* magazine in August 1976.

"Hedonism," "narcissism," "cult of the self," exclaimed Christopher Lasch a few weeks later in an essay in *The New York Review of Books*. (Later its substance would be included in his influential book *The Culture of Narcissism*.)

"Do these exhortations," asked the sociologist Daniel Bell, "add up to anything more than a longing for the lost gratifications of an idealized childhood?"

The attack on the new spiritualism, largely the work of established journalists and academics, intensified the problems surrounding the crisis of faith. Though critics enthusiastically documented, in Lasch's words, "a way of life that is dying—the culture of competitive individualism," they expressed little interest in what they conceded might be "the signs of new life." "Narcissism," insisted Lasch, "holds the key to the consciousness movement and to the moral climate of contemporary society." Such conclusions oversimplified the alternatives. "The popular media . . . judge the entire 'consciousness circuit' by its worst excesses of silly self-indulgence and commercial opportunism," protested Roszak. "*All* meditation is cast in the mold of TM— high-priced and easy do; *all* spiritual leaders are portrayed as incipient fascist masters; *all* religious disciples are lumped together with mindless *Moonies*."

Critics of the new consciousness also presented a view of recent American history that was peculiarly unhistorical. Emphasizing the discontinuity between the political protests of the Vietnam era and the prevailing spiritual malaise, establishment commentators introduced the tidy distinctions of decades—the violent sixties versus the narcissistic seventies—to explain the contemporary mood. "After the political turmoil of the sixties," wrote Lasch in a typical statement, "Americans have returned to purely personal preoccupations." Though Lasch lamented the loss of a sense of history, the separation of decades suggested a corollary message that helped to explain its happy acceptance: social protest, it implied, belonged safely to the past. This sense of historical disjunction thus served to uphold the existing social arrangements.

Despite the cynicism of its critics, however, the consciousness revolution of the seventies involved a quest not simply for personal salvation, but more fundamentally for a sense of cosmic connection. "The plants, the whales, the stars, institutions, sanity," explained former New Left activist Michael Rossen in 1973; "all call on us to discard our old impressions of them." Rejecting a world view that placed preeminence on the human condition— rationality, individualism, objectivity—the new cosmology attempted, as philosopher Jacob Needleman observed, "to heal the fragmentations and divisions that separate man from nature, man from man and man from God." It involved, said Roszak, "the search—at once both desperate and gleeful—for a new reality principle to replace the waning authority of science and industrial necessity."

Flourishing outside the established mainstream, proponents of the new consciousness denied the allegations of narcissism and selfishness—asserted their very opposites: the innocence of human nature and its ability to nourish communities that transcended the meaninglessness of the existing social order. "Each living being is a swirl in the flow, a formal turbulence, a 'song,'" wrote Gary Snyder in the introduction to his 1975 Pulitzer Prize-winning volume of poetry *Turtle Island.* "Anglos, Black people, Chicanos, and others beached up on these shores all share such views at the deepest levels of their cultural traditions. . . . Hark again to those roots, to see our ancient solidarity, and then to the work of being together."

14

"ON THE BOTTOM"

The Cultures of Outgroups

THE CRISIS OF FAITH PERCOLATED through the entire structure of society. But the consequences of institutional failure—the inflation of living costs and the decline of the quality of services—spread unevenly, affecting most grievously those social groups that were traditionally vulnerable to economic decline. Although the majority of the poor in the United States were whites, racial minorities constituted a disproportionate share of people living in poverty. In 1977, 8.9 percent of whites were officially classified as poor; but 22.4 percent of Hispanics and 31.3 percent of blacks lived below the poverty line. Women and young people of all races also faced exceptional economic and social problems. "We are on the bottom," declared black sociologist Harry Edwards. "If America falls, it will fall on us."

AMERICAN INDIANS

While the rising cost of energy played havoc with the economy, ironically the poorest of Americans hoped to profit by the diminished resources. For centuries, American Indians had been pushed into the least valuable lands—until, in the seventies, the energy crisis awakened public awareness to the value of underground reserves. Beneath the arid surfaces rested 5 percent of the nation's untapped oil and natural gas, 25 to 40 percent of United States uranium, and as much as one-third of the western coal. "We want

to contribute to meeting America's goals of energy independence," assured Navajo leader Peter MacDonald, "but America
will not be permitted to march to that goal as it marched to the
Pacific—over the backs of this country's native peoples." "We ask
now quietly and constructively," said MacDonald in the week that
Carter proclaimed the "moral equivalent of war." "We will not
ask much longer; we will withhold future growth at any sacrifice if
that is necessary to survival."

The awarding of mineral leases to large energy companies, a
legal responsibility of the Bureau of Indian Affairs, provided the
reservation tribes with paltry royalties—an average of twelve cents
per ton of coal, for example—which enabled corporations to reap
huge profits while exhausting the Indians' capital reserves. Determined to halt this economic invasion, the Northern Cheyennes of
Montana initiated a precedent-breaking suit in 1973 and won the
right to suspend and renegotiate mineral allocations. In 1977, the
courts upheld a similar decision by the Crow people, and these
legal victories emboldened the Navajo of the Southwest to obtain
new leases, which brought higher cash returns as well as additional
employment for tribal members. The mineral-rich tribes, taking
OPEC as their model, formed in 1975 the Council of Energy
Reserve Tribes (CERT), an alliance of twenty-five tribes to assure
"prudent management" of economic development. Snubbed by
the Carter administration, CERT chairman MacDonald opened
direct negotiations with OPEC in 1977, which prompted the
federal government to reverse its policy. With government grants,
CERT began a comprehensive inventory of native American reserves, trained Indians in energy management, and offered technical assistance to the separate tribes.

The assertion of native American control over mineral wealth
was paralleled by an aggressive defense of treaty rights by tribes
throughout the nation. In Maine, the Passamaquoddy and Pe-
nobscot tribes laid claim to 12.5 million acres seized illegally in the
nineteenth century and agreed in 1978 to settle for $37 million
and the right to expand their reservations by one hundred thousand acres. The Chumash of California staged a three-day protest
to prevent gas development on the sacred lands at Point Conception, winning the right to monitor excavations and protect burial
grounds. A series of legal cases in 1979 required Rhode Island to
return eighteen hundred acres to the Narragansetts; awarded the

Sioux $17 million plus interest, totaling over $100 million, for "dishonorable dealing" in the acquisition of the sacred Black Hills in South Dakota; guaranteed the fishing rights of the Chippewa and Ottawa on the Great Lakes; and assured that the tribes of the Pacific Northwest could control half the annual fish catch of Puget Sound. "The only real question in most of these claims," commented John Echo Hawk of the Native American Rights Fund, "is quantifying the claims."

Such optimism about legal victories underestimated the force of a powerful white backlash. In 1976, the General Accounting Office of Congress reported a startling program of sophisticated genocide by the Indian Health Service—the sterilization of thousands of American Indian women, estimated as high as one-quarter of the native American female population, without consent. "They took away our past with a sword and our land with a pen," protested one woman. "Now they're trying to take away our future with a scalpel." Other government agencies, such as the FBI, continued to harass militant Indians, and the Justice Department's Law Enforcement Assistance Administration listed AIM as one of the five most dangerous groups in the United States.

The growing economic importance of native American rights intensified white resistance to treaty claims. In 1976, businessmen, ranchers, commercial fishermen, resort owners, sportsmen, and many non-Indian residents of reservation land joined forces in the Interstate Congress for Equal Rights and Responsibilities to challenge tribal control of American Indian property. Criticizing government "handouts," anti-Indian groups advocated termination of the government's reservation policy; they argued that "all citizens should bear equally the responsibilities and burdens of citizenship." Sympathetic congressmen from the western states responded to such pressure by introducing legislation to limit American Indian claims and encourage assimilation. Fearful of offending western voters, most of whom supported Ford in 1976, the Carter administration also refused to endorse native American interests.

The emergence of a white backlash together with the resurgence of American Indian aspirations for economic development aggravated a persistent internal conflict between American Indian traditionalists who were determined to preserve tribal customs, and assimilationists who advocated the rapid acceptance of mainstream values. "The coal can stay just where it is until they find a way to get it out without wrecking everything else," said Cheyenne president Allen Rowland in suspending strip-mining operations. "We need progress. . . . But we're against the kind of progress that comes in and takes everything you have and leaves you with big holes in the ground." "A tribe is a people who live together in a special way," explained a Crow Indian. "You don't do that in a coal pit."

On the Navajo reservation, smoke pollution caused by coal-burning power plants devastated the landscape. "My sheep are dying," lamented one woman. "Their noses bleed. The baby goats do not grow up. . . . This is the biggest, baddest disease ever visited on mankind." In 1978, the tribal council rejected a new coal gasification plant. Equally serious were the environmental and health problems caused by mining uranium. The dumping of radioactive tailings, according to a Department of Energy report of 1978, doubled the risk of lung cancer for nearby residents. "It's more than a matter of continued exploitation of our remaining land and resources," objected John Redhouse. "It's also an issue of spiritual and physical genocide." Modernization also threatened traditional values. "In a generation, the resources will be played out," warned Redhouse, "and you'll have a few native American sheiks and an impoverished mass."

To dramatize the peril, American Indian activists commenced "the Longest Walk," in 1978, a five-month three-thousand-mile protest march from San Francisco to Washington, D.C. "We are here," stated AIM's Clyde Bellecourt, "to let America know that everything hasn't been given away, that everything hasn't been stolen from us, that we are still a way of life that survives." Endorsed by the congressional black and Hispanic caucuses, American Indian protesters lobbied against eleven "anti-Indian" bills that challenged water, hunting, and fishing rights as well as a National Equal Opportunity Act designed to terminate all treaty relations. But they succeeded only in winning passage of the American Indian Religious Freedom Act, which protected from government interference certain spiritual practices, such as the use of peyote and the transportation of sacred objects.

This assertion of American Indian spiritual rights represented part of a larger rebirth of native American culture. "Forty years ago," remarked a Crow college professor, "Indians would deny their religions because they didn't want to be persecuted. But now, Crow grandparents are teaching their children the old ways." Seeking to break the cycle of dependence on government policy, AIM established "survival schools" to transmit cultural traditions and the basic skills of hunting, fishing, and sacred purification. "I put my life on the line for Indian pride at Wounded Knee," explained Lorelei Means, whose school in Rapid City, South Dakota, promised an alternative to reservation education. "We teach . . . that Indians are fighting for their survival as people. . . . Our kids will grow up proud to be Indian." "When the energy crisis closes the Safeway store," added AIM's Bellecourt, "our children will be able to survive."

The renaissance of American Indian culture required a vigilant rejection of assimilationist temptations. The publication of Ruth Beebe Hill's best-selling novel, *Hanta Yo*, in 1979, purportedly an authentic dramatization of native American history, brought cries of protest from American Indian scholars who denounced its celebration of white values of individualism. By contrast, native American Leslie Marmon Silko offered *Ceremony*, a lyrical novel about the dangers of assimilation and the native American's respect for community and the balance of nature. "We shall learn all these devices the white man has," promised a Northern Cheyenne newspaper. "We shall master his machinery, his inventions, his skills, his medicine, his planning. But we'll retain our beauty and still be Indian!"

ASIANS AND LATIN AMERICANS

While American Indians struggled to retain their identity, ethnic communities from Asia were reinforced by a rising tide of new immigration from the Philippines, Korea, China, and, especially after 1975, Indochina. This influx complicated the problems of cultural assimilation. Although Chinese Americans enjoyed relative prosperity, many remained unhappily trapped in residential ghettos, such as San Francisco's Chinatown. Fewer than 8 percent, according to a 1980 study, found their lives "very interesting, very enjoyable, very full, very rewarding or very hopeful." Despite continued contact with Chinese culture, American Chinese, as Maxine Hong Kingston's prizewinning book, *The Woman Warrior*, suggested, felt a strong attraction toward mainstream American values. Japanese Americans, with strong assimilationist traditions, maintained less contact with their homeland, largely because prosperity in Japan contributed to a decline of immigration. But newcomers from Korea, the Philippines, and Indochina (including more than half a million refugees admitted after 1975) found severe economic deprivation that was aggravated by language barriers and the residual anger of the Vietnam war. "They paid me $314 a month to kill them," protested one veteran, ignoring the political distinctions among Vietnamese, "and now they're taking my tax money to get them on their feet here."

Latin American ethnics, far more populous than Asians, experienced similar problems interacting with the dominant culture. Like Asians, they came from diverse backgrounds—Cuba, Puerto Rico, Central America, primarily Mexico as well as the Chicano Southwest. But despite these obvious cultural differences, government officials usually lumped them together as "Hispanics." "The dominant cultural group will have to understand the nuances of differences," admonished Luisa Ezqueno of San Francisco. "To the Anglo, we may all look alike . . . , but it doesn't work that way." Differences in language and culture often excluded Spanish-speaking ethnics from the mainstream, though by the late seventies more Latinos had penetrated the middle class and adopted its conventional life-style. But many Latinos explicitly rejected that alternative and announced a preference for an autonomous culture.

Most numerous of the Latino cultures—and consequently the most politically influential—were the Mexican Americans who comprised about ten million people, not counting the "undocumented aliens" who contributed perhaps another ten million. With a relatively young population and a resultant high birth rate, together with about four hundred thousand legal immigrants each year and an equal number of illegal aliens, Chicano population growth far exceeded national averages. The economic status of Hispanics—the official differences between the various Latino groups were not statistically significant—reflected the problems of cultural disenfranchisement. Unemployment rates remained 45 percent higher than that of whites, slightly better than the statistics for blacks. Hispanic men working full time earned 71 percent of the white male rate; Hispanic women, more likely to be unemployed than men, also concentrated in lower-paying jobs and earned only 86 percent of the white female rate.

Concerned about the economic consequences of illegal immigration, the Carter administration presented a program to stem the flow in 1977. Under the plan, the administration offered amnesty to all illegal aliens who arrived before 1970, promised conditional right-to-work privileges (but no welfare) for immigrants before 1977, and proposed a toughening of the border patrol to prevent further violations. But the White House ignored the deep sense of community among Chicanos. "It's an attack on all Spanish-speaking, brown-skinned people," protested a union organizer of undocumented workers. "Let's stop the whole racist game of talking about an amnesty that's going to make slaves and second-class citizens out of undocumented workers," argued the chairman of the Committee on Chicano Rights. "If they're good enough to work then they're good enough to have some rights."

"Sure, some of them are as unruly, dishonest and immoral as some of their American neighbors," wrote John Ehrlichman, who had met many illegal aliens in prison. "But most of them are quality people." When the White House plan languished in Congress, Carter accepted political defeat, saying "It's more complicated than the SALT talks."

Although Mexican Americans remained economically deprived and politically fragmented, Chicanos asserted a sense of cultural autonomy with renewed vigor. Chicano wall art—ranging from spray-painted slogans of machismo to elaborate murals of cosmic suffering—portrayed, in the words of artist Willie Herron, "the tear of two cultures, the feeling of violence and the feeling of being ripped apart by them." In 1978, Luis Valdez's theater production *Zoot Suit*, a bold affirmation of Chicano identity, set attendance records in Los Angeles. "Fight back," snaps the mythic hero El Pachuco. "Show the world a Chicano has balls. Stand up to them with some style."

This celebration of male culture concealed a burgeoning feminist movement among Chicanas. Finding inspiration not in the Anglo women's movement, but within a Chicana tradition, feminists redefined machismo as an expression of cultural independence. "We are no longer going to stand around and pray that things will be better for us than they were for our mothers," insisted a Mexican American student. "Now we are organizing and demanding what is rightfully ours alongside our Chicano men." Despite such assertions, however, Chicanas remained subject to what they perceived as "triple oppression": victimized as women, Chicanas, and also by their own men, earning less than males, attaining lower educational levels, and acquiring fewer benefits from affirmative action programs. But the problems of machismo, they suggested, were inseparable from the larger cultural dilemma. "Underneath all that bravado," noted Angela de Hoyos in her poem "Words Unspoken":

> quakes a hopeless desperado
> who longs to win a battle
> now and then.

The cultural isolation of Chicanos reinforced a sense of identity. "*Chicanismo* reflects a deep, perhaps irreparable alienation of Mexican Americans from Anglo-American society," observed a Chicano political scientist. "The naïve trust of the past has been replaced with cynicism, frustration and intense anger." The separation from assimilationist influences also encouraged positive affirmation of a unique Chicano vision. "Chicanos are singing," remarked poet Sergio Elizondo, "singing and revealing the reality of our lives and our artistic presence that we have always kept relatively hidden." From this spirit emerged a new optimism about the future. "We are tired of being taken for granted and treated like aliens in our own land," asserted a Chicano politician in California. "But we're in a new era. . . . The next decade is the era of the Chicano."

BLACK AMERICANS

The expectations of Chicanos contrasted with the bleak mood within the black community. On the tenth anniversary of the 1968 Kerner commission report, public opinion surveys showed that whites perceived themselves increasingly tolerant of blacks and comfortable with racial equality. In a reversal of divine revelation, for example, the Mormon church ended a 148-year-old policy by opening the priesthood to "all worthy male members . . . without regard for race or color." Stressing the rise of a black middle class, University of Chicago sociologist William Julius Wilson argued in a controversial book, *The Declining Significance of Race*, that racial prejudice no longer explained the problems of black poverty and that the major conflicts stemmed from inequalities among blacks. A dramatic increase in the number of black elected officials (from 103 in 1964 to 1,469 in 1970 to 4,311 in 1977) and the proliferation of black professional and business groups testified to notable occupational advancement. But a majority of blacks denied any progress in eliminating racial discrimination and doubted there was "a real hope of ending it in the long run." "Blacks as a group are still behind whites," stated historian Manning Marable; "no amount of statistical doubletalk will obscure this fundamental fact."

The perpetuation of black poverty reflected a combination of ills—racial, sexual, and structural. Stated simply, blacks continued to earn less money than whites and the gap between average black and white incomes increased after 1969. The departure of industry from urban centers and the rise of a service economy forced blacks to take lower-paying jobs and to accept part-time work in the absence of full employment. More frustrating was the lack of any work at all: black unemployment rates remained at least twice as high as whites—for men and women, teenagers and adults. Average family income in black male-headed households improved slightly in the seventies, but still remained 20 percent lower than white male-headed families. By 1980, however, 40 percent of black families were headed by women (as compared to 12 percent for whites) and even a growing parity of incomes between black women and white women could not compensate for the lower levels of *all* female earnings. As a result, two-thirds of black families living in poverty were headed by women.

The plight of black women also reflected changing cultural circumstances. Rising divorce rates, a phenomenon shared with whites, accentuated the problems of poverty. "I had my children first and thought about it later," admitted a Chicago welfare mother. "It never occurred to me I'd be raising them without a man." But as victims of male domination as well as racism, many black women viewed separation from men as a positive assertion of independence. "Female-headed households in the black community, regardless of economic status, are not always formed by default," suggested poet Audre Lorde. "Black women today share a history of bonding and strength." Despite traditions of extended family support, however, the black woman's struggle for identity often collapsed under the weight of necessity.

The persistence of severe social problems within the black community illuminated the failure of government to fulfill the liberal expectations of the sixties. Johnson's war on poverty had collided first with the financial drain of Vietnam, later with the conservative ideology of Republican administrations. But although blacks voted overwhelmingly Democratic in 1976, the Carter administration rejected increased government spending for social programs in the interests of fiscal austerity. "It's not enough to do better than Nixon or Ford," protested Vernon Jordan of the National Urban League. "An open style without substantive change is not enough. Black people and poor people resent the stress on balanced budgets instead of balanced lives." Fearful of inflation, however, Carter refused to modify his program. "I don't think you'll be very happy," he told black leaders of his budget plans. "I am prepared to take the consequences."

Recognizing the importance of rejuvenating the inner cities, Carter presented a "comprehensive national urban policy" in 1978, which included an urban development bank, tax incentives, and coordinating councils. "The gravest flaw in past federal policy," he declared in reaffirming the limits of direct government aid, "was not that we failed to spend money. It was that too many programs were ineffective." But the program scarcely affected the political economy of the cities, providing only $734 million of new funding, creating slightly more than fifty thousand jobs, and offering few boosts to the local tax base. Limited as it was, the program failed to pass through Congress. Nor did the federal government respond to a HUD study which showed that blacks continued to face racial discrimination in housing. "We have seen successive executive orders proclaiming equality," admitted Secretary Patricia Harris, "but we have seen no diminution of inequity."

The failure of liberal reform aggravated the problems of public education. As the urban environment deteriorated, families continued to retreat from the central cities, further reducing employment opportunities, eroding the urban tax base, and intensifying the racial imbalance of public schools. In Los Angeles, the proportion of whites in the school district dropped to 29 percent by 1980; in Chicago, it slid from 27 percent in 1975 to 18 percent five years later; in St. Louis and Detroit, whites comprised less than one-fifth of the school population. "There are simply not enough white children to go around," explained Dr. Willis Hawley, a specialist in school integration issues. While sociologists debated the relationship between mandatory busing and white flight, school boards increasingly resisted forced desegregation. The willingness to challenge court-ordered busing reflected a subtle but significant shift in judicial orthodoxy. In the Denver school desegregation cases of 1973, the Supreme Court had ruled that evidence of some segregation strongly implied discrimination throughout the system, requiring thorough remedies. But four years later, in a case involving the Dayton, Ohio, school board, the Court held that "isolated" violations did not justify districtwide changes. Emboldened by this decision, school boards in Chicago, St. Louis, Pittsburgh, and Los Angeles strove to block mandatory busing. "Compliance," concluded Secretary Harris, "cannot be secured by voluntary means." As the seventies ended, numerous school districts succeeded in preventing pupil busing to achieve racial balance.

The legal dimensions of racial discrimination culminated in 1978 in a much anticipated Supreme Court ruling involving affirmative action in higher education. To assure the entry of a minimum number of minority students each year, the University of California medical school at Davis had established a quota system. When Allan Bakke, a white student with distinguished academic credentials, was denied admission, despite higher grades than some successful minority applicants, he sought redress in the courts. By raising the question of quotas and group remedies, the case challenged a liberal truism that individuals ought to be treated equally before the law. Yet traditions of racial injustice, equally unpalatable to liberals, could not be denied. As the case approached a determination, public attention focused on these sensitive issues. Already *Bakke* had drawn fifty-eight supporting briefs, a record number in Court history. Perhaps the Supreme Court "will find a way to blur the edges of the controversy and reaffirm the important values raised by both sides," wrote *Washington Post* columnist Meg Greenfield on the eve of the ruling. "You say that is fudging the issue? Fine. It ought to be fudged."

The final ruling appealed to those mixed instincts. By a 5–4 vote, the Court denied the legality of fixed racial quotas and ordered the admission of Bakke to medical school. But by an equally narrow vote, a different majority held that racial factors could be considered in a general assessment of admission standards. Both sides promptly claimed victory. But the *Bakke* legacy remained ambiguous. "The decision will go down in history," stated Harvard law professor Alan Dershowitz, "not for what it did but for what it didn't do. It neither legitimized racial quotas nor put down affirmative action programs." The next year, the Court denied the suit of Brian Weber, billed as the "blue-collar Bakke," against affirmative action programs in employment.

Despite its legal ambiguities, the *Bakke* decision symbolized an undeniable shift in public attitudes toward racial issues. "We're seeing a national backlash against the movement toward economic and racial equality," charged Vernon Jordan, "a backlash fueled by selfish vindictiveness that threatens to fragment our society." "Allies who walked with us so that we could drink water," agreed Benjamin Hooks, president of the NAACP, "—when there was no economic threat to them—find it increasingly difficult to walk with us today." More ominous was the resurgence of the Ku Klux Klan, which increased its membership by some 50 percent after 1975.

Such trends contributed to a sense of oppression within black society. "Unless black people are given relief," Jordan warned, "it will be impossible for them to contain their despair or for them to sublimate their anger through the political process." A power blackout in New York City in July 1977 quickly ignited what Mayor Abraham Beame called "a night of terror." For twenty-five hours, poor, mostly black, crowds ravaged the city, looting over thirteen hundred stores, damaging property worth over $14 million, injuring hundreds of police, and provoking almost four thousand arrests. "Being that the lights are out and the niggers are going hungry," explained one black youth, "we're going to take what we want—and what we want is what we need." According to public records, 55 percent of arrested looters were unemployed; 64 percent had been previously arrested for other offenses. "The ingredients are there," warned Jordan in 1979, "—the same ingredients that led to the rioting in the 1960s." Racial tension exploded again in 1980, caused by a combination of economic distress and police violence, and it turned the city of Miami into an inferno.

The frustration of black aspirations revealed basic limits of American society, the inability of the economy to generate jobs or of government programs to provide adequate relief. "It's no longer a question of sitting in at a lunch counter, but rather the rising price of a shrinking hamburger," suggested Eddie Williams of the Joint Center for Political Studies. "It's not whether there's equal opportunity to get a job, but whether there's a job to be got." "What we find," concluded Earl Shinhoster, southern regional director of the NAACP, "is [an] inward turn, blacks turning within their own community and their own institutions as a sort of defense." Blacks could take solace, perhaps, in the realization that their fate was linked inextricably with the structure of the larger society. "What happens to Afro-Americans eventually happens to all Americans," observed Harry Edwards. "It just happens to Afro-Americans first."

YOUTH CULTURE

The failure of the American dream, the collapse of opportunity, the loss of a genuine future, struck hardest at the least influential social groups—the youth of all cultures. Americans between the ages of sixteen and twenty-four accounted for half the nation's unemployment, suffered jobless rates three times the national average, and worked, when they could find jobs, in the lowest-paying occupations. For young people, moreover, the problems of racial and sexual discrimination magnified dramatically. Estimates of black teenage unemployment exceeded 50 percent, while earnings for full-time full-year workers were about half that of adults. "I go lookin' for work when I hear where somebody's hirin'," explained a black teenager in Detroit. "But it just ain't the jobs for somebody like me. What you expect?"

Such circumstances reflected a critical breakdown in social relations across the generations, a failure to transmit cultural commitments or to offer opportunities for change. Suggestive of this breach of values was a Supreme Court decision of 1977 denying youngsters the same rights as common criminals. "The prisoner and the school child stand in wholly different circumstances," insisted Justice Lewis Powell in upholding the use of corporal punishment in public schools. "This decision gives a green light to the cane and the rod, the paddle and the fist," protested columnist Ellen Goodman. "It is bizarre, though, at a moment when we are obsessed with violence—violence on television, violence in the streets—that we continue to allow adults to teach it in the classroom by the most potent method of all: example."

The indifference of adults to the problems of the young encouraged the emergence of a distinct youth culture that could survive, almost by definition, only through antisocial behavior. More than half the serious crimes committed in the United States—murder, rape, assault, robbery, burglary, larceny, and motor vehicle theft—were perpetrated by people aged ten to seventeen. Eleven percent of all high school seniors admitted smoking marijuana every day and two-thirds indulged at least three times a week. "We're going to slowly disappear—get doped up or put in jail or shot," stated a black fifteen-year-old in Detroit. "Something's goin' to happen to all of us, 'cause, see, for us right now all the stuff in the street—dope, guns, fast money—we see people makin' tops doin' that every day. We're gonna want a piece of the rock, too. Nobody wants to walk around poor."

Focusing this discontent was the classic institution of the youth culture: the gang. "A *cholo* [gang member] is a guy who has had a lot of hard breaks in life and doesn't have anything else to run to except his gang," remarked actor Danny Alvarez, a former gang member. "He has a lot of heart and he is loyal to his friends. His gang is the only thing he knows."

"You learn young that you don't be on the streets by yourself," stated a Chicana from East Los Angeles, "you just don't." In urban areas, children and adolescents developed a sophisticated sense of territoriality—Chicanos called themselves "homeboys"— and guarded their turf from outside assault. Such groups remained an integral part of the community structure, providing goods and services outside the law, while rigorously defending their cultural identity. "The whole trip," said a Chicana, "is to come on tough, and not to be afraid—no matter what."

Within the youth culture, sexual relations reinforced a sense of community. According to the Alan Guttmacher Institute, by age nineteen, four-fifths of males and two-thirds of females had experienced sexual intercourse, with an average age of initiation at sixteen. These statistics mirrored a greater tolerance for sexual activity throughout society. But while middle-class parents encouraged their children to use modern methods of birth control, many teenagers remained ignorant or indifferent to these practices. As a result, teenage pregnancies leaped to one million each year, a 10 percent increase between 1973 and 1978. These pregnancies accounted for over four hundred thousand abortions in 1977, one-third of the total abortions in the United States. (Women between ages twenty and twenty-four comprised half of all abortion patients.) But 21 percent of pregnant teenagers gave birth out of wedlock and 87 percent of these kept their children. Among poor groups, pregnancy served as an alternative to dependence on adult authority. "They conceive babies, they have their babies,

they keep their babies," observed Harry Edwards of black teen-
aged mothers. "and thereby they establish indisputably not only
their membership in humanity but their place among women." "It
makes you feel like somebody to have a baby call you 'mama,'"
suggested Harvard psychiatrist Alvin Poussaint. For these young
mothers, however, options for advancement shrank dramatically,
contributing to a cycle of poverty that placed unmarried women
on the bottom of the economic scale.

The frustrations of youth culture left its members vulnerable
to appeals for assimilation into the social mainstream, a temptation presented through the most influential medium of youth—
music. In the popular hit "(I Just Can't Wait Till) Saturday," for
example, singer Norma Jeane described the disco scene as sufficient reward for a boring job. Promising to liberate the spirit with
the chant dance, dance, dance, the disco beat simultaneously
spawned a $4-billion-a-year entertainment industry that included,
besides the sale of records and tapes, disco clothing, accouter-
ments, clubs, cruises, skating rinks, and over two hundred dedicated radio stations. "We're in a period of the McDonald's
of music," conceded Melba Moore, whose hit song was "You
Stepped into My Life." "I don't know what *good* is anymore."

Fundamental to the disco craze was a pervasive pressure to
conform to adult standards. Disco guidebooks not only taught
complicated dance patterns, but also offered advice about how to
dress, how to gain admission to snobbish clubs ("Never, never,
never wear a slogan T-shirt"), and how to imitate the comport-
ment of celebrities. This emphasis on decorum appealed to a middle-class youth attracted by materialistic trappings. The most
popular expression of the disco world, for example, Hollywood's
Saturday Night Fever, reinforced a conservative message of confor-
mity, expensive dress, and self-discipline. Only by embracing these
traditional American values could the youthful ethnic hero,
played by John Travolta, hope to attain the upward mobility implied in leaving his working-class origins in Brooklyn for a new life
in Manhattan.

For a youth culture trapped in poverty, however, the expensive values of disco rang false. Urban teenagers instead responded
enthusiastically to a series of gang movies that offered alternative
themes. *The Warriors*, a glorification of gang territoriality, emphasized the futility of upward mobility, while *Boulevard Nights*,
filmed with an entire Chicano cast in East Los Angeles, affirmed

the validity of ethnic culture. "The point of the movie," said producer Tony Bill, "is not to leave the community so you don't have to suffer the harshness or evils of it, but to deal with the alternatives in that life-style. At the end of the movie the main characters are not moving to Beverly Hills." Both antiestablishment films proved sufficiently effective to provoke youthful audiences to violence and vandalism, resulting in several deaths and outraging municipal authorities, who managed in some cities to ban future screenings. Hollywood responded to this pressure by shelving other movies that described gang life.

The assertion of youth culture culminated in a popular enthusiasm for music that defied social convention—punk rock and new wave. Both reflections of English working-class youth, groups like the Sex Pistols minimized style, fashion, and lyric in a gut protest against established values. Wearing safety pins and chains, punk/new wave aficionados parodied the changing styles of haute culture and swayed to a nondance "pogo" beat that denied the commercialization of rhythm. Musicians like Elvis Costello and Tom Robinson explicitly meshed social-protest lyrics with a style of resistance. But the most defiant song of youth culture—sufficiently incendiary to be banned by several radio stations—was Pink Floyd's "Another Brick in the Wall":

> We don't need no education
> We don't need no thought control . . .
> Teacher, leave those kids alone

WOMEN'S CULTURE

The repudiation of adult values by American youth mirrored a growing despair among feminists about the possibility of social improvement. By the late seventies, the eager optimism of the women's liberation movement had mellowed slowly into what was called, more simply, the women's movement or, more statically, women's culture. This transformation of nomenclature reflected less a loss of fervor and idealism than it did a realization that the dominant structures of society would not easily accommodate fundamental changes in sexual relations. Frustrated by reformism, American women turned increasingly to each other for sustenance and growth.

But they made no surrender. "We are here to move history

forward," proclaimed the National Women's Conference, some two thousand elected delegates and eighteen thousand additional observers, held in Houston, Texas, in November 1977. "We are sisters. . . . We share the common language and experience of American women who throughout our Nation's life have been denied the opportunities, rights, privileges and responsibilities accorded to men." Pursuing a federal government mandate to "identify the barriers that prevent women from participating fully and equally in all aspects of national life," the Houston convention adopted a comprehensive program for social reform ranging from passage of the ERA and child-care centers to the defense of the rights of minorities and homosexuals. Most impressive to observers was the quality of political exchange, the sacrifice of special interests for harmony, the search for consensus, what Gail Sheehy called "the politics of empathy."

Women left Houston heartened by the sense of a new community. "It was a total high to . . . discover so many people who agree on so many issues," remarked a delegate from New Jersey, "and finding that I am not alone." "Houston was a rite of passage," suggested Eleanor Smeal, president of the National Organization for Women. "A giant self-esteem bath," commented Sheehy, "out of which they stepped refreshed and recommitted for the long march ahead."

At Houston, feminists also met their opponents in force. "The American people do not want the ERA," Phyllis Schlafly told a cheering counterrally attended by eight thouand supporters. "And they do not want government-funded abortion, lesbian privileges or the federal government to set up institutions for universal child care." Lottie Beth Hobbs, head of Women Who Want to Be Women, dismissed "the one-world, humanist, feminist, socialist philosophy" and prayed for a return of simpler values. Inside the convention, antiabortionists shrieked disapproval of feminists' demands to control their bodies. "Houston will finish off the women's movement," predicted Schlafly.

The full power of the antifeminist backlash emerged over the most controversial aspect of women's rights: abortion. The 1973 Supreme Court ruling upholding abortion had run far ahead of national public opinion, stifling a heated debate almost before it began. But a determined right-to-life movement, supported by the Roman Catholic hierarchy and fundamentalist Protestants, exerted enormous public pressure to block implementation of federal policy. In 1977, seven-tenths of non-Catholic hospitals still made no provisions for abortion services and only a minority of physicians and about half the nation's gynecologists performed such procedures. Most women consequently obtained abortions in specialized clinics. But militant antiabortionists attacked these facilities, too, invading operating rooms, establishing picket lines, and firebombing clinics in several cities. "How do you equate the *life* of an unborn infant with the *social well-being* of a mother, a father, a family?" asked Eunice Kennedy Shriver in a letter to *The New York Times*.

Failing moral persuasion, the antiabortionists moved to change the law. In 1976, Representative Henry Hyde introduced an amendment to the annual HEW appropriation bill forbidding the use of medicare funds for purposes of abortion, except when the mother's life was endangered. To the surprise of feminists, the Supreme Court upheld the measure in 1977. By curbing federal funding, the provision merely thwarted the needs of the poor. "There are many things in life that are not fair," commented President Carter, "that wealthy people can afford and poor people can't." The expiration of the HEW budget reopened the debate. Unable to agree about definitions and limitations, the House failed twenty-five times to reach a compromise, while the Senate endorsed more liberal standards. "It seems . . . unconscionable for this national moral deadlock to be broken over the backs of the poor," protested Ellen Goodman. "We see a moral question turned into an economic question." But Congress continued to restrict medicare money for abortions, permitting funding only for cases of rape, incest, or risk to the mother's life and physical health. Furious at this dilution of principles, Hyde voted against the compromise, "unwilling," he said, "to trade unborn life for a health condition." In 1978, Congress extended the Hyde provision to other federal appropriation bills, blocking paid abortions for military personnel and their dependents, and for Peace Corps volunteers; it also permitted employee health insurance programs to cancel abortion coverage. Such restrictions effectively denied about one hundred thousand abortions each year.

Curtailment of abortion services, however, contradicted the flow of public opinion. According to numerous public surveys, support for abortion increased among all social groups. An extensive study by the National Opinion Research Center found that by 1980, between 82 and 91 percent of the sample approved abortion for so-called "hard" reasons—rape, mother's health, or child defects—while about 50 percent endorsed abortions on grounds of poverty, unwanted children, or illegitimacy, an increase of 32 percent since 1965. Only 7 percent opposed abortion on any grounds. Despite government restrictions, the number of abortions increased in 1978 and remained primarily an alternative for young, white, unmarried women. To feminists, such patterns only magnified the danger of the right-to-life movement.

Challenging the constitutionality of the Hyde amendments, women filed a class action suit to reverse the legislative defeats. In a dramatic ruling in January 1980, Judge John Francis Dooling held that medicare restrictions, by imposing "an unduly burdensome interference with the pregnant woman's freedom to decide," violated constitutional rights. But the following June, by a 5–4 vote, the Supreme Court overturned the decision. "Although government may not place obstacles in the path of a woman's exercise of her freedom of choice," the majority declared, "it need not remove those not of its own creation. Indigency falls in the latter category." Feminists were outraged, viewing the decision as "a cornerstone of fascism." "There truly is another world 'out there,'" dissented Justice William Brennan, "the existence of which the court . . . either chooses to ignore or fears to recognize."

The defeat of abortion rights for the poor underscored women's lack of political power. Despite the Houston agenda, the federal governmnt failed to pass legislation establishing shelters for battered women, denied social security for housewives, and retained veterans' preferences on civil service ratings. In 1978, Congress approved funding for job training for "displaced homemakers," an estimated three million middle-aged women made suddenly independent by divorce or widowhood. A series of Supreme Court decisions also upheld women's rights to equal social security benefits, employment seniority, pension plans, and alimony. But a comprehensive legal statement of female equality remained elusive. On a case-by-case basis, said NOW's Smeal, "we'll be working on this until the year 3000."

Central to women's legal defense was the ratification of the ERA. "It's the bedrock issue," explained law professor Ruth Bader Ginsburg; otherwise "the Supreme Court has no gun at its head." But despite 60 percent approval in public opinion surveys, the constitutional amendment remained three states short of ratification as the deadline for passage approached in March 1979. Mustering the spirit of Houston, feminist organizations launched a massive public-relations crusade to extend the date of ratification. In July 1978, sixty-five thousand women converged on Washington, D.C., to lobby for the unprecedented extension. "As Edith Bunker I don't have equal rights," stated television's most popular housewife in support of the measure. "As Jean Stapleton I don't either." Responding to such pressure, Congress authorized the change, allowing three additional years for the amendment's journey through the legislatures.

The extension of the time limit only emboldened the anti-feminist side. "ERA would nullify any laws that make any distinction between men and women," maintained former Senator Sam Ervin in helping to defeat the measure in North Carolina. "When the good Lord created the earth, he didn't have the advice of Bella Abzug and Gloria Steinem." For eight consecutive years, the Illinois legislature refused its assent, despite a feminist boycott that claimed to have cost the state millions of dollars in tourist trade. "The defeat of the equal rights amendment," said a gleeful native daughter, Phyllis Schlafly, "is the greatest victory for women's rights since the women's suffrage amendment of 1920.... we must renew our efforts and develop the quality of perseverance so that we win in the battle for God, family and country." Equally confident about the mind of the Lord, the Mormon church excommunicated Sonia Johnson for advocating the ERA on the grounds she was "not in harmony with church doctrine concerning the nature of God." Such attitudes dimmed the feminist outlook. "I can't predict passage now," conceded lawyer Ginsburg, "but I can predict passage by the year 2000."

The political weakness of American women reflected—and in turn reinforced—their economic subordination. Although more women attained higher education—by 1980 exceeding the total enrollment of men—and greater admission into professional schools, most women congregated in low-paying jobs that *Ms.* magazine labeled "the pink collar ghetto"—sales, secretarial, and food services, many of which offered only part-time employment. In 1979, women's incomes still represented only 57 percent of male earnings, while unemployment rates exceeded male averages

by about 20 percent. Responding to legal pressure, several prominent corporations, such as *Reader's Digest* and *The New York
Times*, agreed to out-of-court settlements ending discrimination
and accepting affirmative action. But the gaping wage differential
represented not only the denial of equal pay for equal work, but
more subtly the assumption that certain tasks, traditionally performed by women, were inherently less valuable. A federal court
ruled in 1979 that unequal pay for "comparable"—but not the
"same"—work constituted no violation of the law. In 1981, however, the Supreme Court reversed that interpretation.

The slowness of government change increased feminist distrust of the political process. President Carter, obliged by law to
respond to the Houston program, refused to endorse any potentially inflationary proposals and instead emphasized the appointment of women to 21 percent of his executive positions, "an
all-time high." "The issues aren't going to go away," retorted Bella
Abzug, head of the President's National Advisory Committee for
Women, "and neither are we." Bristling at this internal dissent,
Carter inflamed the situation by abruptly firing Abzug in 1979.
"This is symbolic of the way women's issues are treated," complained Nancy Neuman of the League of Women Voters, "—as a
joke." Twenty-six members of the Advisory Committee promptly
resigned in protest.

Disillusionment with government reform forced a reevaluation of feminist expectations. "There will be no liberation by next
summer," admitted Jane O'Reilly in 1979, "or even in the summer
after that." Angry at Carter's insensitivity, the executive board of
NOW announced its opposition to the Democratic incumbent no
matter who opposed him. "It would be ridiculous," said a startled
Betty Friedan on learning of the extreme position, "—there is no
way NOW would be for somebody like Connally or Reagan."
Symbolic of the frustration of feminist goals was the announcement in April 1980 of the largest charitable contribution ever received by NOW—a $500,000 bequest from television producer
Norman Lear to establish a monument to a woman who never
existed—the Edith Bunker Memorial Fund. "Edith's life was enriched by women's struggle for equality," said Lear with no hint of
irony. Nor did Jean Stapleton flinch at her sudden nonexistence; it
"makes my television death significant," she said.

The invisibility of feminist achievement coincided with a resurgence of traditional stereotypes. In fashion design, the disco style celebrated spike heels, tight pants, transparent tops, and sleek dresses made of body-hugging fabrics—clothing that restored the image of women as sex objects. "Feminists all over the country have admitted to me that they enjoy looking pretty and dressing up," maintained Betty Friedan. "I *never* stopped going to the beauty parlor." On television, the appearance of "jiggly" programming—"Charlie's Angels," "The American Girls," and "The Love Boat"—flaunted beautiful women wrapped in little more than sexual innuendo. More subtly, advertisers merged traditional female roles with an apparently liberated style, replacing sexy models with "mature" women to peddle a variety of household products. "The trend," explained one modeling executive, "is to emulate someone real instead of an illusion on a pedestal." A wave of sadomasochistic images in advertising—I'M "BLACK AND BLUE" FROM THE ROLLING STONES, exclaimed a tortured woman on a Los Angeles billboard,—AND I LOVE IT!—belied the innocence of sexual stereotypes.

The visual treatment of women as sex objects barely concealed more violent impulses. In the late seventies, the reporting of such crimes as rape, wife-beating, and child abuse reached alarming proportions. In response to this rise of sexual aggression, women moved to protect themselves, opening crisis centers and shelters for victims of rape and battery. Women also won reforms of rape laws that presumed the complicity of victims; some states allowed wives to charge husbands with such crimes. In a widely publicized case in Salem, Oregon, a jury acquitted John Rideout of raping his wife in 1978. The next year, a similar Nebraska law went untested when the accused husband, released on bail, murdered his wife. These challenges to male violence, however unsuccessful in the courts, reflected new psychological findings that advised women to resist rather than succumb to sexual assault. "The thing not to do is act utterly passive," suggested Dr. Mary Lystand, chief of the National Center for the Prevention and Control of Rape. "A woman who behaves as if she were weak and defenseless appears to increase her risk of rape."

Women also succeeded in establishing the seriousness of sexual assault. When Judge Archie Simonson of Madison, Wisconsin, excused rape as a "normal reaction"—"the way women dress and act these days," he said from the bench, "they often provoke men to commit sexual acts"—feminists organized a recall election in 1977 that replaced Simonson with a woman judge. A Connecticut judge who condoned rape—"you can't blame somebody for trying"—was censured by a judicial review committee. Confronted by victims of male violence, the legal system occasionally showed greater compassion for crimes of revenge. In three highly publicized cases of the mid-seventies, three minority women—a black (Joanne Little), a Hispanic (Inez Garcia), and an American Indian (Yvonne Wanrow)—won partial vindication after murdering male attackers, though the Garcia case required two trials and Wanrow plea-bargained after gaining a new hearing. But juries remained skeptical of women who killed husbands and lovers, despite long histories of battering and sexual abuse, giving the lie to what Jane Alpert called "the illusion that women criminals receive preferential treatment in the courts or in the daily press." "Even when I knew I would have to go to prison," said one woman, "I felt as if a stone had been lifted off my head." "I am definitely a prisoner, a murderer and a convict," conceded another avenging wife. "But I'm also a victim. I've been in prison all my life."

The celebration of male power nevertheless remained a vital component of popular culture. Pornographic media, forming a $4 billion a year industry aimed primarily at men, emphasized the vulnerability of women to male sexuality, appealing to fantasies of domination. "Pornography," suggested Helen Buckingham, a prostitute writing for the National Task Force on Prostitution, "is an expression of man's desire to have the effect on women that he knows he does not, in reality, have." At a time of growing female independence, pornography served to reaffirm traditional power relations. "The ubiquitous public display of dehumanized images," observed Ellen Willis in *Rolling Stone*, "is a sexist, misogynist society's answer to women's demands to be respected as people rather than exploited as objects." Popular magazines such as *Playboy* proudly extended this dehumanization to "girl next door" images, while *Hustler* magazine installed a regular feature in which readers published photographs of family members and friends. "The most terrible thing about pornography," remarked Andrea Dworkin, "is that it tells male truth."

While male fantasy emphasized power, women, by contrast, satisfied sexual longings in a vast outpouring of romantic fiction, particularly historical romance, a genre that replaced the dehumanized bodies of male pornography with passionate involvement. Appealing primarily to female readers, titles like *Royal Bondage, Sweet Savage Love,* or *Love's Sweet Torment* sold 20 million copies a year. This fiction, like pornography, glorified female passivity, often using rape scenes to exempt heroines from sexual complicity. Yet the missing ingredient of male fantasy—genuine passion—distinguished the genre. "Love, with a capital L," observed novelist Rob Swigart, "is the religion of the protagonists, an adolescent fervor vaguely defined." Sex, in this mode, remained surprisingly personal.

Repelled by the proliferation of pornography, conservative groups attacked the commercialization of sex. Taking advantage of the 1973 Supreme Court ruling which permitted local jurisdictions to define community standards, a Memphis, Tennessee, court found *Deep Throat*'s Harry Reems guilty of obscenity, even though the actor had never entered the state before his trial. In Wichita, Kansas, a jury convicted the editor of *Screw* magazine for mailing copies to local subscribers, while in Cincinnati, Ohio, *Hustler* publisher Larry Flynt received a lengthy jail sentence on similar charges. "Women have got to lose their hangups about displaying their bodies," protested Flynt shortly after his conversion to Christianity by faith healer Ruth Carter Stapleton, sister of the President. Found guilty by another Georgia court, Flynt avoided other indictments when unknown assassins shot him in the street, leaving him paralyzed below the waist. The legal backlash raised liberal cries against censorship. "Mr. Flynt is an exploiter of low taste, perhaps a corrupter of deeper values," editorialized *The New York Times.* "But our opinion has no bearing on his freedom to publish." Yet in 1978, the Supreme Court ruled that George Carlin's comedy routine "Dirty Words" could be banned from the airwaves, even though it was not obscene but merely "offensive."

The issue of sexual censorship touched directly on feminist concerns. Historically, conservatives had used obscenity laws to prevent dissemination of birth control information, and in 1978 a Montana school district banned the feminist health publication *Our Bodies, Ourselves.* "I'm sick and tired of hearing the cry of censorship," stated a Helena prosecutor. "We've genuflected at the altar of free speech for too long." Fearing the wrath of the purity crusade, feminists drew a fine distinction between sexual freedom and pornography. "Erotica is about sexuality," explained Gloria Steinem, "but pornography is about power." "Pornography's basic message is dominance, not reciprocity," wrote Robin Morgan. "It defines sex as male aggression and the female body as a target for conquest." Convinced that the elimination of pornographic images would change the realities of sexual relations, women picketed movie theaters and sex shops. In San Francisco, Women Against Violence in Pornography and Media organized a bold "Take Back the Night" parade to reclaim their rights to the streets. "We are going to walk together," exhorted Andrea Dworkin, "because in every sense none of us can walk alone."

The feminist crusade against pornography epitomized a new collective consciousness among American women. "Our bodies and minds are inseparable in this life," wrote Adrienne Rich, "and when we allow our bodies to be treated as objects, our minds are in mortal danger." Women worked to transcend historical divisions that separated them along lines of race, class, and age. "Sisterhood and female friendship burn down the walls of male-defined categories and definitions," argued philosopher Mary Daly, and offered an "expanding room of our own."

Celebration of sisterhood exploded in this culture—emerging in feminist music, poetry, literature, painting, the affirmation of female spirituality. Symbolic of this renaissance was artist Judy Chicago's elaborate tribute to women's history, "The Dinner Party," a five-year collective project that required the mastery of traditional women's arts—porcelain painting and embroidered tapestry—to evoke a pervasive female presence. In fiction, Marilyn French's best-seller *The Women's Room* traced the evolution of women's consciousness from the isolation of the feminine mystique of the fifties to the camaraderie of mutual support. In literature, moreover, in Alix Kates Shulman's *Burning Questions*, Marge Piercy's *Vida*, or Diane Johnson's *Lying Low*, youthful women faced authentic social choices and experienced the crises of identity previously reserved for men.

Respect for a women's community bridged the traditional chasm between generations, the classic love-hate relationships between mothers and daughters, and replaced feelings of animosity with growing understanding and empathy. "The way we weave the web of emotion between ourselves and others," conceded Nancy Friday in her popular book *My Mother/My Self*, "is patterned on what we had with her." Daughterhood—not motherhood—seemed to form the basis of reconciliation, transcending women's anger at their mothers for failing to shield them from patriarchal authority. "When a woman comes to recognize the Daughter in her Self, in her mother, she comes in touch with true tradition," suggested Mary Daly. "Sharing this recognition, mothers and daughters become sisters in struggle. They become friends again."

This rediscovery of spiritual connections affirmed a primal unity of the life cycle, illuminated an ancient marriage between women and nature, and linked the emerging feminist consciousness to a heightened ecological awareness. "As Gyn/Ecologists," stated Daly, "we feel a deep communion with our natural environment. We share the same agony from phallocentric attack and pollution as our sister the earth." "The earth lives as we do," said artist Michelle Stuart, "elastic, plastic, vulnerable." Beyond this shared suffering, women identified an alternative cosmic community. "We are all a part of this motion, we say, and the way of the river is sacred, and this grove of trees is sacred," affirmed Susan Griffin in *Women and Nature*, "and we ourselves, we tell you, are sacred."

WOMEN AND YOUTH of all cultures; blacks, Chicanos, native Americans; Cubans, Puerto Ricans, Salvadorans; Chinese, Vietnamese, Filipinos—most lived at the edges of the mainstream culture—in ghettos, barrios, ethnic enclaves, in rooms of their own. Not by choice always, but by necessity, most lived outside the political structure, on the margins of the economy, beyond the lure of assimilation. There, they formed alternative cultures—not subcultures of some larger whole—distinct, if overlapping, worlds around which their lives revolved. They heard presidential promises, watched thwarted government programs, suffered the exigencies of foreign policy and austerity. Still, they struggled as they endured, hopeful of some ultimate acceptance.

15

"NEW COMBINATIONS
FOR INTIMACY AND SUPPORT"

Beyond the Nuclear Family

THE STRUGGLE TO PRESERVE A SENSE
of cultural identity and to assure the continuity of values focused
on the most intimate and most imperiled of American institutions—the family. While audiences laughed at the Bunkers in conflict and *Ms.* magazine published a liberated marriage contract,
the broadcast on public television of a documentary series, "An
American Family," in 1973 captured national attention by its raw
exposure of a pervasive crisis in domestic relations. "Oh, we're
mad at each other all the time," admitted the frustrated husband,
Bill Loud. "You're married all the time," replied his friend. Behind the unblinking cameras, viewers saw the Loud family collapse
at the seams, a twenty-year marriage on the rocks, the oldest son
an avowed homosexual, a house full of teenagers aimless in their
commitments. "These people touch without meeting," stated the
program's publicity sheet, "meet without touching."

The disintegration of the Loud family reflected a national
divorce rate that doubled from 2.5 divorces per thousand people
in 1966 to 5 per thousand ten years later. "Divorce has become so
common," remarked Nena O'Neill, coauthor of the popular *Open
Marriage*, "that it is almost a necessary initiation into adult relationships." A 1978 Gallup survey of teenage attitudes toward
divorce found that two-thirds of the nation's youth endorsed separation on grounds of incompatibility. "Why on earth," responded
a sixteen-year-old girl, "should they struggle on if they just can't

make a go of it?" In the sixties, the stigma of divorce had helped destroy the presidential ambitions of Nelson Rockefeller, but by 1980 only the most assiduous Hollywood bodywatchers cared to comment about the marital background of the Republican standard-bearer. Ronald Reagan became the first divorced President in American history.

The fragility of American marriages evoked serious concern about the future of society. "We need a better family life to make us better servants of the people," President Carter told members of his new administration. "So those of you living in sin I hope you'll get married. Those of you who have left your spouses, go back home. And those of you who don't remember your children's names, get reacquainted." But presidential prestige could not prevent the divorce of Carter's top adviser, Hamilton Jordan, or that of his oldest son, Chip. The frequency of divorce, agreed historian Christopher Lasch, reflected a deep psychological malaise—a fear of commitments, a pervasive pessimism about human obligations. "It is," he wrote, "the world view of the resigned."

Besides the rising divorce rate, social statisticians noted other important changes in American family patterns. The marriage rate, which had steadily increased in the sixties, began to drop in 1972, reaching a low of ten marriages per thousand people in 1976. Young adults, wary of marital failure, increasingly delayed their wedding dates, causing a notable rise in the average age of first marriage, to 22.1 years for women and 24.6 years for men in 1980, a full year higher than in 1975 and nearly two years higher than the averages of the fifties. These marital decisions also affected the nation's birthrate, which dropped from 18.4 per thousand in 1970 to 14.8 per thousand in 1975. By 1973, the nation's fertility rate slipped below the 2.1 child-per-woman ratio required for the natural replacement of the population and hovered about 1.8 for the remainder of the decade. Among married women in their twenties, the rate of childlessness increased so dramatically that census bureau demographers speculated that a generation of liberated women had not merely delayed motherhood but had chosen to remain forever childless. By middecade, the traditional yardstick used by the Department of Labor to define a "typical" household—a working father, a domesticated mother, and two children—represented a mere 7 percent of all American families.

These new statistical patterns—the decline of marriage, the

diminishing importance of children—underscored the failure of the traditional family to serve as a bastion of emotional commitment—as Lasch phrased it, "a haven in a heartless world"—at a time of severe economic pressure and changing social values. "Parents are not abdicating," suggested Harvard psychologist Kenneth Keniston, "they are being dethroned by forces they cannot influence, much less control." As economic stress forced more family members into the work force, other external agents—television, advertising, welfare organizations—entered the private domicile to undermine family relations. "There must now be a family *beyond* the family so many are struggling to escape," advised Theodore Roszak. "Because if there is not, then we will not achieve any sort of liberation by destroying the family; we will only finish unattached and drifting."

THE JEREMIADS about the fate of the traditional family minimized the importance of new domestic forms. "What we are witnessing is not the death of the family as such," argued futurist Alvin Toffler, but "the end of the nuclear family . . . as the ideal model for society." "What families are doing," explained Jane Howard after surveying the varieties of households, "is changing their size and their shape and their purpose." "People are living together in new combinations for the intimacy and support that constitute a family," NOW's Muriel Fox told a National Assembly on the Future of the Family, "—unmarried adults with or without children, single-parent families, multigenerational communes, various new groupings of the elderly." Such trends, said Roszak, "point in a common direction—toward homes that can hold their own against the pressures of the urban-industrial dominance."

The rise of single-person households seemed to epitomize the collapse of family relations. Between 1970 and 1979, the number of people living alone increased by 60 percent, comprising 23 percent of all households by 1980. Though a portion of these statistics reflected the longevity of elderly people, especially widows, capable of maintaining their own domiciles, the number of people living alone under age thirty-five increased by over 200 percent. Besides popularizing a world of "swinging singles" preoccupied with leisure activities, the enlarged market power of independent adults had important consequences for the entire economy. In urban areas, the demand for separate housing contributed to a severe shortage of apartments which, with the emphasis on smaller units, encouraged the migration of families to suburbia. These shifts further weakened the economies of cities and depleted public school systems. A "Singles Expo" held in California in 1978 boasted not only seminars on "Finding That Perfect Mate," but also exhibited new specialized products, such as soup-for-one and small appliances, for the single consumer. Convenience foods aimed at singles eliminated another family staple—table scraps— which stimulated a burgeoning animal food industry. "Those young adults are having children later and less often," explained an investment analyst, "and a dog or a cat makes a nice baby substitute." A sophisticated pet food industry, taking advantage of such feelings, introduced products that claimed to accommodate nutrition to the changing life cycle of the pampered pets.

Despite such excesses, however, the singles style appeared less a permanent choice than what census specialist Arthur Norton called a "transitional living phase." Two-thirds of all single Americans had once married, and independent living for them often represented only a temporary interlude before the commencement of another durable relationship. Only about one-third of single adults had never married and many indicated a desire to do so eventually. "I would consider marriage if the right person comes along," a twenty-nine-year-old woman said in a typical explanation to an interviewer, "but I would not give up my career for it." "When I get married," stated an unattached man, "I would like it to be permanent." Such statements suggested that people still longed for lasting intimacy and companionship, even while rejecting conventional arrangements. "Independence is no longer the crucial issue," wrote Karen Durbin about "the new intimacy." "We can risk love without wondering if we'll end up getting obliterated in the process."

The fascination with the nation's divorce rate often obscured another striking statistic: four-fifths of separated people chose to remarry within three years. Divorce "is not the end of family life, it is a change," said census official Paul Glick. "More people now accept divorce as a transition state to new family life." Yet nearly one-half of second marriages also failed within three and a half years (third marriages averaged only a year and a half). "The myth is that if you get married and if it doesn't work, you get married again," explained Davidyne Maylees, author of *Rewedded Bliss*. "That second marriage is the same but better. But the fact is it's not the same and it's harder." But despite its frequent futility, the passion for remarriage indicated the strength of traditional values, the desire for old-fashioned stability, regardless of the difficulty of implementation. In 1970, 96 percent of all Americans admitted a commitment to the ideal of two people spending their lives together; ten years later, the figure remained exactly 96 percent.

The changes forced by divorce nevertheless acquired an independent momentum, especially in families with children. "In her experience," Ellen Goodman wrote about a child of divorce in a column titled "The Illusion of Permanence," "families often stretched out in long chains of step-parents and half-siblings—chains forged out of broken and rewedded marriage bonds. That was the way things were." Forty percent of the children born in the seventies, according to census estimates, would spend some time in a single-parent household, 90 percent of which would be headed by women. Among urban blacks, traditions of extended families helped to blunt the problems of poverty, divorce, and children born outside marriage. "It's kind of a family tradition," acknowledged one unmarried mother, "for us to get pregnant in our senior year of high school." Instead of being stigmatized by "illegitimacy," such children found a ready acceptance within enlarged households.

The frequency of divorce, cohabitation, and remarriage among white middle-class couples now produced new extended families composed of what Maylees labeled "polyparents and children." Based upon shared custody, liberal visitation rights, and interlocking offspring (half-children and stepchildren), these family networks shared responsibility and nurturance, offering children alternative roles and support. "For every one of the children whose family was tangibly, irrevocably 'destroyed,' " observed Goodman, "there was another whose family had been extended, in steps, or step-parents."

The transformation of traditional marriages encouraged the proliferation of couples who lived together without legal sanction. During the seventies, the number of households established by unmarried couples tripled to 1.6 million, one-quarter of which contained children. Though cohabitation remained illegal in seventeen states, the practice no longer offended public opinion. In 1977, the Department of Housing and Urban Development announced its acceptance of unmarried couples (and homosexual couples) for public housing, provided they exhibited a "stable family relationship." Even conservative family films, such as *Rocky*, portrayed unmarried couples living together without making moral judgments. "Our biggest inconvenience," remarked one man, "is that we don't know what to call each other."

"Most of the problems unmarried couples have—sex, money, power, the need for space," observed an experienced marriage counselor, "—are the same ones married couples mention." Yet without the stability of law, unmarried couples perceived a greater urgency to resolving conflicts that might otherwise remain unexamined. "Couples living together are more likely to try and work out the differences between them," explained one psychiatrist. "There is a fear of losing each other." In an age of speedy, no-fault divorce, unmarried status provided an even easier escape. But an estimated one-third of couples who lived together eventually married, and an ever-growing proportion of such relationships survived and flourished.

Because of their outlaw status, unmarried couples faced special problems at the time of separation. But in a precedent-breaking decision involving actor Lee Marvin and his cohabitant Michelle Triola Marvin, the California Supreme Court ruled in 1977 that couples who engaged in sexual relationships outside marriage did not lose their standing before the law. "The mores of the society have indeed changed so radically in regard to cohabitation," the court held, "that we cannot impose a standard based on alleged moral considerations that have apparently been so widely abandoned by so many." Though Michelle Marvin lost her claim that an implicit marriage contract existed (California law denied the legality of common law status), she won a rehabilitation settlement worth two years of her highest previous salary. Similar "palimony" settlements in other states revealed an important shift in family law, placing contractual obligations above moral issues.

The reorientation of family commitments stimulated new enthusiasm for child rearing, particularly among more mature women. The nation's birthrate, which had plummeted steadily for twenty years, stabilized in 1975 and increased slightly in the next four years. Surveys by the census bureau in 1980 found that birth expectations among women aged eighteen to twenty-four had remained constant since 1976, averaging two children each; only 11 percent said they expected to have no children. And the number of women in their early thirties having a first child leaped 37 percent, while women in the thirty-five to thirty-nine age bracket showed a 22 percent increase. "It used to be that when a woman decided not to have a baby at age 35, that was it," explained Kathy Weingarten, coauthor of a study of "late-timing" parents. "Now, women at age 42 are still asking themselves the question." Such possibilities illuminated significant changes in obstetric procedure—the perfection of the amniocentesis test, which revealed the chromosomal state of the unborn child; the availability of abortions, which minimized the necessity of bearing a deformed fetus; and a dramatic increase in the number of Cesarean deliveries by nearly 100 percent as doctors attempted to reduce birth-related abnormalities.

The explosion of late births represented a major reevaluation of the female life cycle by the first generation of women to demand equal rights outside the home. Though the pursuit of careers often forced women to adopt traditionally male life patterns—the rejection of domesticity for work—the achievement of economic stability together with the approach of menopause produced a shift in values. "I'm up against the clock," stated one career woman. "If I don't have a child now, it will be too late." Mature women, many of them unmarried, viewed child rearing as an extension of their independence. "Their babies were their own gifts to themselves," reported Weingarten, "—a profound statement to themselves and to the world about who they were." Unlike housewives of the past, most older mothers expected to return to work.

The willingness of women to merge careers with child rearing revealed not only a shift of values, but also a new urgency to earn a living. The great expansion of female-headed households simply forced mothers into the work force. During the seventies, moreover, the major growth industries of the American economy—food, health, and business services that provided 40 percent of all new private jobs between 1973 and 1980—were traditionally "women's work." Such jobs often offered only part-time employment at minimum wages (explaining why women's incomes remained a fraction of male earnings), limited opportunities for advancement, and few union protections. But they did allow flexible scheduling, enabling women to juggle family responsibilities with careers. By 1976, only 40 percent of the nation's jobs produced sufficient income to support a family, forcing the employment of married women to bolster household earnings. As a result, one half of American mothers participated in the labor force, and 43 percent of women with pre-school-age children were working.

The increase in the number of working mothers had important consequences for domestic life. Child care, traditionally the responsibility of mothers, moved increasingly beyond the family. In the absence of government programs or workplace facilities, mothers devoted substantial portions of their paychecks to private day-care centers or professional baby-sitters. A survey conducted by Columbia University sociologist Sheila Kammerman found that children of working mothers "may experience three, four or even more kinds of care in an average week, as they spend a part of the day in nursery school, another portion with a family day-care mother (or two different such women) and are brought to and from these services by a parent, a neighbor, or some other person." But in poorer families, the majority of which were female headed, children found no more surrogate supervision than the television screen, logging an estimated twelve to sixteen thousand hours by age sixteen. Working mothers also changed family consumption patterns, preferring fast-food emporiums, convenience products, and microwave ovens to save time. Aware of women's feelings of guilt for neglecting traditional functions, advertisers increasingly appealed to women who, as Enjoli fragrance put it, "bring home the bacon and fry it in a pan."

Despite the necessity of two-income families, American men were slow to fill the breach in child care. In 1976, Dr. Benjamin Spock, author of America's number-one best-seller in the twentieth century (except for the Bible), *Baby and Child Care*, published a major revision "to eliminate the sexist biases that help to create and perpetuate discrimination against girls and women." Responding to the pressures of feminists, Spock insisted that "the father's responsibility is as great as the mother's." But opinion surveys found that while men overwhelmingly approved of working mothers, most continued to define basic domestic chores, such as cleaning the toilets, as women's tasks. "All right, Edith, you go right ahead and do your thing," Archie Bunker expressed the sentiment. "But just remember that your thing is eggs over easy and crisp bacon."

The expansion of female roles nevertheless forced many men to reevaluate their lives, "Goodbye, John Wayne," proclaimed T-shirts at a National Conference on Men and Masculinity, held in the wake of the feminist meeting at Houston. "I am not a success object." As wives established independent careers, men increasingly circumscribed their own ambitions to accommodate their families, rejecting job transfers and overtime work. "The new executive," asserted a corporation headhunter, "draws the line at uprooting the family."

These changes in male careers, still only an incipient trend, suggested the revolutionary implications of women's liberation—the emergence of androgynous roles. "Men do not need to exude machismo," insisted psychologist June Singer, "or women to pretend a naïve and dependent character." Just as women rushed to enter the work force, liberated men now welcomed the chance to become more domestic. "You're going to see a great wave of men dropping out," predicted a bank worker who switched roles with his wife. "Let her support the family for a while, and let me find myself." "I'll work three days a week at the boiler plant and my wife will go back to nursing nights," explained another family innovator, "and between us we'll take care of the kids."

Such attitudes fostered growing concern among men about their relationships with their children. "These things have been kept from us like a dark secret," admitted Avery Corman, author of the novel *Kramer vs. Kramer*. "We've been lean-jawed and macho all these years and the women's movement has created a climate that allows us to express our feelings." Although only one-fifth of divorced fathers contributed to child support, the issue of child custody emerged as a central concern for advocates of male liberation. "Nothing galvanizes men into action more," stated the director of Men's Rights, Inc., "than going home to find a policeman with an injunction that bars a father from seeing his own kids." But while the courts no longer automatically awarded child custody to mothers, only about 10 percent of children of divorce lived with their fathers.

Changes in family patterns remained closely tied to the structure of the workplace. Although most companies remained unconcerned about the domestic problems of employees, some innovative corporations, such as Boston's Stride Rite, opened daycare centers for workers' children. Other businesses experimented with "flexitime" schedules, which allowed workers to arrive and depart at their convenience, provided that they worked during "core" periods and fulfilled standard job obligations. Such schedules helped parents integrate work-related commitments with family responsibilities. A 1978 survey of 805 participating companies, involving approximately 3 million workers, found that flexitime reduced absenteeism, raised employee morale, and, surprisingly, increased productivity. Success with flexitime encouraged experimentation with working at home. "The important thing is getting your job done," explained an executive of the Weyerhaeuser lumber company. "It's incidental to us where you do it." The miniaturization of electronic technology—telephone systems, word processors, and computers—promised to accelerate the arrival of what Alvin Toffler called "the electronic cottage" of the future.

THE RIGIDITY OF MOST CORPORATIONS, however, created severe economic and psychological distress for some 25 million Americans over the age of sixty-five. "Like housewives," observed sociologist Arlie Hochschild, "the old find themselves in a society in which money determines value. Yet they, as a group, remain outside the money economy. Their doings are not worth money, and therefore 'not worth anything.' " Victims of enforced retirement and fixed incomes, people at age sixty-five found themselves facing an average of sixteen years of life without value. "Most of us," protested *Newsday* columnist Lou Cottin, "worked hard all our lives to achieve poverty and an almost total loss of status." In the seventies, the aged began to challenge this invisibility.

Concern for the elderly reflected a sheer growth of numbers. As life expectancy in the United States increased to 69.5 years for white men and 77.2 for white women (blacks averaged nearly five years less), the size of the over-sixty-five population leaped by nearly 20 percent during the seventies. Nearly half these people lived with spouses in independent households and 25 percent more lived alone. Often separated by long distances from relatives, older people turned to each other for companionship and support, seeking redress of collective grievances. "Old people feel they have to look out for themselves," explained the president of the National Association of Retired Federal Employees. Joining organizations such as the American Association of Retired People (which quadrupled its membership to nearly 12 million) and the more militant Gray Panthers, elderly Americans attacked national policies that diminished their importance. "Most organizations tried to adjust old people to the system," objected Gray Panther founder Maggie Kuhn. "The system is what needs changing."

Protesting enforced retirement, older Americans lobbied for the end of age discrimination. "Are we so victimized by our own stereotypes," asked Representative Claude Pepper, at seventy-seven the chairman of the Select Committee on Aging, "that we only recognize as elderly those televised characters who are toothless, sexless, humorless, witless and constipated?" "Which of you," actor John Wayne challenged a congressional committee, "is going to step up and put me out to pasture?" Such appeals reinforced a growing concern among business leaders about the high economic costs of early retirement. "The real challenge is to find a way to make older people more productive," said one management consultant worried about the lagging economy. "We are not yet sufficiently rich as a society to say that we will carry a major proportion of healthy, wise, experienced individuals without their contributing something." As a larger proportion of the population claimed social security benefits, the cost of the program shifted to younger workers required to pay higher payroll taxes. When the social security system began in the thirties, approximately nine active workers supported each retiree; by the seventies, the proportion slid to four workers per retiree. Demographers warned that the aging population would drive the system to bankruptcy. In response to these diverse pressures, Congress extended the age of mandatory retirement from sixty-five to seventy in 1978. Most workers, long bored with their jobs, had no intention of staying in harness. But one-third indicated an interest in retaining their positions, while others hoped for new careers and supplementary earnings.

Older Americans also organized to obtain improvements in government-supported health care. The medicare program, established under Johnson's Great Society, provided some payments for hospitalization. But the elderly emphasized the importance of assisting the homebound. Besides well-reported abuses within the nursing-home industry, gerontologists found a correlation between confinement and senility. Institutionalization, reported Robin Henig, "is the surest way to speed the decline of memory and to hasten confusion and disorientation." Such problems perhaps explained the common failure of nursing-home patients to recover. "Old people believe that entry into nursing homes is a prelude to death," noted Lou Cottin—and for good reason, since only 19 percent ever returned home. But appeals for home-delivered health care drowned in the Carter administration's efforts to fight inflation.

Older Americans also challenged the popular stereotypes that pervaded the mass media. "Our faces are blank and expressionless, our bodies are bent over and the 'senior shuffle' is just a step away from the embalming room," complained Lydia Bragger of the Gray Panthers' media watch. "We are shown as stubborn, rigid, inflexible, forgetful and confused . . . dependent, powerless, wrinkled babies, unable to contribute to society." Such criticism encouraged the appearance of more positive images of the aged. In Hollywood, the remarkable comeback of vaudeville veteran George Burns provided the impetus for a series of films—*The Sunshine Boys, Going in Style*—which portrayed old people as serious, if frustrated, persons. On television, Hugh Downs's talk show, "Over Easy," successfully appealed to "those of us who feel that growing older is not quite the same as growing old." "Wrinkles are just as natural a part of life as diaper rash and acne," concluded Russell Baker, "and a lot more comfortable to boot."

The new militance of gray power stimulated a reappraisal of the aging process, transforming what had been assumed to be a time of debility into a fulfilling stage of life. "It is a time to discover inner richness, for self-development and spiritual growth," suggested Gay Gaer Luce, who in 1974 helped to found the California-based SAGE (Senior Actualization and Growth Exploration), a consciousness-raising group centered on exercise and meditation. "Out of this inner growth come our sages, healers, prophets, and models for generations to follow." Wisdom, not senility, became a goal for the elderly. "Old age is not illness, it is a timeless ascent," affirmed author May Sarton. "As power diminishes, we grow toward more light."

THE CHANGE OF ATTITUDE toward the elderly paralleled a rising awareness of another often invisible social group, the nation's homosexuals, who, like the aged, represented about 10 percent of the population. With the liberalization of sexual values, gay Americans more easily left the shadows of the closet to proclaim the legitimacy of homosexual life-styles and to force "straight" society to reconsider ingrained prejudices. In 1973, the American Psychiatric Association, revising a traditional diagnosis, denied that homosexuality was a "mental disorder" and urged full civil rights for homosexuals. At the national women's conference in Houston, feminists embraced their lesbian sisters in a controversial vote of solidarity. Thrilled by the gesture, lesbians launched a roomful of lavender balloons that carried a simple, increasingly obvious message: WE ARE EVERYWHERE.

The demand for public acceptance of homosexuals constituted an affirmation not so much of sexual preference as it did of one's identity. "It's not a closet," suggested David Goodstein, editor of the gay newspaper *The Advocate*, "but a tunnel." "It isn't something that you do once and it's over," explained a lesbian college instructor. "You are constantly coming out. It becomes the work of your life." Assertions of gay pride nourished a sense of community, feelings of commitment and belonging. "The more of us that do it," said the college teacher, "the more support the next person who's going to come out has."

The emergence of a gay life-style triggered a demand for homosexual rights. Activists dated the beginning of gay militance to a hot June day in 1969 when New York City police invaded a homosexual bar, the Stonewall Inn, and angry patrons fought back. In subsequent years, numerous municipalities enacted ordinances extending equal protection to homosexuals, and a gay-rights bill lingered in Congress. Gay lobbyists met with Carter's aide Margaret Costanza to seek the right to serve in the military, FBI, CIA, and the State Department, the first official homosexual delegation to be greeted at the White House. Though Carter rejected the pressure, he acknowledged the legal rights of gays. "I don't feel that society, through its laws, ought to abuse or harass the homosexual," he stated on Father's Day 1977.

These assertions of gay rights threatened an orthodox morality that viewed homosexuality not merely as deviant but as sinful and prompted a powerful backlash that swept the nation in 1977. The issue coalesced first in Miami, Florida, soon after the city adopted a law prohibiting discrimination against homosexuals. "The ordinance condones immorality, and discriminates against my children's rights to grow up in a healthy, decent community," charged singer Anita Bryant, who quickly launched a Save Our Children movement to overthrow the measure. "Before I yield to this insidious attack on God and His laws," she announced, "I will lead such a crusade to stop it as this country has not seen before."

"If homosexuality were the normal way," Bryant added, "God would have made Adam and Bruce."

Fighting back, gay activists defined the issue as a defense of civil rights. "Miami is our Selma," claimed one gay activist, alluding to the black crusade of the sixties. "We are asking people to go into the election booth and decide whether a minority should be discriminated against," objected Leonard Matlovich, who had sued the Air Force for discharging him on grounds of homosexuality. "What if the people of Selma, Alabama, had been asked to vote on equal rights for blacks in 1964?" But Bryant renounced an economic attack on gays, provided they "do not come out of the closet." "What this means should be absolutely clear," replied Jean O'Leary and Bruce Voeller, codirectors of the National Gay Task Force: "Gay women and men . . . [must] join a conspiracy to pretend we don't exist, so that other people can lie to children."

In June 1977, Miami voters spoke—by a two-to-one margin rejecting the antidiscrimination ordinance. The outcome outraged liberals throughout the nation. "Terribly wrong," commented San Francisco Mayor George Moscone, as five thousand of his city's homosexuals marched in protest. In New York City, angry gays paraded the streets chanting, "Gay rights now!" But the electoral defeat undermined homosexual confidence. "Gays won't come out in Miami because the city is hostile to them," stated one public-opinion analyst; "the city remains hostile because no one will come out." Exulted Anita Bryant, "The 'normal majority' have said, 'Enough! Enough! Enough!' " and she promised to lead a national crusade "to repeal similar laws . . . which attempt to legitimize a life-style that is both perverse and dangerous."

Three weeks later, homosexuals throughout the country celebrated the anniversary of the Stonewall insurrection by staging mass demonstrations in support of gay rights. "Out of the closet into the streets," cheered marchers in a gay pride parade that extended twenty-seven blocks through New York City. "No more Miamis," they declared. "Anita, we would rather fight than switch." But the anger of gay men, targeted primarily at Bryant, alarmed lesbian feminists who detected an "underlying gynophobia" in the failure to attack the men, the churches, and the corporate interests that supported the singer's campaign. "It should be obvious," Adrienne Rich reminded a separate gathering of lesbian protesters, "that no woman in male-dominated society can wield the public influence ascribed to Anita Bryant, unless men say she shall do so."

Division within the homosexual communities—distrust between lesbians and gay men, disagreements between homosexuals who urged anonymity and exhibitionists who flaunted their preferences—left this group vulnerable to further attack. In October 1977, the Supreme Court refused to review a Washington state law that permitted the dismissal of homosexual teachers. "Now I have greater hope that God has given America a space to repent," concluded Bryant, "and that this will slow down the forces that are attempting to destroy the foundations of this country—the family unit." In the spring of 1978, the spirit of Miami spread to St. Paul, Minnesota, to Wichita, Kansas, to Eugene, Oregon—cities in which popular referenda repealed existing antidiscrimination laws. "Come out," pleaded a lesbian of St. Paul. "Everyone should come out. The best way to educate the public is for all gay people to identify themselves."

As the antihomosexual movement gained momentum, the defense of gay rights shifted in 1978 to two traditionally tolerant areas: Seattle, Washington, and California. In a hotly contested municipal election, Seattle voters overwhelmingly rejected an attempt to repeal a law protecting civil rights regardless of sexual orientation, and two thousand gays staged a candlelight parade to say, "Thank you, Seattle." In California, a statewide initiative to ban homosexual teachers offended liberals and conservatives alike. "It has the potential of infringing on the basic rights of privacy and perhaps even constitutional rights," warned former Governor Reagan. "It . . . has the potential for real mischief." The measure failed by over one million votes. San Francisco, with one of the largest homosexual communities in the country, boasted a gay supervisor, Harvey Milk, first elected in 1977, and a gay rights ordinance signed by Mayor Moscone in 1978.

Even in liberal San Francisco, however, a substantial constituency criticized gay rights and a conservative police department resented the mayor's prohibition of the harassment of homosexuals. The only supervisor to vote against the antidiscrimination measure was a former policeman named Dan White who had campaigned against "splinter groups of radicals, social deviates, incorrigibles." Unable to influence municipal policy, White overcame his political impotence with the help of a police special .38 and a dozen hollowed bullets, assassinating Moscone and Milk in their offices in November 1978. "If a bullet should enter my brain," Milk had prophetically tape-recorded his own eulogy, "let that bullet destroy every closet door." Stunned by the attack, San Franciscans quietly mourned their liberal leaders. But despite the smoking gun, White managed a successful legal defense on grounds of "diminished mental capacity"—a temporary insanity caused, in part, by overeating junk food. The sentence: seven years, eight months, with the possibility of early parole. The verdict ignited the fury of the gay community, sparking a night of violence. "Dan White's getting off is just one of a million things that happen in our lives: the beatings, the murders, the people driven to suicide by the hostility of straights," stated an angry rioter. "Dan White's straight justice is just the last straw. We're not a bunch of fairies. We can be as tough as they were in Watts." The next night, ironically Milk's birthday, San Francisco gays held a peaceful vigil in his memory.

Responding to the antihomosexual backlash, gays attempted to mobilize their political strength. In 1978, they installed a full-time lobbyist in Washington, D.C., to thwart hostile legislation and defend gay interests. The following year, some one hundred thousand homosexuals paraded in the nation's capital to support protective legislation. Working within the political structure, gays sent thirty-seven avowed homosexuals to the Democratic national convention in 1980, two to the Republican convention, and obtained verbal support from third-party candidate John Anderson. "We're taking advantage of the most powerful closet we have," remarked Jean O'Leary, "the voting booth."

The attack on homosexual rights underscored the uniqueness of the gay life-style. In most major cities, gays could participate in a distinct community network—find professional services, religious organizations, social activities, and, as one New York City homosexual boasted, "never see a straight person again." Though heterosexuals usually emphasized the sexual preference of gays, homosexuals insisted on the importance of less tangible values, feelings of love and mutual affection. "To be gay," suggested a middle-aged man, "is to be of a certain undefined, but very strong kind of temperament." Even in purely sexual terms, according to a laboratory study conducted by Masters and Johnson, homosexuals placed priority on "the exchange of pleasure at all levels of sexual excitement" rather than on the exclusive goal of orgasm that typified heterosexual coupling. "We are two people who shouldn't be together," explained a lesbian mother. "This takes us to places we've never been before; it makes for an experimental vulnerability that deepens the intimacy between us."

The importance of emotional commitment among gays contradicted popular images of homosexual promiscuity, stereotypes that led to gay protests against the Hollywood film *Cruising*. Though unattached homosexual men (and, to a lesser extent, lesbians) supported a booming industry of gay bars, baths, and social clubs that encouraged casual sexual encounters, homosexual couples described a pattern of stable relationships. A nationwide survey conducted by Mary Mendola reported that 83 percent of lesbians had exclusive sexual relations with their partners and 14 percent more had only occasional outside affairs; among gay men, Mendola found that 37 percent maintained exclusive relationships and 49 percent sought occasional affairs, figures that compared with the results of recent heterosexual surveys. Beyond sexual experiences, two-thirds of the respondents defined themselves as primarily committed to their mates. But despite greater openness, homosexual marriages remained outside the law.

The strength of the gay community raised questions, similar to those faced by ethnic minorities, about the risks and advantages of assimilation into mainstream society. "I look at the gay movement as one which will, hopefully, self-destruct," admitted a black man. "I would like to see the movement bring social alienation and discrimination to an end; then we can go on being what we are." Others feared that dispersal into the larger society would attenuate a unique and vital culture that linked civil rights to a larger search for community and commitment. "Gay liberation may really be the ultimate revolution," suggested a lesbian college instructor in San Francisco, "because when gay people are free, when all people are free to love whomever we wish, when love can be expressed openly to children, to older people, to people of the same sex, to animals, to trees, to the earth . . . , we'll be on the road to being a species that is worthy of this planet. . . . This is part of the gift that gay people have to offer the world."

THE RISE OF GAY LIBERATION, the appearance of an elderly coalition, the creation of alternative living arrangements—all testified to a powerful drive among Americans in the seventies for personal commitments that transcended traditional family institutions. Yet these social experiments—vulnerable, besieged, incomplete—remained trapped within the limitations established by the dominant society—by the rules of the workplace, the quality of health care, a morality locked into the last century. For the innovators, as with ethnic minorities, the temptations for assimilation, for quiet surrender, often proved irresistible, causing the compromise of genuine alternatives on grounds of convenience or propriety. Establishment critics saw in these gestures no more than extreme individualism, and they berated a selfish generation dedicated to endless gratification. Such comments misread more fundamental meanings.

The liberation of sex, for example—the toleration of premarital, extramarital, polygamous, and gay relations—moved rapidly in the seventies from the celebration of random promiscuity—Erica Jong's "zipless fuck"—to a search for stable relations. The films of Woody Allen, the transition from *Play It Again, Sam* (1972) to *Annie Hall* (1977) and *Manhattan* (1979), documented the replacement of orgasmic thrill with the need, never quite fulfilled and consequently funny, for enduring emotional bonds. A Harris poll conducted for *Playboy* magazine found that a majority of men defined their ideal lover as "someone to be totally open and honest with," while only 23 percent preferred "someone who is sexually exciting." "Without commitment," one woman told an interviewer, "sex doesn't get any better than the first time you have it with someone." Unsatisfied by impersonal sexuality, many Americans chose no sex at all, starting what therapists perceived as a trend toward asexuality. "Celibacy partly represents my self-esteem," maintained one woman. "I'm celibate because I want more than sex." But most celibates saw their moratoria from sex as temporary, a time to seek more serious attachments. "I'm taking a sabbatical from sex now," said a divorced man, "to sort out my feelings." "I haven't given up sex at all," stated another. "I'm just looking for the right person to share it with."

This longing for connection permeated the popular culture, an earnest desire easily corrupted by the corporate structure with goals of its own. In a curious merger of motives—the search for attachment and aggressive hucksterism—it affected the most basic aspects of life. Clothing, for example, passed beyond the subtleties of mere body language. It spoke directly: designer labels, silkscreen art, T-shirts with slogans, political statements, personal messages, brand names. As free-floating billboards, they expressed the most blatant invasion of American capitalism into the private sphere—the purchase not of products but of advertisements. Such marketing manipulation, what advertisers called "personal brand identity" (PBI), exploited a subliminal antipathy to social isolation. "If you don't give your brand a PBI," advised advertising executive Larry Light, "the consumer will." In a similar way, the proliferation of "personal" bumper stickers—I'D RATHER BE SAILING, TEACHERS DO IT WITH CLASS, HONK FOR JESUS—also proclaimed an explicit group identity. Such mobile totems served not only to link individuals with products and causes, but more importantly with other like-minded people—the kind who might smoke Camels, save whales, or go to church. "We need something special, something distinctive," said an adman in search of a logo, "something that says this is our team."

The pursuit of community stimulated new respect for the value of friendship, webs of relationships that provided collective support and warmth. A 1978 survey found that five out of six people had at least one confidant outside their households with whom they "would feel comfortable discussing just about any private problem." "The population which is not married is by no means bereft," concluded Angus Campbell of the Survey Research Center at the University of Michigan. "The 'lonely crowd' seems to be made up of people who have a surprising number of relatives and close friends with whom they are in frequent contact."

"My friends are my family," wrote Jane O'Reilly one Christmas, "and we will provide for each other."

"The movement itself had become 'family,'" said Betty Friedan of her network of liberated friends.

"The only stable element is friendship," agreed gay writer Edmund White.

"By some complex alchemy," suggested Jane Howard, "we must transform our friends into relatives. If blood and roots don't do the job, we must look to water and branches."

16

"LOOKING FOR AN ANCHOR"

History, Science, and the Natural Order

"WHEN YOU START TALKING ABOUT family, about lineage and ancestry," remarked the nation's most famous genealogist, "you are talking about every person on earth." On the eve of the 1976 presidential election, he had published his own family history, *Roots*, and almost immediately Alex Haley's saga of black America seized the popular imagination. In January 1977, during a bitter cold spell that froze the nation indoors, the ABC network transformed Haley's genealogical explorations into a riveting eight-day miniseries that attracted the largest audience in history. Over 130 million people, more than half the country's population, watched at least one segment of the series. Boosted by television, Haley's book sold sixty-seven thousand copies in one day, over nine hundred thousand in a single month.

The extraordinary popularity of *Roots* revealed a burgeoning enthusiasm for American history that had been building since the beginning of the decade. Stimulated first by the commercialization of nostalgia—reruns, trivia contests, fifties fads—then by the politically mandated Bicentennial, which fostered over sixty-four thousand community projects and activities, Americans eagerly celebrated the national past as mass entertainment. Typical of this escapism was the exuberance for historical romance, a literary taste that supported such pulp best-sellers as John Jakes's *Kent Family Chronicles*, which claimed over 30 million copies in print between 1974 and 1980. Such passions disturbed academic historians, who were concerned not only with declining classroom enrollments, but also with what they considered the trivialization of the past—in the words of Christopher Lasch, "the severance of the sense of historical continuity."

The fascination with American history, however, represented more than a retreat from the present, more than the substitution of fantasy for fact. It revealed a more fundamental pursuit: the desire for connection in time. "One of the real problems in this country these days," observed Jimmy Carter on the campaign trail in the year of the Bicentennial, was "the lack of roots, the mobile society, the constant moving from here to there—and, you know, the absence of anything that lasts in people's lives." Seeking ballast, Americans looked backward for a sense of direction. "There's a recognition that we've reached a turning point in our national history," observed Wilton Dillon of the Smithsonian Institution. "It's a good time to discover who we are." "People are floating," agreed Jeane Eddy Westin, author of *Finding Your Roots*, "looking for an anchor."

As Americans yearned for connection, librarians, archivists, historical societies, even the Daughters of the American Revolution, reported a renewed interest in genealogical research. Each week, the National Archives received twenty-three hundred requests for information. Once considered the domain of the elderly, genealogical research now appealed to the nation's youth. "Membership is getting younger," admitted the DAR, "—surprising, but true." To encourage such activity, the Boy Scouts of America introduced a new merit badge in genealogy. Sensing the trend, the nation's travel industries urged vacationers to retrace the steps of their ancestors (TAKE OUR ROUTES TO YOUR ROOTS, advertised Continental Trailways; "All of us come from somewhere else," summoned Pan American Airlines in a series of "two heritage" commercials). "The craze for genealogy probably . . . is connected with the epidemic of divorce," suggested Jane Howard. "If we can't figure out who our living relatives are, then maybe we'll have more luck with the dead ones."

Beyond genealogy, the search for historical roots held special appeal for social groups traditionally excluded from the national chronicle of greatness—ethnic and racial minorities, women, gays, and radicals. Just as Alex Haley's personal odyssey to Africa demonstrated the vitality of an alternative black history capable of surviving the most odious oppression of racism and slavery, other dispossessed groups sought a historical legacy to affirm their contemporary identity. "Maintaining history as the exclusive province of the elite," explained Sherna Gluck, in an oral history of five American suffragists, "not only denies most women a sense of their past but inevitably diminishes the significance they attach to their own lives." Inspired by Haley, grass-roots organizations, such as the Radical Elders Oral History Project, the San Francisco Gay History Project, as well as regional and local historical societies, sponsored a variety of activities—ranging from scholarly research in local archives to tape recording the reminiscences of the elderly—to reclaim the past.

The passion for oral history revealed a new respect for the spoken word. Unlike the written language, oral history diminished the importance of an expert intermediary, reduced the process of historical inquiry to its simplest form: the acquisition of raw experience. To cultural minorities, oral history symbolized a liberation from standard versions of the American past, offered interpretations that often differed from the narrative of professional historians who usually served the established society. At a time when educators observed a decline of literacy, oral history testified to the strength of cultural diversity. "Indian oral history is a recognition of what has moral value," suggested Simon Ortiz of the Acoma people of New Mexico. "Passing on that oral history to another generation is an affirmation of that value. . . . Indian oral history has not been acceptable to American society not because it has been unwritten but because the Indian system of moral value has not been accepted."

The reverence for oral traditions paralleled a popular interest in other nonliterary documentation—artifacts and relics, photographs, and films. Blurring the traditions of art and anthropology, major museums throughout the country staged gigantic exhibitions of antique artifacts—"Ice Age Art," "Sacred Circles," "The Treasure of Tutankhamun"—which attracted millions of spectators to glimpse centuries-old objects of human creation. "They are so fresh," noted Thomas Hoving of New York's Metropolitan Museum about the ancient Egyptian art, "they kind of wipe out time." The desire to transcend the passage of time, to share the historical moment, also underlay a contemporary enthusiasm for photography. "When we are nostalgic," observed Susan Sontag, "we take pictures." The freezing of time in a frame, the popular curiosity for photographic exhibits and anthologies, the rediscovery of nineteenth century camera pioneers and the subjects they immortalized—all illuminated a new sensitivity to the history of ordinary people, to ancestors previously invisible and unsung. The respect for the common past helped revitalize the documentary tradition in motion pictures. Women film makers, often excluded from the Hollywood mainstream, produced a series of dramatic films—*Harlan County, Union Maids, Rosie the Riveter, Babies and Banners*—that expressed the varieties of women's history and documented a radical tradition.

The enthusiasm for the past also stimulated interest in the historical environment, the context of history. "It is more important . . . to be able to say that certain events happened *here* and *there*," suggested American Indian author Vine Deloria, "rather than *when*." "Everybody is into roots now, since Haley," agreed Chicano novelist Rudolfo Anaya. "I see the roots of my soul grasping the earth. . . . The sense of culture, of tradition, of history was always around us." Revealing a new appreciation for the historical presence, Americans in the late seventies rejected the liberal euphoria for urban renewal, the demolition of old buildings, and instead affirmed the value of historical preservation. In a landmark case in 1978, the Supreme Court upheld the right of New York City to prevent the remodeling of historic Grand Central Station, arguing that "these buildings and their workmanship . . . embody precious features of our heritage . . . [and] serve as examples of quality for today." By the end of the decade, architectural renovation represented a major theme in urban planning. "Buildings, like people, must be allowed to age, develop and change," suggested architects Jane and Benjamin Thompson. "We should not attempt to freeze history but rather attempt to enhance its flow."

The re-creation of the past—the resurrection of artifacts, the personal encounter of oral history—transformed the historical process into a cosmic adventure, established connections with what the poet Gary Snyder called "the Old Ways, which are outside of history, and forever new." "It's a spiritual experience," exulted Lynn Donovan after recording the life histories of elderly women of San Francisco. The personal interaction of history, the intimacy across the generations, nourished a feeling of community, a shared experience that transcended secular chronology and defied the limitations of traditional scholarship. History became an emotional commitment, a conversation, the feel of polished wood, that linked the present with the symbols of the past. Said Alex Haley of the typical encounter between the old and the young, between grandparent and child, "It's sort of like stardust."

THE SEARCH FOR HISTORICAL CONTINUITY—for a community in time—closely paralleled an equally profound quest for connections in space, for a sense of achieving harmony with the fundamental structure of nature. During the seventies, scientific investigation of the history of the universe introduced subtle but important changes in the way people viewed their relationship to the cosmos. Where science in the sixties offered the promise of endless frontiers and infinite mobility—typified by the peregrinations of the multinational crew of the *Enterprise* on television's popular "Star Trek"—the most intriguing research in the field of astrophysics in the seventies emphasized the possibility of a world of absolute limits: the black hole. As superdense masses of collapsed matter, the hypothetical black hole contained gravitational forces so powerful that even light could not escape its grip. By definition, then, black holes remained a hypothesis of the scientific imagination.

The implications of the black hole theory, however, reflected broader cultural concerns. "Never before," suggested Princeton physicist John Wheeler, "did we think that matter could be so ephemeral." "Imagine, you take an enormous mass and shrink it down to nothing," proposed Harvard astrophysicist Jonathan Grindley. "A very disturbing idea." The image of a collapsing star—Isaac Asimov called it "the collapsing universe"—may have had special appeal to a people who were beginning to appreciate the limits of their own power to expand across the globe. Equally important was the theoretical possibility that the presence of black holes—if they existed at all—might represent sufficient density in the universe to exert a gravitational force capable of slowing and ultimately reversing the expansion of all matter from its cosmic center. Instead of an infinitely larger world-view, the black hole conjured up the alternatives of limits and retreat.

These metaphysical possibilities coincided with the appearance of some highly visible evidence that reinforced the world of limits. In 1975, a Viking spaceship, packed with ingenious experimental apparatus, extinguished a centuries-old dream of finding life on Mars. The earth's nearest planetary neighbor, commented Lewis Thomas, was "stone dead, the deadest place any of us has ever seen, hard to look at without flinching." This message of limited horizons echoed even more dramatically when another NASA launched project, the 77.5-ton orbiting space station known as Skylab, encountered unexpected shifts in the solar magnetic field and fell to earth four years earlier than promised, in 1979. Coming just one month after the fiery crash of a DC-10 airplane because of technological faults, the unpredictable descent of Skylab produced worldwide shivers at the inability of scientists to control their creations and reinforced a sense of earthboundness.

The gloomy prospects of human survival beyond the earth's gravitation inspired a popular belief in the existence of alternative life forms in outer space. A Gallup poll conducted in 1978 discovered that 57 percent of the public—70 percent of people under thirty—believed in the reality of unidentified flying objects (UFOs) and that one in nine claimed to have experienced a "sighting." Yet American attitudes toward extraterrestrial life remained highly ambivalent. In exploiting the fascination with nonhuman beings, Hollywood's *Star Wars* portrayed the invading society as menacing to humanlike people. The film *Close Encounters of the Third Kind* contrasted jubilant space explorers with the remainder of mankind, trapped by the earth's gravity. This sense of the earth as a home, a refuge for harried travelers, dominated science fantasies of the late seventies: the television production "Battlestar Galactica" and the movies *Superman* and *Alien*. In 1978, the film version of "Star Trek," once the epitome of the frontier culture, introduced a plot about defending the earth from invasion and in a remarkable time-warp ending confronted earthlings not with exotic creatures from beyond but with the voice of an earlier human launch.

The acceptance of the earth as a home for mankind reflected a growing awareness of the interconnectedness of all living things, a realization that the life process constituted less an evolutionary hierarchy than it did a web of organic relations. At the most advanced levels of research, physicists described a microcosmic world composed of high-energy matter that had no objective reality, but rather exhibited "tendencies to exist." Such "tendencies" depended upon the relationship between particles and the environmental context (which included the presence of the observer). Inhabited by quarks and leptons which had characteristics of "spin," "strangeness," and "charm," this subatomic world mirrored the living cosmos described by microbiologists, patterns of life sustained by the interdependence of eukarites, parasites, and viral organisms. "It is this huge reservoir of microlife," wrote biologist Url Lanham, "that produces the so-called ecological balance in nature." "The living and nonliving parts of ecosystems," suggested ecologist Eugene Odum, "are so interwoven into the fabric of nature that it is difficult to separate them." In this tightly knit cosmos, human existence depended upon the preservation of a shared environment.

The uniqueness of the earth's habitat accentuated the dangers of human intervention, the fear of irreversible destruction. In 1975, a federal task force on the Inadvertent Modification of the Stratosphere warned that unrestrained use of aerosol sprays, triggered by fluorocarbons, threatened to destroy the ozone layer that shielded the earth from radiation. "The idea that little puffs from spray cans could endanger the great ozone belt that surrounds the earth [seemed] preposterous," admitted *The New York Times*. But in 1977, federal agencies ordered a ban on such devices because of "unacceptable risk to individual health and to the earth's environment." Unlike the earlier furor over the SST, in which large corporations had heavy economic stakes, this prohibition found the leading manufacturer of aerosol spray valves, Robert Abplanalp, "rejoicing over the ban." "We've managed to put together something [new] with tried and true engineering principles," explained Nixon's closest friend, "that totally changes the nature of the aerosol business." Fluorocarbon refrigerants, however, were not outlawed, even though they contributed 40 percent of the dangerous emissions.

The effects of unrestrained technology had sobering repercussions. "Toxic chemical waste," advised Representative John Moss, "may be the sleeping giant of the decade." In 1973, an error in packaging animal food supplies in Michigan resulted in the accidental contamination of 30,000 head of cattle, 3,500 pigs, and 1.5 million chickens—all of which had to be killed—as well as a substantial human population which suffered unknown injury, including the toxification of breast milk. At Love Canal, near Niagara Falls, New York, residents noticed a wave of odd occurrences: a peculiar stench filled the air, trees turned black, children detonated multicolored sparks by crashing stones against the pavement, and the number of miscarriages and babies born with birth defects soared ominously—all probably the result of chemical wastes buried underground thirty years before. "We request a reprieve from death row," pleaded one resident, diagnosed with cancer and whose children suffered from liver abnormalities. Though President Carter designated the region an emergency area, many residents remained trapped by the economic cost of moving. "There are ticking time bombs all over," concluded an official of the Environmental Protection Agency. "We just don't know how many potential Love Canals there are."

Americans also became increasingly self-conscious of the effects of human activity on more vulnerable species. Concerned about the indiscriminate slaughter of whales, dolphins, and baby seals, environmental activists attempted to block the annual sea harvests and instituted boycotts of Japanese imports to protest the killings. Such gestures remained largely symbolic. In a celebrated case of 1978, the Supreme Court halted construction of the nearly completed Tellico Dam in Tennessee on the grounds that it imperiled the tiny snail darter, an endangered species protected by congressional legislation. "There will be little sentiment to have this dam standing before an empty reservoir," dissented Justice Lewis Powell, "serving no purpose other than a conversation piece for incredulous tourists." In a reversal of policy that reflected the heavy economic investment in the project, Congress voted to complete the dam in 1979.

The problems of tampering with the environment nevertheless raised new fears of an ecological catastrophe. Such concern, partly an expression of popular distrust of the scientific establishment, shifted in the seventies from the field of physics to biology. These changes emerged graphically in two versions of the classic science fiction film *Invasion of the Body Snatchers*. Despite the title, the first version, made in 1956, ascribed strange behavioral phenomena to radiation contamination (a familiar subject of fifties horror), whereas the remake, released in 1978, stressed biological issues, the dangers of genetic manipulation and, in one shocking depiction of a dog with a human face, the possibility of cloning. Ira Levin's popular novel about Hitlerian clones, *The Boys from Brazil,* linked the scientific nightmare with the specter of fascism. "This is not just science fiction," advised a Baptist minister about the risks of biological research. "Genetic engineering for the worst of reasons is a possibility in this world."

The warnings came first from within the scientific community. "New kinds of hybrid plasmids or viruses, with biological activity of unpredictable nature, may eventually be created," announced two experimental biologists in the prestigious *Science* magazine in 1973. "Certain such hybrid molecules may prove hazardous to laboratory workers and to the public." As biological research unveiled the mysteries of deoxyribonucleic acid (DNA), the chemical coding of heredity, scientists approached the possibility of recombining genetic structures to create new forms of life. Such experimentation held the promise of eliminating genetic defects or of producing efficient strains of edible vegetation. But some scientists shrank from the implications of their research. "The probability of creating a dangerous genetic agent . . . is real," maintained Liebe Cavalieri of the Sloan-Kettering Institute for Cancer Research, "and there is no way to test for the danger."

Fearful of some cataclysmic hubris, the nation's leading biologists hesitated to proceed. For the first time since World War II, when American physicists agreed not to publish research relating to atomic energy, the scientific leadership adopted a voluntary moratorium on further inquiry. But some scientists, confident in their ability to control experiments, protested this invasion of the freedom of research. To resolve the crisis, 150 biologists attended a historic meeting at Asilomar, near Monterey, California, in February 1975, to debate the issue—and they discovered they could not agree. They settled for compromise. "Ignorance," they admitted, "has compelled us to conclude that it would be wise to exercise the utmost caution. Nevertheless, the work should proceed with appropriate safeguards." "Scientists alone decided to impose the moratorium," protested Senator Edward Kennedy, "and scientists alone decided to lift it." In the spring of 1976, the National Institutes of Health issued a series of voluntary guidelines to assure a modicum of public safety. But dissident scientists rallied local communities near research laboratories to express public distrust of the controversial work. In Cambridge, Massachusetts, a citizens' review board monitored strict municipal guidelines and nearly approved a ban on risky research. "Only one accident is needed," insisted biologist Cavalieri, "to endanger the future of mankind."

Such dissent failed to slow the pace of genetic research. By the end of the decade, American scientists had succeeded in cloning portions of human chromosomes and had created hybrid human cells to produce pure antibodies. Using the technique of gene-splicing, commercial researchers at the General Electric company invented a living bacterial organism capable of digesting oil, and in a landmark decision of 1980, the Supreme Court upheld the issuing of a patent for such microorganisms. "Biologists have become, without wanting it, the custodians of great and terrible power," concluded biologist Robert Sinsheimer. "It is idle to pretend otherwise."

The terror of an uncontrolled biological holocaust, lurking close to the skin of the culture, erupted with unexpected violence during the summer of the Bicentennial. In the spirit of the national birthday, a contingent of American Legion war veterans converged in Philadelphia to celebrate and reminisce. "It was an ordinary convention, just like any other," noted one district commander. But within days, some of the veterans developed raging fevers, complained of chest congestion and exhaustion; in an epidemic of unknown causes, twenty-nine men died. "Whatever it is," pronounced one virologist, "it's one of the most dangerous things in the world." Within the next two years, the disease struck at least six more times; it claimed 118 victims and two deaths in a small area of Manhattan in September 1978. After a year of investigation, doctors at the Center for Disease Control identified the mysterious rod-shaped bacteria responsible for the epidemic. But its origins and its treatment remained obscure.

Amid the panic of Legionnaire's disease, epidemiologists intensified public fear by predicting the invasion of a highly contagious form of swine flu which they said threatened to decimate the population. Taking advice from such noted authorities as Jonas Salk and Albert Sabin, President Ford announced a national program "to inoculate every man, woman and child in the United States." But when insurance companies refused to underwrite the pharmaceutical manufacturers of the flu vaccine, health officials used the scare of Legionnaire's disease to push a limited liability law through Congress. One year later, reported a Harvard autopsy on the swine flu program, "cheeks flush, brows furrow, voices crack"—not from the symptoms of flu, but from embarrassment: "the killer never came." Worse, the inoculation of some flu vaccine itself proved dangerous, causing over five hundred cases of Guillein-Barré syndrome, a devastating neurological disorder that took twenty-three lives. In December 1976, the entire program was unceremoniously scrapped, showing, concluded the Harvard study, "how little experts understand."

At the beginning of the decade, Michael Crichton's novel *The Andromeda Strain* analyzed the danger of introducing an alien virus on the wings of a space ship returning to earth. "If there should be life on the moon," Lewis Thomas concurred, "we must begin by fearing it. We must guard against it, lest we catch something." But Crichton's story turned out happily; the menacing invader underwent rapid mutation into a benign form, self-destroying its capacity for evil. Such confidence about the evolutionary cycle contrasted starkly with popular anxieties at the end of the decade. In the remake of *Invasion of the Body Snatchers*, a terrified shriek signaled the end of human prospects, while the film *Alien*, pitting extraterrestrial life against a human space crew, epitomized not so much science fiction as it did sheer horror. Where Crichton envisioned a world of optimistic mobility, these later films dramatized the realistic constraints of gravity, a reaffirmation of human roots on earth.

THE POTENTIAL FOR BIOLOGICAL CATASTROPHE stimulated a thorough reevaluation of the relationship of the human body to the natural environment. "We are ignorant about how we work," admitted Lewis Thomas, "about where we fit in, and most of all about the enormous imponderable system of life in which we are imbedded as working parts." In orthodox allopathic medicine, disease symbolized invasion from outside, illness constituted a pattern of symptoms, and the physician served as an expert combatant to defeat an invisible foe. But a growing awareness of ecological principles, of the integration of all living forms within a web of relations, encouraged the emergence of alternative theories of health. "Nature is an interactive friend," explained Richard Miles, a pioneer in the holistic health movement, "and disease is a feedback process . . . which informs the individual that some life process is off-course." From this perspective, suggested Kenneth

Pelletier, an authority on psychosomatic medicine, "health is not the absence of disease but a state of optimum functioning."

The belief that good health reflected natural processes reinforced popular suspicions about medical intervention in normal life activities. As physicians introduced sophisticated technologies to monitor the birth process and implemented a drastic rise in cesarean deliveries, for example, parents increasingly sought alternative birth care—buying pregnancy diagnostic kits, learning muscle control and breathing techniques to replace medication, relying upon midwives for spiritual as well as medical support, and delivering children in special birth centers or at home. Despite opposition from the medical profession and the occasional prosecution of midwives for malpractice, statistical studies showed that home deliveries proved at least as safe as hospital care. "At home, people feel in control of the process. In the hospital they fear they won't be," explained Dr. Milton Estro, an advocate of home birth. "But these are the negative reasons. For a lot of people, it just feels right to have a baby in the intimacy of their home. Birth is not just a medical process, it is one of the penultimate experiences of life."

The articulation of alternative medical opinion, besides provoking raging battles within the healing professions, confused popular attitudes about the treatment of disease, causing some people to flee all orthodox advice and others to seek security in sophisticated technology. The issues emerged in an unplanned dialectic between two celebrated literary critics, each diagnosed with a potentially fatal disease: Susan Sontag and Norman Cousins. "There is a peculiarly modern predilection for psychological explanations of disease," chided Sontag, a recent cancer patient, in emphasizing the reality of physical illness. "Psychologizing seems to provide control over the experiences and events . . . over which people have in fact little or no control." Cousins, by contrast, responded to a diagnosis of degenerative muscular disease with a regimen of self-care based on raising his spirits by watching old comedies and by taking large doses of vitamin C. "The will to live is not a theoretical abstraction," he concluded upon recovery, "but a physiologic reality with therapeutic characteristics."

These differences about the nature of illness mirrored a major debate about the origins of the most dreaded malady of the age: cancer. The traditional view, implemented in the National Cancer

Act of 1971, presumed the existence of specific viral causes of disease. "Cancer in its many forms is undoubtedly a natural disease," maintained F.J.C. Roe, consultant to the American Industrial Health Council. "It is probably one of nature's many ways of eliminating sexually effete individuals who would otherwise, in nature's view, compete for available food resources without advantage to the species as a whole." Countering this Darwinian view was mounting evidence that many forms of cancer resulted from environmental factors: cigarette smoking, nutritional additives, toxic wastes. A study of occupational health commissioned by the Department of HEW in 1978 concluded that at least 20 percent of all cancers in the United States "may be work related." Such findings suggested that the "cure" of cancer required nonmedical remedies.

New attitudes toward the causes of disease encouraged the acceptance of alternative treatments, particularly the expansion of preventive medicine. At the beginning of the twentieth century, the major causes of death involved infectious diseases—influenza, pneumonia, tuberculosis, gastroenteritis—and preventive measures required massive public programs of inoculation, draining of swamps, and purification of water. By the seventies, the major diseases—cancer, cardiovascular problems, and cerebrovascular lesions—suggested environmental origins: smoking, nutrition, lack of physical stamina, and stress. In these cases, preventive medicine necessitated personal solutions. There existed "an individual moral obligation to preserve one's own health," said John Knowles of the Rockefeller Foundation, "—a public duty if you will."

These imperatives ignited an enormous explosion of physical fitness in the seventies. Running, bicycling, swimming, calisthenics, and handball—all relatively inexpensive activities, easily accessible, which could, most importantly, be indulged in by men and women together—awoke the nation from the torpor of spectator sports and rejuvenated a $2 billion a year athletic-supply industry based on the democratization of fitness. "I hear American puffing," parodied *Newsweek* in a cover story about the exercise rage, "the varied exhalations I hear/Those of joggers . . . in pursuit of transcendental highs. . . . /Puffing with open mouths, their strong cardiovascular harmonies." Jim Fixx's *The Complete Book of Running* topped the national best-seller lists for months; *Runner's World* magazine's annual shoe-evaluation issue sold half a million copies in 1978; popular marathons attracted thousands of participants. "We are discovering," exclaimed George Leonard, author of *The Ultimate Athlete*, "that every human being has a God-given right to move efficiently, gracefully and joyfully."

This cult of athletics, unlike traditional sports, minimized the importance of competition, stressed instead the ecstasy of physical awareness. The invention of cooperative games, the popularity of yoga, the emergence of Asian martial arts, such as aikido and t'ai chi, all evidenced a new concern for integrating the body and the soul, the athlete with the rhythms of nature. Some critics saw such innovations as "the trivialization of sports," mere expressions of narcissism and self-gratification. But participants extolled the values of spiritual connection. "Pressing us up against the limits of physical exertion and mental acuity," insisted George Leonard, "sports may open the door to infinite realms of perception and being." "It's a super feeling," maintained Senator William Proxmire, a five-mile-a-day runner, "like being immortal." "A good run," said a woman jogger in New York City, "makes you feel sort of holy."

The passion for physical fitness also led to a reassessment of the main reason for running: American eating habits. Although the fast-food industry enjoyed unprecedented growth in the seventies—McDonald's sold one billion hamburgers every five months; Kentucky Fried distributed 2.3 billion pieces of chicken a year—public-opinion surveys revealed increasing concern about the poor quality of the national diet. "Too much fat, too much sugar or salt . . . are linked directly to heart disease, cancer, obesity, and stroke, among other killer diseases," announced Senator McGovern in a report on American nutrition. "Six of the ten leading causes of death in the United States have been linked to our diet." Seeking to reverse eating habits that depended upon processed food and artificial additives, health-conscious consumers initiated what *The Wall Street Journal* called a "back-to-basics trend" based on home baking and fresh, often homegrown vegetables. Flour sales, which had declined steadily for twenty years, turned upward in 1973, while canned meat, fish, and poultry dropped 25-to-60 percent. "The number of home gardeners is increasing astronomically," reported television's green thumb, Jim Crockett, in 1979. "It's a reflection of the whole movement toward a more natural existence."

Concern about the standard American diet focused on eliminating ingredients that added little except calories and high blood pressure. After failing to persuade parents about the alleged dangers of homemade baby food, the industry capitulated to consumer pressure and removed extra salt and sugar from its products in 1977. "We're doing what the medical establishment and scientists say we should be doing," conceded a Beech-Nut executive. "But it also represents an awareness of what the mother will buy." Determined to gain control of their diets, Americans consumed an ever larger number of cookbooks, typified by Julia Child's shift from complicated French cuisine to simpler native diets. "The trend is toward lighter, seasonal dishes prepared with a minimum of fuss," observed Julie Dannenbaum of Philadelphia's Creative Cooking school. Worried about the overconsumption of alcohol, American drinkers embraced two booming new industries—low calorie beer and sparkling water. "Eating," decided Ellen Goodman, "had become the last bona fide sin in America."

Changes in diet and exercise had salutary effects on the state of American health. According to the National Center for Health Statistics, death rates decreased significantly in the seventies, particularly those caused by strokes and cardiovascular disease. Between 1969 and 1977, the death rate from heart disease declined 19.2 percent for men, 24.1 percent for women. Public awareness of risk, suggested a survey by the Metropolitan Life Insurance Company, "may be credited with the trend toward greater moderation in living habits." "If you make mistakes, after a while nature is going to give you a little slap," concluded Dr. Harold Bloomfield, a holistic health practitioner. "But if you start to go along with nature, pay attention, and enjoy that flow of effortless naturalness coming through you, you start to enjoy higher and higher levels of being and wellness."

THE CELEBRATION OF the natural order assumed that Americans could transcend the limits of industrial society, restore some primal attachment to the order of nature. "The most dangerous tendency in modern society," warned author Wendell Berry, "is the tendency toward encapsulation of human order—the severance, once and for all, of the umbilical cord fastening us to the wilderness or the Creation." Yet the weight of history already separated contemporary Americans from the textures of the land, the sea, and the stars. Although most people yearned for some ultimate connection, they remained enmeshed in the structure of the twentieth century. Told about the wonders of natural food, Archie Bunker expressed a common irony: "You can't get anything more natural than baloney."

Vulnerable to the confusion between nature and culture, between natural and artificial, consumers faced an array of mass metaphors that exploited their most profound needs. If "going natural" for women meant the rejection of cosmetics, the discarding of brassieres and underwear, the fullness of unstyled hair, corporate advertisers seduced the unwary with lingerie such as Nakeds ("Because you're sexier without a stitch on"); "clean fresh" perfumes like Revlon's Charlie which offered the "natural look"; hairstyles "given more natural coloring by reverse streaking," eyebrows "reshaped, made more natural." "The chemicals we make are no different from the ones God makes," explained the Dow company, once notorious as the manufacturer of napalm. "There is an essential unity between chemicals created by God and chemicals created by humans. . . . Birds, for example, are extraordinarily beautiful products produced by God." "The natural cigarette is here!" announced the R. J. Reynolds company in introducing the brand Real in 1977. Low-calorie "light" beer, one of the most innovative products of the decade, cultivated a similar "natural" image. Commented one brewery adman, "It's the sin without the penalty."

The ambiguity about the nature of "natural" raised moral issues that extended beyond the deceit of advertising or the sinfulness of alcoholic beverages. By defining as natural nearly everything that existed, corporate rhetoric not only thwarted a popular impulse for alternatives, but also denied individual responsibility for the shaping of the social order. Shielded behind images of nature—wild horses, leafy greens, or mountain vistas—such disavowals defended society from change. But the idea that existing social arrangements were natural contradicted traditions of social reform, the ability of liberals like Hubert Humphrey to identify corporate economics as the "old-time sin" or the recognition by Dolores Huerta of the United Farm Workers union "that wrong is wrong . . . that there's evil in the world and that you have to fight evil." By the late seventies, however, middle-class Americans often doubted the clarity of those judgments, perceived instead a world in which evil itself had become natural.

The fascination with evil in popular culture exposed a haunting ambivalence about the rapid social changes of the past decade. Sadomasochistic fashion photography, depictions of violence in department-store windows, the abiding luster of Nazi symbols and black leather (particularly among gay men)—in short, the social acceptability of situations of terror, illuminated an incomplete reconciliation to changing sexual values, to the liberation of women and the emergence of homosexuals as significant forces in society. Images of evil arose as psychic reminders of the risk of social upheaval. The popularity of horror novels expressed similar fears. In Anne Rivers Siddons's gothic *The House Next Door*, for example, a series of moral catastrophes—two respectable men caught in homosexual embrace, two other neighbors caught in heterosexual embrace, a horrible marriage sewn together only by the secret of an illegitimate child—circumstances that seemed eminently familiar in the maelstrom of domestic relations in the seventies, led to an unusual conclusion: "The house did it, the house *made* them do it!" In the same spirit, a purportedly nonfiction book, *The Amityville Horror*, attributed a ghastly mass murder to ancient ghosts that "inflict evil when the opportunity presents itself."

Belief in the naturalness of evil permitted a deliberate reversal of moral authority. In a series of Hollywood movies, *The Exorcist*, *The Omen*, *Carrie*, *The Shining*, seemingly innocent children confronted strange demonic powers, found themselves borne along by forces they neither wanted nor understood. Projections of adult fantasy, such visions transcended time, evaded social issues, flourished beyond moral effort and responsibility. "All the monsters we've created in fiction," admitted horror-film maker George Romero, "represent our own evil. We create them so we can kill them off, thereby justifying ourselves—it's a kind of penance, a self-exorcism." "People who cease to believe in God or goodness altogether still believe in the devil," suggested Anne Rice in the novel *Interview with the Vampire*. "Evil is always possible."

THE IMAGINATION OF EVIL, framed in fiction and fantasy, concealed a more dreadful—and more realistic—horror nestled at the center of the national conscience: the Vietnam war. "The American people tend to put unpleasant and unsuccessful events far beyond them as quickly as possible," observed the Reverend Theodore Hesburgh of Notre Dame in 1977. "Now one rarely speaks about the war or hears about it." Such amnesia buffered the country from the agony of its history. "However," added Hesburgh, "the American people cannot commit to oblivion the malevolent experience of the one quarter of all Americans who directly confronted that war and the many heartrending personal decisions it demanded." By the late seventies, the Vietnam war—or, more precisely, some versions of the war—reappeared, in journalism (Michael Herr's *Dispatches*; C. D. B. Bryan's *Friendly Fire*); memoir (Philip Caputo's *A Rumor of War*); fiction (Tim O'Brien's *Going after Cacciato*); and film (*The Boys of Company C, Coming Home, Go Tell the Spartans, The Deer Hunter*, and *Apocalypse Now*). Still, behind metaphor and symbol, the evil of Vietnam remained buried.

This burden of silence rested squarely on the war's veterans. "Going to war is a landmark experience in the life of an individual," stated Robert Muller, a former Marine lieutenant, "but in the case of Vietnam you learned very quickly to repress it, keep it secret, shut up about it, because people either considered you a sucker or some kind of psychopath who killed women and children. . . . It's unnatural." "They came back," recalled Dave Christian, perhaps the most decorated American soldier in Vietnam, "and people said, 'Forget it. Block out Vietnam. What you did was worthless.' It twisted a lot of guys."

In this silence, the horror of the war fed upon itself, causing deep turmoil for the military survivors. "At my age I should be worrying about getting dressed up fancy, making some bread, and learning to disco," said one veteran. "Instead, I'm worrying about not having any emotions." For Vietnam veterans, unlike soldiers in earlier wars, the symptoms of stress moldered for years, belatedly sending waves of survivors back to VA hospitals. In a study of five hundred Vietnam veterans, psychologist John Wilson reported that 80 percent of the men "cried, or got extremely angry, or were almost at times in a rage state because this was the first time they had gotten all this stuff off their chests." "The best medicine a country can give its veterans is love and understanding," suggested Purdue's Charles Figley, "—and it didn't."

As the war receded from public discourse, however, Americans made an uneasy peace with the men who fought in Vietnam.

A 1979 Harris poll found that most people viewed Vietnam veterans as victims, not perpetrators, of a senseless war. These changing sentiments persuaded Congress to authorize Operation Outreach, a nationwide counseling service to deal with the specific problems of Vietnam survivors. The veterans also aroused public attention to a lingering malady of the war that claimed unknown numbers of victims: the toxic effects of the defoliant Agent Orange. "Like women and blacks," commented psychiatrist Robert Jay Lifton in 1979, "Vietnam vets are emerging and demanding dignity. They are bouncing back—not just licking their wounds, but declaring their worth." "We don't need parades, plaques and certificates," agreed Randy Fowler of the veterans group Flower of the Dragon, "just respect and recognition."

The difficulty of accepting Vietnam veterans mirrored an equally awkward reconciliation with those citizens who had once bitterly opposed them, the survivors and victims of the antiwar movement. Under appeal, the Kent State trial continued through the courts, keeping a smoldering anguish alive until, at last, both sides welcomed relief. In an out-of-court settlement reached in January 1979, the state of Ohio awarded six hundred thousand dollars to compensate the victims, and Governor James Rhodes and twenty-seven national guardsmen released a statement acknowledging that "the tragedy of May 4, 1970, should not have occurred." "We have learned through a tragic event," responded the Kent survivors and the victims' parents, "that loyalty to our nation and its principles sometimes requires resistance to our government and its policies—a lesson many young people, including the children of some of us, had learned earlier."

At the university, the slaying remained a focus of dissent. In the mid-seventies, plans to erect a gymnasium at the site of the shootings provoked mass demonstrations against the desecration. The university commissioned sculptor George Segal to construct a monument to the tragedy, but in 1978 abruptly rejected it, on the grounds that "an apparent act of violence"—the sculptor showed Abraham poised with a knife above Isaac—was "inappropriate to commemorate an act of violence." A counterproposal to build a stone arch drew student scorn. "We have no room in our lives for tombstones," protested a group of architecture majors, "only living monuments to remind us that we each must help to make things better."

Such tempests belied any easy accommodation to the nation's history, to the roots and reality of evil. "We still haven't had an accounting," protested veteran Bobby Muller. "Why did it happen? People always say it was a waste, but, when you ask why it was a waste, you get 50 different stories. Let's talk about it. You cannot take 55,000 lives away—and that amount of money spent—and never give an accounting for everything that happened. *Why did Vietnam happen?*"

"It is depressing," wrote film critic Michael Covino, "that not a single full-length Vietnam War film has even come close to suggesting the overwhelming truth about the war: that the United States, an enraged giant, practically wasted an entire peasant country."

"We must face the fact," insisted veteran Stephen Phillip Smith, "that we fought a war for nothing, that our time and money and heroism went for nothing, and that those men who sacrificed their lives and limbs, or lost the ability to move or think, did so for absolutely nothing. The only dignity left is in telling the truth and hoping other generations will learn from it."

17

"AN AGE OF FEW HEROES"

The New Populists, the New Right, and the Search for the Lost America

On the thirteenth day of January 1978, a slowly spreading cancer clutched away the life of the last great symbol of American liberalism—former Vice President Hubert Horatio Humphrey. "For 30 years," eulogized President Carter, "his voice was heard from one end of the country to the other—most often in defense of the oppressed, the hungry, the victims of poverty and discrimination." Through the storms of controversy and personal defeat, the buoyant Minnesotan had preserved a fervent belief in the ability of government to alleviate social misery, and he had advocated, too, amid angry dissent, the importance of upholding the American way of life around the world. "I have no apologies for the federal government doing things," he told a reporter shortly before his death. "Who's going to take care of the environment, establish standards? . . . We've got to have federal government activity. The only question is not the size of the government, but does it work?" Four times Humphrey had tried—and failed—to occupy the White House. But, preached his protégé, Vice President Mondale, "he achieved something much more rare and valuable than the nation's highest office. He became his country's conscience."

The death of Hubert Humphrey (followed one year later by the demise of his liberal Republican counterpart, Nelson Rockefeller), portended the end of an era. Forty-five years after the inauguration of Franklin Delano Roosevelt, the nation no longer shared Humphrey's vision of a magnanimous federal government providing leadership for the hinterlands. "The moral test of government," said Humphrey in one of his last public appearances, "is how it treats those who are in the dawn of life, the children; those who are in the twilight of life, the aged; and those who are in the shadows of life, the sick, the needy and the handicapped." By such standards, liberal dreams often remained unfulfilled, despite heavy public expenditures for education, health, and welfare.

Frustrated by the failure of government policy, critics from the right and the left—for decidedly different reasons—joined in denouncing the liberal vision. "We've broken all the ground in all areas of human activity—the environment, outer space, human rights, civil rights, women's rights—right across the board," stated Richard Lesher, president of the conservative Chamber of Commerce. "We're just now waking up to the fact that government is ill-equipped to deal with many of these problems."

"In the crisis that's lying ahead," suggested Milton Kotler, director of the National Association of Neighborhoods, a coalition of community groups, "there's a new recognition that the country's not going to be saved by experts and bureaucrats. It's going to be saved by some moral vision and some moral hope coming from the grassroots and the neighborhoods." "We are not," announced antiwar veteran Gary Hart in running successfully for reelection to the Senate, "a bunch of little Hubert Humphreys."

CONVINCED OF THE INADEQUACIES of federal programs, political activists turned increasingly to more manageable arenas—state, local, and neighborhood organizations. "The day of the state has come and gone," remarked Colorado Governor Richard Lamm, "—and come back again." By the late seventies, over 20 million Americans participated in some form of neighborhood improvement group, joining consumer advocates, labor organizers, independent farmer organizations, and proponents of alternative technology to form a massive grass-roots movement aimed at restoring the vitality of community democracy. "Most Americans . . . tend to think that political history is made only by great men—Kennedys or Kings, maybe, but not ordinary people," remarked Mike Ansara, organizer of the Massachusetts citizens group Fair Share. "A lot of what we are doing is challenging that notion and getting people over that tremendously debilitating sense of powerlessness and cynicism."

The contrast between liberal reformism sponsored by the federal government and the new community populism emerged dramatically in the revitalization of urban neighborhoods. While the nation's major cities continued to lose population to the suburbs and rural areas, communities throughout the country repudiated the traditional remedies of urban renewal—the razing of whole neighborhoods to be replaced by commercial structures or public housing projects—and instead chose to rebuild and restore existing dwellings. Reflecting the popular enthusiasm for cultural roots, such rehabilitation often began as a personal project—dictated partly by economics, partly by a preference for traditional architecture. But individual enterprise soon spread to larger community issues involving taxation, financing, zoning, and public services. "We came to restore old houses," stated the founder of St. Louis's Lafayette Square Restoration Committee, a pioneering program in urban homesteading, "but we wound up restoring the neighborhood."

These commitments often clashed with government and business policies that had contributed to urban decline and led many community builders to become political activists. The common practice by banks and insurance companies to "redline" deteriorating neighborhoods as bad investment risks, for example, blocked the funding necessary to rebuild old dwellings, reoccupy abandoned structures, and improve public spaces. But local pressure organizations, such as Chicago's Citizens Action Program, launched alternative "greenlining" campaigns which persuaded lending institutions in many cities to end such neighborhood-destroying activities. Another effective tactic was the formation of community credit unions, which expanded the equity base and so facilitated the acquisition of small loans for renovations. In Colorado, the state government initiated a program that distributed public deposits to encourage banks to undertake "social lending." "We don't ask them to do business differently," explained a Philadelphia advocate, "only with an open and rational mind."

The attempt to protect communities from the intrusive power of the federal government and large corporations stimulated nationwide experimentation with alternative technologies, particularly in the area of energy resources. "If we're going to conserve energy as a nation," argued Dick Fiddler of Seattle's Office of Energy, "we've got to start at the local level." To maximize available resources, local governments and private organizations introduced innovative technologies, ranging from burning wood chips in Vermont, garbage in Milwaukee, and geothermal heat in Idaho, to limit energy dependence. At the frontiers of research, organizations such as the New Alchemy Institute at Cape Cod, the California Office of Alternative Technology, and the Shelter Institute in Maine repeatedly demonstrated the validity of small-scale technology in providing superior levels of food, shelter, and energy. Decentralized economies, partially freed from corporate control, promised to ensure local autonomy. "It's a question of getting the available technology into the proper hands," maintained Richard Kazis of the Institute for Self-Reliance. "Like the question of whether we can develop photovoltaic cells before the energy corporations get hold of the technology." But such enthusiasm could not prevent large businesses from gaining control of valuable patents in the race to develop solar technology.

The belief in community democracy encouraged the proliferation of grass-roots organizations that worked for social betterment. "We try to get people in touch with their own anger," stated Ernie Cortes, a community organizer who helped found effective mass coalitions in San Antonio, Texas, and in East Los Angeles. "What we mean by anger is being your brother's keeper. It means building a new community." In Massachusetts, a state-wide citizens group, Fair Share, harnessed popular antagonism toward rising automobile insurance rates and forced the legislature to rebate extra premiums and to rescind probusiness legislation. "We tried to get back to real, everyday things, to a calm style," explained one organizer, formerly active in the antiwar movement. "We switched issues from Vietnam and Cambodia and just moved in with the community." In rural Minnesota, the construction of a high-voltage power line aroused bitter resistance in the conservative farm country, culminating in mass protests supported by the local Catholic churches.

"I hate to tell you my position during the Vietnam war," admitted Gloria Woida, a leader of the Minnesota movement. "I was totally against all that protesting, but now I see that war as the same as what . . . the Government is doing to us with that power line. I realize we're all at the mercy of government."

"I keep hearing that everything's dead and there's no big

cause since civil rights and the Vietnam War," observed Gale Cincotta, head of National People's Action, a nationwide neighborhood coalition. "But that's a myth. There's a neighborhood movement that started in the sixties. It's not as dramatic with everybody out in the streets, but it's steadily gaining strength in every city and state. The base was there and people reached the point where they just had to do something."

"The media is selling us on this notion of apathy and paralysis in the country," objected former antiwar activist Sam Lovejoy. "Bullshit. The movement did not die. It did the most intelligent thing it could do: it went to find a home. It went into the community. It's working, unnoticed, in the neighborhood. They're starting to blossom and make alliances, connections."

Such passions usually focused on disparate local issues—a particular grievance, such as utility rates, that galvanized traditional liberals and conservatives to community action. But one issue had nationwide implications—the spread of nuclear reactors. On George Washington's birthday in 1974 ("I cannot tell a lie," he crowed, "I did knock down the cherry tree"), Lovejoy single-handedly toppled a five-hundred-foot tower designating the site of a planned nuclear power plant in Montague, Massachusetts. "Communities have the same rights as individuals," he announced upon surrendering to the police. "We must seize back control of our community." Amid considerable publicity, a local jury acquitted Lovejoy, boosting a grass-roots antinuclear protest that stretched from coast to coast. "This movement is built from the bottom up," commented a member of the antinuclear Clamshell Alliance. "Here the movement starts with the town. There is no other way."

Mustering public support, opponents of nuclear power attempted to restrict further proliferation through popular initiatives. In 1976, antinuclear measures appeared on ballots in California, Oregon, Washington, Colorado, Montana, Arizona, and Ohio. Attacked by lavishly funded advertisements from the nuclear power industry, the proposals failed everywhere. But public distrust of nuclear power, virtually unknown a decade earlier, had gained a self-perpetuating momentum. "We're feeling very disillusioned about the legal and legislative channels for stopping nuclear power," stated a member of San Francisco's People Against Nuclear Power. "Our new method is disciplined, nonviolent direct action."

The small beach community at Seabrook, New Hampshire,

population 5,700, wanted no part of nuclear power, voting, despite promises of tax relief and new jobs, against a proposed plant in 1976. As ground-breaking ceremonies continued anyway, residents joined the Clamshell coalition in adopting passive resistance tactics perfected during the civil rights movement of the sixties. And, as in that earlier struggle, the uncompromising response of public authorities to nonviolent protest widened the appeal of the antinuclear crusade. In 1976, occupiers at the planned site, known as the Seabrook Ten, received six-month jail sentences for civil disobedience. "Ignorance of the law is no excuse," admitted one defendant, "but ignorance of the dangers of nuclear power is also no excuse." In 1977, as the sit-in tactics continued, national guardsmen arrested over fourteen hundred protesters and the costly incarceration further inflamed public opinion, inspiring even larger antinuclear rallies the next year. Such protests soon mushroomed around the country, and to the forefront came veterans of earlier populist crusades—Benjamin Spock, Daniel Ellsberg, Dennis Banks, Tom Hayden, Jane Fonda, and hordes of supporters.

This burgeoning dissent awakened public suspicions, reminiscent of the antiwar movement, about government credibility. The calamity at Three Mile Island in 1979 aroused new doubts about official assurances of nuclear safety. That spring, moreover, a jury verdict against a Kerr-McGee nuclear facility in Oklahoma vindicated the long-suppressed allegations of the deceased Karen Silkwood, confirming fears that nuclear plants were not only technologically deficient, but also poorly protected against theft and subversion. "The history of the nuclear power industry," Ralph Nader told a throng of over a hundred thousand gathered at Capitol Hill in May 1979 to protest nuclear energy, "is replete with cover-ups, deceptions, outright lies, error, negligence, arrogance, greed, innumerable unresolved safety questions and a cost-plus accounting that taxes our citizens as consumers and taxpayers. There has to be a better, safer way to heat water."

The opposition to nuclear power focused on practical matters of health, safety, and cost, but its philosophical underpinnings also evoked a distinct vision of the future of American society. Where nuclear energy involved the continued expansion of industrial capitalism along with elaborate government regulatory administration, the antagonists envisioned, in the words of California Governor Jerry Brown, "a world with limits to its resources and a country with limits to its power and economy." This alternative view rejected the centralized authority inherent in nuclear energy, preferring inexpensive and ecologically sensitive technologies, such as solar power, to free individuals and communities from both big business and big government. Challenging what economist E. F. Schumacher called "the forward stampede" of modern society, the antinuclear position assumed, more simply, that "small is beautiful."

The great popularity of Schumacher's ideas about the development of small-scale technology reflected not merely its ecological wisdom, but also a moral appeal based on traditional Christian principles, specifically the teachings of the Roman Catholic church to which Schumacher had recently converted. Where mainstream Catholicism of the sixties seemed to embrace the presidential summons toward New Frontiers and endless mobility, surveys of Catholic opinion in the seventies reported a preference for the more rooted values of family, neighborhood, and community and a casual style of interaction "rather than formal, bureaucratic, direct techniques." In the late seventies, church attendance among young adult Catholics suddenly increased by 10 percent, reversing a long downward trend. "To be Catholic," wrote Michael Novak, "is not so much to belong to an organization as to belong to a people. It is . . . to have a differentiated point of view and sensibility." Such values often clashed with the pressures of assimilation, individualism, and advancement. "One of the penalties of upward mobility," conceded Catholic novelist Mary Gordon, "is a sense of guilty indebtedness to the old neighborhood."

The ideal of small personal communities permeated the writings of numerous ecologically oriented commentators, such as Theodore Roszak and Ivan Illich—who, incidentally, shared Catholic antecedents—and closely paralleled the traditional values of an organic society. "The problem is to re-establish neighborhood and community responsibility," suggested Governor Brown, a former Catholic seminarian. "But it's difficult, given the fact that everybody's moving around, shifting jobs, driving 30 or 40 miles a day." "We need a politics of smallness," agreed Michael Novak. "Think small. It is a time for small states and quiet ways." Calling for "creative social disintegration," Roszak urged "a new sense of our organic reciprocity with the land" and appealed for a spirit of "conviviality . . . as a culminating relationship between free and unique persons." To the question "What can I actually *do*?" Schumacher offered the plain homily, that "each of us work to put our own inner house in order."

THE REPUDIATION OF LIBERALISM by community populists paralleled a reinvigorated attack on the same system by its traditional enemies—the conservative right. "For the average American, the message is clear," stated Ronald Reagan: "Liberalism is no longer the answer—it is the problem." Long hostile to bureaucracy and rising taxes, opponents of the liberal state successfully transformed public frustration at government inefficiency into a mass movement to slash property taxes and curb administrative waste. "You are the people," declared Howard Jarvis, a seventy-five-year-old curmudgeon who led the crusade for California's Proposition 13 in 1978, "and you will have to take control of the government again or else it is going to control you." Tax reforms of the sixties combined with runaway real-estate values in the seventies placed a mounting burden of taxation on California homeowners. Yet while assessments escalated rapidly, the state government held a $4 billion surplus. Proposition 13, a ballot initiative supported by 1.5 million signatures, offered to reduce assessments, limit property taxes to one percent of full value, and prevent the easy passage of new taxes. "Give the politicians a budget," suggested one pro-13 advertisement, "instead of a blank check."

Despite the opposition of state government and the generous contributions of big business, which feared the disruptive effects of a massive tax cut, Californians voted to make bureaucracy accountable, approving the initiative by a 2–1 margin. Overnight, homeowners gained tax relief worth hundreds, sometimes thousands, of dollars, while the state's largest corporations saved multimillion-dollar levies. "Let us hope that California's message will be heard loud and clear . . . across the nation," exclaimed the exile of San Clemente, who saved $27,500 on his $2 million home. "People everywhere want to reduce government spending, the burden of taxes, and the spiral inflation which is the cruelest tax of all." After initial shock at the landslide defeat, liberals announced that the state surplus would salvage the sunken budgets. "We have our marching orders from the people," said Governor Brown in belatedly endorsing the initiative. "This is the strongest expression of the democratic process in a decade."

The ratification of Proposition 13 seemed to herald a conservative backlash against liberal programs. "Across the country," charged Senator McGovern in a farewell address as president of Americans for Democratic Action, "politicians . . . are seeking a mandate to govern by running against government itself." "This isn't just a tax revolt," insisted President Carter's pollster, Pat Caddell. "It's a revolution against government." Conservatives in other states promptly introduced similar tax-cutting proposals, sometimes in language identical to Proposition 13. The measure, former Governor Reagan told a Chicago audience, "triggered hope in the breasts of the people that something could be done . . . a little bit like dumping those cases of tea off the boat in Boston harbor."

Such pronouncements contradicted the drift of public opinion. While Proposition 13 demonstrated widespread dissatisfaction with inefficiency, waste, and unresponsiveness, taxpayers indicated little desire to reduce public services. "The American people have not become more conservative in their attitudes toward government," explained political scientist Everett Ladd after analyzing a spate of opinion surveys. "The heart of the indictment is a call not for *less* government but for *better* government." In Idaho and Nevada, which like California had experienced soaring property taxes, voters did approve similar cutbacks. But elsewhere, in Oregon, Michigan, Colorado, Nebraska, the public rejected tax and spending limitations, and in other states, such as New Jersey and Tennessee, voters accepted budgetary ceilings without attacking existing structures. Given an opportunity in 1980 to reduce state income taxes in an initiative labeled Jarvis II (liberals called it "Jaws II"), California voters chose to preserve the fiscal status quo. "The tax revolt is not taking us on a conservative trip to the right," concluded Robert Teeter, former pollster for President Ford. "This is a moderate country."

The populist rhetoric of reduced taxation nevertheless lent legitimacy to a conservative fiscal crusade led by big business to stop tax reform. Though President Carter promised to improve a tax system he considered a "disgrace to the human race," his plan to eliminate corporation loopholes encountered stiff resistance from a well-financed business lobby that demanded tax cuts to stimulate capital investment. "Proposition 13 gave us a lift," conceded one business adviser. "It helped give tax reduction a broader credibility." A proposal to reduce all taxes by one-third found little favor in the Democratic Congress. But mounting pressure from business to reduce capital gains taxes overcame liberal dissent. The resulting Revenue Act of 1978 gave three-quarters of all tax reductions to the wealthiest two percent of the nation's taxpayers. "It used to be that business would hire a tax counsel to get a special tax break," remarked Bob Brandon, director of Ralph Nader's Tax Reform Research Group. "Now they don't get special tax breaks; they change the whole system." It was, protested Senator Kennedy, "the worst tax legislation approved by Congress since the days of Calvin Coolidge and Andrew Mellon."

The ability of big business to engulf the taxpayers' revolt illuminated the growing power of a hitherto ignored force in American politics—the New Right. Four decades after the New Deal, orthodox conservatives, such as columnist William Buckley and the Republican party establishment, had made an uneasy peace with liberal programs. "The right wing in America," explained Garry Wills in *Confessions of a Conservative*, "is stuck with the paradox of holding a philosophy of 'conserving' and an actual order it does not want to conserve." The New Right, by contrast, dismissed these ideological contradictions. "We are radicals who want to change the existing power structure," said Paul Weyrich, who with the financial backing of brewer Joseph Coors founded the Committee for the Survival of a Free Congress in 1974. "We are not conservatives in the sense . . . [of] accepting the status quo."

The New Right ironically drew strength from social discontents similar in some ways to those that motivated community populists—a distrust of liberal economics and the expansion of government bureaucracy. But while opposing centralized power, the new conservatives paradoxically created tightly disciplined political organizations, often knit together not only by common goals, but also by interlocking leaderships and bureaucracies as well as the computerized operations of direct mail expert Richard Viguerie, so-called "godfather" of the New Right. Unlike the populists, moreover, the New Right condemned the liberalization of moral values. Appealing to single-issue voters opposed to gun control, abortion, homosexuality, pornography, and the ERA, this vocal minority promised to restore a world of simple virtues, an old America based on family, church, and the work ethic.

To revitalize the capitalistic spirit, conservatives embraced the panacea of laissez faire economics. "Instead of government serving to create a climate of opportunity," argued Representative Jack Kemp of New York, "government has become the competition. . . . the other team—and it's winning!" Adopting the theories of Arthur Laffer, a maverick economist at the University of Southern California, Kemp joined Senator William Roth in proposing a drastic 30 percent cut in federal taxes designed to stimulate investment, boost productivity, and simultaneously end inflation and unemployment. Conservative economics also attacked the proliferation of government regulations—environmental rules, health and safety requirements, consumer protection standards—as additional drags on capital investment. Conservative public interest law groups supported suits to prevent enforcement of administrative rules that challenged business goals. In 1978, for example, the conservative Mountain States Legal Foundation helped persuade the Supreme Court that federal inspectors could not enter business facilities without a proper search warrant. "If we could eliminate the unnecessary regulation of business," insisted Ronald Reagan, "we could cut the rate of inflation in half." Such prospects appealed to a public troubled by a world of limits. "No frontier need be closed for long," promised Kemp. "The creative genius that has always invigorated America is still there, submerged, waiting like a genie in a bottle to be loosed."

The optimism of the New Right contrasted with the cranky tone of a group of ex-liberal intellectuals who constituted the "neoconservatives"—Irving Kristol, Norman Podhoretz, Daniel Bell, Nathan Glazer, and Senator Daniel Moynihan. Still committed to the principles of the welfare state and the pursuit of the cold war, neoconservatives objected to specific government policies initiated in the sixties. Glazer's *Affirmative Discrimination*, for example, emphasized that opportunity traditionally applied to individuals, not to social groups, and that equality before the law mandated no equality of result. "Unlike the New Right," explained Kristol, "we have no interest in, and little sympathy for, methods of direct democracy like initiatives and referenda." "A society has vitality," argued Bell, "if it has a strong establishment." In such publications as *The Public Interest* and *Commentary*, these writers denounced affirmative action, feminism, and post-Vietnam isolationism. But the very elitism that spawned their independent position starved the neoconservatives of their logical constituencies.

The democratization of conservative ideas hinged on more basic metaphors, the revival of an old American mythology about the self-made man. Despite persistent inflation, unemployment, and the decline of real wages in the seventies, public opinion surveys found that most poor Americans still believed in the possibility of upward economic mobility and feared, most of all, that government taxation would curtail opportunity. Two-thirds of the public in 1978 consequently favored cuts in the capital gains tax, even though the main beneficiaries would be business investors. These attitudes percolated through the larger society, thanks to two dramatic success stories—one that appealed to blacks, the other to working-class whites.

A black newspaper called him "a Patty Hearst in reverse," and a prominent leftist writer dismissed him as a "Bicentennial coon," but exiled Black Panther polemicist Eldridge Cleaver, a fugitive on murder charges, returned to the United States in 1975 confident that he could win his freedom. "With all its faults," he declared, "the American political system is the freest and most democratic in the world." Cleaver promptly announced his conversion to evangelical Protestantism and made plans to manufacture expensive codpiece trousers. Released on bail, he emerged in public lectures to extol "the limitless possibilities of the American dream." "For 22 years I studied and practiced the communist ideology," he admitted. "Then I came face to face with a different kind of revolutionary. His name is Jesus Christ." Daniel Moynihan donated five hundred dollars to his cause, and Norman Podhoretz, in a conservative version of "radical chic," hosted a fund-raising party on his behalf. "People say I've changed," noted the former minister of information, "but they forget how America has changed." Plea-bargaining to assault charges dating from a 1968 shootout with Oakland, California, police, Cleaver threw himself at the mercy of the court. "I feel you have changed for the better," replied Judge Winton McKibben in sentencing the returned prodigal to probation and two thousand hours of community service. A gleeful Cleaver promised to "bring the gospel of Jesus Christ to bear on all activities."

"You're just a working stiff," scoffed Archie Bunker's boss on the loading dock. Someone was always yelling at him to move crates, and just to make ends meet he had to drive a cab at night.

But, announced Archie in 1977, "I wanna raise myself up. I want my name on somethin' more than just a lunchpail." When the proprietor of the neighborhood tavern retired, Archie forged his wife's signature to obtain a bank mortgage. "He resented me because he never had a chance to better himself," explained his son-in-law in a rare moment of support. "Well, now he's got that chance. In Archie's mind it's a chance for him to be somebody. I don't think you can take that away from him." In the spirit of the delinquent Benjamin Franklin who ran away from home to build a fortune, "All in the Family" followed the hero of the television workingmen into a new setting, the fulfillment of one middle class dream, a saloon of his own: Archie's Place.

THE CELEBRATION OF the old American values coincided with an impassioned effort by the New Right to restore an old moral order. Threatened by the rapid spread of alternative social values—the decline of traditional marriage, the rise of sexual liberation movements, demands for equal opportunity and affirmative action—fundamentalist Christian sects vowed to extirpate a "secular humanism" that they claimed was destroying the country. "Moral decadence is a very serious problem today," stated Gary Jarmin of the lobby group Christian Voice, "and politics is a big reason for these problems." "Everywhere we turn," agreed the organization's director, Robert Grant, "Christian values are assaulted and are in retreat. As Christians, we are not going to take it anymore." "This country is fed up with radical causes," insisted Jerry Falwell, preacher-host of television's "Old-Time Gospel Hour," "fed up with the unisex movement, fed up with the departure from basics, from decency, from the philosophy of the monogamous home." Although public opinion polls demonstrated that a majority of Americans rejected the social values of these religious conservatives, special-interest minorities assumed inordinate importance, especially at a time when political participation in the larger population continued to decline. "I don't want everyone to vote," admitted Weyrich during the 1980 campaign. "Our leverage in the election quite candidly goes up as the voting population goes down. We have no responsibility, moral or otherwise, to turn out our opposition."

The defense of traditional morality began in the bosom of the family. "The Bible clearly states," announced Edward Hindson's *The Total Family*, a book endorsed by Falwell, "that the wife is to submit to her husband's leadership and help him fulfill God's will for his life. . . . She is to submit to him just as she would submit to Christ as her Lord." On such grounds, Protestant fundamentalists joined Phyllis Schlafly's Eagle Forum to lobby the state legislatures against passage of the ERA. "Homosexuality is a perversion, not an alternative life-style," maintained Falwell in a "Clean Up America" campaign that eagerly supported the preaching of Anita Bryant. "Abortion on demand is legalized murder," he said in backing the right-to-life movement. "You can stop the moral landslide," Falwell exhorted. "We can turn back the tide of situation ethics."

The protection of the family from outside interference required special vigilance against the favorite institutions of liberal infiltration—the mass media. "Pornography," argued Falwell, "particularly in television and literature, is brainwashing the American people into accepting as normal what is abnormal." According to the Reverend Don Wildmon, founder of the National Federation for Decency, television audiences witnessed over eleven thousand sexually suggestive comments each year (over eighteen thousand if "skin scenes" counted), a 45 percent increase in profanity between 1978 and 1979, and a preponderance of sexual activity outside marriage. Such findings bolstered a nationwide boycott of the sponsors of televised sexuality and succeeded in persuading Sears, Roebuck to drop "Charlie's Angels" and "Three's Company" and the Kentucky Fried Chicken chain to shift its support to blander programming.

The moral conservatives also challenged the attitudes of professional educators who tried to influence the thinking of their charges. "As long as we've got schools in this country," warned a West Virginia textbook protester in 1975, "we're going to have to realize that there are people who are trying to destroy our basic concepts." The introduction of school books that accepted premarital sex and abortion, for example, or that used language considered obscene, often violated community standards. Organizing protests, parent groups succeeded in censoring teaching materials, school publications, and library lists. The fear of cultural subversion also justified opposition to school busing and the employment of homosexual teachers. "The children in your neighborhood are in danger," cried the Christian Voice in describing a host of public school policies that constituted "just a fraction of a master plan to destroy everything that is good and moral here in America."

The revival of traditional morality extended beyond the doors of any single denomination or political group, increasingly influencing people opposed to liberal change, and it transformed public opinion about an old bone of moral contention—the practice of capital punishment. In the heyday of liberal reform, a 1966 Gallup poll found that more Americans opposed capital punishment than favored it (47 percent to 42 percent), an opinion that encouraged the Supreme Court to rule in 1973 that existing death penalty laws were imposed "wantonly and freakishly" and were consequently unconstitutional. By 1976, however, public opinion had changed and an overwhelming majority, according to a Gallup survey, now supported the death penalty (65 percent to 28 percent). "We hold," said the Supreme Court in a clarification of its thinking, "that the death penalty is not a form of punishment that may never be imposed." Though the Court disallowed state laws that demanded mandatory sentencing and insisted that "death is grossly disproportionate and excessive punishment" for the crime of rape, it encouraged "an individual decision . . . in capital cases."

The first victim of these changing postures ironically contributed to its public acceptance. Charged with two murders in Utah, defendant Gary Gilmore refused to appeal the death sentence. "Weak bad habits . . . have left me somewhat evil," he explained. "I don't like being evil and . . . desire to not be evil anymore." In January 1977, a state firing squad effectively ended a ten-year moratorium on capital punishment that itself represented a moral bulwark against legal executions. By 1977, public opinion polls found that the majority favoring capital punishment had increased. Such feelings, surveys found, remained constant even if people believed the practice had no deterrent effect. "The motives for the death penalty may indeed include vengeance," suggested sociologist Ernest van den Haag. "Legal vengeance solidifies social solidarity against lawbreakers and probably is the only alternative to the disruptive private revenge of those who feel harmed." In May 1979, the state of Florida reaffirmed those primal standards by electrocuting convicted murderer John Spenkelink in the first involuntary execution since 1967.

The resurgence of traditional values triggered the expansion of conservative churches dedicated to reversing the drift of modern society. Through television and radio pulpits, preachers like Falwell, Pat Robertson, James Robison, and Jim Bakker reached an estimated 100 million Americans each week. This vast electronic church urged its members to support conservative causes, even as it undermined traditional religious institutions and the local church. The broadcast preachers also created an electronic feedback system of telephone lines and direct mail facilities that enabled them to garner, along with their converts, over $30 million a year to finance church activities. "We have enough votes to run the country," claimed Robertson. "And when the people say, 'We've had enough,' we are going to take over." Forming in 1979 what he called the "Moral Majority," Falwell launched a coalition of religious groups, primarily evangelical Protestants, as one of his supporters reported, "to mobilize at least two million Americans to work for pro-God, pro-family policies in government." "Get them saved, baptized, and registered," Falwell advised his ministerial colleagues.

THE POLITICIZATION OF organized religion provided moral fervor in the rebirth of conservative politics. Following the Watergate scandals, Congress had limited the size of individual campaign contributions, forcing candidates to develop a mass base of support. Such revisions increased the importance of communications specialists, such as the conservative Viguerie, who solicited funds from likely contributors. "Direct mail has allowed conservatives to by-pass the liberal media, and go directly into the homes of the conservatives in this country," Viguerie told the Conservative Political Action Conference in 1977. "There really is a silent majority in this country, and the New Right now has learned how to identify them and communicate with them and mobilize them." By targeting appeals to specific constituencies, such techniques allowed politicians to disregard the traditional party structures.

The attempt to minimize corporation interference in elections by limiting business contributions also caused powerful and unexpected reverberations when the Supreme Court ruled that political expenditures, as a form of public speech, could not be limited by Congress, and that corporations, as legal entities, shared these constitutional rights with private citizens. Business groups responded by organizing ever larger numbers of independent political action committees (PACs)—from 89 in 1974 to 821 in 1978 to more than 1,300 in 1979—to support favored candidates and causes. "They are multiplying like rabbits," warned Senator Kennedy, "and they are doing their best to buy every Senator, every Representative and every issue in sight." "It's just as much a civic responsibility," replied one executive, "as helping the Heart Fund." Permitted by the high court to participate in referenda campaigns, corporations often outspent citizens groups to protect vested interests. "If corporate interests can dominate both legislatures and referenda with their dollars," advised Mark Green, director of the Public Citizens Congress Watch, "then the golden rule of politics prevails—he who has the gold rules."

An invigorated alliance between corporate conservatives and the New Right produced unexpected results in the elections of 1978. With voters disdaining traditional party labels, conservative coalitions orchestrated elaborate campaigns against such liberal incumbents as Dick Clark of Iowa, Floyd Haskell of Colorado, and Thomas McIntyre of New Hampshire, toppled liberal governor Michael Dukakis of Massachusetts in the primaries, and danced on the grave of Humphrey's Democratic-Farmer-Labor organization by beating the entire ticket in Minnesota. In these contests, single-issue conservatives, such as antiabortion groups, often exerted a small but crucial margin of difference. "The people have had enough," stated Iowa's new senator, Roger Jepsen. "They are conservatives for change." Even moderates, such as Illinois Senator Charles Percy, slipped to the right to avoid defeat, and several Democratic candidates represented the conservative wing. Asked a glum White House aide after the final tally, "How would you like to be Frank Church or George McGovern in 1980?"

Sensing the changing winds, Democratic leaders quickly asserted their own brand of conservatism. At the party's midterm convention in December 1978, President Carter unveiled a tight anti-inflationary budget which demanded "short-term sacrifices." In California, Governor Brown, victorious in a landslide after embracing Proposition 13, endorsed the summoning of a national constitutional convention to force a balanced budget, an unprecedented means of altering the Constitution that already had been approved by some thirty states. "It is time to get off the treadmill," declared Brown, "to challenge the assumption that more government spending automatically leads to better living." Such statements defied the tenets of traditional liberalism, opening deep rifts within the Democratic coalition. "The Administration's budget," retorted Senator Kennedy in staking out an alternative position, "asks the poor, the black, the sick, the young, the cities and the unemployed to bear a disproportionate share of the billions of dollars of reductions in Federal spending." "I did not become Speaker of the House," agreed Tip O'Neill, "to dismantle the programs I've worked all my life for."

The widening split within the Democratic party fired the imagination of the conservative opposition.

"We've changed the focus of politics in America from their ground to our ground," boasted Representative Kemp. "We've shifted from the defensive to the offensive. They're now arguing on our turf."

"We're the liveliest, most energetic political action force in America today," declared Representative Robert Bauman, chairman of the American Conservative Union. "Our time has come."

"We have moved the entire Democratic Party across the horizon, at least if you believe their rhetoric," said Ronald Reagan. "The people of America are demanding what we've always stood for."

"Perhaps we had to watch as the Democrats tried to prove that government could do everything," suggested Senate Minority Whip Ted Stevens, "—in order to show it could not."

"About the only thing that might stand a chance getting through with this bunch," said a White House aide, "is higher defense spending."

Committed to restoring the old America, the new conservative leadership flatly rejected a foreign policy of limits—loathed détente, the Panama Canal treaties, and SALT II—and demanded implementation of the B-1 bomber, the neutron bomb, and a modernized navy. "Unless the international performance of the United States improves substantially over what has become the norm in recent years," advised Kemp, "we shall all bear the burden of failure directly." The most powerful nation on earth, argued the conservatives, could ill afford to appear timid. "Shouldn't we stop worrying whether someone likes us," suggested Reagan shortly before announcing his presidential candidacy in 1979, "and decide once again we're going to be respected in the world?"

THE OLD HOLLYWOOD COWBOY, dead of cancer in 1979, personified that lost respect. "John Wayne was bigger than life," eulogized President Carter. "In an age of few heroes, he was the genuine article." One month before his death, Congress had authorized a gold medal struck in his honor, a token that easily blurred the man and his numerous roles. "Celebrating the dead John Wayne," observed *Newsweek* critic Jack Kroll, "America was celebrating one of its gallant dead dreams—a dream of unflagging national virility, courage, moral righteousness and stone-fisted sincerity." In recent years, such virtues had won sparse applause. "That little clique back there in the East has taken great personal satisfaction reviewing my politics instead of my pictures," Wayne told fellow actor Ronald Reagan. "But one day those doctrinaire liberals will wake up to find the pendulum has swung the other way." Writing Wayne's obituary for *Reader's Digest*, Reagan found solace in that defiant prophecy. "Duke Wayne symbolized . . . the force of the American will to do what is right in the world," averred the presidential hopeful. "He could have left no greater legacy."

As the decade drew to a close, Americans stood at the crossroads of possibility. The revival of conservatism and the simultaneous proliferation of community organizations represented competing versions of the future. Each appealed to the frustrations of the age—the failure of government to assure economic stability, to provide social justice, to fulfill a sense of national purpose—and each insisted that the American people, left to their own devices, could better resolve these troublesome issues. But as conservatives forecast a world of endless opportunity and growth, the community populists predicted an era of roots and limits. To implement these rival visions, conservatives moved, naturally, to control the established institutions, while populists sought alternative bases of support at the grass roots. With such diverse tactics, both movements ironically could achieve success at the same time. The conflict between federal authority and community power, between the leadership groups and the citizenry, between advocates of social change and defenders of the old morality—this fundamental tension of values—would persist. Its resolution would constitute the nation's major dilemma in the eighties.

INTO THE EIGHTIES

18

"TWO AMERICAS"

1980: Another Silent Majority

ON A LOVELY AUTUMN DAY IN NEW England, October 20, 1979, the once most powerful people in the country gathered, like ghosts from the past, to pay tribute to their fallen leader. At Columbia Point, overlooking the waters of Boston harbor, they dedicated a monumental glass and concrete library to the memory of John F. Kennedy. In the presence of the nation's most famous family, surrounded by the veterans of Kennedy's New Frontier—Dean Rusk, Robert McNamara, Arthur M. Schlesinger, Jr., Kenneth Galbraith, Pierre Salinger—the ceremony evoked memories of a lost age of infinite possibility. The end of the seventies, by contrast, seemed a time of narrow hope.

"The world of 1980 is as different from what it was in 1960," observed President Carter, "as the world of 1960 was from that of 1940. . . . We have a keener appreciation of limits now, the limits of government, limits on the use of military power abroad, the limits of manipulation without harm to ourselves [of] a delicate and balanced natural environment. . . . And we face," he explained, "centrifugal forces in our society and in our political system—forces of regionalism, forces of ethnicity, of narrow economic interest, of single issue politics—[that] are testing the resiliency of American pluralism and of our ability to govern."

Another voice rose to challenge the President's bleak diagnosis. "Those thousand days are like an evening gone," said Senator Edward Kennedy, the slain President's last surviving brother. "But they are not forgotten. . . . In dedicating this library to Jack, we can recall those years of grace, that time of hope. The spark still glows," he insisted. "The journey never ends. The dream shall never die."

KENNEDY'S ENTHUSIASM RAN against the currents of public opinion. A Harris poll taken that month found that two-thirds of Americans expected inflation to accelerate in the near future, and a majority doubted that government would act to control the runaway economy. A Yankelovich survey reported that the number of Americans who believed that the nation had entered an era of enduring shortages increased from 40 percent at middecade to 62 percent at its end, and the Gallup organization announced that 55 percent of the public believed that "next year will be worse than this year." "We are fast coming to a turning point in our history," agreed a 72 percent majority. "The land of plenty is becoming the land of want."

Determined to transform this sense of despair into a political crusade, Kennedy launched a bid for the presidency. Leading Carter by a two-to-one popularity margin among Democrats, the Massachusetts senator attacked the President's retreat from liberal action, describing unemployment, not inflation, as the major economic issue, demanding executive leadership to control prices and wages, and proposing a magnanimous plan for national health insurance. "The only thing that paralyzes us today is the myth that we cannot move," he said. "If Americans are pessimistic, it is because they are also realistic. They have made a fair judgment on how government is doing—and they are demanding something better."

Kennedy's insurgency, however, soon stumbled across another old snare of Democratic liberalism—the militance of loyal cold warriors. On November 4, 1979, exactly one year before the next presidential election, Iranian revolutionaries seized the American embassy in Teheran and mocked the power of the United States. Overnight, outraged public sentiment rallied behind the President. Kennedy, still suspect for his moral failure in the drowning accident of a campaign worker at Chappaquiddick in 1969, now aggravated his problem by criticizing the President's foreign policy. "Because the Shah . . . ran one of the most violent regimes in the history of mankind" and had stolen "umteen billions of dollars" from his people, Kennedy asked why the White House opposed the extradition of the deposed ruler. The outburst aroused new doubts about Kennedy's integrity and rapidly eroded his support. "If the Vietnam era taught us anything," retorted Kennedy, "it is precisely that when we do not debate our foreign policy, we may drift into deeper trouble." But Carter, using the hostage crisis as an excuse to avoid campaigning, adopted a "Rose Garden" strategy that limited his public appearances to formal White House functions, thereby enhancing his presidential image. By mid-December, he had supplanted Kennedy as the Democratic favorite.

For Carter, the seizure of the hostages justified a growing militance in foreign policy. In submitting the SALT II treaty the previous summer, he had advocated a 25 percent increase in military expenditures over the next five years. The President now approved a once-vetoed nuclear aircraft carrier and also endorsed the development of an expensive MX mobile missile system designed to confound Soviet weaponry. Beginning in 1978, Carter had called for additional appropriations for civil defense, and in 1979 he announced support of military draft registration to prepare the nation for war. "We must understand," he declared after the capture of the hostages, "that not every instance of the firm application of the power of the United States is a potential Vietnam."

Carter's new militance paralleled the politics of another Democratic underdog, Harry S Truman, who in 1948 had followed the advice of Clark Clifford in exaggerating the cold war to disarm the domestic opposition. Carter, having consulted with Clifford, used the Soviet invasion of Afghanistan in December 1979 to announce that the United States faced "the most serious threat to world peace since the Second World War." Heating up the cold war, the President ordered an embargo on high-technology and grain exports to the Soviet Union, and in January 1980 asked Senate Majority Leader Robert Byrd to postpone debate on the embattled SALT II agreement. To assert world leadership, the White House appealed to American allies to boycott the Olympic games scheduled for Moscow in July 1980. "Afghanistan has given Carter a useful excuse . . . to reveal publicly [a] much earlier decision," protested Barry Commoner in assuming leadership of a dissident Citizens Party. "He has sacrificed the hope for peace . . . on the altar of his own political ambition."

The rekindling of the cold war ironically highlighted the poverty of Carter's foreign policy. As negotiations failed to gain release of the hostages, the President belatedly opted for military force, ordering a poorly planned rescue mission that ended ignominiously when American aircraft crashed and burned in an Iranian desert. The fiasco, a near duplication of the failure to free the Mayaguez crew in 1975, underscored the futility of big stick diplomacy, and a frustrated Secretary of State Vance, the administration's main exponent of détente, resigned in disgust. Nor did the President's economic and moral sanctions against the Soviet Union produce diplomatic benefits. Raising the stakes, Carter issued Presidential Directive 59 in July 1980, a major shift in nuclear war strategy that retargeted American weapons from Soviet cities to missile sites, ostensibly to permit limited nuclear wars, but also providing what amounted to a first-strike capability. Coming in the wake of three highly publicized computer failures which briefly placed military forces on the verge of war, the new policy demonstrated the administration's resolve to restore what conservatives charged was a decline of American power.

Carter's emphasis on foreign policy in 1980 effectively undermined the Kennedy candidacy. Refusing to campaign, the President avoided a Democratic confrontation, settling for primary victories in state after state. While disenchantment with the incumbent enabled Kennedy to carry several large states, Democratic party rules about proportional representation minimized their political impact. A brief run by California Governor Jerry Brown had no discernible effects. When all the primaries were tallied, Carter had captured 51 percent of the vote, Kennedy only 38 percent. But despite Carter's hold on a clear majority of Democratic delegates, Kennedy refused to quit, pleading stubbornly with the nominating convention to reject party reforms that bound delegates to the primary results. Unannounced Democratic candidates, hoping for a Carter-Kennedy stalemate, also endorsed an open convention. Carter's fortunes sank markedly with revelations that his brother, Billy Carter, had served as an extralegal lobbyist for Libya, raising questions about White House complicity. But the President refused to surrender and Kennedy succeeded only in forcing the adoption of a liberal party platform. The prolonged bickering nevertheless accentuated divisions within the Democratic camp. By July 1980, Carter's approval ratings in the Gallup poll had again plummeted to 32 percent.

THE TRIUMPH OVER DEMOCRATIC LIBERALISM left the President vulnerable to attacks from Republicans, who possessed more obvious conservative credentials. Though Carter restored the language of the cold war, candidate Reagan compared the rhetorical response to "Mr. Chamberlain . . . tapping the cobblestones of Munich." "The United States appears so lost in uncertainty or paralyzed by propriety," complained Richard Nixon in his 1980 book, *The Real War*, a work quoted frequently (without attribution) by Reagan's speechwriters, "that it is either unable or unwilling to act." "Our allies are losing confidence in us," said Reagan, as the Western European nations ignored Carter's plea for an Olympic boycott, "and our adversaries no longer respect us."

Carter's half-hearted conservatism in handling the economy also aroused Republican scorn. Though the President flatly rejected price and wage controls, his support of recessionary tactics to stop inflation provoked suspicion and anger within the business community. As an antidote to corporate pessimism, Republican candidates advocated additional tax incentives for business, the elimination of costly government regulations, the liberation of the free enterprise system. More simply, Reagan called for "a crusade . . . to take government off the backs of the great people of this country, and turn you loose again to do the things that I know you can do so well, because you did them and made this country great."

Such hyperbole dominated the agenda of the Republican party. Four years after his defeat by Gerald Ford, Reagan claimed leadership of a rising conservative tide. Challenged for the nomination by other conservatives—Philip Crane, John Connally, George Bush, Robert Dole, Howard Baker—he easily exceeded their popularity and overcame his major handicap of age (Reagan turned sixty-nine during the New Hampshire primary race) by campaigning assiduously and proving his good health. More skillful than the demolition of the Republican right was Reagan's move toward the party center, the muting of criticism of such irreversible programs as social security and the Panama Canal treaties, belated acceptance of the federal bailout of Chrysler, the cultivation of geniality and moderation to negate residual images of right-wing extremism. So deft was this maneuver that the only liberal Republican in the race, maverick Representative John B. Anderson, soon departed in defeat to start an independent third-party candidacy.

Central to the conservative revival was the promise of restoring American greatness:

"This is the greatest country in the world," read one Reagan advertisement. "We have the talent, we have the drive, we have the imagination. Now all we need is the leadership."

"There's nothing the American people cannot do when we try," exhorted former President Ford. "Let's never doubt America's greatness."

"Ronald Reagan's America would be back to grassroots principles and old-fashioned American ideals," stated one New Jersey supporter, "back to the traditional values that made America great."

"They say that the United States has had its day in the sun, that our nation has passed its zenith," charged Reagan in his acceptance speech. "I utterly reject that view."

In capturing the Republican nomination, the Reagan leadership placed preeminence on party unity. Though a vocal right wing forced the adoption of a conservative platform—rejecting the ERA, abortion, gun control, and busing—the party standard-bearer, after flirting briefly with Ford, chose Trilateralist Bush as a running mate, assuring corporate conservatives of his loyalty to big business. Jerry Falwell's Moral Majority might describe the campaign as "a holy war," and the National Conservative Political Action Committee would raise a $7.5 million war chest to defeat liberal renegades. But Reagan himself saluted the New Deal, quoting from Franklin Roosevelt's Democratic acceptance speech of 1932 and urging Americans "to recapture our destiny." "Franklin Delano Reagan," headlined *The New York Times*.

THE CONTEST BETWEEN Reagan and Carter exposed a wide range of differences—some personal, some political, some merely metaphorical. Both candidates made minor blunders—Reagan smearing the President with regional ties to the Ku Klux Klan; Carter unleashing vitriolic attacks that blemished himself with "meanness"—and both predicted calamitous results if their opponents prevailed. As the campaign progressed, however, the politicians disagreed not only about personalities, but also about foreign policy, national security, the economy, the importance of federal power. "In a fumbling way," remarked Elizabeth Drew, "Reagan and Carter have ended up making this election campaign one that focuses on the big issues." But not until the last week of the contest did the rivals meet in a televised debate that attracted some 100 million viewers. There, ideological differences appeared with crystal simplicity. Carter, running on his record, endorsed a world view based on limits. "We have demanded that the American people sacrifice," he said, "and they have done very well." Reagan, promising the nation greatness, denied that austere prospect. "This country doesn't have to be in the shape that it is in," he maintained. "We do not have to go on sharing in scarcity." Recalling better times, both politicians backed toward the future.

Through the tumultuous campaign, public opinion analysts discovered one disconcerting fact: whatever the candidates said or did, however much money poured into advertising and travel, voter sentiment scarcely budged after Labor Day. In late October, most pollsters found the adversaries running neck and neck, a race too close to call. And they noticed, too, another unusual phenomenon, that a high proportion of the electorate remained undecided about any choice. This deadlock reflected not so much voter apathy as a widespread dislike of the available fare. "The question is not which one is the best," explained one Akron, Ohio, voter, "but which one is the least worst." "Oh, thank God," preached a Massachusetts minister on election eve, "only one of them can get elected!"

Unobserved by the pollsters, however, was a sudden break in the logjam. Standing beside Carter during the television debate, Reagan acquired a new presidential stature, a visibility that added legitimacy to his cause. By not actually "losing" to Carter, he became an acceptable alternative to the status quo. "Ask yourself, are you better off than you were four years ago?" Reagan proposed. "If you don't think that this course that we've been on for the last four years is what you would like to see us follow for the next four, then I could suggest another choice that you have." Public opinion, frustrated by Carter's inertia, now turned toward Reagan. A late shift in the hostage crisis—the "October surprise" feared by the Reagan camp—proved abortive, intensifying anti-Carter feeling. The drift to Reagan swiftly reached floodtide.

"This isn't an election," said Drew, "it's an earthquake." While President Carter attracted 41 percent of the popular vote and Anderson claimed seven percent, Reagan garnered 51 percent of the electorate, commanded 489 electoral votes to Carter's 49, and led his party in a national landslide that saw Republicans gain control of the Senate for the first time since 1953, add thirty-three seats in the House of Representatives, and seize four additional governorships of the states. As Carter fell, so did other key Democrats: Senators McGovern, Church, Bayh, Culver, and Nelson as well as a spate of House leaders. Also purged was a group of scandal-tainted legislators—Talmadge and the Abscam operatives—and Wayne Hays, who failed to stage a comeback. Concluded Carter's pollster Pat Caddell, "It's a fed-up vote."

Though the New Right, led by Falwell, Viguerie, and Weyrich, quickly claimed credit for the outcome, voting analysis suggested that the Reagan landslide reflected less a shift in the ideological winds than it did a rejection of incumbency. By election day, inflation ran at 12 percent, interest rates reached 15½ percent, unemployment touched 8 million people, and workers' real wages had declined almost 3 percent in twelve months—all tangible evidence of Carter's political failings—and the captivity of fifty-three Americans in Iran accentuated the impotence of government. According to a *New York Times*/CBS survey of voters leaving the polls, 38 percent chose Reagan because it was "time for a change," only 11 percent because "he's a real conservative." "It's the first time I ever voted Republican," explained a Michigan voter, part of the one-third of Democrats who deserted the President. "But I'm sick and tired of the mess that's going on in this country." "This is no big thing," soothed historian Richard Wade, once a McGovern strategist. "Carter was a lousy President."

The Republicans' claim to a political mandate also ignored fundamental trends in American voting which suggested different conclusions. Though Reagan's popular vote exceeded the combined Carter-Anderson totals, the size of victory remained smaller than those of Eisenhower, Johnson, and Nixon in 1972. Moreover, Anderson held the margin of difference in thirteen states, some of which would otherwise have turned Democratic. (The impact of Anderson's campaign on Democratic strategy—the refusal, for example, of Carter to debate Reagan earlier in the race—was, of course, unanswerable. Anderson also attracted 230,000 separate donations, triple the number of contributors to the Democratic National Committee.) Reagan, like Nixon before him, did succeed in breaking the traditional New Deal coalition, diminishing Carter's support among liberals, union members, Jews, and Catholics. But blacks and Hispanics voted overwhelmingly Democratic and women divided between the parties. In explaining their choices, two-thirds of the voters stressed economic issues—taxes, unemployment, and inflation. Yet in the congressional races, 92 percent of the incumbents who sought reelection regained their seats. "We'll be a majority party," admitted Representative Kemp, "when we implement the policies . . . we have promised. If we fail, this will not turn out to be a significant election."

The most striking statistic, however, was the continued decline in voter participation, which fell to 52.3 percent. When combined with Anderson's seven percent—clearly a protest vote—a majority of the citizenry rejected *both* Carter and Reagan! The repudiation of the ballot, a particularly strong tendency among the poor, less educated, and the young, reflected not merely a frustration at the specific choices, but at the structure of power itself.

"I don't like the job Carter has done," explained one nonvoter. "I don't like Reagan—he's too conservative. And they keep saying that voting for Anderson is throwing your vote away."

"I didn't want to be responsible for electing either one," said one eighteen-year-old.

"The politicians," observed a twenty-year-old black man in San Francisco, "ain't got nothing to do with me."

"The way it was last night," explained a nonvoting black about Carter's early concession, "it proves voters don't mean nothing. The polls are still open, and . . . Carter has already said, 'I surrender.'"

Amid Reagan's sense of triumph, such data were easily ignored. Asked at his first press conference as President-elect if he could reassure citizens who felt disenfranchised by his politics, Reagan replied, "Well, I don't think that anyone is disenfranchised by my views."

Persuaded of his mandate, Reagan staged an extravagant inauguration festival designed to uplift the national spirit. Coinciding with the release of the hostages from Iran, the change of administrations provided a unique moment for patriotic splendor—yellow ribbons wrapped around the old apple tree, the Stars and Stripes rippling in the winds, brass bands, parades, the full military regalia. "It is time for us to realize," advised the new President, "that we are too great a nation to limit ourselves to small dreams," and he urged Americans to "begin an era of national renewal." But even this inaugural address belied an important countertrend. "In this present crisis," said the apostle of the laissez faire state, "government is not the solution to our problems; government is the problem."

THE ELECTION OF RONALD REAGAN dramatized a subtle but profound transformation within American culture, a virtual revolution in popular attitudes about the traditional institutions of American society. This change involved not so much a new politics, or a shift in desired programs, or even the emergence of a conscious ideology. Rather, it reflected a spreading realization that the government of the United States and the leadership groups that supported it no longer functioned as an integral component of the American identity. "There are increasingly two Americas," explained Dennis Kucinich, one-time mayor of Cleveland, Ohio: "the America of multinationals dictating decisions in Washington, and the America of neighborhoods and rural areas, who feel left out."

This division between a formal establishment and the larger population increasingly affected economic relations. "Today . . . two overlapping economies are competing with each other for people's allegiance," wrote Peter Gillingham, a disciple of E. F. Schumacher, "to prove which over time can help the largest number of people to make their livelihood in ways they find rewarding." Instead of measuring productivity by traditional GNP standards (the "exhausting economy"), an alternative "renewing economy" based on barter, secondhand merchandise and, above all, home-produced goods and services permitted a different type of prosperity for a small but growing proportion of Americans. Indicative of this pattern was a historic reversal of population migration in the seventies. For the first time since 1820, small towns and rural areas grew faster than the nation's metropolitan centers. In the sixties, rural areas lost 2.8 million people; in the seventies, they gained 8.4 million, a 15.4 percent increase. "We're at the end of an age," remarked one woman whose family had left an urban center for rural West Virginia. "But at least from a temporary standpoint, we have the security of providing for our-selves." "Conservatives and radicals have a lot of things in com-mon, actually," agreed a neighbor. "They say we can do with less, and they do."

The separation of Americans from the major traditions of society represented a psychological leap far more fundamental than any geographical relocation. The shattering of the old con-sensus, begun in the sixties and accelerated by Vietnam, Water-gate, and OPEC, demystified the symbolic connections that bound Americans to their leaders and institutions. Awareness of the failure of traditional culture permeated the society. The crea-tion of effective alternatives required more hesitant steps.

Not voting reflected an obvious form of removal. The rejec-tion of orthodox economic rewards also laid the basis for further change. The belief that "hard work always pays off" appealed to 58 percent of the public in the late sixties but fell to only 43 percent by the end of the seventies, a dramatic reassessment that said less about blocked opportunities than it did about the inade-quacy of traditional "payoffs." Other opinion polls found that 75 percent of Americans no longer accepted boring work "as long as the pay is good"; 65 percent felt an employee could reject a job transfer to another city; 63 percent said employees could refuse promotions; and 78 percent claimed they would not leave a job they enjoyed for higher wages elsewhere. "Increasing numbers of Americans," concluded survey analyst Daniel Yankelovich, "partic-ularly the young, are questioning . . . the value of giving a particu-lar kind of hard work in exchange for a particular set of economic benefits."

Such negative reactions reinforced the emergence of an alter-native consciousness. New attitudes toward the family, toward birth and health and death, toward nature and natural resources, toward the sacred and the spiritual—all formed the foundations of a new culture. Nor were such changes merely individualized ac-tivities (though they appeared often in fragmented ways). Increas-ingly, Americans established connections with kindred people. According to Yankelovich surveys, this "Search for Community" trend "deeply involved" 47 percent of Americans—nearly half the nation by the beginning of the eighties—and suggested the emer-gence of a new social ethic based on personal commitment.

These redefinitions of American culture arose most easily

among the politically dispossessed. "I've been all over the country," stated activist Sam Lovejoy, "and I have not been into one community where I did not meet people exactly like me."

"The women's movement didn't start in Washington," recalled Gloria Steinem after the Reagan election, "and it won't be stopped by it."

"We're sharpening our weapons and waiting to see what happens," explained M. Carl Holman of the National Urban Coalition. "We're in for some tough times, but it might just have a tonic effect."

The tenacity of these alternative movements assured the continuation of conflict with the forces of reaction. Although the New Right exulted in the triumph of conservative candidates in 1980, a majority of Americans continued to support such liberal measures as abortion, the ERA, gun control, and national health insurance. The White House, Congress, the judiciary might become citadels of conservative strength. But among Americans outside the structure of power—in the heart of the culture—the outcome seemed less tidy and less certain. "In unexpected quarters, those, hitherto quiescent, are finding voice," observed broadcaster Studs Terkel. "In a society and time, with changes so stunning and landscapes so suddenly estranged, the last communiques are not yet in."

FOR MOST AMERICANS—for nonvoters and protest voters, for cultural minorities and community organizers, even, ironically, for the conservative right, the "era of renewal" depended less on active leadership than on the spirit of the people. On that autumn day in 1979, when the aging New Frontiersmen dedicated the Kennedy library at Columbia Point, the rising generation spoke through Robert Kennedy's son, Joseph P. Kennedy III: "We all know that inflation bears down hardest on the poor," said young Kennedy, invoking the "moral courage" of his father and uncle on behalf of the disadvantaged—migrant workers, Chicanos, American Indians, Eskimos, the poor of Appalachia, and plain working people—all of whom, he observed, "too often get a raw deal from those thinking of themselves as their betters, their leaders. . . . I hope the rest of us keep our eyes open during the 1980s."

NOTES

CHAPTER 1: "THE ALLEGIANCE OF YOUTH"

The fullest study of Nixon's foreign policy is Tad Szulc, *The Illusion of Peace* (New York, 1978), which may be supplemented with William Shawcross's *Sideshow: Kissinger, Nixon and the Destruction of Cambodia* (New York, 1979). The relationship between foreign policy and domestic politics is elucidated clearly in Alexander Kendrick, *The Wound Within* (Boston, 1974) and Jonathan Schell, *The Time of Illusion* (New York, 1976). Agnew's speeches are collected in John R. Coyne, Jr., *The Impudent Snobs: Agnew vs. the Intellectual Establishment* (New Rochelle, N.Y., 1972). A convenient summary of the events at Kent State University in 1970 is James Michener, *Kent State: What Happened and Why* (New York, 1971).

PAGE

5 "Sort of laughed": Michael Mullen, October 25, 1969, quoted in *Ms.*, January 1977, p. 72.

6 "We've got those liberal": Quoted in Szulc, *Illusion of Peace*, p. 158.

7 "Nothing would please me": Coyne, *Impudent Snobs*, p. 292.

8 "The new-style young": Quoted in Michener, *Kent State*, pp. 242–43.

9 "Sure I'm against": Quoted ibid., p. 307.

11 "Just imagine they are wearing": Coyne, *Impudent Snobs*, p. 320

11 "Megalomania": Len Keyser, *Hollywood in the Seventies* (San Diego, 1981), p. 100.

13 "This is madness": *Newsweek*, May 11, 1970, p. 25.

13 "We recognize": Quoted in Schell, *Time of Illusion*, pp. 89–90.

13 "We do not harbor": Quoted in Bill Warren, *The Middle of the Country* (New York, 1970), pp. 43–46.

13 "It is now our task": Quoted in Michener, *Kent State*, p. 21.

14 "worse than the Brown Shirts": Quoted ibid., p. 251.

14 "no accident": Quoted ibid., p. 260.

14 "These students are going": Quoted in Peter Davies, *The Truth About Kent State* (New York, 1973), p. 29.

15   "heating up the climate": Quoted in Schell, *Time of Illusion*, p. 99.
15   "youth in its protest": Quoted ibid.
16   "were unnecessary": *The Report of the President's Commission on Campus Unrest* (New York, 1970), pp. 289, 450, 4, 9.
16   "I saw the same disbelief": Quoted in Warren, *Middle*, p. 61.
17   Letters to the editor: Excerpted in Michener, *Kent State*, pp. 436–47.
18   "Kent State": Quoted in Shawcross, *Sideshow*, pp. 157–58.
19   "I call it a common": Coyne, *Impudent Snobs*, p. 519.
20   "The Constitution is larger": Quoted in Peter Schrag, *Test of Loyalty* (New York, 1974), p. 26.
20   "I feel about as alienated": Quoted in Warren, *Middle*, p. 155
20   "I feel too much": Quoted ibid., p. 123.
20   "I realized that my sympathy": Quoted in Michener, *Kent State*, p. 390.
20   "I felt the futility": Personal interview with author.
21   "They feel they must": *Report of the President's Commission*, p. 5.

2: "TO OPEN ONE'S EYES"

The feminist revival is examined in William H. Chafe, *Women and Equality* (New York, 1977), Carl N. Degler, *At Odds* (New York, 1980), and Sheila M. Rothman, *Woman's Proper Place* (New York, 1978). For the origins of the women's liberation movement, see Sara Evans, *Personal Politics* (New York, 1979). An important anthology of feminist essays is Robin Morgan, ed., *Sisterhood Is Powerful* (New York, 1970). A personal history of involvement is Jane Alpert, *Growing up Underground* (New York, 1981).

PAGE
22   "serious militant leftists": Jane Alpert, "Mother Right: A New Feminist Theory," *Ms.*, August 1973, pp. 55, 88–94. Except as noted, all references to Alpert are from this article.
22   "The anger of youth": *New York Times*, November 14, 1969, p. 1.
23   "to take off": Alpert, "Mother Right," p. 88.
23   "I was a woman": Ibid., p. 89
23   "We had come to the group": Ibid., p. 90.
23   "We have suddenly": Jane O'Reilly, "The Housewife's Moment of Truth," *Ms.*, premier issue [1971], p. 54.
24   "The initial feminist": Vivian Gornick, *Essays in Feminism* (New York, 1978), p. 1
25   "It's disgusting": Quoted in James Michener, *Kent State: What Happened and Why* (New York, 1971), p. 404.
25   "If I've had": Quoted ibid., p. 406.
25   "According to most men": Anselma Dell'Olio, "The Sexual Revolution Wasn't Our War," in Francine Klagsbrun, *The First Ms. Reader* (New York, 1973), p. 124.
25   "The Achilles' heel": Ibid., p. 126
26   "When women feel powerless": *Our Bodies, Ourselves* (Boston, 1971), p. 9.

26 "If hostility to men": Martha Shelly, "Notes of a Radical Lesbian," in Morgan, *Sisterhood*, p. 346.

26 "Pregnancy is barbaric": Shulamith Firestone, *The Dialectic of Sex* (New York, 1970), p. 198.

26 "a process of the female": *Ladies' Home Journal*, August 1970, p. 66.

26 "a terrifying": *Our Bodies*, p. 123.

27 "a woman's liberty": Quoted in *Scientific American*, January 1970, p. 50.

27 "Our legs, busts": *Our Bodies*, p. 4.

28 "even the most liberated": Harriet Lyons and Rebecca W. Rosenblatt, "Body Hair: The Last Frontier," in Klagsbrun, *Ms. Reader*, p. 148.

28 "radical-liberals . . . wore": John R. Coyne, *The Impudent Snobs: Agnew vs. The Intellectual Establishment* (New Rochelle, N.Y., 1971), p. 363.

30 "The *Times* can congratulate": *New York Times*, December 22, 1970, p. 33. See also Robin Morgan, *Going Too Far* (New York, 1977), p. 91.

30 "Miss Alpert, a petite": *New York Times*, May 5, 1970, p. 34.

30 women's most effective weapon: Morgan, *Sisterhood*, pp. 213-17.

31 "Let me make one thing": Quoted in *Ms.*, premier issue, p. 82.

31 "Now I lie": Joan Didion, *Play It as It Lays* (New York, 1970), p. 10.

31 "who seem to shrivel": Alexandra Symonds, "Phobias after Marriage," in Jean Baker Miller, *Psychoanalysis and Women* (New York, 1973), pp. 289, 302.

32 "the trauma of": Robert Seidenberg, "The Trauma of Eventlessness," in Miller, *Psychoanalysis*, p. 355.

33 "I've suffered more": *Ms.*, premier issue, p. 75.

34 "This is not a bedroom war": *New York Times*, August 27, 1970, p. 1.

35 "It's not a matter": *Ladies' Home Journal*, August 1970, p. 50.

35 "Eliminating the patriarchal": Klagsbrun, *Ms. Reader*, p. 270.

36 "Even the brightest": Joan Didion, "The Women's Movement," *The White Album* (New York, 1979), p. 113.

36 "The women's movement": *New York Times*, August 27, 1970, p. 30.

37 ". . . all of us": Robin Morgan, "Letter to a Sister Underground," *Monster* (New York, 1972), pp. 59, 61.

37 "The sleepwalkers": Adrienne Rich, "When We Dead Awaken," in *On Lies, Secrets, and Silence* (New York, 1979), p. 35.

37 "Because the Women's Movement": Alpert, "Mother Right."

3: "THIS TERRIBLE DIVISION BETWEEN US"

Nixon's southern strategy is described in Leon Panetta and Peter Gall, *Bring Us Together* (Philadelphia, 1971) and two books by Richard Harris, *Justice* (New York, 1970) and *Decision* (New York, 1971). John Langston Gwaltney's *Drylongso* (New York, 1980) provides an excellent description of black culture. For the state of American prisons, see Jessica Mitford, *Kind and Usual Punishment*

(New York, 1973). The best account of Attica is Tom Wicker, *A Time to Die* (New York, 1975),

PAGE

38 "They're starting to treat their own children": *New York Times*, May 8, 1970, p. 19.

38 "The contrast." Quoted in Panetta, *Bring Us*, p. viii.

38 "the anger, outrage": *Commission on Campus Unrest*, p. 98.

39 "This country cannot": "What Has Happened to America?" *Reader's Digest*, October 1967, p. 51.

40 "Until we have order": Congressional Quarterly, *Nixon: The Second Year of His Presidency* (Washington, D.C., 1971), p. 67.

40 "It is hard for the average": Quoted in Harris, *Justice*, p. 103.

40 "a symbolic assurance": Quoted ibid., p. 111.

41 "the respect and": Congressional Quarterly, *Second Year*, p. 68.

41 "The issue of race": *The Memoirs of Richard Nixon* (New York, 1978), I, p. 540.

41 "cold, calculated political": Congressional Quarterly, *Second Year*, p. 70.

42 "nationally, not just": Congressional Quarterly, ibid., p. 69.

42 "It's almost enough": Quoted in Rowland Evans and Robert D. Novak, *Nixon in the White House* (New York, 1971), p. 149.

42 "There are those who want instant": Congressional Quarterly, *Nixon: The First Year of His Presidency* (Washington, D.C., 1970), p. 25A.

44-45 "I understand the bitter feelings": Quoted in Schell, *Time of Illusion*, p. 83.

45 "essentially regional legislation": Congressional Quarterly, *First Year*, p. 51.

45 "The time for racial": Quoted in Laurence Shoup, *The Carter Presidency and Beyond* (Palo Alto, Cal., 1980), p. 81.

46 "forced integration": Quoted in Richard J. Margolis, "Last Chance for Desegregation," *Dissent*, XIX (1972), p. 249.

46 "the patience of many": Congressional Quarterly, *Second Year*, p. 70.

46 "to give the moral leadership": Quoted in Mark R. Levy and Michael S. Kramer, *The Ethnic Factor* (New York, 1972), p. 26.

46 "You will be better advised": Quoted in Harris, *Justice*, p. 206.

46 "If the cities": Quoted in Robert L. Allen, *Black Awakening in Capitalist America* (New York, 1969), p. 226.

47 "People who own": Quoted ibid., p. 230.

47 "We believe that": Congressional Quarterly, *Second Year*, p. 69.

48 "There's been lots": Ibid., p. 68.

48 "There could be no more": Ibid.

49 "The evidence of attention": Daniel Moynihan, *The Politics of a Guaranteed Income* (New York, 1973) p. 243.

49 "Money for social programs": Quoted in James W. Button, *Black Violence* (Princeton, N.J., 1978), p. 98.

49 "I think this is an institution": Quoted in Harris, *Justice*, p. 161.

50 "expose, disrupt, misdirect": Quoted in Lowell Bergman and David

Weir, "Revolution on Ice," *Rolling Stone*, September 9, 1976, pp. 42, 46.

50 "the greatest threat": Quoted ibid., p. 46.

50 "The Black Panthers": Quoted in Button, *Black Violence*, p. 137.

50 "Richard Nixon is an evil": *Newsweek*, December 15, 1969, p. 37.

51 "They are fighting": Quoted in Mitford, *Kind and Usual*, pp. 256–57.

52 "No one can remember": Samuel Melville, *Letters from Attica* (New York, 1972), p. 70

52 Tom Wicker observed: Wicker, *A Time to Die*, p. 6.

53 "All the rules": ibid., p. 174.

53 "WE are MEN": Wicker, *A Time to Die*, pp. 401, 126.

53 "We are not beasts": Ibid., p. 126.

53 "There was the whole rule": Quoted in Alexander Kendrick, *Wound Within* (Boston, 1974), p. 339.

53 "Kent State psychology": Wicker, *A Time to Die*, p. 222.

53 "the swiftest": Quoted in Kendrick, *Wound Within*, p. 339.

53 "I was amazed at Kent State": Quoted in Wicker, *A Time to Die*, p. 369.

53 "In prison": Congressional Quarterly, *Historic Documents 1972* (Washington, D.C., 1973), p. 784.

54 "We are a year closer": Quoted in Moynihan, *Politics*, p. 279.

54 "Our cities and ghettos": George McGovern, *An American Journey* (New York, 1974), p. 9.

54 "the end of an era": *Time*, August 27, 1973, p. 10.

54 "We've rejected the rhetoric": Quoted in William J. Wilson, *Power, Racism, and Privilege* (New York, 1973), p. 149.

55 "The next generation": *Newsweek*, February 23, 1970, p. 30.

55 "Black men have no": Quoted in Gwaltney, *Drylongso*, p. 1.

55 "I get tired": Quoted ibid., p. 19.

4: "NO ONE CALLS IT THE WORKING CLASS"

A fine analysis of the problems of the white working class is Stanley Aronowitz, *False Promises* (New York, 1973). Nixon's appeal to white workers is explained in Schell, *Time of Illusion*. Richard P. Adler's *All in the Family* (New York, 1979) is an excellent anthology of the controversy surrounding the program.

PAGE

56 "The country is virtually": *New York Times*, May 7, 1970, pp. 24, 19.

57 "We just wanted to show": *Newsweek*, May 25, 1970, pp. 34–35.

57 "They went through": Quoted in James Michener, *Kent State: What Happened and Why* (New York, 1971), p. 396.

58 "nobody calls it": Pete Hamill, "The Revolt of the White Lower-Middle Class," in Louise Kapp Howe, ed., *The White Majority* (New York, 1970), p. 11.

58 "they are almost the only": Fred J. Cook, "Hard-Hats: The Rampaging Patriots," *Nation*, June 15, 1970, p. 717.

59 "I'm working my ass off": Quoted in Peter Schrag, "The Forgotten American," *Harper's*, August 1969, p. 28.

59 "I work my ass off": Quoted in Hamill, "Revolt," pp. 11–12.

59 "There's a lot": Quoted ibid.

59 "The whole goddamn country": Quoted in Richard Polenberg, *One Nation Divisible* (New York, 1980), p. 228.

59 "get the same breaks": Quoted in Andrew Levison, *The Working Class Majority* (New York, 1974), p. 162.

59 "If I had the chance": *New York Times*, May 8, 1970, p. 16.

60 "You can't turn on the television": Ibid.

60 "Why the hell": Quoted in Hamill, "Revolt," p. 14.

60 "What is our answer?": Daniel Moynihan, *Politics of a Guaranteed Income* (New York, 1973), p. 107.

60 "This country is going": Quoted in Schell, *Time of Illusion*, p. 124.

60 "The time has come": John R. Coyne, *The Impudent Snobs: Agnew vs. the Intellectual Establishment* (New Rochelle, N.Y., 1972), p. 362.

60 "You hear them night after night": Quoted in Schell, *Time of Illusion*, p. 127.

62 "the creative liberals": Quoted in Adler, *All in the Family*, p. 87.

62 "the words of their subterranean": Quoted ibid, p. 91.

62 "I wish there were more": Quoted ibid., p. 236.

62 "What's great about": Quoted ibid., p. 240.

62 "Dad is like Archie": Quoted ibid., p. 234.

63 "I think they enjoy": Quoted ibid., p. 241.

63 "I think a couple": Quoted ibid., p. 235.

64 "Work will always": Coyne, *Impudent Snobs*, p. 304.

64 "the right and the ability": Richard Wilson, ed., *Setting the Course* (New York, 1970), p. 368.

64 "a golden growth industry": Theodore White, *The Making of the President: 1972* (New York: 1973), p. 207.

64 "The blue collar worker": *Work in America: Report of a Special Task Force to the Secretary of HEW* (Cambridge, Mass., 1973), p. 32.

64 "I was just in the right place": Quoted in Richard Sennett and Jonathan Cobb, *The Hidden Injuries of Class* (New York, 1972), pp. 193–94.

65 "The workplace": Quoted in Agio Salpuka, "Unions: A New Role?" in Jerome M. Rosow, *The Worker and the Job* (Englewood Cliffs, N.J., 1974), p. 108.

65 Subsequent analysis: Levison, *Working Class Majority*, pp. 128–30.

66 "I can look back": Quoted in Studs Terkel, *Working* (New York, 1974), p. 589.

66 "They're different": Quoted in Levison, *Working Class Majority*, p. 214.

66 "I'm getting the shit": Quoted in Aronowitz, *False Promises*, p. 21.

66 "When you talk about that watch": Quoted in Terkel, *Working*, p. 191.

67   "The melting pot": Coyne, *Impudent Snobs*, p. 190.
67   "The Ethnic American": Quoted in Stanley Feldstein and Lawrence Costello, eds., *The Ordeal of Assimilation* (Garden City, N.Y., 1974), p. 440.
67   "Our children": Quoted in Joseph Ryan, ed., *White Ethnics* (Englewood Cliffs, N.J., 1973), p. 6.
69   "They learned the Puritan": *Time*, October 30, 1972, p. 23.
70   "not because he's": Ibid., May 25, 1970, p. 21.
70   "They know God": Ibid., October 30, 1972, p. 23.

5: "POLITICS IS EFFRONTERY"

A detailed account of the 1972 election is Theodore White's *The Making of the President: 1972* (New York, 1973). McGovern's speeches are collected in *An American Journey* (New York, 1974). Foreign policy issues are discussed in Tad Szulc, *The Illusion of Peace* (New York, 1978). A convenient collection of public documents is Congressional Quarterly, *Historic Documents 1972* (Washington, D.C., 1973).

PAGE

72   "I shall seek to call": McGovern, *American Journey*, pp. 6, 8.
72   "Vietnam is the wound": Quoted in Evans and Novak, *Nixon in the White House* (New York, 1971), p. 383.
72   "is a moral and political": Quoted in White, *Making of the President*, p. 150.
72   "Don't give me another": Quoted in George McGovern, *Grassroots* (New York, 1977), pp. 104–105, 107.
75   "What we have done": Quoted in Szulc, *Illusion of Peace*, p. 413.
75   "What we see": Quoted ibid.
75   "the hemisphere community": Quoted ibid., p. 643.
77   "This new escalation": Quoted in White, *Making of the President*, p. 134.
77   "I think it": Quoted ibid.
77   "a major confrontation": Quoted ibid.
77   "We are headed": Quoted in Szulc, *Illusion of Peace*, pp. 557–58.
78   "Everywhere we went": Quoted ibid., p. 588.
78   "If we have SALT": Quoted ibid., p. 594.
79   "the Moscow primary": *Newsweek*, June 12, 1972.
80   "I'm not going to comment": Quoted in John W. Dean, III, *Blind Ambition: The White House Years* (New York, 1976), p. 102.
80   "since there would be no possibility": Norman Mailer, *St. George and the Godfather* (New York, 1972), p. 178.
80–81 "The choice is between going forward": Congressional Quarterly, *Documents 1972*, pp. 652–53.
81   "Four years ago": Ibid., p. 712.
81   "Agnew is a monster": Quoted in Jonathan Schell, *The Time of Illusion* (New York, 1976), p. 284.

81   "I shall not dwell": Quoted ibid., pp. 718, 724–25.

82   "For the last five weeks": Mailer, *St. George*, p. 228.

82   "After all most editors": Gordon L. Weil, *The Long Shot* (New York, 1973), p. 231.

83   "A good woman": Quoted in James M. Perry, *Us and Them: How the Press Covered the 1972 Election* (New York, 1973), p. 96.

83   "to solve the problem": Quoted ibid., p. 100.

83   "The American people": Quoted in White, *Making of the President*, p. 121.

83   "The George Wallace victory": Quoted in Perry, *Us and Them*, pp. 116–17.

84   "an angry cry": Quoted ibid.

84   "the Establishment Center": Quoted in White, *Making of the President*, p. 150.

84   "I wish I could": Arthur H. Bremer, *An Assassin's Diary* (New York, 1973), p. 107.

84   "mentally ill persons": *New York Times*, May 21, 1972, p. 1.

84   "He seems like a shallow": *New York Times*, May 17, 1972, p. 29.

84   "He must have been": *New York Times*, May 16, 1972, p. 34.

84   "if not before": *New York Times*, August 1, 1972, p. 8.

85   "Nixon doesn't have to give": *New York Times*, August 2, 1972, p. 16.

85   "It was the horror": Mailer, *St. George*, pp. 18–19.

85   "reformed us out": Quoted in White, *Making of the President*, p. 213.

86   "Anybody who would": Quoted ibid., p. 219.

87   "completely unacceptable to": *New York Times*, June 5, 1972, p. 26.

87   "of dictators, dope-runners": McGovern, *American Journey*, p. 54.

88   "the President of the United States": Quoted in Szulc, *Illusion of Peace*, p. 616.

88   "He's become an apologist": Quoted in Weil, *Long Shot*, pp. 152–53.

88   "I feel a little like Al Smith": *Time*, October 30, 1972, p. 23.

89   "a sneak attack": Quoted in Kristi Witker, *How to Lose Everything in Politics Except Massachusetts* (New York, 1974), p. 29.

89   "The blue collar worker": Quoted in Andrew Levison, *The Working Class Majority* (New York, 1974), p. 170.

90   "The low voter turnout": Shirley Chisholm, *The Good Fight* (New York, 1973), preface.

90   Subsequent analysis: Norman H. Nie et al., *The Changing American Voter* (Cambridge, Mass., 1976), pp. 277–79.

90   "the other side": *New York Times*, November 14, 1972, p. 36.

90   "Vietnam is the shared": Quoted in McGovern, *Grassroots*, p. 245.

6: "THE WAR ISN'T OVER"

The Vietnam peace settlement is examined in Tad Szulc, *The Illusion of Peace* (New York, 1978), and William Shawcross, *Sideshow: Kissinger, Nixon and the*

Destruction of Cambodia (New York, 1979). For the problems of returning veterans, see Robert Jay Lifton, *Home from the War* (New York, 1973), Paul Starr, *The Discarded Army* (New York, 1973), and Lawrence M. Baskir and William A. Straus, *Chance and Circumstance* (New York, 1978). The annual volumes of the Congressional Quarterly series, *Historic Documents*, provide convenient access to public events.

PAGE

91   "No man would have welcomed": *New York Times*, January 24, 1973, p. 16.

91   "His tragedy—and ours": *New York Times*, January 23, 1973, p. 25.

91   "We had to realize": Quoted in Lifton, *Home*, p. 446.

92   "There was no dancing": *New York Times*, January 25, 1973, p. 24.

92   "I'm not going to get": Ibid., p. 25.

92   "This is a false ending": Quoted in Lifton, *Home*, p. 446.

92   "All I know": *New York Times*, January 24, 1973, p. 17.

92   "You can tell that bastard": Quoted in Lifton, *Home*, p. 450.

92   "Abusing executive privilege": Congressional Quarterly, *Documents 1973*, p. 89.

94   "The justification": Quoted in George McGovern, *Grassroots* (New York, 1977), p. 254.

94   "until the will of the people": Quoted in Shawcross, *Sideshow*, p. 284.

94   "Congress cannot sanction": Quoted ibid., p. 285.

95   "There was a time": Quoted in Lifton, *Home*, p. 141.

95   "As far as I'm concerned": Quoted in Starr, *Discarded Army*, p. 4.

95   "We've lost more over there": *New York Times*, January 25, 1973, p. 25.

95   "You're forgetting a lot of people": Quoted in Starr, *Discarded Army*, p. 4.

96   "It isn't peace": Quoted in Lifton, *Home*, p. 447.

96   "We are honored": *New York Times*, February 13, 1973, p. 1.

96   "It's almost too wonderful": Ibid., p. 14.

96   "When anyone can say": *New York Times*, February 17, 1973, p. 18.

96   "We are over-publicizing": *New York Times*, March 3, 1973, p. 16.

97   "I find it a little": *New York Times*, February 24, 1973, p. 12.

97   "the South did not lose": *New York Times*, February 13, 1973, p. 14.

97   "We walked out": *New York Times*, March 3, 1973, p. 16.

97   "It's about time": Ibid.

97   "What's disturbing": Ibid.

97   "How many veterans": Ibid.

97   "suckers, having to risk": Quoted in Baskir and Straus, *Chance*, p. 6.

97   "Coming back to America": Quoted in Starr, *Discarded Army*, p. 30.

98   "I was busted": Quoted in Baskir and Straus, *Chance*, p. 158.

98   "One time [in] Vietnam": Quoted in Lifton, *Home*, p. 122.

98   "The vets are the only": Quoted in John Bryan, *This Soldier Still at War* (New York, 1975), p. 85.

99   "malcontents, radicals, incendiaries": Quoted in Lifton, *Home*, pp. 208–09.

99   "They did not hear": Quoted in Peter Schrag, *Test of Loyalty* (New York, 1974), p. 54.

100   "I would certainly prefer": Congressional Quarterly, *Documents 1973*, p. 541.

100   "a new feeling": Congressional Quarterly, *Documents 1972*, p. 891.

101   "The average American": Ibid.

101   "contemptuous of the real needs": Congressional Quarterly, *Documents 1973*, p. 171.

101   "The President's in the driver's seat": Ibid.

101   "The authority of Congress": Quoted in Jonathan Schell, *The Time of Illusion* (New York, 1976), p. 314.

7: "NOT AS STEPCHILDREN OR WARDS"

Richard Polenberg's *One Nation Divisible* (New York, 1980) provides a solid background on the problems of minorities and women. A brief statistical overview is Sar A. Levitan et al., *Minorities in the United States* (Washington, D.C., 1975). For American Indians, see Vine Deloria, Jr., *Behind the Trail of Broken Treaties* (New York, 1974); Tony Castro's *Chicano Power* (New York, 1974) is a good introduction to that subject; the problems of blacks are analyzed in Sar A. Levitan et al., *Still a Dream* (Cambridge, Mass., 1975).

PAGE

103   "is like that of a foster child": Quoted in Maurilio Vigil, *Chicano Politics* (Washington, D.C., 1978), epigraph.

103   "everyone must have the opportunity": Congressional Quarterly, *Documents 1973*, pp. 232–33.

104   "We have bet": *New York Times*, March 5, 1973, p. 1.

105   "To call for new treaties": *New York Times*, January 12, 1973, p. 36.

105   "If we all die": Quoted in Bill Zimmerman, *Airlift to Wounded Knee* (Chicago, 1976), p. 125.

106   "another indication": *New York Times*, June 1, 1973, p. 38.

106   "We believe we": Ibid.

106   "Culture is fine": Quoted in Raymond J. DeMallie, "Pine Ridge Economy," in Sam Stanley, ed., *American Indian Economic Development* (The Hague, 1978), p. 310.

106   "within the competitive": Lorraine Turner Ruffing, "Navajo Economic Development" in Stanley, *American Indian*, p. 53.

106   "The Indian was good": *New York Times*, March 5, 1973, p. 26.

106   "A member of the reservation": Lowell John Bear, "Morongo Indian Reservation," in Stanley, *American Indian*, p. 195.

107   "We . . . have made": Quoted in Castro, *Chicano Power*, p. 5.
107   "Attack until the [Anglo] invader": Quoted in Manuel P. Servin, *An Awakened Minority: The Mexican Americans* (Beverly Hills, Cal., 1974), p. 236.
107   "We are first in janitors": Quoted in F. Chris Garcia, *La Causa Politica* (Notre Dame, Ind., 1974), pp. 9–10.
107   "If it works for him": Quoted in Thomas M. Martinez, "Advertising and Racism" in Edward Simmen, *Pain and Promise: The Chicano Today* (New York, 1972), p. 94.
108   "Spanish-speaking voters": Quoted in Castro, *Chicano Power*, p. 213.
108   "The two-party system": Quoted in Elizabeth Sutherland Martinez and Enriqueta Longeaux y Vasquez, *Viva La Raza!* (Garden City, N.Y., 1974), pp, 268, 271.
108   "This country is based": Quoted in Castro, *Chicano Power*, p. 213.
108   "to foster the free enterprise system": Vigil, *Chicano Politics*, p. 147.
108–09   "the principle of self-determination": Quoted in Castro, *Chicano Power*, p. 190.
109   "I hate the white ideal": Quoted in Simmen, *Pain and Promise*, p. 129.
109   "The barrio is a refuge": Robert Ramirez, "The Woolen Scrape" in Simmen, *Pain and Promise*, p. 42.
109   "a systematic failure": Quoted in Alfredo Mirande and Evangelina Enriquez, *La Chicana* (Chicago, 1979), p. 132.
109   "The poor people": Quoted in Castro, *Chicano Power*, p. 62.
110   "There may be a change": Quoted in Roger Wilkins, "The Sound of One Hand Clapping," *New York Times*, May 12, 1974, p. 45.
110   "Racism comes much more naturally": Quoted ibid., p. 44.
111   "The real danger": Quoted ibid., p. 43.
112   "Black Americans": Shirley Chisholm, *The Good Fight* (New York, 1973), pp. 144–45.
113   "Like blacks": Erica Jong, "The Artist as Housewife," in Klagsbrun, *Ms. Reader*, p. 120.
113   "It's just unholy": *New York Times*, March 21, 1973, p. 47.
113   "A Total Woman": Marabel Morgan, *The Total Woman* (Boston, 1975), p. 55.
113   "We are triumphantly": Quoted in Robin Morgan, *Going Too Far* (New York, 1977), p. 191.
114   "The assumption": Adrienne Rich, *On Lies, Secrets and Silence* (New York, 1979), p. 109.
114   "Knowing our place": Morgan, *Going Too Far*, p. 165.
114   "the objectification": Rich, *On Lies*, p. 110.
114   "Pornography is the theory": Morgan, *Going Too Far*, p. 169.
114   "Until all women": Jill Johnston, *Lesbian Nation* (New York, 1973), p. 166.
114   "The Women's Liberation Movement": Quoted in Toni Morrison, "What the Black Woman Thinks About Women's Lib," *New York Times Magazine*, August 22, 1971, p. 15.

115 "I just wish white women": Quoted in Chisholm, *Good Fight*, p. 108.
115 "Chicanas have no more faith": Quoted in Gilberto Lopez y Rivas, *The Chicanos* (New York, 1973), p. 170.

8: "PINCH, SQUEEZE, CRUNCH OR CRISIS"

The origins of the energy crisis are explained in Barry Commoner, *The Poverty of Power* (New York, 1976). His *The Closing Circle* (New York, 1971) is a good introduction to the environmental movement. The problems of the economy are analyzed in Fred L. Block, *The Origins of International Economic Disorder* (Berkeley, Cal., 1977) and Gardner C. Means et al., *The Roots of Inflation* (New York, 1975).

PAGE
118 "The Arab cutback": *New York Times*, October 18, 1973, p. 18.
118 "a very stark fact": Congressional Quarterly, *Documents 1973*, pp. 9, 15.
118 THINGS WILL GET WORSE: *New York Times*, November 11, 1973, IV, p. 3.
119 "I think there was gas": *New York Times*, March 18, 1974, p. 16.
119 "A country that runs on oil": *New York Times*, April 1, 1973, III, p. 15.
120 "Conservation is not": Quoted in Tad Szulc, *The Illusion of Peace* (New York, 1978), p. 450.
120 "future wastes": *Scientific American*, September 1971, p. 42.
120 "If ever any": Ibid., p. 157.
121 "Energy won't get": Quoted in Theodore White, *The Making of the President: 1972* (New York, 1973), p. 478.
121 "It is not the philosophy": Quoted in Dennis C. Pirages and Paul R. Ehrlich, *Ark II: Social Responses to Environmental Imperatives* (New York, 1974), p. 34.
121 "Popeye is running out": Congressional Quarterly, *Documents 1973*, p. 465.
121 "We should not be misled": Ibid., p. 468.
122 "a major new endeavor": Ibid., p. 921.
122 "He is really calling": *New York Times*, November 9, 1973, p. 27.
122 "He has too readily": Ibid.
122 "is an especially pernicious": Commoner, *Poverty of Power*, p. 77.
122 "I am not afraid": Quoted in James Rathlesberger, *Nixon and the Environment* (New York, 1972), p. 102.
123 "Call it pinch": *New York Times*, January 16, 1974, p. 27.
123 "the only practicable": Ralph E. Lapp, "Nuclear Salvation or Nuclear Folly?" *New York Times Magazine*, February 10, 1974, p. 73.
123 "We can't live": *Time*, November 5, 1973, p. 100.
123 "The consequences of potential": *New York Times*, August 21, 1974, p. 14.
123 "We don't worry": *New York Times*, March 18, 1974. p. 1.

124 "The present course": Commoner, *Closing Circle*, pp. 217–18.
124 "There is a new kind": Quoted in Frederick R. Anderson, *NEPA in the Courts* (Baltimore, 1973), p. 205.
124 "a spectacular gesture": *Scientific American*, May 1970, p. 18.
125 "Ecology has become": *Newsweek*, January 26, 1970, p. 31.
125 "a new social ethic": Ibid., p. 47.
125 "would have a lonely": Lewis Thomas, *The Lives of a Cell* (New York, 1974), p. 7.
125 "have broken out": Commoner, *Closing Circle*, p. 13.
126 "The Establishment sees this": *Newsweek*, May 4, 1970, p. 27.
126 "The increase of": *New York Times*, March 18, 1971, p. 28.
126 "the bird watchers": *New York Times*, March 25, 1971, p. 24.
127 "that all the things": Quoted in Rowland Evans and Robert D. Novak, *Nixon in the White House* (New York, 1971), p. 176.
128 "I am now a Keynesian": Quoted ibid., p. 372.
128 "Robin Hood": Quoted in Leonard Silk, *Nixonomics* (New York, 1972), p. 74.
128 "It's us they is always": Quoted in Gus Tyler, "White Workers: Blue Mood," in Joseph Ryan, *White Ethnics* (Englewood Cliffs, N.J., 1973), p. 124.
129 "to improve this country's": Quoted in Emma Rothschild, *Paradise Lost: The Decline of the Auto-Industrial Age* (New York, 1973), p. 56.
129 "a nation of hamburger": Quoted in Richard J. Barnet and Ronald E. Muller, *Global Reach* (New York, 1974), pp. 305–06.
129 "Too much was at stake": Quoted ibid., p. 243.
129 "The logic of the 1973": *Congressional Quarterly, Documents 1973*, p. 45.
130 "damn fools": Ibid., p. 427.
130 "Doing something about meat": *New York Times*, April 2, 1973, p. 30.
130 "an awareness that": Quoted in Jeremy Brecher and Tim Costello, *Common Sense for Hard Times* (New York, 1976), p. 111.
130 "How much can these people": *New York Times*, April 3, 1973, p. 36.
130 "Why, I've been boycotting": *New York Times*, April 4, 1973, p. 28.
130 "He's the Marie Antoinette": *New York Times*, April 5, 1973, p. 38.
131 "It's going to be the housewives": *New York Times*, April 4, 1973, p. 28.
131 "Everybody thinks that Phase III": *Congressional Quarterly, Documents 1973*, p. 578.
131 "We have been caught": Quoted in Rufus E. Miles, Jr., *Awakening from the American Dream* (New York, 1976), p. 45.
131 "1973 was a good year": *New York Times*, January 9, 1974, p. 19.
132 "There is going to be panic": *New York Times*, January 3, 1974, p. 30.
132 "I'm helpless": *New York Times*, February 2, 1974, p. 15.
132 "A lot of people": *New York Times*, February 24, 1974, III, 13.
132 "Things have got to get": Ibid.

132 "I used to keep": *Newsweek*, March 4, 1974, p. 58.

132 "You always used to think": Ibid.

132 "There's nothing left": Ibid., p. 60.

132 "The wheat deal": Ibid.

132 "We are in for a hell": Ibid., p. 58.

133 "Teachers and social science": Quoted in Caroline Bird, *The Case Against College* (New York, 1975), p. 48.

133 "I'm resentful, bitter": Quoted in Richard B. Freeman, *The Overeducated American* (New York, 1976), p. 86.

133 "I have absolutely no prospects": Quoted ibid.

133 "all people with welfare cards": Congressional Quarterly, *Documents 1974*, p. 247.

133 "It's too bad": Quoted in Edmund G. Brown and Bill Brown, *Reagan: The Political Chameleon* (New York, 1976), p. 175.

133 "it certainly didn't sound": Quoted in Robert Brainard Pearsall, ed., *The Symbionese Liberation Army: Documents and Communications* (Amsterdam, 1974), p. 91.

133 "The gravity of our current": Congressional Quarterly, *Documents 1974*, p. 420.

134 "clearly excessive": *New York Times*, May 4, 1974, p. 49.

134 "inquiry into the human": Robert L. Heilbroner, *An Inquiry into the Human Prospect* (New York, 1974), p. 21.

135 "What is at stake": E. F. Schumacher, *Small Is Beautiful* (New York, 1973), p. 245.

135 "diet for a small": Francis Moore Lappe, *Diet for a Small Planet* (New York, 1971).

135 "Free people": Ivan Illich, *Toward a History of Needs* (New York, 1978), p. 118.

135 "If you want to know": Philip Slater, *Earthwalk* (Garden City, N.Y., 1974), pp. 94–95.

9: "ANIMALS CRASHING AROUND IN THE FOREST"

The major documents and public statements regarding Watergate have been conveniently assembled in Congressional Quarterly, *Watergate: Chronology of a Crisis* (Washington, D.C., 1975); unless otherwise noted, all references come from this well-indexed source. Two other useful summaries are the New York Times, *The End of a Presidency* (New York, 1974), and the Washington Post, *The Fall of a President* (New York, 1974). The Agnew affair is covered in Richard M. Cohen and Jules Witcover, *A Heartbeat Away* (New York, 1974).

PAGE

139 "An inflated and erroneous conception": Congressional Quarterly, *Watergate*, I, p. 81.

140 "We have absolutely": Quoted in *End of a Presidency*, pp. 153–54.

140 "Watergate did not demonstrably": Theodore White, *The Making of the President: 1972* (New York, 1973), p. 399.

140 "For it would be no less": Ibid., pp. 493-94.

141 "conscious conspiracy to": Lester A. Sobel, *Presidential Succession: Ford, Rockefeller & the 25th Amendment* (New York, 1975), p. 62.

141 "to get practical control": Congressional Quarterly, *Watergate*, I, p. 58.

142 "Under the doctrine": Quoted in Sobel, *Presidential Succession*, p. 58.

142 "Executive poppycock": Quoted in *End of a Presidency*, p. 188.

142 "twist slowly, slowly": Ibid., p. 173.

142 "Right now the credibility": Congressional Quarterly, *Watergate*, I, p. 26.

143 "the most important": Congressional Quarterly, *Documents 1973*, pp. 550-51.

143 "two of the finest": Ibid., p. 503.

145 "Watergate has taken": *New York Times*, June 8, 1973, p. 17.

145 "I was hoping": Quoted in J. Anthony Lukas, "Preamble," *New York Times Magazine*, January 13, 1974, p. 8.

145 "We were all": Quoted ibid.

145 "An outrage": Congressional Quarterly, *Documents 1973*, p. 697.

145 "I wouldn't have minded": Ibid., p. 507.

145-46 "If we make the most": *The Memoirs of Richard Nixon* (New York, 1978), II, p. 272.

146 "White people like to have books": Quoted in John Langston Gwaltney, *Drylongso* (New York, 1980), p. 100

146 "At this time in world history": Barbara W. Tuchman, *Practicing History* (New York, 1981), p. 299.

146 "One senses a laxness": Congressional Quarterly, *Documents 1973*, pp. 725-26.

148 "If President Nixon defied": Congressional Quarterly, *Watergate*, II, p. 35.

148 "It may well be that the biggest threat": Quoted in Frank Mankiewicz, *U.S. v. Richard M. Nixon* (New York, 1975), p. 100.

148 "I am innocent": Quoted in Cohen and Witcover, *Heartbeat*, p. 153.

148 "masochistic persons": Quoted ibid., p. 187.

148 "the full equivalent": Quoted ibid., p. 343.

149 "Dear Ted": Congressional Quarterly, *Documents 1973*, p. 830.

149 "scurrilous and inaccurate": Ibid., p. 837.

149 "the monarchical life-style": *Fortune*, October 1973, p. 143.

149 "People have got to know": Quoted in *End of a Presidency*, p. 234.

149 "We've demonstrated that we can replace": *Time*, October 22, 1973, p. 15.

149 "For nearly five years": *Time*, November 12, 1973, p. 11.

149 "Big Deal": Ibid.

150 "Ford has the reputation": Elizabeth Drew, *Washington Journal* (New York, 1975), p. 41.

150 "As emphatically and as strongly": Quoted in Sobel, *Presidential Succession*, p. 43.

150 "incantation of the doctrine": Congressional Quarterly, *Documents 1973*, p. 842.

151 "The President has defied": *Time*, November 5, 1973, p. 14.

151 "This sounds like a Brown-shirt": Ibid.

151 "The office of the President": *Time*, October 29, 1973, p. 12.

151 WAS THE ALERT: *Time*, 5, 1973, p. 21.

152 "dangerous emotional instability": Congressional Quarterly, Watergate, II, p. 82.

152 "He must leave office": Ibid., p. 108.

152 "I have passed the point": Ibid., p. xv.

152 "Coincidence, coincidence, coincidence": Ibid., p. 93.

152 "The public is fed up": Ibid.

152 "irredeemably": *Time*, November 12, 1973, pp. 20–21.

152 "a virtually unbroken": Quoted in Sobel, *Presidential Succession*, p. 43.

152 "The truth is": *Time*, November 12, 1973, p. 37.

153 "Integrity is the bottom line": Congressional Quarterly, *Documents 1973*, pp. 970–71.

153 "There are other things": J. Anthony Lukas, "I Am Not a Crook," *New York Times Magazine*, January 13, 1974, p. 65.

153 "We *know* that there is corruption": Quoted in Mankiewicz, *U.S. v. Nixon*, p. 113.

154 "Uncertainties make business": *New York Times*, January 6, 1974, p. 22.

154 "a very positive": *New York Times*, July 10, 1974, p. 23.

154 "not because they feel": *New York Times*, February 13, 1974, p. 16.

155 "mounting his electronic throne": Congressional Quarterly, *Documents 1974*, p. 288.

156 "Nobody is a friend": New York Times, *The White House Transcripts* (New York, 1974), p. 5.

156 "stonewall attitude": Quoted in Sobel, *Presidential Succession*, p. 178.

156 "the broadest but thinnest": Quoted ibid., p. 179.

157 "Make no mistake": Quoted in Drew, *Washington Journal*, p. 334.

157 "I am not going to sit here": Barbara Jordan and Shelby Hearon, *Barbara Jordan: A Self Portrait* (New York, 1979), pp. 186–87.

157 "You have left no stain": Quoted in Drew, *Washington Journal*, p. 350.

157 "Richard Nixon did many things": Garry Wills, *Confessions of a Conservative* (Garden City, N.Y., 1979), p. 113.

159 "Out of the traumatic": *New York Times*, August 10, 1974, p. 3.

159 "You don't get to the top": *New York Times*, August 9, 1974, p. 5.

159 "In terms of morality": Quoted in Mary T. Hanna, *Catholics and American Politics* (Cambridge, Mass., 1979), p. 90.

160 "We assume that politicians": Adrienne Rich, *On Lies, Secrets, and Silence* (New York, 1979), p. 186.

10: "MODEL T IN THE WHITE HOUSE"

Gerald Ford's autobiography, A Time to Heal (New York, 1979), reprints many presidential speeches and summarizes the history of the administration. The annual volumes published by the Congressional Quarterly, Historic Documents, remain a convenient source for public affairs.

PAGE

161   "He's the smartest guy": Quoted in Richard Reeves, A Ford, not a Lincoln (New York, 1975), p. 28.

161   "there is no whiff": New York Times, The End of a Presidency (New York, 1974), p. 76.

162   "a throwback": Quoted in Lester A. Sobel, Presidential Succession: Ford, Rockefeller & the 25th Amendment (New York, 1975), p. 213.

162   "He's been hung": New York Times, August 24, 1974, p. 1.

162   "profoundly hypocritical": New York Times, September 25, 1974, p. 1.

162   "serious mistake": New York Times, November 23, 1974, p. 16.

162   "a sour smell": Quoted in Reeves, A Ford, p. 107.

163   "earned reentry": Quoted in Robert T. Hartmann, Palace Politics: An Inside Account of the Ford Years (New York, 1980), pp. 214-15.

163   "They want me to shuffle": Quoted in Lawrence M. Baskir and William A. Straus, Chance and Circumstance (New York, 1978), p. 215.

163   "I think we gave them": Quoted ibid., p. 224.

163   "Gerald Ford is an awfully nice man": Quoted in John Osborne, White House Watch: The Ford Years (Washington, D.C., 1977), p. 53.

165   "Don't try to reach agreements": Quoted in Arthur Macy Cox, The Dynamics of Détente (New York, 1976), p. 162.

165   "to call upon America": Congressional Quarterly, Documents 1975, p. 491.

165   "I am against it": Quoted in Ford, Time to Heal, p. 292.

165   "backward, not forward": Quoted ibid.

166   "So at last it has come": "Punch," San Francisco Chronicle, April 13, 1975, p. 1.

166   "recriminations": Congressional Quarterly, Documents 1975, p. 263.

166   "to close ranks": Ibid., p. 266.

166   "What we need now": Ibid., pp. 274-75.

166   "carry the nostalgia": Robin Morgan, Going Too Far (New York, 1977), p. 223.

166   "We have been piously commanded": Quoted in Jan Barry and W. D. Ehrhart, Demilitarized Zones (Perkasie, Pa., 1976), p. 166.

166   "Let no potential adversary": Congressional Quarterly, Documents 1975, p. 251.

167   "In an era of turbulence : Ibid., p. 262.

167   "Although South Vietnam": Ibid., p. 252.

167   "At some point the United States": Quoted in Ford, *Time to Heal*, p. 268.

167   "I was not consulted": Congressional Quarterly, *Documents 1975*, p. 311.

167   "We never anticipated it": Quoted in Roy Rowan, *The Four Days of Mayaguez* (New York, 1975), p. 217.

168   "It was wonderful": William Shawcross, *Sideshow; Kissinger, Nixon and the Destruction of Cambodia* (New York, 1979), p. 434.

168   "a daring show": Quoted ibid., p. 435.

168   "It did not only ignite confidence": Quoted in Rowan, *Four Days*, p. 223.

168   "close cooperation . . . continued": *New York Times*, May 16, 1975, p. 3.

168   "not only a flagrant violation": Congressional Quarterly, *Documents 1974*, p. 806.

168   "In the CIA": Philip Agee, *Inside the Company* (New York, 1975), p. 596.

169   "I think a President": Congressional Quarterly, *Documents 1976*, p. 127.

169   "wrongful uses of power": Congressional Quarterly, *Documents 1976*, p. 324.

169   "A great nation": Ford, *Time to Heal*, p. 334.

170   "self-determination, majority": Congressional Quarterly, *Documents 1976*, p. 290.

170   "I'm certainly not appeased": *New York Times*, November 4, 1975, p. 1.

170   "stimulated new doubts": Quoted in Ford, *Time to Heal*, p. 320.

171   "I recognize when power": *New York Times*, December 9, 1974, p. 45.

171   "be bland . . . and blind": *New York Times*, December 8, 1974, p. 72.

171   "My little Argentine": *New York Times*, December 2, 1974, p. 42.

171   "I can't type": Congressional Quarterly, *Documents 1976*, p. 366.

171   "emotional and psychological": Ibid., p. 368.

172   "the worst inflation": Quoted in Ford, *Time to Heal*, p. 147.

172   "wage and price controls": Congressional Quarterly, *Documents 1974*, p. 765.

172   "public enemy number one": Ibid., p. 773.

172   "make a list": Ibid., p. 879.

172   "We have not one but two": Ibid., p. 870.

172   "any policy that brings": Ibid., p. 861.

172   "Inflation is social dynamite": Ibid., p. 868.

173   "Clean up your plate": Quoted in Reeves, *A Ford*, pp. 161–62.

173   "a 180 degree turn": Congressional Quarterly, *Documents 1974*, pp. 976, 979.

173   "Americans are no longer": Congressional Quarterly, *Documents 1975*, p. 28.

174   "voluntary restrictions simply": Ibid., p. 18.

174   "The worldwide nuclear industry": Elizabeth Drew, *American Journal* (New York, 1977), p. 9.

174 "People are disturbed": Interview in *Forbes* magazine, October 1, 1975, p. 22.
174 "ominous signs": Congressional Quarterly, *Documents 1975*, p. 637.
175 "We must reject": Congressional Quarterly, *Documents 1976*, p. 28.
175 "As the cities of the Northeast": Quoted in Drew, *American Journal*, p. 60.
176 "no single tradition": Quoted in J. Harvie Wilkinson III, *From Brown to Bakke* (New York, 1979), p. 225.
176-77 "I have consistently opposed": Quoted in Jon Hillson, *The Battle of Boston* (New York, 1977), pp. 35-36.
177 "The real issue isn't education": Quoted ibid., p. 31.
177 "Young people": Congressional Quarterly, *Documents 1975*, p. 71.
177 "There is no longer justice": Quoted in Hillson, *Battle of Boston*, p. 262.
178 "There is a gut feeling": Quoted in Drew, *American Journal*, p. 62.
178 "If our leaders abandon us": Manning Marable, *From the Grassroots: Essays Toward Afro-American Liberation* (Boston, 1980), p. 42.
178 "For us": *New York Times*, March 22, 1976, p. 18.
178 "No longer is the female": Congressional Quarterly, *Documents 1975*, pp. 55-56.
179 "that nigger is as guilty": Quoted in Hillson, *Battle of Boston*, pp. 121-22, 126.
179 "People were fed up": *New York Times*, November 6, 1975, p. 1.
179 "They have repudiated this fraudulent": *New York Times*, November 5, 1975, p. 22.
179 "My goal is to stop living": *New York Times*, November 15, 1974, p. 1.
179 "Melville was dead": *New York Times*, January 14, 1975, pp. 14-15.
179 "Any jury we": Quoted in Joseph Kelner and James Munves, *The Kent State Coverup* (New York, 1980), p. 26.
180 "We don't blame": Quoted ibid, pp. 254-55.
180 "There is a double standard": *Time*, April 21, 1975, p. 58.
180 "The time has come": *New York Times*, November 18, 1975, p. 37.
180 "Attica lurks": *New York Times*, December 31, 1976, pp. 1, 10.
180 "Most are still ensconced": *New York Times*, August 24, 1975, III, p. 1.
181 "One must believe": Congressional Quarterly, *Documents 1975*, p. 689.
181 "will foster respect": *New York Times*, December 31, 1976, p. 1.
181 "You have to enforce": Quoted in Kelner and Munves, *Kent State Coverup*, p. 257.
181 "I'm not that person": *New York Times*, January 14, 1975, p. 15.
181 "The war continues": Quoted in Nora Sayre, "Kent State: Victims, Survivors, Heirs," *Ms.*, September 1975, p. 56.
181 "I saw a hand coming up": *New York Times*, September 6, 1975, p. 1.
181 "This country is a mess": *New York Times*, September 6, 1975, p. 26; September 20, 1975, p. 12; September 12, 1975, p. 1; September 6, 1975, p. 12; September 24, 1975, p. 28; December 18, 1975, p. 27.

182   "Urban guerrilla": *New York Times*, September 19, 1975, p. 1.
182   "radical feminism": *New York Times*, September 20, 1975, p. 14.
182   "The coming revolutionary struggle": Quoted in Vin McLellan and Paul Avery, *The Voices of Guns* (New York, 1977), p. 456.
182   "a psychiatric profile": *New York Times*, September 20, 1975, p. 1.
182   "For months": Quoted in McLellan and Avery, *Voices of Guns*, p. 417.
182   "It was a kind of ultimate protest": *New York Times*, September 26, 1975, p. 16.
182   "In every case of violent political protest": *Playboy*, June 1976, p. 70.
183   "just might have triggered": *New York Times*, January 19, 1976, p. 26.
183   "No one has been charged": *New York Times*, December 13, 1975, p. 15.
183   "Whatever happened": *New York Times*, January 19, 1976, p. 26.
183   "I cannot vouch": Woody Allen, *Side Effects* (New York, 1980), p. 89.
184   "Such movies distract people": Quoted in Len Keyser, *Hollywood in the Seventies* (San Diego, 1981), p. 183.
184   "The common wisdom": *Newsweek*, July 4, 1976, p. 13.
184   "The country is old": Gloria Steinem, "Cheer Up," *Ms.*, July 1976, p. 47.
184   "The feeling of the day": Drew, *American Journal*, pp. 282–83.

11: "CALCULATED APPEALS AND EMPTY PROMISES"

The fullest coverage of the election of 1976 is Jules Witcover, *Marathon* (New York, 1977). The major statements of the candidates are collected in *The Presidential Campaign, 1976*, 4 vols. (Washington, D.C., 1978). The best transcription of the Ford-Carter debates appears in Lloyd Bitzer and Theodore Reuter, *Carter vs. Ford* (Madison, Wis., 1980). The annual volumes of the Congressional Quarterly, *Historic Documents*, provide a useful context.

PAGE
185   "Basically I found": Quoted in Witcover, *Marathon*, p. 126.
186   "Great dreams still": *Presidential Campaign*, I, i, pp. 3–4, 10.
186   "The people are about as fed up": Ibid., II, i, pp. 83, 85.
187   "There is no need for lying": Jimmy Carter, *Why Not the Best?* (Nashville, Tenn., 1975), p. 128.
187   "We might have the most incredible": Quoted in Kandy Stroud, *How Jimmy Won* (New York, 1977), p. 166.
187   "That word would be": Quoted in Martin Schram, *Running for President: 1976* (New York, 1977), p. 155.
188   "The bickering, squabbling": Quoted in Witcover, *Marathon*, p. 247.
188   "not [to] avoid": *Presidential Campaign*, I, i, p. 11.
189   "the Lon Chaney": James Wooten, *Dasher* (New York, 1979), p. 32.
189   "it indicates . . . that people": *Presidential Campaign*, I, i, p. 99.
189   "He has more positions": Robert Shogan, *Promises to Keep* (New York, 1977), p. 43.

189 "I am personally opposed": *Presidential Campaign,* I, i, pp. 93, 97, 105–06.

189 "an emotional issue": Quoted in Schram, *Running,* p. 76.

189 "Who is Jimmy": Quoted in Witcover, *Marathon,* p. 344.

189 "close, personal, intimate": Quoted in Schram, *Running,* pp. 98–99.

189 "We knew the thing": Quoted in Witcover, *Marathon,* p. 202.

190 "We have our own built-in State Department": Quoted in Laurence Shoup, *The Carter Presidency and Beyond* (Palo Alto, Cal., 1980), pp. 29–30.

190 "a splendid learning opportunity": Carter, *Why Not the Best,* p. 127.

190 "Stories in the *New York Times*": Quoted in Schram, *Running,* p. 55.

191 "His basic strategy": Quoted in Christopher Lydon, "Jimmy Carter Revealed," *Atlantic Monthly,* July 1977, p. 51.

191 "elusive enough to": Quoted in Shoup, *The Carter Presidency,* p. 83.

191 "I would not be where I am": Quoted ibid., p. 68.

191 "The hierarchy of the Democratic party": Quoted in Stroud, *How Jimmy Won,* p. 262.

192 "Everybody is now saying": *New York Times,* June 7, 1976, p. 23.

192 "peeled the veil": *Presidential Campaign,* I, i, p. 19.

192 "Wallace and Carter": Drew, *American Journal,* pp. 121, 127.

192 "blue-eyed Jimmy": *New York Times,* July 6, 1976, p. 21.

192 "None of us": Ibid.

192 "He'll be like most other white": *New York Times,* March 28, 1976, p. 52.

192 "apathy and cynicism": *New York Times,* April 18, 1976, p. 36.

192 "Blacks have always known": Andrew Young, "Why I Support Jimmy Carter," *Nation,* April 3, 1976, pp. 397–98.

193 "This is a Christian": Quoted in Drew, *American Journal,* p. 99.

193 "Why every Negro I ever met": Quoted in Haynes Johnson, *In the Absence of Power* (New York, 1980), p. 118.

193 "He caught a lot of black politicians": *New York Times,* July 6, 1976, p. 21.

193 "I see nothing wrong": Quoted in Witcover, *Marathon,* pp. 302–07.

193 "Is there no white politician": Quoted in James David Barber, *The Pulse of Politics* (New York, 1980), p. 196.

193 "We've created a Frankenstein": Quoted ibid.

193 "A disaster": Quoted ibid.

193 "For a man who chooses": Quoted in Stroud, *How Jimmy Won,* pp. 278–79.

194 "The burden is on Jimmy": *New York Times,* April 9, 1976, p. 37.

194 "I've always been able": Quoted in Witcover, *Marathon,* p. 307.

194 "It would be ironic": Quoted in Barber, *Pulse,* p. 197.

194 "Candidates who make an attack": Quoted in Witcover, *Marathon,* pp. 293–94.

195 "One thing I don't need": Quoted in Schram, *Running,* pp. 133–34.

195 "One of them has been campaigning": Quoted in Witcover, *Marathon,* p. 340.

195   "A lot of conventional thinking": *New York Times*, June 4, 1976, p. A12.

195   "Whether you are a Governor": "Playboy Interview: Jerry Brown," *Playboy*, April 1976, p. 72.

196   "set the stage": *New York Times*, June 1, 1976, p. 41.

196   "the monster bureaucracy": *New York Times*, July 15, 1976, p. 26.

196   "There are new": Ibid.

196   "There's no sense": *New York Times*, June 8, 1976, p. 23.

197   "a national community": *New York Times*, July 13, 1976, p. 24.

197   "Millions of Americans": *New York Times*, July 15, 1976, p. 24.

197   "President who pardoned": Quoted in Witcover, *Marathon*, p. 368.

197   "My name is Jimmy Carter": Congressional Quarterly, *Documents 1976*, pp. 598–603.

197   "Surely the Lord": Quoted in Witcover, *Marathon*, p. 370.

197   "Our nation's capital": Quoted ibid., p. 92.

198   "It doesn't change my view": *New York Times*, November 21, 1975, p. 20.

198   "a foreign policy": Quoted in Ford, *Time to Heal*, p. 361.

198   "Americans are hungry": Quoted in Witcover, *Marathon*, p. 46.

198   "Balancing the budget": *Newsweek*, March 24, 1975, p. 20.

198   "the best thing in the world": Quoted in Ford, *Time to Heal*, pp. 297–98.

198   A DISGRACE: Quoted in Witcover, *Marathon*, p. 58.

198   "Gerald Ford's problem": Ibid., p. 392.

199   "When you lose such a close race": Quoted in Witcover, *Marathon*, p. 396.

199   "Under Messrs. Kissinger": Ibid., p. 402.

199   "When it comes to the canal": *New York Times*, February 29, 1976, p. 42.

200   "This was no long, loud cheer": Quoted in Malcolm D. MacDougall, *We Almost Made It* (New York, 1977), p. 80.

200   "There is no substitute": *New York Times*, August 20, 1976, p. 12.

201   "In 1976 . . . issues": Stroud, *How Jimmy Won*, p. 277.

201   "vicious and unprovoked": *New York Times*, August 19, 1976, p. 1.

201   "disreputable tyrant": *New York Times*, September 16, 1976, p. 45.

202   "I do not favor a blanket": Quoted in Stroud, *How Jimmy Won*, pp. 343–44; Lawrence M. Baskir and William A. Straus, *Chance and Circumstance* (New York, 1978), p. 229.

202   "One of the incumbents": Quoted in Bitzer and Reuter, *Carter vs. Ford*, pp. 21–22.

202   "Trust must be earned": Ford, *Time to Heal*, p. 400.

202   "Like a moderately dull marriage": Norman Mailer, "The Search for Carter," *New York Times Magazine*, September 26, 1976, p. 21.

203   "It was done in the best schoolyard style": Quoted in MacDougall, *We Almost Made It*, p. 181.

203   "I'll tell you what the coloreds want": Quoted in Bitzer and Reuter, *Carter vs. Ford*, p. 398.

203   "He had no interest": Quoted ibid.

203 "Democratic wars": Quoted ibid., p. 37.
203 "Some people considered": Quoted ibid., p. 411.
203 THE BLOOPER HEARD: *Time*, October 18, 1976, p. 10.
204 "It's something out of Alice": Ibid.
204 "The traveling press": Quoted in *Playboy*, November 1976, pp. 66, 86.
204 "How can you put confidence": Quoted in Mailer, "The Search for Carter," p. 76.
204 "*Playboy* is known": Quoted in Witcover, *Marathon*, p. 568.
204 "In what is widely conceded": Quoted in Bitzer and Reuter, *Carter vs. Ford*, p. 195.
205 "I wish—Lord": *Time*, November 26, 1976, p. 20.
206 "I consider it my duty": *Time*, November 15, 1976, p. 20.
206 "I don't vote": Ibid.
206 "I'm not apathetic": Ibid.
206 "to use the Republican": *New York Times*, November 3, 1976, p. 17.
206 "I think the sun's rising": Quoted in Shogan, *Promises to Keep*, p. 15.

12: "A CRISIS OF CONFIDENCE"

The first hundred days of the Carter administration are described in Robert Shogan, *Promises to Keep* (New York, 1977). Haynes Johnson's *In the Absence of Power* (New York, 1980) explores the larger problems of politics under Carter. The Congressional Quarterly's collection of sources, *Historic Documents*, continues through 1978.

PAGE

207 "Our people were sick at heart": *Presidential Campaign, 1976*, 4 vols. (Washington, D.C., 1978), I, ii, p. 1126.
207 "This is not the time": *New York Times*, January 21, 1977, p. A22.
208 "One result was certain": Johnson, *Absence of Power*, pp. 134-35.
208 "the revolving door": Congressional Quarterly, *Documents 1977*, p. 30.
208 "What has been Mr. Lance's": Clark R. Mollenhoff, *The President Who Failed* (New York, 1980), p. 51.
209 "If after the inauguration": Robert Scheer, "Jimmy, We Hardly Know Y'All," *Playboy*, November 1976, p. 192.
209 "Conservatives with high integrity": Quoted in Shogan, *Promises to Keep*, p. 88.
209 "It is now clear": Quoted ibid., p. 92.
210 "a return of the confidence": *Newsweek*, May 2, 1977, p. 32.
210 "If this were France": *Time*, November 20, 1978, p. 42.
210 "This was a routine matter": Congressional Quarterly, *Documents 1978*, p. 53.
211 "This is the most profound": *Time*, November 20, 1978, p. 16.
212 "Nixon had his enemies list": *Newsweek*, October 24, 1977, p. 37.
212 "the Eptitude Question": Ibid.
212 "He is a soothing": Quoted in Johnson, *Absence of Power*, p. 242.

212 "It's the saddest day": Quoted in Lawrence M. Baskir and William A. Straus, *Chance and Circumstance* (New York, 1978), p. 231.

213 "The most disgraceful thing": Quoted ibid.

213 "If I had known this would happen": *Newsweek*, January 31, 1977, p. 29.

213 "I don't intend to pardon": Congressional Quarterly, *Documents 1977*, p. 186.

213 "more likely to be poor": *New York Times*, January 22, 1977, p. 1.

214 "We must replace": Quoted in Jeremiah Novak, "The Trilateral Connection," *Atlantic Monthly*, July 1977, p. 58.

214 "the American people": Quoted in Shogan, *Promises to Keep*, pp. 127, 221–22.

214 "Washington's claims to teach": Quoted ibid.

214 "Carter painted himself": *Newsweek*, July 17, 1978, p. 22.

214 "It's not worth going into": *Newsweek*, July 24, 1978, p. 19.

215 "disgusted the entire": Quoted in Shogan, *Promises to Keep*, p. 220.

215 "the ghosts of Attica": *Newsweek*, March 21, 1977, pp. 27, 16.

215 "Taking hostages": Ibid., pp. 25–26.

215 "Dealing *viva voce*": *Newsweek*, April 4, 1977, p. 15.

216 "face the fact": Congressional Quarterly, *Documents 1977*, p. 106.

216 "This country did not conserve": *Newsweek*, April 18, 1977, p. 73.

216 "a windfall loss": *Newsweek*, May 2, 1977, p. 12.

216 "Our problem isn't a shortage": *Newsweek*, June 13, 1977, p. 14.

216 "It's like it was": *New York Times*, April 22, 1977, p. B6.

217 "I don't feel much like talking": Quoted in Barry Commoner, *The Politics of Energy* (New York, 1979), p. 24.

217 "The moral equivalent of the Vietnam": *Newsweek*, October 10, 1977, p. 30.

217 "the moral . . . Sominex": *Newsweek*, November 21, 1977, p. 40.

217 "Further delay will only lead": Congressional Quarterly, *Documents 1978*, p. 11.

217 "I don't see the inevitability": *Newsweek*, April 24, 1978, p. 36.

217 "To think of alternative energy": Lester C. Thurow, *The Zero-Sum Society* (New York, 1980), p. 38.

217 "It's time for it to compete": *Newsweek*, April 24, 1978, p. 42.

218 "I have not given up on": Quoted in Johnson, *Absence of Power*, p. 293.

218 "Market conditions do not warrant": Congressional Quarterly, *Documents 1978*, p. 792.

218 "honor the 55": *Time*, February 26, 1979, p. 60.

218 "The world has never known": Quoted in Mark Stephens, *Three Mile Island* (New York, 1980), p. 4.

218 "We were damn lucky": *Newsweek*, November 5, 1979, p. 54.

219 "We cannot simply shut down": *New York Times*, July 17, 1979, p. 1.

219 "The members don't pay any attention": *Newsweek*, June 4, 1979, p. 20.

219 "They put their heads": *Newsweek*, May 21, 1979, p. 24.

219 "The average motorist": *Newsweek*, May 14, 1979, p. 89.

219 "It's sort of like sex": *Newsweek*, May 21, 1979, p. 24.

220 "When the President and all them senators": *Newsweek*, July 2, 1979, p. 24.

220 "The future of the Democratic Party": *Newsweek*, July 9, 1979, p. 18.

220 "If I give this speech": Quoted in Jack W. Germond and Jules Witcover, *Blue Smoke and Mirrors: How Reagan Won and Why Carter Lost the Election of 1980* (New York, 1981), p. 29.

220 "All the legislation in the world": *New York Times*, July 16, 1979, p. A10.

221 "If OPEC tries to blackmail us": *San Francisco Examiner and Chronicle*, July 6, 1980, p. 9.

222 "The increase in the federal budget": Congressional Quarterly, *Documents 1977*, p. 127.

222 "no new programs": *Newsweek*, May 16 1977, p. 44.

222 "there is *no* way": Ibid.

222 "We already have so much capacity": *Newsweek*, January 9, 1978, p. 55.

223 "You just can't have a free-enterprise system": *Newsweek*, August 13, 1979, p. 55.

223 "would have a falling-dominoes effect": *Newsweek*, October 29, 1979, p. 22.

223 "The people who made": Ibid.

223 "You can't figure your real return": *Newsweek*, May 29, 1978, p. 68.

224 "my own word of honor": Congressional Quarterly, *Documents 1978*, p. 661.

224 "We must face": Ibid., p. 688.

224 "few believed that the Carter plan": Ibid., p. 684.

224 "Using high interest rates": *Seven Days*, December 8, 1978, p. 7.

224 "Sometimes a party must sail": Congressional Quarterly, *Documents 1978*, p. 775.

224 "equality of sacrifice": *Time*, February 15, 1979, p. 9.

224 "There are no economic miracles": *Time*, February 11, 1980, p. 54.

225 "Fairness, not force": Congressional Quarterly, *Documents 1977*, p. 591.

225 "The fatal flaw": *Newsweek*, September 19, 1977, p. 50.

226 "There is *no* Panama Canal": *Newsweek*, September 5, 1977, p. 38.

226 "If the treaties are rejected": *Newsweek*, February 13, 1978, p. 18.

226 "After receiving thousands": Walter LaFeber, *The Panama Canal* (New York, 1979), p. 231.

226 "The Panama Canal": *Newsweek*, October 8, 1979, p. 49.

226 "We're trying to carve out"; *Newsweek*, August 20, 1979, p. 39.

226 "Normalization": Congressional Quarterly, *Documents 1978*, p. 784.

226 "a major blow": *New York Times*, December 16, 1978, p. 10.

227 "an outright abuse": *Time*, January 1, 1979, p. 39.

227 "Peace will not be assured": Congressional Quarterly, *Documents 1977*, p. 740.

227 "We, like our forebears": Congressional Quarterly, *Documents 1978*, p. 232.

227–28 "If we spend all our time jawboning": *Newsweek*, May 29, 1978, p. 21.

228 "SALT II will not end": *New York Times*, June 19, 1979, p. A13.

228 "The danger is real": *Newsweek*, June 25, 1979, p. 33.

229 "We stood toe-to-toe": *Newsweek*, Octocer 15, 1979, p. 64.

230 "a scapegoat": *Newsweek*, August 27, 1979, p. 20.

230 "the credibility of the United States": *Newsweek*, September 3, 1979, pp. 18–19.

230 "We've learned our lessons": Congressional Quarterly, *Documents 1978*, p. 709.

231 "There is no way we could get": *New York Times*, February 15, 1979, p. A16.

231 "This is a volatile world": *Time*, February 26, 1979, p. 18.

231 "The 10,000 Iranian students": *Newsweek*, June 4, 1979, p. 43.

231 "How would you like it": Ibid.

232 "My initial reaction": *Newsweek*, November 19, 1979, pp. 61–62.

232 No MORE IRANIAN: *Time*, November 26, 1979, p. 21.

232 "It is a time not for rhetoric": *Time*, November 19, 1979, p. 14.

232 "It would not be possible": *Newsweek*, December 10, 1979, p. 39.

232 "If one works for years": *Newsweek*, November 19, 1979, p. 62.

13: "TO HEAL THE FRAGMENTATIONS"

PAGE

235 "over the last": Sissela Bok, *Lying: Moral Choice in Public and Private Life* (New York, 1978), pp. xviii, 258.

235 "The social incentives": Ibid.

236 "Watergate, then the energy": *New York Times*, January 11, 1974, p. 13.

236 "The Cosmic Flopperoo": *New York Times*, January 15, 1974, p. 37.

236 "deepening disillusionment": Quoted in *Daedalus*, Spring 1974, p. 192.

236 "Too often, as we know": Quoted in Nena and George O'Neill, *Shifting Gears* (New York, 1974), p. 34.

236 "most often excluded": *Daedalus*, Spring 1974, p. 199.

236 "using up our intellectual": *Time*, February 26, 1973, pp. 75–76.

236 "the possibility of a decline": *Daedalus*, Spring 1974, p. 12.

237 "further decline in the role": Congressional Quarterly, *Documents 1973*, p. 782.

237 "The general public": *Scientific American*, January 1976, p. 16.

237 "There is an essential element": *Daedalus*, Spring 1974, pp. 42, 31.

237 "I think present-day reason": Robert M. Pirsig, *Zen and the Art of Motorcycle Maintenance* (New York, 1974), pp. 164–65.

237 "rationality has to include": *Time*, April 23, 1973, p. 84.

237 "He had built empires": Pirsig, *Zen*, p. 372.

238 "What we have mistakenly come to think": John Holt, *Instead of Education* (New York, 1976), p. 16.

238 "the hidden curriculum": Ivan Illich, *Toward a History of Needs* (New York, 1978), pp. 23, 70.

238 "Next to the right to life": Holt, *Instead of Education*, p. 4.
238 "The most serious aspect of vandalism": Congressional Quarterly, *Documents 1975*, p. 208.
238 "It's just that we're not interested": *Newsweek*, April 26, 1975, p. 97.
238 "The kids are just fed up": Ibid.
239 "Diplomas and tests": Quoted in Illich, *Toward a History*, p. 84.
239 "The embarrassing thing": Caroline Bird, *The Case Against College* (New York, 1975), pp. 134–35.
239 "prevailing sadness": Ibid., pp. 9–10.
239 "History is in crisis": *Journal of American History*, September 1975, p. 557.
239 "The 'lessons' taught": Quoted in Christopher Lasch, *The Culture of Narcissism* (New York, 1978), p. xiv.
240 "Conventional thinking about": Congressional Quarterly, *Documents 1975*, p. 640.
240 "The cause of the medical malpractice crisis": *New York Times*, May 14, 1975, p. 42.
240 "you're doing nothing to curtail": *New York Times*, May 20, 1975, p. 28.
240 "malpractice is the number one problem": *New York Times*, June 15, 1975, p. 44.
241 "The time has come to recognize": *New York Times*, January 26, 1976, p. 20.
241 "Because of the suppression": Quoted in Samuel S. Epstein, *The Politics of Cancer* (San Francisco, 1978), p. 106.
241–42 "extremely grave questions": Ibid., p. 311.
242 "There is no way you can continue": *New York Times*, February 3, 1976, p. 12.
242 "The magnitude of the risks": Ibid.
242 "generic problems that were well known": *New York Times*, February 11, 1976, p. 1.
242 "Neither the nuclear bomb": Barry Commoner, *The Poverty of Power* (New York, 1976), p. 97.
242 "Still obsessed by thoughts of death": Woody Allen, *Without Feathers* (New York, 1975), p. 4.
242 "Life does end": Gail Sheehy, *Passages* (New York, 1976), p. 136.
242 "A patient reaches a point": Elisabeth Kübler-Ross, *On Death and Dying* (New York, 1969), pp. 116, 118.
243 "Death is not a sudden": Lewis Thomas, *The Lives of a Cell* (New York, 1974), p. 50.
243 "The time had come": Phyllis Battelle, " 'Let me sleep': The Story of Karen Ann Quinlan," *Ladies' Home Journal*, September 1976, p. 72.
243 "The hope of recovery": Congressional Quarterly, *Documents 1976*, p. 198.
243 "She's been returned": B. D. Colen, *Karen Ann Quinlan* (New York 1976), p. 23.
244 "I should've been given the privilege": *New York Times*, April 9, 1974, p. 49.

244   "the most romanticized": Quoted in John E. O'Connor and Martin A. Jackson, *American History/American Film* (New York, 1979), pp. 268–69.

244   "When they're cheering": Quoted ibid.

244   "my metaphor for America": *Newsweek*, June 30, 1975, pp. 46–48.

245   "The voices are nasal": John Sayles, "I-80 Nebraska, M. 490–M. 205," in William Abrahams, *Prize Stories of the Seventies* (Garden City, N.Y., 1981), p. 233.

245   "The whole world is just becoming": Quoted in Ted Morgan, "MH² recycles our garbage," *New York Times Magazine*, October 3, 1976, p. 54.

245   "You must have planted": Ibid., p. 41.

245–46   "there is something sick, sick": *Newsweek*, May 3, 1976, p. 54.

246   "The constant revision": O'Neill, *Shifting Gears*, p. 14.

246   "The life structure": Daniel J. Levinson et al., *The Seasons of a Man's Life* (New York, 1978), p. 49.

246   "Times of crises": Sheehy, *Passages*, p. 21.

247   "a time of religious": Quoted in Jacob Needleman and George Baker, eds., *Understanding the New Religions* (New York, 1978), p. 49.

247   "From all sides there is a prospect": Quoted ibid., p. 47.

247   "The Catholic church": Quoted ibid., p. 340.

247   "very sure"; Andrew M. Greeley, *The American Catholic* (New York, 1977), pp. 127–28.

247   "to awaken the God who sleeps": Quoted in Needleman and Baker, *Understanding the New Religions*, p. 62.

248   "Do you know the devil": Quoted in Daniel Cohen, *The New Believers* (New York, 1975), p. 83.

248   "Nobody who ever talked with a witch": Theodore Roszak, *The Unfinished Animal* (New York, 1975), p. 11.

248   "a nation whose trust": Charles Y. Glock and Robert N. Bellah, *The New Religious Consciousness* (Berkeley, Cal., 1976), pp. 5, 13.

248   "America is destined": *New York Times*, September 20, 1974, pp. 44–45.

248   "I feel changed": Frederick Sontag, *Sun Myung Moon and the Unification Church* (Nashville, Tenn., 1977), p. 54.

249   "It was radical Christianity": Quoted in Marshall Kilduff and Ron Javers, *The Suicide Cult* (New York, 1978), p. 76.

249   "the number one problem": *San Francisco Bay Guardian*, March 31, 1977, p. 7.

249   "We committed an act": *Newsweek*, March 26, 1979, p. 53.

249   "the cult would": Robert Jay Lifton, "The Appeal of the Death Trip," *New York Times Magazine*, January 7, 1979, p. 27.

249   "elicited one of the most overwhelmingly negative": George Gallup, Jr., and David Poling, *The Search for America's Faith* (Nashville, Tenn., 1980), p. 28.

249   "a retreat from the worlds": Peter Marin, "The New Narcissism," *Harper's*, October 1975, pp. 45, 46, 48.

250 "It's the Me-Decade": Tom Wolfe, "The 'Me' Decade and the Third Great Awakening," *New York*, August 23, 1976.

250 "Hedonism," "narcissism": Christopher Lasch, "The Narcissist Society," *New York Review of Books*, September 30, 1976, pp. 8–9.

250 "Do these exhortations": Daniel Bell, *The Cultural Contradictions of Capitalism* (New York, 1976), p. 144.

250 "a way of life that is dying": Lasch, *Culture of Narcissism*, p. xv.

250 "Narcissism holds the key": Lasch, "Narcissist Society," p. 9.

250 "The popular media": Theodore Roszak, "Expanding on the new consciousness," *San Francisco Bay Guardian*, January 20, 1977, pp. 7–8.

250 "After the political turmoil": Lasch, *Culture of Narcissism*, p. 4.

251 "The plants, the whales": Michael Rossman, *New Age Blues* (New York, 1979), p. 23.

251 "to heal the fragmentations": Jacob Needleman, *A Sense of the Cosmos* (Garden City, N.Y., 1975), p. 162.

251 "the search—at once both desperate": Theodore Roszak, *Person Planet* (Garden City, N.Y., 1978), p. xxi.

251 "Each living being": Gary Snyder, *Turtle Island* (New York, 1974).

14: "ON THE BOTTOM"

Page

252 "We are on the bottom": Harry Edwards, *The Struggle That Must Be* (New York, 1980), p. 335.

252–53 "We want to contribute": *Newsweek*, March 20, 1978, pp. 60–61.

253 "We ask now quietly": Quoted in Philip Reno, *Mother Earth, Father Sky, and Economic Development* (Albuquerque, N.M., 1981), p. 117.

254 "The only real question": *New York Times*, July 9, 1979, p. 10.

254 "They took away our past": Bruce Johansen and Roberto Maestas, *Wasi'chu: The Continuing Indian War* (New York, 1979), p. 71.

254 "all citizens should bear equally": Quoted in Mark Kellogg, "Indian Rights," *Saturday Review*, November 25, 1978, p. 27.

255 "The coal can stay": Quoted ibid., p. 24.

255 "A tribe is a people": Quoted ibid., p. 26.

255 "My sheep are dying": Quoted in Johansen and Maestas, *Wasi'chu*, p. 142.

255 "It's more than a matter": Quoted ibid., pp. 164–65.

255 "In a generation": Quoted in Howell Raines, "American Indians: Struggling for Power and Identity," *New York Times Magazine*, February 11, 1979, p. 24.

255 "We are here to let America know": *New York Times*, July 16, 1978, p. 22.

255 "Forty years ago": *Newsweek*, April 9, 1979, p. 98.

256 "I put my life on the line": Quoted in Susan Braudy, " 'We Will Remember' Survival School," *Ms.*, July 1976, p. 78.

256   "When the energy crisis": Raines, "American Indians," p. 28.

256   "We shall learn all these devices": Kellogg, "Indian Rights," p. 27.

256   "very interesting, very enjoyable": *San Francisco Examiner and Chronicle*, August 10, 1980, p. 9.

257   "They paid me $314 a month": *Newsweek*, September 10, 1979, p. 22.

257   "The dominant cultural group": Jonathan Kirsch, "Chicano Power," *New West*, September 11, 1978, p. 36.

258   "It's an attack": Quoted ibid., p. 38.

258   "Let's stop the whole racist game": Quoted ibid.

258   "Sure, some of them are as unruly": John Ehrlichman, "Mexican Aliens Aren't a Problem," *Esquire*, August 1979, p. 64.

258   "It's more complicated": *Newsweek*, July 4, 1977, p. 16.

258   "the tear of two cultures": Maureen Orth, "The Soaring Spirit of Chicano Arts," *New West*, September 11, 1978, p. 41.

258   "Fight back": Quoted in Kirsch,"Chicano Power," p. 40.

258   "We are no longer going to stand around": Sylvia Alicia Gonzales, "The Chicana Perspective" in Arnulfo D. Trejo, ed., *The Chicanos* (Tucson, Ariz., 1979), p. 95.

259   "Underneath all that bravado": Quoted in Alfredo Mirandé and Evangelina Enríquez, *La Chicana* (Chicago, 1979), p. 184.

259   "*Chicanismo* reflects a deep": Trejo, *Chicanos*, p. 114.

259   "Chicanos are singing": Quoted in Bruce-Novoa, *Chicano Authors* (Austin, Tex., 1980), p. 81.

259   "We are tired of being taken for granted": Quoted in Kirsch, "Chicano Power," p. 36.

259   "all worthy male members": *New York Times*, June 10, 1978, p. 1.

260   "Blacks as a group": Manning Marable, *From the Grassroots: Essays toward Afro-American Liberation* (Boston, 1980), p. 212.

260   "I had my children first": *Wall Street Journal*, August 28, 1980, p. 1.

260   "Female-headed households": Audre Lorde, "We Need Only Look," *Ms.*, February 1979, p. 70.

261   "It's not enough to do better": *Newsweek*, August 8, 1977, p. 16.

261   "I don't think you'll be very happy": *Time*, December 18, 1978, p. 5.

261   "The gravest flaw": Congressional Quarterly, *Documents 1978*, p. 242.

261   "We have seen successive executive orders": *New York Times*, April 18, 1978, p. 24.

261   "There are simply not enough": "This World," *San Francisco Examiner and Chronicle*, September 7, 1980, p. 29.

262   "Compliance cannot be secured": "This World," *San Francisco Examiner and Chronicle*, October 28, 1979, p. 12.

262   "will find a way to blur": J. Harvie Wilkinson III, *From Brown to Bakke* (New York, 1979), p. 298.

262   "The decision will go down in history": *New York Times*, June 29, 1978, p. A22.

263   "We're seeing a national backlash": *Newsweek*, August 14, 1978, p. 13.

263 "Allies who walked with us": "This World," *San Francisco Examiner and Chronicle*, January 6, 1980, p. 26.

263 "Unless black people are given relief": *Time*, December 18, 1978, p. 15.

263 "Being that the lights are out": *Newsweek*, July 25, 1977, p. 18.

263 "The ingredients are there": *New York Times*, January 18, 1979, p. 10.

263 "It's no longer a question": *Time*, December 18, 1978, pp. 15–16.

263 "What we find is [an] inward turn": *New York Times*, December 30, 1979, XII, p. 6.

264 "What happens to Afro-Americans": Edwards, *Struggle That Must Be*, p. 305.

264 "I go lookin' for work": *Newsweek*, August 7, 1978, p. 22.

264 "The prisoner and the school child": Congressional Quarterly, *Documents 1977*, p. 294.

264 "This decision gives a green light": Ellen Goodman, *Close to Home* (New York, 1979), pp. 188–89.

265 "We're going to slowly disappear": *Newsweek*, August 7, 1978, p. 22.

265 "A *cholo*": Quoted in Georgia Jeffries, "The Low Riders of Whittier Boulevard," *American Film*, February 1979, p. 58.

265 "You learn young": Quoted in Suzanne Murphy, "A Year With the Gangs of East Los Angeles," *Ms.*, July 1978, p. 56.

265 "the whole trip": Quoted ibid.

265 "They conceive babies": Edwards, *Struggle That Must Be*, p. 318.

266 "It makes you feel like somebody": *Newsweek*, August 7, 1978, p. 22.

266 "We're in a period": *Newsweek*, April 2, 1979, p. 58.

266 "Never, never, never": Kitty Hanson, *Disco Fever* (New York, 1978), p. 37.

267 "The point of the movie": Jeffries, "Low Riders," p. 63.

267 "We are here to move history": *The Spirit of Houston: An Official Report to the President* (Washington, D.C., 1978), p. 15.

268 "the politics of empathy": Gail Sheehy, "Women in Passage," *Redbook*, April 1978, p. 250.

268 "It was a total high to discover": *Time*, December 5, 1977, p. 19.

268 "Houston was a rite": Ibid.

268 "A giant self-esteem bath": Sheehy, "Women in Passage," p. 250.

268 "The American people": Congressional Quarterly, *Documents 1977*, p. 863.

268 "the one-world": Sheehy, "Women in Passage," p. 246.

268 "Houston will finish off": *Spirit of Houston*, p. 119.

269 "How do you equate the *life*": *New York Times*, December 16, 1977, p. A30.

269 "There are many things in life": Frederick S. Jaffe et al., *Abortion Politics* (New York, 1981), p. 132.

269 "It seems . . . unconscionable": Goodman, *Close to Home*, p. 79.

269 "unwilling to trade": Jaffe, *Abortion Politics*, p. 132.

270 "an unduly burdensome": Ibid., p. 189.

270 "Although government may not place": Quoted in "This World," *San Francisco Examiner and Chronicle*, July 6, 1980, p. 7.

270 "a cornerstone of fascism": *New York Times*, July 1, 1980, p. B9.

270 "There truly is another world": "This World," *San Francisco Examiner and Chronicle*, July 6, 1980, p. 7.

270 "we'll be working on this": *Newsweek*, April 30, 1979, p. 69.

270 "It's the bedrock issue": Ibid.

271 "As Edith Bunker": "Hollywood Mobilizes for the ERA," *Ms.*, June 1978, p. 56.

271 "ERA would nullify": *Time*, February 26, 1979, p. 19.

271 "The defeat of the equal rights amendment": "This World," *San Francisco Examiner and Chronicle*, October 28, 1979, p. 34.

271 "not in harmony": *New York Times*, December 6, 1979, p. A26.

271 "I can't predict": *Newsweek*, April 30, 1979, p. 75.

272 "The issues aren't going to go away": *Time*, November 27, 1978, p. 30.

272 "This is symbolic": *Time*, January 29, 1979, p. 19.

272 "There will be no liberation": Jane O'Reilly, *The Girl I Left Behind* (New York, 1980), p. xviii.

272 "It would be ridiculous": *New York Times*, December 11, 1979, p. D22.

272 "Edith's life was enriched": *New York Times*, April 11, 1980, p. 16.

272 "makes my television death": Ibid.

273 "Feminists all over": Quoted in Judy Klemesrud, "The Year of the Lusty Woman," *Esquire*, December 19, 1978, p. 33.

273 "The trend is to emulate someone real": *Newsweek*, March 19, 1979, p. 59.

273 "The thing not to do": *San Francisco Examiner and Chronicle*, November 30, 1980, p. 12.

273 "normal reaction": Marcia Rockwood and Mary Thom, "Rape-Proof," *Ms.*, March 1979, p. 80.

274 "you can't blame somebody": *New York Times*, March 29, 1979, p. B4.

274 "the illusion that women criminals": Jane Alpert quoted in a publicity release for Ann Jones, *Women Who Kill* (New York, 1980).

274 "Even when I knew I would have to go to prison": Jones, *Women Who Kill*, p. 320.

274 "I am definitely a prisoner": *People* magazine, July 1980, p. 67.

274 "Pornography is an expression": Deidre English, "The Politics of Porn," *Mother Jones*, April 1980, p. 19.

274 "The ubiquitous public display": Quoted in Laura Lederer, ed., *Take Back the Night: Women on Pornography* (New York, 1980), p. 191.

274 "the most terrible": Ibid., p. 289.

275 "Love with a capital L": *San Francisco Bay Guardian*, January 18, 1979, p. 15.

275 "Women have got to lose their hangups": *New York Times*, February 2, 1978, p. 16.

275   "Mr. Flynt is an exploiter": *New York Times,* February 16, 1978, p. 38.

275   "I'm sick and tired": Norma Tirell, " 'Our Bodies . . .' Too Bawdy for Montana?" *Ms.,* January 1979, p. 21.

276   "Erotica is about sexuality": Gloria Steinem, "Erotica and Pornography," *Ms.,* November 1978, pp. 54–55.

276   "Pornography's basic message": Robin Morgan, "How to Run the Pornographers out of Town," *Ms.,* November 1978, p. 55.

276   "We are going to walk together": Quoted in Lederer, *Take Back the Night,* p. 290.

276   "Our bodies and minds": Adrienne Rich, *On Lies, Secrets, and Silence* (New York, 1979), p. 233.

276   "Sisterhood and female friendship": Mary Daly, *Gyn/Ecology: The Metaethics of Radical Feminism* (Boston, 1978), p. 380.

276   "The way we weave": Nancy Friday, *My Mother/My Self: The Daughter's Search for Identity* (New York, 1977), p. 22.

277   "When a woman comes to recognize": Daly, *Gyn/Ecology,* p. 347.

277   "As Gyn/Ecologists": Ibid., p. 409.

277   "The earth lives": Lucy Lippard, "A New Landscape Art," *Ms.,* April 1977, p. 68.

277   "We are all a part of this motion": Susan Griffin, *Woman and Nature: The Roaring Inside Her* (New York, 1978), p. 186.

15: "NEW COMBINATIONS FOR INTIMACY AND SUPPORT"

PAGE
278   "Oh, we're mad at each other": Ron Goulart, *An American Family* (New York, 1973), p. 130.

278   "These people touch without meeting": Quoted in Pat Loud and Nora Johnson, *Pat Loud: A Woman's Story* (New York, 1974), p. 136.

278   "Divorce has become so common": Nena O'Neill, *The Marriage Premise* (New York, 1977), p. 213.

278   "Why on earth should they struggle": *San Francisco Examiner,* May 10, 1978, p. C11.

279   "We need a better family life": Quoted in Haynes Johnson, *In the Absence of Power* (New York, 1980), p. 150.

279   "It is the world view": Christopher Lasch, *Haven in a Heartless World* (New York, 1977), p. 139.

280   "Parents are not abdicating": *Newsweek,* May 15, 1978, p. 64.

280   "There must now be a family": Theodore Roszak, *Person Planet* (Garden City, N.Y., 1978), p. 143.

280   "What we are witnessing": Alvin Toffler, *The Third Wave* (New York, 1980), p. 227.

280   "What families are doing": Jane Howard, *Families* (New York, 1978), p. 15.

280 "People are living together": Betty Friedan, "Feminism Takes a New Turn," *New York Times Magazine*, November 18, 1979, p. 92.

280 "point in a common direction": Roszak, *Person Planet*, p. 153.

281 "Those young adults": "Scene," *San Francisco Examiner and Chronicle*, March 4, 1979, p. 3.

281 "transitional living phase": *New York Times*, March 20, 1977, p. 1.

281 "I would consider marriage": Ibid.

281 "When I get married": Ibid., p. 59.

281 "Independence is no longer the crucial issue": Karen Durbin, "What Is the New Intimacy," *Ms.*, December 1978, p. 48.

281 "is not the end": Quoted in Jane O'Reilly, *The Girl I Left Behind* (New York, 1980), p. 63.

281 "The myth is that if you get married": *Los Angeles Times*, May 7, 1978, III, p. 24.

282 "In her experience": Ellen Goodman, *Close to Home* (New York, 1979), p. 154.

282 "It's kind of a family tradition": Quoted in Howard, *Families*, p. 86.

282 "polyparents and children": *Los Angeles Times*, May 7, 1978, III, p. 24.

282 "For every one of the children": Goodman, *Close to Home*, p. 155.

283 "stable family relationship": *New York Times*, May 29, 1977, p. 22.

283 "Our biggest inconvenience": *Newsweek*, August 1, 1977, p. 46.

283 "Most of the problems": Ibid., p. 49.

283 "Couples living together": Ibid.

283 "The mores of the society": Quoted in Toni Ihara and Ralph Warner, *The Living Together Kit* (Berkeley, Cal., 1978), p. 34.

284 "It used to be": *New York Times*, September 29, 1980, p. D11.

284 "I'm up against the clock": Friedan, "Feminism," p. 40.

284 "Their babies were their own gift": *New York Times*, September 29, 1980, p. D11.

285 "may experience three": Quoted in Friedan, "Feminism," p. 94.

285 "bring home the bacon": Bernice Kanner, "Back Page," *Ms.*, March 1980, p. 104.

285 "to eliminate the sexist biases": Benjamin Spock, *Baby and Child Care* (New York, 1976), p. xix.

285 "All right, Edith": Kanner, "Back Page," p. 104.

285 "Goodbye, John Wayne": Carole Kleiman, "Goodbye, John Wayne?", *Ms.*, April 1978, p. 45.

286 "The new executive": *Newsweek*, January 16, 1978, p. 54.

286 "Men do not need to exude": June Singer, *Androgyny* (Garden City, N.Y., 1976), p. 33.

286 "You're going to see a great wave": Friedan, "Feminism," p. 98.

286 "I'll work three days a week": Ibid.

286 "These things have been kept from us": *Newsweek*, January 16, 1978, p. 54.

286 "Nothing galvanizes men": *U.S. News & World Report*, December 8, 1980, p. 52.

287 "The important thing": Quoted in Toffler, *Third Wave*, p. 214.
287 "Like housewives the old find themselves": Arlie Russell Hochschild, *The Unexpected Community* (Berkeley, Cal., 1978), p. xii.
287 "Most of us worked hard": Lou Cottin, *Elders in Rebellion* (Garden City, N.Y., 1979), p. xiii.
287 "Old people feel": *New York Times*, October 24, 1977, p. 19.
287 "Most organizations tried to adjust old people": *Time*, June 2, 1975, p. 51.
288 "Are we so victimized": *New York Times*, September 9, 1977, p. A12.
288 "Which of you is going to step up": *Newsweek*, July 18, 1977, p. 79.
288 "The real challenge": *Newsweek*, February 28, 1977, p. 52.
288 "is the surest way to speed": Robin Henig, "Exposing the Myth of Senility," *New York Times Magazine*, December 3, 1978, p. 167.
288 "Old people believe that entry into nursing homes": Cottin, *Elders in Rebellion*, p. 57.
289 "Our faces are blank": *New York Times*, October 30, 1977, IV, p. 4.
289 "those of us who feel that growing older": *New York Times*, November 14, 1977, p. 66.
289 "Wrinkles are just as natural": *New York Times*, November 19, 1977, p. 21.
289 "It is a time to discover inner richness": Gay Gaer Luce, *Your Second Life* (New York, 1979), p. 7.
289 "Old age is not illness": *New York Times*, January 20, 1978, p. A21.
290 "It's not a closet": Quoted in Edmund White, *States of Desire: Travels in Gay America* (New York, 1980), p. 31.
290 "It isn't something that you do once": Quoted in Nancy Adair and Casey Adair, *Word Is Out* (San Francisco, 1978), p. 213.
290 "The ordinance condones immorality": *New York Times*, January 19, 1977, p. A14.
290 "Before I yield to this insidious attack": *New York Times*, April 11, 1977, p. 39.
291 "If homosexuality were the normal way": *New York Times*, May 10, 1977, p. 18.
291 "Miami is our Selma": *Newsweek*, June 6, 1977, p. 16.
291 "We are asking people": Ibid.
291 "What this means should be absolutely clear": *New York Times*, June 7, 1977, p. 35.
291 "Terribly wrong": *New York Times*, June 9, 1977, p. D16.
291 "Gays won't come out in Miami": Quoted in White, *States of Desire*, p. 191.
291 "The 'normal majority' ": *Time*, June 20, 1977, p. 59.
291 "to repeal similar laws": *New York Times*, June 8, 1977, p. 1.
291 "underlying gynophobia": Adrienne Rich, *On Lies, Secrets, and Silence* (New York, 1979), pp. 223–24.
291 "It should be obvious": Ibid.
292 "Now I have greater hope": *New York Times*, October 4, 1977, p. 24.
292 "Come out": Quoted in White, *States of Desire*, p. 176.

292   "It has the potential": *San Francisco Chronicle*, September 23, 1978, p. 7.

292   "splinter groups of radicals": Quoted in White, *States of Desire*, p. 50.

293   "If a bullet should enter": Randy Schilts, *The Mayor of Castro Street: The Life and Times of Harvey Milk* (New York, 1982), p. 372.

293   "Dan White's getting off": Quoted in Warren Hinckle, "Dan White's Final Solution," *San Francisco Review of Books*, December 1979, pp. 15-16.

293   "Dan White's straight justice": Ibid.

293   "We're taking advantage": *San Francisco Examiner and Chronicle*, August 3, 1980, p. B3.

293   "never see a straight person": *New York Times*, October 25, 1977, p. 41.

293   "To be gay": Quoted in Adair, *Word Is Out*, p. 246.

293   "the exchange of pleasure": William H. Masters and Virginia E. Johnson, *Homosexuality in Perspective* (Boston, 1979), p. 65.

293   "We are two people": Quoted in Durbin, "New Intimacy," p. 48.

294   "I look at the gay movement": Quoted in Adair, *Word Is Out*, p. 158.

294   "Gay liberation may really be the ultimate": Quoted ibid., p. 260.

295   "someone to be totally open": Quoted in Daniel Yankelovich, *New Rules: Searching for Self-Fulfillment in a World Turned Upside Down.* (New York, 1981), p. 252.

295   "Without commitment": Quoted in Gabrielle Brown, *The New Celibacy* (New York, 1980), p. 115.

295   "Celibacy partly represents": Ibid., p. 122.

295   "I'm taking a sabbatical": *New York Times*, May 1, 1978, p. A18.

295   "I haven't given up sex": Quoted in Brown, *New Celibacy*, p. 95.

296   "If you don't give your": Quoted in "Charlie Haas on Advertising," *New West*, November 5, 1979, p. 48.

296   "We need something special": Michael J. Arlen, *Thirty Seconds* (New York, 1980), pp. 55-56.

296   "would feel comfortable": Angus Campbell, *The Sense of Well-Being in America* (New York, 1981), p. 105.

296   "The population which is not married": Ibid., 227.

296   "My friends are my family": O'Reilly, *Girl I Left Behind*, p. 12.

296   "The movement itself": Friedan, "Feminism," p. 102.

296   "The only stable element": White, *States of Desire*, p. 264.

296   "By some complex alchemy": Howard, *Families*, p. 262.

16: "LOOKING FOR AN ANCHOR"

PAGE

297   "When you start talking about family": *Time*, February 7, 1977, p. 72.

298   "the severance": Christopher Lasch, *The Culture of Narcissism* (New York, 1978), p. 68.

298 "One of the real problems": Quoted in James Wooten, *Dasher* (New York, 1979), pp. 59–60.

298 "There's a recognition": *Newsweek*, September 13, 1976, p. 84.

298 "People are floating": *Newsweek*, July 4, 1977, p. 26.

298 "Membership is getting younger": *Los Angeles Times*, November 13, 1977, IX, p. 12.

298 "The craze for genealogy": Jane Howard, *Families* (New York, 1978), p. 44.

299 "Maintaining history": Sherna Gluck, *From Parlor to Prison: Five American Suffragists Talk about Their Lives* (New York, 1976), p. 4.

299 "Indian oral history": Roxanne Dunbar Ortiz, *The Great Sioux Nation* (Berkeley, Cal., 1977), p. 14.

299 "They are so fresh": *Time*, December 16, 1978, p. 79.

299 "When we are nostalgic": Susan Sontag, *On Photography* (New York, 1977), p. 15.

300 "It is more important": Vine Deloria, Jr., *The Metaphysics of Modern Existence* (New York, 1979), p. 25.

300 "Everybody is into roots now": Quoted in Bruce-Novoa, *Chicano Authors* (Austin, Tex., 1980), pp. 185–86.

300 "these buildings": Congressional Quarterly, *Documents 1978*, pp. 455–56.

300 "Buildings, like people": Quoted in Jeanne Davern, *Architecture: 1970–1980* (New York, 1980), p. 202.

300 "the Old Ways": Gary Snyder, *The Old Ways* (San Francisco, 1977), p. 66.

300 "It's a spiritual experience": Lynn Donovan, lecture at Stanford University, May 3, 1978.

301 "It's sort of like stardust": *Time*, February 7, 1977, p. 72.

301 "Never before did we think": *Time*, September 4, 1978, p. 50.

301 "Imagine, you take an enormous mass": Ibid., p. 53.

301 "the collapsing universe": Isaac Asimov, *The Collapsing Universe* (New York, 1977).

302 "stone dead": Lewis Thomas, *The Medusa and the Snail* (New York, 1979), p. 134.

303 "It is this huge reservoir": Url Lanham, *The Sapphire Planet* (New York, 1978), p. 103.

303 "The living and nonliving parts": Quoted in William Ophuls, *Ecology and the Politics of Scarcity* (San Francisco, 1977), p. 22.

303 "The idea that little puffs": *New York Times*, May 18, 1977, p. A24.

303 "unacceptable risk": *New York Times*, May 12, 1977, p. 1.

303 "rejoicing over the ban": *New York Times*, May 13, 1977, p. D1.

303 "Toxic chemical waste": Quoted in Michael H. Brown, "Love Canal, U.S.A.," *New York Times Magazine*, January 21, 1979, p. 23.

304 "We request a reprieve": Ibid. p. 44.

304 "There are ticking time bombs": *Newsweek*, August 21, 1978, p. 25.

304 "There will be little sentiment": Congressional Quarterly, *Documents 1978*, p. 450.

305 "This is not just science fiction": Quoted in Jeremy Rifkin, "Recom-

binant DNA" in Rita Arditti et al., *Science and Liberation* (Boston, 1980), p. 156.

305 "New kinds of hybrid plasmids": Quoted in Richard Hutton, *Bio-Revolution* (New York, 1978), p. 45.

305 "The probability of creating": Rifkin, "Recombinant," p. 148.

305 "Ignorance has compelled us to conclude": Quoted in Michael Rogers *Biohazard* (New York, 1977), p. 83.

305 "Scientists alone decided to impose": Quoted ibid., p. 149.

306 "Only one accident": Quoted in Rifkin, "Recombinant," p. 152.

306 "Biologists have become": *Time*, April 18, 1977, p. 32.

306 "It was an ordinary convention": *Newsweek*, August 16, 1976, pp. 16–17.

306 "Whatever it is": Ibid.

306 "to inoculate every man": Quoted in Philip M. Boffey, "Soft Evidence and Hard Sell," *New York Times Magazine*, September 5, 1976, p. 8.

306 "cheeks flush, brows furrow": Congressional Quarterly, *Documents 1978*, pp. 672–73.

307 "If there should be life on the moon": Lewis Thomas, *The Lives of a Cell* (New York, 1974), p. 6.

307 "We are ignorant about how we work": Lewis Thomas, "Biomedical Science and Human Health," *Daedalus*, Summer 1977, p. 170.

307 "Nature is an interactive friend": Quoted in Berkeley Holistic Health Center, *The Holistic Health Handbook* (Berkeley, Ca., 1978), p. 20.

308 "health is not the absence of disease": Kenneth R. Pelletier, *Holistic Medicine* (New York, 1979), p. 5.

308 "At home, people feel in control": *Seven Days*, October 13, 1978, p. 26.

308 "There is a peculiarly modern predilection": Susan Sontag, *Illness as Metaphor* (New York, 1978), p. 55.

308 "The will to live": Norman Cousins, *Anatomy of an Illness* (New York, 1979), p. 44.

309 "Cancer in its many forms": Quoted in Samuel S. Epstein, *The Politics of Cancer* (San Francisco, 1978), p. 299.

309 "may be work related": Congressional Quarterly, *Documents 1978*, p. 636.

309 "an individual moral obligation": Quoted in Pelletier, *Holistic Medicine*, p. 8.

309 "I hear America puffing": *Newsweek*, May 23, 1977, p. 78.

310 "We are discovering that every human being": Ibid.

310 "the trivialization of sports": Lasch, *Culture of Narcissism*, p. 108.

310 "Pressing us up against the limits": George Leonard, *The Ultimate Athlete* (New York, 1975), pp. 39–40.

310 "It's a super feeling": *Newsweek*, May 23, 1977, p. 81.

310 "A good run": Quoted in James F. Fixx, *The Complete Book of Running* (New York, 1977), p. 15.

310 "Too much fat": Quoted in Pelletier, *Holistic Medicine*, p. 145.

310 "back-to-basics": *Wall Street Journal*, May 29, 1975, p. 1.

310 "The number of home gardeners": *Newsweek*, June 11, 1979, p. 86.

311 "We're doing what the medical establishment": *Newsweek*, March 21, 1977, p. 72.

311 "The trend is toward lighter": Quoted in John Mariani, "The New Food Establishment," *Food and Wine*, June 1980, p. 11.

311 "Eating had become the last": Ellen Goodman, *Close to Home* (New York, 1979), p. 44.

311 "May be credited with the trend": *San Francisco Examiner*, August 12, 1979.

311 "If you make mistakes": Quoted in Larry Geis et al., *The New Healers: Healing the Whole Person* (Berkeley, Cal., 1980), p. 20.

311 "The most dangerous tendency": Wendell Berry, *The Unsettling of America: Culture and Agriculture* (San Francisco, 1977), p. 130.

312 "given more natural coloring": Maureen Lynch, "Making Yourself Over," *Ladies' Home Journal*, February 1980, pp. 97, 99.

312 "The chemicals we make are no different": Quoted in David Dickson and David Noble, "By Force of Reason" in Thomas Ferguson and Joel Rogers, eds., *The Hidden Election* (New York, 1981), p. 268.

312 "It's the sin": *Business Week*, October 13, 1975, p. 118.

312 "old-time sin": Congressional Quarterly, *Documents 1974*, p. 872.

312 "that wrong is wrong": Quoted in Manuel P. Servín, *An Awakened Minority: The Mexican Americans* (Beverly Hills, Cal., 1974), p. 294.

313 "The house did it": Anne Rivers Siddons, *The House Next Door* (New York, 1978), p. 212.

313 "inflict evil": Jay Anson, *The Amityville Horror* (Englewood Cliffs, N.J., 1977), p. 195.

313 "All the monsters we've created": Quoted in Len Keyser, *Hollywood in the Seventies* (San Diego, 1981), p. 199.

313 "People who cease to believe in God": Ann Rice, *Interview with a Vampire* (New York, 1976), p. 12.

313-14 "The American people": Quoted in Lawrence M. Baskir and William A. Straus, *Chance and Circumstance* (New York, 1978), p. xi.

314 "Going to war": Quoted in Bernard Weinraub, "Now, Vietnam Vets Demand Their Rights," *New York Times Magazine*, May 27, 1979, pp. 30, 33.

314 "They came back and people said": Quoted ibid., p. 68.

314 "At my age I should be worrying": "Punch," *San Francisco Examiner and Chronicle*, August 12, 1979, p. 2.

314 "cried or got extremely angry": Quoted ibid.

314 "The best medicine": *Newsweek*, November 12, 1979, p. 49.

315 "Like women and blacks": Ibid.

315 "We don't need parades": Ibid.

315 "the tragedy of May 4, 1970": Quoted in Joseph Kelner and James Munves, *Kent State Coverup* (New York, 1980), pp. 269-70.

315 "We have learned through a tragic event": Ibid.

315 "an apparent act": *Newsweek*, September 11, 1978, p. 99.

315 "We have no room in our lives": *Daily Kent Stater*, March 7, 1980.
316 "We still haven't": Weinraub, "Vietnam Vets," p. 32.
316 "It is depressing": *East Bay Express* (Oakland, Cal.), July 6, 1979, p 4.
316 "We must face the fact": Steven Phillip Smith, "Apocalypse? Not Yet," *New West*, October 8, 1979, p. 73.

17: "AN AGE OF FEW HEROES"

The expansion of community activism is described in Harry C. Boyte, *The Backyard Revolution* (Philadelphia, 1980). A good survey of urban reform is Robert Cassidy, *Livable Cities* (New York, 1980). Robert Kuttner's *Revolt of the Haves* (New York, 1980) elucidates the complexities of the taxpayers' rebellion. A fine explanation of the new conservatism is Alan Crawford, *Thunder on the Right* (New York, 1980). For the intellectual reaction, see Peter Steinfels, *The Neo-Conservatives* (New York, 1979).

PAGE
317 "For 30 years": *Newsweek*, January 23, 1978, p. 16.
317 "I have no apologies": Quoted in Haynes Johnson, *In the Absence of Power* (New York, 1980), p. 78.
317 "he achieved something": Congressional Quarterly, *Documents 1978*, p. 5.
318 "The moral test": *Newsweek*, January 23, 1978, p. 23.
318 "We've broken all the ground": Johnson, *Absence of Power* (New York, 1980), p. 236.
318 "In the crisis that's lying ahead": Quoted in Boyte, *Backyard Revolution*, p. 69.
318 "We are not a bunch of little": David S. Broder, *Changing of the Guard* (New York, 1980), p. 75.
318 "The day of the state": Quoted in Kevin Phillips, "The Balkanization of America," *Harper's*, May 1978, p. 46.
318 "Most Americans . . . tend to think": Quoted in Broder, *Changing of the Guard*, p. 144.
319 "We came to restore old houses": Quoted in Cassidy, *Livable Cities*, p. 6.
319 "We don't ask them to do business differently": Quoted ibid., p. 211.
319-20 "If we're going to conserve energy": *Newsweek*, October 8, 1979, p. 34.
320 "It's a question of getting": Quoted in Boyte, *Backyard Revolution*, p. 146.
320 "We try to get people": Quoted ibid., p. 67.
320 "We tried to get back to real, everyday things": Quoted ibid., p. 34.
320 "I hate to tell you": *New York Times*, July 22, 1979, p. 14.
320 "I keep hearing": Quoted in Boyte, *Backyard Revolution*, p. 33.
321 "The media is selling us": Quoted in Studs Terkel, *American Dreams: Lost and Found* (New York, 1980), pp. 460-61, 458.

321   "Communities have the same rights": Quoted in Harvey Wasserman, *Energy War: Reports from the Front* (Westport, Conn., 1979), p. 29.

321   "This movement is built": Quoted ibid., p. 52.

321   "We're feeling very disillusioned": *Newsweek*, May 23, 1977, p. 25.

322   "Ignorance of the law": Quoted in Wasserman, *Energy War*, p. 57.

322   "The history of the nuclear power industry": "This World," *San Francisco Examiner and Chronicle*, May 13, 1979, p. 7.

323   "a world with limits": "Playboy Interview: Jerry Brown," *Playboy*, April 1976, p. 79.

323   "the forward stampede": E. F. Schumacher, *Small Is Beautiful* (New York, 1973), p. 146.

323   "rather than formal": Andrew M. Greeley, *The American Catholic* (New York, 1977), p. 213.

323   "To be Catholic": Quoted in Mary T. Hanna, *Catholics and American Politics* (Cambridge, Mass., 1979), p. 2.

323   "One of the penalties of upward mobility": Mary Gordon, "More Catholic Than the Pope," *Harper's*, July 1978, p. 65.

323   "The problem is to re-establish": *Newsweek*, June 19, 1978, p. 28.

323   "We need a politics of smallness": Michael Novak, *The Rise of the Unmeltable Ethnics* (New York, 1973), p. 284.

323   "creative social disintegration": Theodore Roszak, *Person Planet* (Garden City, N.Y., 1978), pp. 289, 271, 291.

324   "What can I actually *do*?": Schumacher, *Small Is Beautiful*, p. 281.

324   "For the average American": Quoted in James C. Roberts, *The Conservative Decade* (Westport, Conn., 1980), p. viii.

324   "You are the people": Quoted in Phil Tracy, "The Jarvis Revolt: Rallying 'Round an Old Man's Obsession," *New West*, May 22, 1978, p. 18.

324   "Give the politicians a budget": Quoted in Kuttner, *Revolt of the Haves*, p. 72.

324   "Let us hope that California's message": Howard Jarvis and Robert Pack, *I'm Mad As Hell* (New York, 1979), p. 119.

324   Nixon's tax: *Newsweek*, June 26, 1978, p. 22.

324   "We have our marching orders": *Time*, June 19, 1978, p. 14.

325   "Across the country": *New York Times*, June 18, 1978, p. 23.

325   "This isn't just": Kuttner, *Revolt of the Haves*, p. 92.

325   "triggered hope in the breasts": New York Times Service, September 24, 1978, p. 23.

325   "The American people": Everett Carl Ladd, "What the Voters Really Want," *Fortune*, December 18, 1978, pp. 41, 48.

325   "The tax revolt": *New York Times*, November 26, 1978, IV, p. 4.

326   "Proposition 13": Quoted in Kuttner, *Revolt of the Haves*, p. 247.

326   "It used to be that business": Quoted ibid., p. 307.

326   "the worst tax legislation": *Time*, October 30, 1978, p. 33.

326   "The right wing": Garry Wills, *Confessions of a Conservative* (Garden City, N.Y., 1979), p. 211.

326   "We are radicals": Quoted in Richard A. Viguerie, *The New Right: We're Ready to Lead* (Falls Church, Va., 1981), p. 56.

327 "Instead of government serving": Jack Kemp, *An American Renaissance* (New York, 1979), p. 6.

327 "If we could eliminate": *New York Times,* January 16, 1979, p. A7.

327 "No frontier need be closed": Kemp, *American Renaissance,* pp. 197, 195.

327 "Unlike the New Right": Quoted in Crawford, *Thunder on the Right,* p. 174.

327 "A society has vitality": Quoted in Steinfels, *Neoconservatives,* p. 67.

328 "a Patty Hearst in reverse": Quoted in T. D. Allman, "The 'Rebirth' of Eldridge Cleaver," *New York Times Magazine,* January 16, 1977, p. 11.

328 "Bicentennial coon": Quoted ibid., p. 31.

328 "With all its faults": *New York Times,* November 18, 1975, p. 37.

328 "For 22 years I studied and practiced": *Newsweek,* February 28, 1977, p. 48.

328 "I feel you have changed": *New York Times,* January 4, 1980, p. 10.

328 "bring the gospel": *San Francisco Chronicle,* January 4, 1980, p. 2.

329 "Moral decadence is a very serious problem": Quoted in Roberts, *Conservative Decade,* p. 92.

329 "Everywhere we turn": Quoted in Robert E. McKeown, " 'Christian Voice': The Gospel of Right-Wing Politics," *Christian Century,* August 15, 1979, p. 781.

329 "This country is fed up": Quoted in Mary Murphy, "The Next Billy Graham," *Esquire,* October 10, 1978, p. 25.

329 "I don't want everyone to vote": Quoted in Thomas Ferguson and Joel Rogers, eds., *The Hidden Election* (New York, 1981), p. 4.

329 "The Bible clearly states": Quoted in Frances FitzGerald, "A Disciplined Charging Army," *New Yorker,* May 18, 1981, p. 74.

330 "Homosexuality is a perversion": Quoted in Murphy, "Next Billy Graham," pp. 30, 25.

330 "As long as we've got schools": Quoted in Crawford, *Thunder on the Right,* pp. 144, 146.

331 "We hold that the death penalty": *Newsweek,* November 29, 1976, p. 35: Congressional Quarterly, *Documents 1977,* p. 521; *Documents 1978,* p. 496.

331 "Weak bad habits": Quoted in Norman Mailer *The Executioner's Song* (New York, 1979), p. 473.

331 "The motives for the death penalty": Quoted in Peter Ross Range, "Will He Be the First," *New York Times Magazine,* March 11, 1979, p. 72.

332 "We have enough votes to run the country": Quoted in Crawford, *Thunder on the Right,* p. 161.

332 "Get them saved": *Time,* October 1, 1979, p. 68.

332 "Direct mail has allowed conservatives": Crawford, *Thunder on the Right,* pp. 45–46.

333 "They are multiplying": *Time,* December 18, 1978, p. 27.

333 "It's just as much a civic responsibility": Ibid.

333 "If corporate interests": *New York Times,* August 20, 1979, p. A17.

333 "The people have had enough": Quoted in Crawford, *Thunder on the Right,* p. 274.

333 "How would you like to be Frank Church": *Newsweek,* November 20, 1978, p. 56.

333 "It is time to get off the treadmill": *Time,* January 22, 1979, p. 29.

334 "The Administration's budget": *New York Times,* January 23, 1979, p. B11.

334 "I did not become Speaker of the House": Ibid.

334 "We've changed the focus of politics": *New York Times,* February 10, 1979, p. 7.

334 "We're the liveliest": *U.S. News & World Report,* February 26, 1979, p. 52.

334 "We have moved the entire Democratic Party": Ibid.

334 "Perhaps we had to watch": *Newsweek,* April 2, 1979, p. 37.

334 "About the only thing": *Newsweek,* November 20, 1978, p. 56.

334 "Unless the international performance": Kemp, *American Renaissance,* p. 181.

334 "Shouldn't we stop worrying": *Newsweek,* October 1, 1979, p. 21.

335 "John Wayne was bigger": *New York Times,* June 13, 1979, p. B10.

335 "Celebrating the dead John Wayne": *Newsweek,* June 25, 1979, p. 76.

335 "That little clique back there in the east": Ronald Reagan "Unforgettable John Wayne," *Reader's Digest,* October 1979, pp. 118–19.

335 "Duke Wayne symbolized": Ibid.

18: "TWO AMERICAS"

Major campaign speeches as well as the transcription of the Carter-Reagan debate are reprinted in the Washington Post's *The Pursuit of the Presidency: 1980* (New York, 1980).

PAGE

339 "The world of 1980": Quoted in *Pursuit of the Presidency,* pp. 233–34.

339 "Those thousand days": *New York Times,* October 21, 1979, p. 31; David S. Broder, *Changing of the Guard* (New York, 1980), p. 78.

340 "next year will be worse": Quoted in Daniel Yankelovich, *New Rules: Searching for Self-Fulfillment in a World Turned Upside Down* (New York, 1981), pp. 182–83, 25.

340 "The only thing that paralyzes us today": Quoted in Jack W. Germond and Jules Witcover, *Blue Smoke and Mirrors: How Reagan Won and Why Carter Lost the Election of 1980* (New York, 1981), p. 78.

340–41 "Because the Shah": Quoted ibid., p. 87.

341 "If the Vietnam era taught us anything": Quoted ibid., p. 146.

341 "We must understand": *Newsweek,* December 24, 1979, p. 21.

341   "the most serious threat to world peace": *New York Times*, January 23, 1980, p. A12.

341   "Afghanistan has given Carter": *In These Times*, February 13, 1980, p. 12.

343   "Mr. Chamberlain . . . tapping": Quoted in Hedrick Smith et al., *Reagan, the Man, the President* (New York, 1980), p. 100.

343   "The United States": Richard Nixon, *The Real War* (New York, 1980), p. 3; for the similarity of language used by Nixon and Reagan, see Bruce Cumings, "Chinatown: Foreign Policy and Elite Realignment" in Thomas Ferguson and Joel Rogers, eds., *The Hidden Election* (New York, 1981), pp. 227–28.

343   "Our allies are losing confidence": Quoted in Smith, *Reagan, the Man*, p. 100.

343   "a crusade . . . to take the government": *Pursuit of the Presidency*, p. 399.

344   "This is the greatest country": Ibid., p. 32.

344   "There's nothing the American people": *New York Times*, July 20, 1980, IV, p. 21.

344   "Ronald Reagan's America": *Pursuit of the Presidency*, p. 162.

344   "They say that the United States": Ibid., p. 416.

344   "a holy war": Quoted in Frances FitzGerald, "A Disciplined Charging Army," *New Yorker*, May 18, 1981, p. 60.

344   "to recapture our destiny": *New York Times*, July 20, 1980, IV, p. 20.

344   "Franklin Delano Reagan": Ibid.

344   "In a fumbling way": Elizabeth Drew, "1980: The Election," *New Yorker*, December 1, 1980, p. 169.

345   "We have demanded": Quoted in *Pursuit of the Presidency*, p. 366.

345   "This country doesn't have to be": Ibid., p. 399.

345   "The question is not which one": Quoted in Steven Roberts, "The Year of the Hostage," *New York Times Magazine*, November 2, 1980, p. 66.

345   "Oh, thank God": Quoted in Gerald Pomper et al., *The Election of 1980* (Chatham, N.J., 1981), p. 113.

345   "This isn't an election": Quoted in Drew, "1980," p. 186.

346   "it's a fed-up vote": Ibid.

346   "time for a change": *New York Times*, November 9, 1980, p. 18.

346   "It's the first time I ever voted Republican": *Newsweek*, November 17, 1980, pp. 31–32.

346   "This is no big thing": Ibid.

347   "We'll be a majority party": *New York Times*, November 7, 1980, p. 23.

347   "I don't like the job Carter has done": *New York Times*, November 5, 1980, p. 14.

347   "I didn't want to be responsible": Ibid.

347   "The politicians ain't got nothing to do": *San Francisco Chronicle*, November 6, 1980, p. 3.

347   "The way it was last night": Ibid.

347 "Well, I don't think that anyone": Quoted in Drew, "1980," p. 197.

348 "There are increasingly": Quoted in Studs Terkel, *American Dreams: Lost and Found* (New York, 1980), p. 349.

348 "Today . . . two overlapping": Quoted in E. F. Schumacher, *Good Work* (New York, 1979), pp. 194–95.

348 "We're at the end of an age": Quoted in Haynes Johnson, *In the Absence of Power* (New York, 1980), p. 132.

349 "hard work": Yankelovich, *New Rules*, p. 39.

349 "as long as the pay is good": Ibid., p. 152.

349 "Increasing numbers of Americans": Ibid.

349 "Search for Community": Ibid., p. 251.

350 "I've been all over the country": Quoted in Terkel, *American Dreams*, p. 461.

350 "The women's movement": *New York Times*, November 7, 1980, p. 10.

350 "We're sharpening our weapons": *Newsweek*, December 1, 1980, p. 39.

350 "In unexpected quarters": Terkel, *American Dreams*, p. xxv.

350 "We all know that inflation": *New York Times*, October 21, 1979, p. 30.

350 "I hope the rest of us": *San Francisco Examiner and Chronicle*, October 21, 1979, p. 14.

· ACKNOWLEDGMENTS ·

On the subject of contemporary history, nearly everyone claims some area of expertise, and I have benefited greatly by generous bestowals of advice and opinion. At a critical stage, my agent Fred Hill encouraged a major reorganization that built the basis of this book. Tom Dubis, Karen Hansen, Rick Mitz, and Paul Preuss kindly donated research material from their areas of interest. Michael Batinski, Rochelle Gatlin, Bill Issel, Michael Kazin, and especially Jules Tygiel read various drafts of the manuscript and offered valuable criticism for its improvement. My editor, William Abrahams, provided the rare combination of enthusiasm and wisdom that inspired the writing as it improved it. To Jeannette Ferrary belongs the remarkable distinction of having lived through the seventies with me twice—and having enriched the experience immensely both times.

396

· INDEX ·